The Emergence of Modern Central Banking from 1918 to the Present

The Emergence of Modern Central Banking from 1918 to the Present

Edited by

CARL-L. HOLTFRERICH,
JAIME REIS and GIANNI TONIOLO

Routledge
Taylor & Francis Group
LONDON AND NEW YORK

First published 1999 by Ashgate Publishing

2 Park Square, Milton Park, Abingdon, Oxon OX14 4RN
711 Third Avenue, New York, NY 10017, USA

Routledge is an imprint of the Taylor & Francis Group, an informa business

First issued in paperback 2016

British Library Cataloguing in Publication Data

The Emergence of Modern Central Banking from 1918 to the
Present
(Studies in Banking History)
1. Banks and banking, Central—History—20th century—
Congresses.
I. Holtfrerich, Carl-L. II. Reis, Jaime. III. Toniolo,
Gianni.
332.1'1'0904

Library of Congress Cataloging-in-Publication Data

The emergence of modern central banking from 1918 to the present/
edited by Carl-L. Holtfrerich, Jaime Reis and Gianni Toniolo.
Papers presented at a conference held in Évora, Portugal, in May
1996
ISBN 1–85928–241–5 (hardback)
1. Banks and banking, Central—History—Congresses.
I. Holtfrerich, Carl-L. II. Reis, Jaime. III. Toniolo,
Gianni, 1942–
HG1811.E45 1999
332.1'1'0904—dc21 99–30101
CIP

Transferred to Digital Printing in 2012

ISBN 978-1-85928-241-0 (hbk)
ISBN 978-1-138-26746-6 (pbk)

Contents

List of Figures

List of Tables

Acknowledgements

The chapters which constitute this volume were originally presented as papers at a conference on 'The Emergence of Modern Central Banking from 1918 to the Present', which was held in Évora, Portugal, in May 1996. The Portuguese central bank, the Bank of Portugal, hosted and organized the meeting as part of its 150th anniversary celebrations and provided generous funding. Financial support was made available equally by the European Association for Banking History, which sponsored the event as part of the ongoing series of highly successful annual conferences that for several years now have been held on various aspects of banking history. (A number of other papers were also presented on this occasion and have since been published by the Association under the title *Bank Archives and the User*.) Thanks are due to both institutions for making the conference possible and to their respective staffs for making it such a success. Our gratitude is also due to the participants at the meeting, in particular to the authors of the papers and their discussants, who did so much to enliven the debate and to shed light into the many obscure corners of a subject on which there is still so much left to be said.

C.L.H.
J.R.
G.T.

Introduction

Carl-L. Holtfrerich and Jaime Reis

This book is the result of a conference, in 1996, on 'The Emergence of Modern Central Banking: 1918 to the Present'. The conference assembled not only scholars of banking history but also archivists, as guardians of historical sources, and bankers. The conference aimed – and so does this volume – at learning from the exchange of ideas and research results on its general subject and at confronting the results of historical research with issues that bankers, especially central bankers, are dealing with in their current business.

A brief look at the history of the *Banco de Portugal* confirms how well the general theme of the conference was chosen. In the nineteenth century, the *Banco de Portugal* was a note-issuing commercial bank whose main business was discounting commercial paper and undertaking foreign exchange transactions. Established as a joint stock company, its shares were held by the public. The shareholders, not the government, elected its Board of Directors.[1] It was only at the end of the nineteenth century that the Bank was granted a monopoly over the note issue in Portugal (1891) and became the bank of the state (1887). Concomitantly, it had to accept a certain loss of independence. In 1888 a government-appointed governor was empowered to veto decisions by the Board of Directors. All the other modern functions and instruments were formally given to the *Banco de Portugal* after 1918, that is during the period on which the conference concentrated. In fact, however, they were gradually emerging from the 1870s onwards as a result of a combination of public and political expectations with the more immediate economic interests of the institution itself, as is shown by Jaime Reis in Chapter 5 (The Bank of Portugal's First Century: From 1846 to the Second World War).

Contemporary central banking thus has a short history, which only starts in earnest at the end of the nineteenth century, but one that is both rich and complex. Every country which has a central bank – and nowadays most do – has had its own distinct experience in this respect. Yet, each country will also have some features in common: the problems that these banks were set up to tackle are basically similar; their institutional architecture tends to follow the same model; and a great deal of international interaction has occurred and increasingly occurs between them. It is precisely the tension between these two poles which makes the study of this subject at once so fascinating and so full of pitfalls and surprises. It is also the reason why it is so important to carry out comparative analysis of how central banks have performed in different countries, at different times and in different economic environments.

In the chapters following this introduction, diversity is certainly widely present. It should not be allowed, however, to obscure the main common developments which have affected the functions, objectives and instruments of monetary policy of central banks everywhere in the course of this century. These will emerge here as the text unfolds and it is therefore useful, before the detail of particular cases is examined, to draw attention to the most important among these common features. Five of them may be singled out for consideration.

1. Central banks have been instrumental in the replacement of full-value gold and silver coin by paper currency in the circulation of money. In the late nineteenth century, such metal coin constituted the bulk of the monetary base and was often the only legal tender. It was issued by the mints of the central governments and any seigniorage gains flowed directly to them. Bank notes, even those of central banks, were then an instrument of credit, the equivalent of a cheque today. Central banks, in this respect, were privileged banks, but nevertheless they faced essentially the same constraints as commercial ones. A central bank, whether or not its notes had acquired the status of legal tender, still had to watch its liquidity position, not only to cover its international obligations within the gold standard system, but also *vis-à-vis* its domestic note issue and depositors. It could not itself just create the money that it was legally obliged to pay out on demand.

   With the onset of the First World War, paper money issued by central banks replaced the full-value metal coin money issued by government mints. Notes became not only legal tender but also ceased to be convertible into gold. The power of central banks over the supply of money was thereby greatly enhanced. Stabilization policy in the modern sense, with a view to the domestic price level and business cycle – in other words, the realization of Knut Wicksell's original ideas and Gustav Cassel's and Irving Fisher's monetary policy recipes – became possible. The Federal Reserve Bank embarked on such a policy in 1923, at the price of violating the rules of the gold standard by sterilizing the gold inflows, and, long before Keynes propagated the idea of stabilizing business cycle fluctuations through fiscal policies, monetary policy had already assumed such a role. As notes had been made inconvertible into gold in most countries, central banks no longer faced a liquidity problem arising from issuing bank notes or from taking deposits. The only liquidity constraint left resulted from the restoration of fixed exchange rates in the 1920s, coupled with currency convertibility between the central banks.

2. In the period following the First World War, central banks assumed new functions besides their traditional discount and lombard business with the private sector. The role of banks became more important, and, simultaneously, there was a reduction in commercial banking activities with private customers, where these still existed.[2] Their role in supervising the business of private commercial banking was extended in many cases and increasingly they assumed regulatory powers. The lender of last resort function, to stabilize the banking system in financial panics, was explicitly or implicitly strengthened. The clearing of bank balances through the operation of the central bank was greatly extended.

   The First World War was also the cause of central banks' increasing involvement in extending credits to their governments. Whenever they could, they channelled government demands for short-term or long-term credits into the private money and capital markets. When this was not possible, they satisfied the governments' demands directly through their own printing presses. The rapid rise in the share of public expenditure in GNP, both during the First World War and in the Great Depression, led to government paper inevitably playing an increasing role in central banks' portfolios.

3. With the emergence of manipulated paper currency standards came an increase in and a refinement of monetary policy instruments. To handle their new role as brokers for government debt, central banks were allowed to trade government paper on the open market, and were entitled to develop the open market policy instrument for the fine-tuning of interest rates and of credit and money supply growth. Since 1933 in the US, and shortly after the Second World War in Germany, central banks were empowered to change minimum reserve requirements and were thus given another tool of monetary policy. Further progress was made with the appearance of the more sophisticated instruments of swap policy. In the Bretton Woods period (1944–71) such instruments used gold and foreign exchange (often to bridge balance of payments surpluses or deficits), and, in the post-Bretton Woods period, swap policies used mainly domestic government paper. Meanwhile the rate for such repurchase agreements has come to replace the discount rate as the leading indicator of money market rates. More new policy instruments could be listed here but these should be enough to delineate the trend.

4. The most characteristic change in central banking worldwide since the First World War can be seen in the foundation on which central bank operations were conducted. Before 1914 central banks operated according to a set of rules, namely those of the gold standard, which were designed to keep exchange rates stable and thus integrate world markets for capital and goods. That globalization was even more pronounced then than it is today has recently been emphasized by Jeffrey Williamson.[3] The securing of price stability was mainly left to the natural limitations on the supply of gold and to the scarcity of credit and money resulting from market operations in continuously growing economies.

   Since 1914, and again since the end of Bretton Woods, central banks have been granted more and more discretionary power to conduct their operations. They have been explicitly assigned domestic economic policy goals, such as the securing of price stability, in the case of the *Bundesbank* and of the European Central Bank, or of price stability as well as maximum growth and employment, in the case of the Fed. In sum, in the age of autonomous stabilization policies, central banks have moved from rules to discretion.

5. While the above mentioned changes have tended to occur persistently in one direction only, one important transformation seems now to have been reversed after decades of experience. Before the First World War in most cases central banks were not only private institution – while today they are mostly government owned – but they were also formally independent of their governments.[4] Around the time of the Second World War, this trend suffered a reverse. In Germany, France, England, Japan, Italy and Sweden, as well as in other countries, central banks were made subordinate to political masters. In the light of the empirical proof that, when independent, such institutions display better results in securing price stability than when they are dependent,[5] governments have recently started to grant more independence again to their central banks. This tendency has now become particularly visible in Europe and has strengthened in the aftermath of the Maastricht Treaty of 1992 and in preparation for the European Monetary Union. No doubt this has been helped by the apparently enduring success recently achieved with the reduction of inflation throughout the countries involved in the process. It is an interesting matter for speculation, however, to know whether this is a reversal in the trend of central bank evolution which is here to stay, or whether time will reveal renewed attempts at the reassertion of political will and control over central banks.

Autonomy *vis-à-vis* the government is in fact the main theme of the first chapter of this book, by Michael Collins and Mae Baker (Bank of England Autonomy: A Retrospective). In it we are reminded of how recent is the reacquisition of autonomy in the case of that most venerable and ancient of central banks, the Bank of England, and how difficult, therefore, it is to assess the durability of this change. The chapter also emphasizes that, from a long-term perspective, the powers which the Bank of England has been enabled to exercise recently are much less far reaching than they were in their heyday, when a broader conception of what should constitute a central bank was in place. One of the problems here is that, in a democratic system, the granting of this independence must be ultimately justified socially, in terms of a 'common good', the definition of which is apt to change over time, as are the means for achieving it which are considered acceptable by parliamentary majorities or the consensus of the nation.

The issue re-surfaces explicitly in Chapter 8, by Pierre L. Siklos (US and Canadian Central Banking: The Triumph of Personalities over Politics?), although in a very different setting, that of North America, and with a different focus. The aim of this chapter is to determine how much of central bank behaviour in the US and Canada, as judged by its autonomy from government and by its macro-economic success, was the consequence of statutory rules and how much the result of the personality of those who were in charge. The conclusion is cautionary: answers depend on the choice of yardstick, and the definition of autonomy depends as much on formal frameworks as on the degree of agreement over policy between governments and central bankers.

Rules are nevertheless an extremely important part of this history. This is so, in particular, when they become a frequent battlefield for political forces and diverging notions concerning the shape and future development of a country's financial system, as happened in Italy during the first half century or so after the creation of the Bank of Italy in 1893. Cosma Gelsomino's account of this in Chapter 6 (The Bank of Italy from its Foundation to the 1950s: Institutional Aspects) brings to light the succession of disputes from which was forged a central bank that, despite this, or perhaps because of it, emerged as a powerful and respected institution. It may have had to follow the government's bidding on crucial occasions but it also got its way on many others, a fact that should make us wary of reaching too hurried a conclusion about how little independence it may have had. Several ingredients helped it along this long road to institutional pre-eminence. As happened in other relatively 'backward' economies, the very fact of this backwardness was one of these ingredients because of the contrast with the 'modern' institution that is the central bank. Other important factors were the stability of leadership; long-serving governors with a clear purpose; and a persistent effort to build technical and administrative capacity where these were often lacking elsewhere. These factors helped the *Banca d'Italia* to stand firm against a backdrop of political and economic instability, changing regimes and rulers, an ever hungry Treasury and a banking system which was rocked from time to time by immense difficulties.

The history of this bank also illustrates how great was the impact of imported models at least for the institutional shape of central banking, if not also for their style of management, in countries which were relatively late in establishing such arrangements. In this respect, however, it is Latin America which is the classical locus in which to examine the role of such importation and, in particular, the manner in which that exotic plant, the Euro/American central bank, set down its roots in foreign soil and adapted as best it could. In Chapter 9 (The Emergence of Central Banks in Latin America: Are Evolutionary Models Applicable?), Carlos Marichal and Daniel Díaz Fuentes take Mexico, Argentina and Brazil as their case studies to draw significant contrasts with the experience on the other side of the Atlantic. In these three countries, central banks not only came late but did not arise out of the gradual transformation of large 'national' banks which had already been close to their respective governments for some time. Such banks did exist there – from at least the 1880s a growing need was being felt for some form of institutionalized centralization of central bank functions, and, by the early twentieth century, some of the latter were indeed in place. But these functions were being carried out by many different bodies (the Treasury, the 'national bank', the money conversion board, etc.), some of them official, others private. Therefore, in spite of the profusion of foreign advice and the visits of the 'money doctors' in the 1920s and 1930s, centralization was hard to achieve. These factors, combined with the financial and monetary instability which so often visited these economies, had a large part to play in the slow arrival of modern central banking. In the case of Brazil, for instance, it took until 1965.

In contrast, in Spain and France, monopolist note-issuing banks have a history which stretches well back into the 1800s. Yet, as is shown by Pablo Martín Aceña and Olivier Feiertag in Chapter 2 (The Delayed Modernization of The Central Banks of France and Spain in the Twentieth Century), these institutions did not become 'modern' central banks until relatively late in the present century. What constitutes 'modernity' or the proper function of such institutions is obviously essential in shaping the answers which can be given in this type of analysis. But no less interestingly, disagreement over these issues was also a part of the very reason for the slow transformation of national into central banks.

Different generations understood their purpose differently and therefore repeatedly adapted them to satisfy the current needs of the main financial actors and the political consensus on how they should be handled. The result was a lack of appropriate instruments (for example, open market operations), uncertainty regarding the place of the central bank in the market, indefinition about its duties and, at times, profound internal divisions about what its role should be. The situation clarified after the 1960s, with the opening up and expansion of the financial system, the pressure of internationalization and the advent of more or less permanent monetary instability.

The case of Sweden, depicted in Chapter 4 by Lars Jonung and Tarmo Haavisto (Central Banking in Sweden and Finland in the Twentieth Century), shows how a precocious financial sophistication and a strong British influence on banking practices during the classical gold standard period, can account in large measure for the clear emergence of the Swedish *Riksbank* as already a central bank before 1914. A similar contemporary experience in financially much less sophisticated Finland, suggests that in this case the process occurred as early as it did due to the traditionally strong Swedish influence in this country. The analysis of these two economies sheds equally interesting light on the post-1945 period, when the tight integration of monetary policy into a much vaster regulatory exercise produced central banks that were instrumentally powerful but subservient to the authorities. Their aim, for the next four decades, was low interest rates and selective credit and capital controls, with a view to ensuring growth and achieving explicit social objectives. Central banking that resembled its earlier model has returned only recently, to take up an earlier theme. It suggests that an independent role coupled with effective influence in markets only becomes possible when the latter themselves become free from intensive State determination and central banks are called upon to do what they are best at, namely regulating the market.

The reconstruction of a country's central bank after a profound political and institutional shock forms the subject of Chapters 3 and 7, both of which are framed in a comparative perspective. In the first of these, Carl-L. Holtfrerich and Toru Iwami (Postwar Central Banking Reform: A German–Japanese Comparison) look at the experience of two countries where earlier financial institutions were practically wiped out by war and where the restoration of the central bank was carried out under the guidance of an external power, namely the US or the Allies, at times indeed even by the very same American officials. Paradoxically, the two outcomes – in Germany, a federal model; in Japan, a centralized one – could not have been more diverse. One reason was that American plans, which were the same in both instances, for historical reasons were quite unrealistic for Japan, whereas they were quite practicable for Germany. No less important, however, was once again the force of politics, another theme which recurs throughout this book. Japanese opposition combined with American uncertainty prevented US plans from coming to fruition in the former country. However, in Germany, the unconditional surrender meant that the Allies took over all central government functions. Politicians in the reconstructed federal states were therefore given much less opportunity to express themselves and when they finally did, a good deal later, their interests by then had come to coincide very much with those of their occupiers.

For the successor states of the Austro-Hungarian monarchy, the problems they faced in the aftermath of the First World War were similar ones. However, they lacked the support of a strong occupation force which was determined to re-establish economic and financial normality, while their own means were too slender to make up for this, as becomes clear in Chapter 7 by Aurel Schubert (The Emergence of National Central Banks in Central Europe after the Break-up of the Austro-Hungarian Monarchy). Foreign assistance, largely from the League of Nations, played an important role, as did regional political forces, although in the case of Czechoslovakia, Hungary and Austria the latter's influence seems to have been mostly negative. Encouraged nevertheless by outside pressures to act independently and maintain the external value of their respective currencies, the new central banks succeeded, against enormous odds, in making substantial contributions towards keeping government finances afloat, taming hyperinflation and staving off the collapse of fragile financial systems. However, they could never overcome fully the problems caused by the poor geo-political design of the countries and the chronic economic problems which, as a result, beset them for two decades.

As Capie and Wood have shown in a recent paper, a truly supranational central bank to exist would have to become a lender of last resort. In the absence of an international currency, no institution has been able therefore to undertake this function.[6] Notwithstanding, there is an important international dimension to the history of central banking which cannot be ignored, and which has gained in significance with the creation of a European Central Bank. Moreover, there are important lessons to be gleaned in this respect from an examination of the two institutions which are considered in Chapters 10 and 11. In the first of these, Harold James (The International Monetary Fund and Central Banking) shows that the International Monetary Fund was never supposed either to create money or to regulate international banking. History bears a heavy responsibility for this given that the institutional design which shaped the IMF was so strongly influenced by the events of the 1930s and by the expectations of the founding fathers that future significant capital movements across borders were unlikely. From the early 1970s, the collapse of Bretton Woods and the rapid growth of an international private capital market changed the economic environment irrevocably. The Fund, on the other hand, responded more or less by 'stumbling' into something which began increasingly to resemble in some respects an international central bank function. Although formally no changes occurred, its attention clearly shifted to markets and its concerns came to focus far more on crisis management and on supervision. In this sense, the emphasis on the production and dissemination of information regarding international financial markets could be seen as a revealing instance of something akin to a surveillance function over them, in a show of embryonic central bank behaviour on an extra-national scale which continues to develop to the present day.

It is perhaps fitting that the last chapter in this volume should focus on the history of the Bank of International Settlements (Sixty-five Years of Central Bank Cooperation at the Bank for International Settlements). As Gunter Baer writes in this chapter: 'cooperation at the BIS is thus to a significant extent a reflection of the history of monetary and financial relations and of how central banks [...] have responded and adapted to new challenges'. Although in it the accent is on cooperation and informal interaction and the narrative revolves around meetings and discussions without tangible conclusions, it would be wrong to underestimate the impact of this institution on events since the 1930s, both worldwide as well as at the national level. Among its achievements, the BIS provided an impressive set of technical facilities which members were able to make use of and which on occasions were of great value in crisis management. Additionally, it fostered a climate of discrete mutual comprehension and collaboration among central banks which in the heady times of globalized markets and floating exchange rates served these banks in achieving their domestic objectives. How much success this institution had can probably never be clearly established but the situations documented in this chapter suggest that without it matters could have been quite different and, in all likelihood, worse.

The studies that this book brings together by no means exhaust their subject, nor was this their aim. They provide, however, a great deal of new data, stimulating and revealing comparisons, new judgements as well as tests for old ones and a variety of analytic approaches, all of which advance our understanding of central banking during the century of its emergence. Central banking history has been massively analysed during this century and the literature on it is enormous. The chapters that follow build on this basis of knowledge but have the further merit of showing how much we still need to learn about a political and economic reality the importance of which throughout this period has not ceased to grow.

Notes

1. See F. Capie, C. Goodhart, S. Fischer and N. Schnadt (eds) (1994), *The Future of Central Banking. The Tercentenary Symposium of the Bank of England*, Cambridge, Cambridge University Press, p. 152.
2. The Fed – the US Federal Reserve Board – was directly founded as a bank of banks in 1913.
3. Jeffrey Williamson (1996), 'Globalization, convergence and history', *Journal of Economic History*, 56.
4. The German *Reichsbank* was an exception but it was made independent in 1922.
5. See A. Cukierman (1992), *Central Bank Strategy, Credibility and Independence: Theory and Evidence*, Cambridge, MA, The MIT Press, pp. 415–31.
6. Forrest H. Capie and Geoffrey E. Wood (1995), 'A European lender of last resort? Some lessons from history', in J. Reis (ed.), *International Monetary Systems in Historical Perspective*, Houndmills and London, Macmillan.

PART I
The Origins of Central Banking

CHAPTER ONE

Bank of England Autonomy: A Retrospective

Michael Collins and Mae Baker

Introduction

A critical function of history is to provide a long-term perspective for current preoccupations, to come up with historical yardsticks against which to measure recent experience. Past economic experience provides one of the essential ingredients needed for a proper assessment of current economic theory and policy. The recent tercentenary of the Bank of England (which first opened for business in July 1694) – as with the 150th anniversary of the Bank of Portugal – has offered one of those traditional occasions for retrospective contemplation on the role of a key agency responsible for the direction of a country's economic policy: the central bank.

The Bank of England's three hundred years have involved many aspects of British financial development but the following four issues have been at the core of its evolution as a central bank:

1. Prudential control of, and responsibility for, money market institutions;
2. Exchange rate policy and international financial cooperation;
3. Monetary control and the maintenance of price stability;
4. Bank/government relations.

This paper concentrates on just one issue, that of Bank/government relations, though, in fact, all are inextricably linked. We are particularly concerned to provide an historical perspective on current moves to establish greater central bank autonomy in the UK. In the next section we make some general introductory remarks about central bank autonomy and the Bank of England's historical experience. The following two sections then deal with the post-war period, treating separately the decades of the 1950s and 1960s which were dominated by Keynesian thinking on macroeconomic management, and the period since the 1970s in which greater weight was given to the role of monetary policy in subduing inflationary pressures. As will become clear, in both these post-war periods the extent of Bank of England autonomy was for the greatest part very muted, though for different reasons. Certainly, post-war experience represents a marked decline in the extent of independence exercised in previous periods. Two further sections explore the reasons for this earlier autonomy and explain the reasons for its decline between the wars. The concluding section briefly outlines the latest changes to Bank of England responsibilities and reiterates the lessons from history: that central bank autonomy has worked in Britain only when non-discretionary rules have bound the central bank's behaviour, and only when politicians have supported both the rules and the Bank's behaviour within them. Up until very recent times, such political backing has been fairly nominal and in an historical context the degree of autonomy exercised by the Bank of England – at least until mid-1997 – has been limited. Inevitably, though, the effects of the changes implemented in the late 1990s are still too recent to allow for a proper assessment.

Central bank autonomy

Over the very long sweep of Bank of England history, the degree of autonomy exercised by Threadneedle Street has been much less in the twentieth century than in the nineteenth. This autonomy was at its greatest prior to 1914. It began to crumble in the inter-war period and was swept aside in the war and post-war era of demand management. It continued suppressed under the monetary uncertainties of the 1970s and the monetarist experiments of the 1980s. Revival of official interest in British central bank autonomy is thus very recent, dating only from the late 1980s.

There is now a broad consensus on two propositions: (1) that low (or zero) and predictable rates of inflation are beneficial; and (2) that over the long term there is no clear trade-off between the rate of inflation and real growth. Therefore, the cost of attaining a low inflation rate over the long term is not severe. In turn, convergence of British views about the desirability of greater independence for the central bank, as a means of attaining lower inflation, arises out of the failure of earlier policy and institutional regimes to achieve the economic goals of low inflation without high unemployment. Another factor has been the apparent success of those few countries overseas which since the war have had constitutionally more independent central banks.[1] In other countries, the extent of central bank autonomy has tended to be positively correlated to lower and less variable rates of inflation, without any noticeable effects (for good or ill) on real macro-economic performance. The most important comparators are West Germany, Switzerland, Japan and the USA – though many doubts have been raised about the true autonomy of the Federal Reserve at different times, not least by Milton Friedman (Friedman, 1962) and, of course, the other countries are all exceptional in a number of important respects and very few would point to their central banks' autonomy as the most crucial element in their economic success. Nevertheless, once the possibility of greater autonomy for the Bank of England became an issue, the existence of alternative models overseas was directly relevant.

Another important factor has been the UK's position in Europe. European monetary union was established on 1 January 1999, with the creation of the 'European Central Bank [which] will formulate a unified monetary policy which independent national central banks will implement' (Read, 1996: 131). Thus, legislative independence must be established for individual central banks as a precondition for joining EMU. The current UK government is intending to join the single currency though not at the first opportunity and, therefore, establishing greater independence for the Bank of England is part of the necessary preparations.

However, in the broader historical context, it has been the breakdown of previous policy regimes and the loss of faith – if not in particular theoretical paradigms, then in the capability of the politico-institutional framework to operate according to theoretical principles – that has provided the impetus for establishing greater central bank autonomy. This paper takes a closer look at the previous regimes, in order to show how they suppressed central bank autonomy and how their passing has led to the possibility of greater independence for the Bank of England.

Bank autonomy and demand management, 1950s and 1960s

The extent of Bank autonomy reached a new low during the period of the so-called 'Keynesian consensus', from the late 1940s to the 1970s. The long-term trend towards greater subordination of the Bank to the state which had become apparent between the wars, was greatly reinforced by wartime experience and this culminated in 1946 with the passing of the Nationalisation Act. In terms of distance between Bank and state, the Act retained some compromises.[2] It did take the Bank into public ownership and passed to the Crown (in practice, the Prime Minister) the power of appointing the Governor, Deputy-Governor and other directors. The term of office for the Governor was set at five years (with eligibility for re-appointment which, in fact, became the norm) but, though appointed by the government, the Governor cannot be removed in mid-term. The Bank did not become a department of state but remained a separate institution under the management of the Governor and Deputy-Governor, with the assistance of the Court of Directors. It thus retained a fair degree of independence over day-to-day institutional affairs, and indeed over the day-to-day implementation of policy, but not over policy itself. In fact, even before the war (when the Bank was still in private ownership) it had become the practice that no change in bank rate would be implemented before the Chancellor of the Exchequer had been fully consulted (and, by implication, approved the change).

More important than the legislative change in the Bank's status was the fact that from the late 1940s, the prevailing ethos of British macro-economic policy negated the requirement for an independent central bank. Successive governments (from both major political parties) embraced an explicit responsibility for managing the economy and this included the conduct of monetary policy. The new macro-economic priorities were the maintenance of high levels of employment and high rates of growth. Price stability was subordinated to these greater goals. However, it was not merely that the new orthodoxy subordinated Bank policy to Treasury policy – that it did – but it went further in necessitating the active participation of the Bank in the management of aggregate demand. At the centre of this new approach was the use of discretionary judgement by those advising policy makers. It is instructive to quote from Richard Sayers, then the leading authority on the Bank (and, with Cairncross, the major presence on the influential Radcliffe Committee which reported on the 'Working of the Monetary System' in 1959). His views show clearly how concepts of central bank autonomy had shifted in the brave new world of pro-active economic management. He welcomed the Bank's ready participation in discretionary demand management, but went much further by arguing that discretion was at the heart of the definition of central banking: [3]

> The essence of central banking is discretionary control of the monetary system ... working to rule is the antithesis of central banking. A central bank is necessary only when the community decides that a discretionary element is desirable. The central banker is the man who exercises discretion, not the machine that works according to rule. [p. 1] ... [W]e must have central bankers to exercise a discretionary influence upon the monetary situation. And it follows that there is no code of eternal rules for them to follow. They have to adapt their ways to the shape of the community's constantly changing financial habits. By comparative study we may, of course, hope to find some generalisations about the behaviour of central banks,

> and the experience of some may offer guarded guidance to others; but we are doomed to disappointment if we look for rules applicable to all times and all places. We have central banks for the very reason that there are no such rules (Sayers, 1957: 1–7).

Given this prevailing view of economic policy and of the part played by government agencies, it is hardly surprising that Bank autonomy all but evaporated. Monetary policy was too important to be left to any agent which was not subject to democratic sanction.

The strong element of policy discretion and the wide acceptance of a political responsibility for monetary matters remained, despite the British government's adherence to the fixed exchange rate regime which had been negotiated at Bretton Woods as part of the international post-war settlement. The Bretton Woods system was not the same animal as the old gold standard, nor did it operate in the same environment. The Bretton Woods conference of 1944 was a response to the disruption and dislocation to international trade and growth resulting from the hostilities of the 1930s and the Second World War. The aim of the conference was to foster international trade and, consequently, growth through stable exchange rates. Each participating country's currency was fixed in terms of gold, but without the requirement for convertibility (only the US$ had convertibility at US$35 per ounce). Moreover, an essential feature was the assumption of the continuation of active intervention by the authorities in foreign exchange markets.

The disruption to domestic economies occasioned by the Second World War resulted not only in loss of international trade and changing patterns of demand, but also a requirement for greater governmental involvement and direction in the use of resources in order to support the war effort. Moreover, this experience of wartime direction of the economy followed a long period in which there was a dwindling of confidence in previously accepted beliefs in the efficacy of the workings of the market economy and of economic agents. This was a period which embraced the inflation of the early 1920s and the heavy unemployment of the 1930s. The post-war years saw, therefore, the emergence of a consensus in favour of a more active governmental role in managing the economy. Eventually, this led to an acceptance of the importance of demand management; of the subordination of price control to the macroeconomic objective of full employment; and of a view of the Bank of England as part of the machinery of state for the implementation of macroeconomic policy. Hence, the loss of central bank autonomy culminating in the Nationalisation Act of 1946.

This is not to say that during the 1950s and 1960s the Bank showed no glimpses of independence. The Bank of England Act of 1946, in fact, left some little room for independent action. It was short on essential detail. Thus, ' ... beyond the enactment of powers of direction, nothing in the legislation indicated ... what the division of responsibility was to be between the Bank and the Treasury ... ' (Cairncross, 1988: 50). Under the legislation the Governor could be 'directed' by the Treasury to take action and the Bank's 'requests' to the commercial banks could be made binding by the Treasury, but the Governor had to be consulted in all cases and the Treasury itself had no power to instruct the commercial banks directly. Moreover, in practice the power of direction has never been exercised against the Bank.

The precise balance of power between Bank and Treasury depended upon particular circumstances and on the perceived success of the Bank's interventions. Lack of success has always been more likely to invite outside interference. For the immediate post-war decades, the events of the mid-1950s can be seen as something of a turning point, for they illustrate both the exercise of independence at that time and its clear limitations.

During the life of the immediate post-war Labour administration, domestic monetary policy was not considered central to overall economic policy, but with the election of the Conservatives in 1951 a more active interest rate policy was introduced and the government, for the most part, was prepared to allow Cobbold (Governor, 1949–61) a free hand. However, things started to go wrong in 1955 (Kynaston, 1995: 48–9). In April the government had introduced an expansionary budget and was expecting the Bank to hold back inflationary pressures through the implementation of a credit squeeze on the banks. The Bank, however, was reluctant to impose quantitative restrictions on the clearing banks. By early summer, the frictions were clear, yet Cobbold not only refused government requests to tighten the squeeze (arguing that the banks would be unable to bear it) but also insisted on the sanctity of current practice whereby the Treasury could only communicate with the commercial banks through the mediation of the Bank of England. In the spring of 1956 the Governor resisted the Prime Minister's suggestion of imposing liquidity ratio requirements on the clearing banks and pointed to the need to cut back government expenditure (Kynaston, 1995: 49). There was a similar clash eighteen months later, between the Governor and Chancellor Thorneycroft. The latter wanted quantitative restrictions on bank lending and modest increases in interest rates, but the Governor reminded the government that the 1946 Act had vested the Bank with the power to 'direct' the commercial banks and he sided with the banks in preferring higher interest rates and no quantitative restrictions. On this occasion, the Treasury conceded and the bank rate was raised to seven per cent in September 1957, despite government views.

But while the Bank may have won this battle, it was losing the war. Within the context of the long history of Bank autonomy, such displays of independence were marginal. The truth is that, in this period the scope for independent action was severely restricted (Fforde, 1992: ch. 10). Demand management encompassed all macro-economic policy and Bank action was not allowed to stray very far. The policy ethos that prevailed from the late 1940s until (at least) the early 1970s subordinated Bank activity to that of the government, to the policy preoccupations of the political party in power.

In the case of the mid-1950s, confusion over policy responsibilities was one factor in the appointment of the Radcliffe Committee. The subsequent Report, published in 1959, strongly affirmed the subordination of the Bank – and of monetary policy – to the Treasury and to the overall aims of discretionary management. 'Monetary policy ... cannot ... pursue its own independent objectives. It is part of a country's economic policy as a whole and must be planned as such ... We are ... dissociating ourselves from a view ... that the central bank should be assured complete independence from political influence' (Radcliffe, 1959: 273). The Wilson Committee, some two decades later, took a similar view (Wilson, 1980: para. 1278).

Indeed the outcome of the problems of the mid-1950s was a belittling of the Bank's autonomy in monetary matters, with the Bank powerless to prevent Conservative pre-election booms or the sharp inflationary expansion of 1971/73 ('Barber boom'), and it was unable to persuade the new Labour government of 1964 to adopt a policy of public sector retrenchment, despite a confrontation between Prime Minister and Governor (Wilson, 1971: 34–8).

To repeat, despite the odd exception, the Bank was very much subordinate to the Treasury at this time.

Bank autonomy since the 1970s

The more recent phase of British monetary history, from the abandonment of fixed exchange rates in 1972, has been one of mixed fortunes for the Bank of England's status and independence. As elsewhere in the West, the breakdown of international monetary arrangements and the unprecedented experience of high and variable rates of inflation during the 1970s gave much greater standing to the role of monetary policy. The emergence of stagflation and the failure of successive incomes policies (which had been designed to moderate rises in general wage costs) were particularly significant in increasing the political acceptance of a macro-economic approach which was more reliant on monetarist principles. For the Bank, the end of the Keynesian consensus not only enhanced the status of its sphere of influence (monetary policy) but also raised the possibility of a reappraisal of a more general issue for autonomous central banking – the appropriate degree of discretion to be exercised by policy-makers.

Enhanced status certainly followed, but not greater independence. In effect, the conduct of monetary policy was considered to be too important politically to leave the Bank freedom to get on with its implementation. This was never so clear as during Mrs Thatcher's premiership when monetary policy was the central plank of the government's economic, anti-inflation programme. She doubted that people of sufficient calibre could be found to run a truly independent Bank. But, more significantly, she felt that the conduct of monetary policy was a political responsibility of government, that at that time (1988) ' ... it would be seen as an abdication by the Chancellor ... an admission of failure of resolve on our part ... ' to pass such responsibilities over to technicians in an independent Bank (Thatcher, 1993: 706).

Thus, even though the theoretical paradigm in which macro policy was then governed was wholly alien to that of the Keynesian advisors of the 1950s and 1960s, the Bank's position, if anything, was even more subservient under the new regime. Indeed, so important was the conduct of monetary policy to Mrs Thatcher that she enhanced the politicization of the Bank during her tenure of office. Her strident espousal of monetarism in the early 1980s was not reciprocated by the Governor, Gordon Richardson. He was perhaps conscious of the fact that the Bank had to cooperate with whichever political party was in power, that the monetarist stance was politically controversial and, in public, he advocated a more watered-down version of 'practical monetarism' (Bank of England, 1978: 31–7; Bank of England, 1984: 63–4, 65–7). Subsequently, when his tenure of office was completed in 1983 the Prime Minister appointed a political sympathizer from outside the Bank, Robin Leigh-Pemberton. Irrespective of his individual and professional merits, at that time the Bank was seen as being far from independent.

In 1988, the Chancellor, Nigel Lawson, raised with Mrs Thatcher the possibility of introducing legislation which would create an independent Bank of England along the lines of the Federal Reserve, a central bank charged with the duty of maintaining the value of the currency. In October 1989 he made known his views publicly, in his resignation speech. His aim had been to give greater credibility to the government's anti-inflation stance, at a time when the earlier commitments to clear monetary targets had fallen by the wayside and at a time – prior to Britain's entry into the ERM – when there was no formal fixed exchange rate policy (Lawson, 1992: 868–9, 1059–60). He thought that, in the short run, an independent Bank would command more credibility in the markets than the government and that, in the long term, the creation of a strong institution, legally obliged to eradicate inflation, would be a powerful force to the good. The proposal, though, was turned down by the Prime Minister and, in the event, measures to give the Bank greater independence had to await Mrs Thatcher's own resignation, in 1990.

Since then, a number of (for the most part) tentative moves by government have enhanced the Bank's relative contribution to the implementation of monetary policy. From November 1993 the Bank has had the right to determine the *timing* of interest rate changes (although the Chancellor still determined the rate itself). Also from April 1994 (on the recommendation of the Treasury and Civil Service Committee of the House of Commons) the minutes of the monthly meetings between Governor and Chancellor on monetary policy began to be published. The rationale behind this move was largely a question of subjecting government to market scrutiny, in that it allowed the public to judge for itself whether or not ministers were acting responsibly if they should choose to ignore the Bank's advice. Also in February 1993 the Bank began publishing its own quarterly *Inflation Report*, and this is now produced without consultation with the Treasury. This move was, in effect, a re-assertion of the central bank's primary concern with the value of the currency. It also provides a regular medium through which the Bank can express its own opinion on inflationary prospects.

The move towards greater autonomy for the Bank of England accelerated with the election of a new Labour government, in May 1997, when it implemented 'the most important institutional and operational changes at the Bank since nationalisation in 1946' (Rodgers, 1997: 1). Importantly, the Chancellor of the Exchequer, Gordon Brown, granted the Bank power over the level and timing of changes in interest rates and he also increased the degree of transparency governing decision making. The Bank was not to determine monetary policy – this is still the preserve of the government – but the Bank was given greater autonomy in deciding how to achieve the objectives of policy. Operationally, the government (subject to parliamentary approval) sets a target rate for annualized inflation and the Bank is obliged to use its new powers over interest rates to hit the target. Decisions on interest rates are taken monthly by a Monetary Policy Committee which consists of the Governor, two Deputy-Governors, and six other members (four appointed by the Chancellor, two by the Governor); if there is a split decision on interest rates, the Governor has the casting vote. Individual voting on interest rate changes, and the arguments behind them, are also published.

Finally, if the inflation rate should deviate by more than one per cent either side of the target limits, the governor has to explain in public through the medium of a letter to the Chancellor of the Exchequer.

As we have already seen, the move towards greater autonomy has arisen for a number of reasons (Capie, Goodhart and Schnadt, 1994; Capie and Goodhart, 1995) but, in the UK, the fundamental motivation arises out of changed economic and political circumstances. In particular, the government's declared objective of eradicating high inflation (of keeping the annual rate below four per cent and pushing it below two per cent by 1997) has needed some sort of policy or institutional underpinning. Greater independence for the Bank is part response to failures elsewhere in monetary policy. There has been no attempt to reinstate the monetary targets of the early 1980s and the earlier debacle of the UK's experience within the European Exchange Rate Mechanism (when the UK authorities were obliged to devalue sterling and leave the ERM in 1992) removed the discipline of formal stable exchange rates for most of the 1990s. In effect, moves towards greater central bank autonomy became more acceptable as previous sources of discipline in monetary policy were abandoned but, until 1997, these remained modest moves only. Central bank autonomy was not a critical plank of government policy in the same way as the Medium-Term Strategy had been in the early 1980s.[4] However, the current Labour government has strongly accelerated the process – it has enhanced the importance of central bank independence within its macro-economic policy and sees it as an essential step towards joining EMU in the early years of the new millenium.

Bank autonomy in perspective: the pre-First World War period

The move towards greater Bank of England autonomy is, thus, very recent – a flower in the snow which could easily be overwhelmed by a new economic storm. The history of the twentieth century shows in a startling way that this is a real possibility. There are many examples from overseas – including Germany between the wars (and not just under fascism) – but it is also true of different periods in British history. Indeed, the Bank of England has only exercised true independence in the years before the First World War and it is instructive to examine the reasons for this, and the reasons why autonomy was lost for most of the twentieth century.

In the decades immediately before the First World War the Bank of England's autonomy was at its zenith. The Bank was free to determine how best to implement exchange rate policy, to influence short-term interest rates and to engage in open market operations. Even though there was some outside criticism and occasional friction with the Treasury over interest rates and commission charges on the government's account, there was no serious challenge to the Bank's operational freedom to implement what foreign exchange and monetary policies there then were. How had this come about?

Constitutional arrangements

The Bank of England was beginning to be recognized as a central bank by the last quarter of the nineteenth century but it was not a department of the state, nor was it owned by the state (Bagehot, 1912).[5] Yet its creation, almost two centuries earlier, had arisen from the requirements of state finances and, throughout the time that the succession to the English throne remained in dispute, it was a pillar of the Protestant Establishment, an institution dominated by the commercial interests of London. The Bank was created as part of the Tunnage Act of 1694, with its powers laid out in a Charter and more clearly defined in the Bank Act of 1697 (Richards, 1929: ch. V; Clapham, 1958: vol. 1, ch. 1). It was a joint-stock company (an Act of 1707 granting it a monopoly of joint-stock banking in England and Wales), capital was privately subscribed, the directors were elected by those proprietors who had subscribed at least £500, and the Governor and Deputy were appointed by the Court from among its own members. The period of office for the Governor was relatively short (two years in most instances). The Bank was a profit-making corporation, with independent income which came partly from commercial banking operations (bill discounting, lending, remittance and clearing services). Formally, therefore, the Bank was autonomous – privately owned, independently managed and generating its own revenue.

It was during the eighteenth century that the Bank's notes became the sole form of bank note circulation in London, although Scottish, Irish and, by the end of the century, a growing number of English provincial banks issued their own notes (except in Lancashire where Bank of England notes were used). Although widely used and generally accepted (for example, in transactions between financial institutions and large commercial concerns), the Bank's notes were not granted legal tender status in England and Wales until 1833. For much of its early history the Bank's business was confined to London, the first provincial offices being opened in 1827.

It is important to realize that the Bank was a commercially-oriented institution that only slowly evolved as a central bank. Critical to this evolution were the Bank's relations with the state, which have always been close. The immediate reason for its creation in 1694 had been

William III's requirement to finance his European military campaigns, with the Bank committing all of the original capital of £1.2 million as a loan to the government. In fact, throughout the first century-and-a-quarter of the Bank's history, the bellicose nature of the British imperial state meant that war or the threat of war was forever present. So, too, was the need to finance such wars and it was the Bank that provided the government with an effective agency through which to sell securities and to deploy resources. In the eighteenth century this was its primary task (Bowen, 1995). It was in these years that the Bank consolidated its position as the government's banker and manager of the National Debt. By 1816 the Bank's loans to the government totalled £14.6 million, backed by equity of some £11.6 million.

Undoubtedly, then, the Bank's financial relationship with the State could expose it to government pressure (though on occasions it could work in the reverse direction, with the Bank, as creditor, having the upper hand). But there were more formal and open opportunities for political interference. The Bank's powers and privileges were contained in its charter and this was formally subject to periodic review by Parliament and, thus, opportunities arose for an appraisal of Bank performance. The second quarter of the nineteenth century, in particular, proved important for a wide-ranging debate about the causes of monetary instability and the Bank's role in provoking it. The debate brought the Bank's actions under close scrutiny, encouraged open hostility from some quarters, and led to its powers being modified. Its monopoly of joint-stock banking was lost and its power to issue notes was closely regulated. In other words, while it may have been formally independent at this stage of its history, it was not free from political buffeting.

The reasons for such 'interference' are informative in the light of what has happened in the twentieth century. Modification of the Bank's powers was part of a much broader attack on 'Old Corruption' and 'Privilege'. One major strand of this movement was a desire to modernize the state bureaucratic machine, and such reform encompassed the Bank as an important agent of the state. Another broad influence, which stretched much further than the Bank, was the pervasive influence of neo-classical/market economics and the broader acceptance of the need to liberalize markets and remove monopoly privileges, such as those enjoyed by Threadneedle Street.

Legal restrictions on Bank discretion

In addition to these broad political and philosophical factors, the Bank was more specifically targeted because of perceived weaknesses and failures in its monetary management.

There was a series of business cycle fluctuations from the 1820s. For many contemporaries the most dramatic features of these fluctuations were the recurrent monetary crises that were associated with the onset of recession. The monetary crises of 1825, 1837, 1839 and 1847 were particularly important in influencing the regulations governing the Bank of England's action. This was a formative period in the development of monetary thought, with a great deal of discussion on the determinants of general price changes and on the effects of the monetary innovation then taking place. It was within this context that the power and influence of the Bank was subjected to close scrutiny and public debate. The legislative outcome was to fix the framework for many of the Bank's activities for the next three-quarters of a century, providing the base on which Victorian and Edwardian monetary orthodoxy became embedded into British political economy (Fetter, 1965). Crucially, it was an orthodoxy that permitted the operation of a largely autonomous central bank.

The cornerstone of this legislative framework was those stipulations that aimed to minimize Bank of England discretion with respect to fluctuations in the stock of money. The Bank's obligations in respect of the exchange rate had been fixed in 1816 and 1819. These meant that the Bank was legally obliged to maintain full convertibility of its notes to gold on demand. In other words, the degree of discretion it could exercise over its note circulation was closely restricted. Moreover, continued dissatisfaction with monetary fluctuations during subsequent decades led to further restrictions on Bank discretion, changes that culminated in the passing of the 1844 Bank Charter Act. This measure was based directly on the principles of monetary regulation espoused by the 'Currency School' of thinkers and it meant that the Bank's note issue (above a fiduciary issue of some £14 million) could vary pound for pound only with fluctuations in its gold reserve. The importance of this measure in making the Bank's note circulation act 'as if it were precious coin' was underpinned in contemporary minds by the wide acceptance of the efficacy of the price/specie flow mechanism which linked international exchanges and ensured price stability (Collins, 1988: ch. 5).

In summary, the legislation of 1816, 1819 and 1844 closely tied the Bank's note issue into the international economy through the gold standard. The legislation, in effect, bound Bank action within clear, legally obligatory 'rules' of behaviour and, in total, these measures severely restricted the amount of discretion the Bank could exercise. The legislation sought to make monetary and exchange policy largely a matter of conforming to well-established rules, not one of judgement.

It was this status as a non-discretionary agent of the gold standard that was critical to the Bank's ability to exercise autonomy in the period before the First World War. Removal of discretion for this privately-owned bank was, in effect, an essential precondition for the Bank winning so much freedom from interference. Being bound by strict rules, its actions could be portrayed as impartial and technical. Of course, the rules, in turn, were justified by the widespread acceptance of the efficacy of the gold standard. The passage of time was important, too, for once it was established that it was in the Bank's province alone to apply the rules, then the passing of each decade strengthened the institutional *status quo*. In this respect the perceived success of the Bank in the late nineteenth century and at the beginning of the twentieth century – the avoidance of financial instability and general pre-eminence of British finance and trade – was also critical. As long as the system was thought to be working successfully there was little call for change from powerful interests.

Looking back over the pre-1914 period, a number of significant points should be stressed. First, political interference with the Bank in the first half of the century arose from dissatisfaction with contemporary Bank performance. Secondly, the reforms of the mid-nineteenth century that set up the regulatory pre-conditions for autonomous central banking were not always welcomed by the Bank itself. To an extent, then, autonomy was thrust on it – initially it wished to retain discretion and it was only later that the Bank recognized that it was the acknowledged sanctity of the 'rules' which helped define its position within the economy. Thirdly, not surprisingly it was the nature of prevailing economic thought that determined the detail of that interference – in this case in favour of minimising discretionary powers over the money supply. As we know, this, in turn, was part of the broad shift towards a *laissez-faire* orthodoxy in the approach of the state to the economy and it meant that there was little inclination on the part of politicians to interfere with the Bank, provided the rules governing its behaviour – and the behaviour itself – were seen as supportive of the market economy. And in the sixty or so years following the mid-nineteenth century legislation the Bank's actions with respect to the exchange rate, money supply and price level were widely perceived as being successful. Obviously frictions did arise (for example, over charges on the government's account and over the share of responsibility between the Bank and the commercial banks in holding gold reserves) but these were peripheral to the main non-discretionary legislative framework which established the Bank's clear autonomy. That did not come under serious attack.

Bank autonomy in perspective: the inter-war period

It is clear from British history that the establishment of unambiguous, non-discretionary rules are a necessary pre-condition for truly autonomous central banking, but it is not a sufficient condition on its own. The history of the inter-war years highlights that a whole complex of factors can hold sway – prevailing political and economic philosophies, the general performance of the economy and the specific performance of the central bank are crucial. Between the wars these factors changed fundamentally and the Bank lost much of its autonomy. As has been stressed, for central bank autonomy to survive there must be generally accepted rules of monetary control; the bank must be seen as acting impartially (non-politically) in interpreting the rules; and it must be considered to be successful in so doing. These conditions, which had held before 1914, all changed in the inter-war years.

At the beginning of the period, however, the portents for a reversion to the pre-war position were strong. Two factors were particularly favourable to the Bank's efforts to re-establish its independence: the Bank's new Governor and the return to the gold standard. Some commentators have correctly pointed to the critical importance in general of the personality of the Governor (especially *vis-à-vis* the Chancellor).[6] At this time the Bank, in fact, had an extremely strong Governor, Montagu Norman, who succeeded Cockayne in 1920 and remained Governor until 1940. He was a forceful, skilful Governor and a jealous guardian of the Bank's freedom from political interference (Sayers, 1986: 643–54). Britain's inter-war experience shows, though, that while the personality of the Governor and his awareness of the Bank's traditions and legal status may well be important in safeguarding autonomy, these, too, are insufficient on their own. A strong Governor is only an insurance against interference if other factors are favourable.

History suggests that the assertion of the impartiality and efficacy of economic theory or rules is also a fickle safeguard of central bank autonomy. At the beginning of the inter-war period, few in Britain who thought of these matters questioned the attractiveness of re-establishing the gold standard and all that it implied about Bank of England behaviour. The Report of the Cunliffe Committee in 1918 was unstinting in its admiration of the pre-war monetary standard and the Bank's role within it (Cunliffe, 1918: 333–9). As Richard Sayers, the Bank's official historian, has expressed it: ' ... the men of 1919 believed that the best monetary system was that of 1913: a world gold standard based on London, with the Bank of England controlling the system ... ' (Sayers, 1986: 111). Moreover, arguments in favour of restoration were greatly reinforced by the inflationary experience of the immediate post-war years when the gold standard had remained temporarily suspended. In fact, opposition to the decision to reintroduce the system in 1925 was limited and ineffectual. The main contrary argument came from Keynes and his objection was to the chosen rate of exchange, not to the principles of operation. Thus, on the face of it, in the 1920s the scene was set for the reimposition of the impartial rules of monetary behaviour that had worked so well before the war, rules which – as has been argued – were essential to ensuring central bank autonomy.

However, this was not to be. In fact, inter-war experience illustrates starkly that what appears to be the most steadfast economic orthodoxy can be overthrown, that fashion in economic matters is changeable. In this case, views on the efficacy of a stable exchange rate regime changed markedly in the light of changed economic circumstances and, as a result, the performance of the old system – and that of the Bank – came under close, critical scrutiny, in a manner unknown since the mid-nineteenth century.

The general circumstances are familiar enough. The volume of British exports suffered a collapse and unemployment rose. Exports (in constant price terms) averaged four-fifths of the immediate pre-war level during the 1920s and were down to an average of just two-thirds of that level in the 1930s. High unemployment rates startled contemporaries – at an average of 12.8 per cent of insured workers in the 1920s and at 16.5 per cent in the 1930s. Industry faced major restructuring and those industries and regions which had been heavily dependent on overseas markets, such as South Wales collieries and Lancashire cotton mills, suffered sharp contraction. The backdrop was a weak international economy, especially after 1929. International monetary collapse saw a run on sterling in 1931, the suspension of the gold standard and the depreciation of the pound – all unthinkable in the decades before the First World War.

A major consequence of the period's economic instability and generally perceived poor performance was an attack on the Bank of England's traditional role in monetary management. Legally charged with maintaining a stable exchange rate and currency convertibility, the Bank became the champion of stable prices and tight money. Such aims led to conflict with those who advocated a more lax monetary stance, one more conducive to expansion at home. In crude terms, a conflict arose between policy measures which might stimulate domestic industry and reduce unemployment and those advocated by the Bank to keep inflation low (or negative) and re-establish international monetary stability as a boost to world trade. It was in these circumstances that the Bank's position as the neutral agent of generally accepted rules of monetary control evaporated. It became easy to portray the Bank as the champion of the City against industry, as the champion of price stability against concern for unemployment, as the champion of external prosperity against internal expansion.[7] The dangers of political interference were obvious.

Criticism of the Bank built up during the 1920s, after sterling convertibility had been restored at the pre-war parity of $4.86, but the demise of central bank autonomy was part of a more general shift in economic thinking that led to fundamental questioning of the rules of monetary regulation. Chronic unemployment and external instability led to diminishing confidence in the efficiency of markets and a reinforcement of the move away from *laissez-faire* economic policy. The 'Keynesian revolution' was part of this, but the loss of faith in markets was more widespread and even affected policy advisers, including officials at the Treasury and at the Bank itself. Throughout the 1930s, for instance, government trade policies were supportive of measures to suppress competition and to encourage supplier collusion, including price fixing (Booth, 1987; Peden, 1988). At the Bank, Norman's industrial interventions are a good illustration of the shift in thinking and he, too, eventually accepted that $4.86 had probably been too high (Collins, 1991: ch. 6).

Such a shift in economic orthodoxy inevitably led to the questioning of the activities of the agents of monetary policy. If the rules governing policy were no longer considered justified and if the Bank was no longer considered to be a neutral arbiter of those rules, Bank freedom of action could no longer be defended. With such a shift in the parameters of prevailing political economy, even a strong Governor such as Norman had to take more cognisance of outside influences and be more accommodating. Events forced the issue and suspension of the gold standard in 1931, rendering the old rules redundant. This removed the constitutional justification of the Bank's autonomy over monetary matters, especially as it was still a privately owned institution with very little accountability to ministers, let alone Parliament. Suspension of the gold standard fundamentally changed the constitutional relationship between the Bank and the Treasury in favour of the latter because it removed the accepted rationale for Bank autonomy. Thus, the stage was set for the nationalization of the Bank after the war and its close incorporation into the state machine of post-war economic management.

Conclusion

Assessment of the effectiveness of the recent attempts to give the Bank of England greater autonomy has to remain very circumspect – it is still early days. As has been shown above, almost immediately on winning the general election in May 1997, the new Labour government granted the Bank of England power to determine the level and timing of changes in the rate of interest although the government retains the responsibility of determining monetary policy. The Bank itself apparently favoured this arrangement.[8] Thus, in the prolonged debate on possible legislative reforms, the then Deputy-Governor, Rupert Pennant-Rea, in 1994 advocated such a division of responsibility between government and Bank (Pennant-Rea, 1995). It was his view that it should be the former's role to determine monetary policy (setting inflation targets, timetables and the like), and the Bank's responsibility should be confined to merely technical matters, determining the best means of achieving government objectives. This is now reality. However, in an historical context, it is a narrow interpretation of Bank duties and it is almost the opposite of what Sayers saw as the essence of central banking. Moreover, the Bank's powers have also been reduced in other ways. In particular, the Bank (in this instance, against its wishes) has lost its traditional supervisory and regulatory powers over the banking sector. These have passed to a new, separate Financial Services Authority. Taken together, these new changes mark a clear diminution of the influence of the Bank.

As regards the likely robustness of the new arrangements, clearly much will depend on future developments concerning the European single currency and the European Central Bank. The stronger the influence of the latter, the weaker that of national central banks such as the Bank of England. The irony is that, the greater the effectiveness of European Monetary Union and of the UK's position within it, the less important will be the Bank of England and the greater the chances of its new-found autonomy remaining intact.

Nationally, of course, central bank autonomy is in the gift of any government with a majority in Parliament. The granting of autonomy to a central bank over the conduct of monetary affairs can only be justified in a democratic society if the Bank's freedom of action is severely limited by a set of rules of behaviour that ensure that it can act only in a prescribed manner for the 'public good'. This implies not only that such a set of rules (European Monetary System?) can be devised but also that they can win widespread political support (domestically, of both Labour and Conservative governments?). It is because of such restrictive conditions that, historically, Bank of England autonomy has been a rather fragile child. Under the gold standard, the unique conditions existed and independence appeared to be very robust. Rules were prescribed, they were widely supported and they were perceived as being successful. This has not been the case subsequently, though on occasions the Bank has exhibited some independence of action. Nevertheless, even if in the near future there is the conjunction of factors that leads to a broad political consensus in favour of more autonomy, the lesson of history (and common sense) is that no set of economic rules is eternal and, of more practical significance, political support for a particular economic paradigm or set of rules is likely to be relatively short-lived. In effect, monetary policy is too important to escape the close attention of democratically-elected governments.

Mrs Thatcher can have the final word. In her autobiography she asserts the need for government to set a target for price stability, and her preferred route is via targets for monetary aggregates. She rejects fixed exchange rates and, significantly, states that a return to a mechanism for price stability ' ... should not entail giving new autonomy to the Bank of England. Ultimately, it is the politicians who must be accountable for economic policy. But they have to learn from the mistakes of the past, so that they and their successors are not condemned to repeat them' (Thatcher, 1995: 570).

Notes

1. Among the assessments of relative performance see Alesina and Summers (1993); Posen (1993); Wood, Mills and Capie (1993); and Doyle and Weale (1994).
2. See Fforde (1992), ch. 1 for detailed changes to drafts of the legislation as they reflected negotiations between the Treasury and the Bank.
3. These quotes are also reproduced in Collins (1993, vol. 3: 218–24).
4. This set out the targets for monetary aggregates and reduction in the Public Sector Borrowing Requirement.
5. Extracts are reproduced in Collins (1993, vol. 1: 238–91).
6. Evidence of Kit McMahon (former Deputy-Governor) and Denis Healey (former Chancellor), Treasury and Civil Service Committee (1994: 11–21 and 49–57 respectively).
7. The best illustration is Keynes (1925), reproduced in Pollard (1970). Also see Pollard's introduction.
8. Evidence of Eddie George (Governor) and Rupert Pennant-Rea (Deputy-Governor), Treasury and Civil Service Committee (1994: 22–37).

References

Alesina, Alberto and Summers, Lawrence H. (1993), 'Central bank independence and macroeconomic performance', *Journal of Money, Credit and Banking*, 24.

Bagehot, Walter (1912), *Lombard Street*, London.

Bank of England (1978), 'Reflections on the conduct of monetary policy' (Governor's lecture), *Bank of England Quarterly Bulletin*, 18, March.

Bank of England (1984), *The Development and Operation of Monetary Policy, 1960–1983*, Oxford. See 'British economic policy over the last decade', pp. 63–4, and 'Setting monetary objectives', pp. 65–7.

Booth, A. (1987), 'Britain in the 1930s: a managed economy?', *Economic History Review*, XL.

Bowen, H.V. (1995), 'The Bank of England during the long eighteenth century, 1694–1820', in Roberts, R. and Kynaston, D. (eds), *The Bank of England, Money, Power and Influence, 1694–1994*, Oxford.

Cairncross, Alec (1988), 'The Bank of England: relationship with the Government, Civil Service and Parliament', in Toniolo, G. (ed.), *Central Banks' Independence in Historical Perspective*, Berlin/New York.

Capie, F., Goodhart, C. and Schnadt, N. (1994), 'The development of central banking', in Capie, F. et al. (eds), *The Future of Central Banking*, Cambridge.

Capie, Forrest and Goodhart, Charles (1995), 'Central banks, macro policy and the financial system: the nineteenth and twentieth centuries', *Financial History Review*, 2.

Clapham, John (1958), *The Bank of England. A History*, Cambridge, 2 vols.

Collins, Michael (1988), *Money and Banking in the UK: A History*, London.

Collins, Michael (1991), *Banks and Industrial Finance in Britain*, London, (new edition, 1995).

Collins, Michael (ed.) (1993), *Central Banking in History*, Aldershot, 3 vols.

Cunliffe (1918), *Committee on Currency and Foreign Exchanges. First Interim Report*, Cd. 9052, Parliamentary Papers 1918, VI, HMSO, London.

Doyle, Christopher and Weale, Martin (1994), 'Do we really need an independent central bank?', *Oxford Review of Economic Policy*, 10 (3).

Fforde, John (1992), *The Bank of England and Public Policy, 1941–1958*, Cambridge.

Fetter, Frank Whiston (1965), *Development of British Monetary Orthodoxy, 1797–1875*, Cambridge, MA.

Friedman, Milton (1962), 'Should there be an independent monetary authority?', in Yeager, L. (ed.), *In Search of a Monetary Constitution*, Cambridge, MA.

Keynes, J.M. (1925), 'The economic consequences of Mr Churchill', reproduced in Pollard, S. (ed.), *The Gold Standard and Employment Policies between the Wars*, London, 1970.

Kynaston, David (1995), 'The Bank of England and the Government', in Roberts, R. and Kynaston, D. (eds), *The Bank of England, Money, Power and Influence, 1694–1994*, Oxford.

Lawson, Nigel (1992), *The View from No. 11: Memoirs of a Tory Radical*, London.

Peden, G. C. (1988), *Keynes, the Treasury and British Economic Policy*, London.

Pennant-Rea, Rupert (1995), 'The Bank of England: yesterday, today and tomorrow', in Roberts, R. and Kynaston, D. (eds), *The Bank of England, Money, Power and Influence, 1694–1994*, Oxford.

Posen, A. (1993), 'Why central bank independence does not cause low inflation: there is no institutional fix for politics', *AMEX Bank Review*.

Radcliffe (1959), *Committee on the Working of the Monetary System. Report*, London, HMSO, Cmnd. 827.

Read, Tessa (1996), 'Creating a central bank for Europe', *Euromoney*, July.

Richards, R.D. (1929), *The Early History of Banking in England*, London.

Rodgers, Peter (1997), 'Changes at the Bank of England', *Bank of England Quarterly Bulletin*, August, 37 (3).

Sayers, R.S. (1957), *Central Banking after Bagehot*, Oxford.

Sayers, R.S. (1986), *The Bank of England, 1891–1944*, Cambridge.

Thatcher, Margaret (1993), *Downing Street Years*, London.

Thatcher, Margaret (1995), *The Path to Power*, London.

Treasury and Civil Service Committee (1994), *First report. The Role of the Bank of England*, London, 2 vols.

Wilson, Harold (1971), *The Labour Government, 1964–1970*, London.

Wilson, Harold (1980), *Committee to Review the Functioning of Financial Services. Report*, London, HMSO, Cmnd. 7937.

Wood, G.E., Mills, T.E. and Capie, F.H. (1993), *Central Bank Independence*, London.

PART II
National Experiences with Central Banking

CHAPTER TWO

The Delayed Modernization of the Central Banks of France and Spain in the Twentieth Century

Olivier Feiertag and Pablo Martín Aceña

Introduction

In the overall process of modernization of note-issuing banks, a feature common to both the Bank of France and the Bank of Spain is that they did not become fully fledged central banks until relatively late in the twentieth century, certainly later than other European banks of issue such as the Bank of England or the *Reichsbank*. This widely held view has been clearly expounded, for example, by Forrest Capie, Charles Goodhart and Norbert Schnadt in their recent study of the phases in the development of the concept and practice of central banking in the industrialized nations (Capie et al., 1994).

This view is based on the postulate, firmly established at least since Walter Bagehot, that the main, if not the sole, criterion of a central bank's modernity is its function as lender of last resort (Collins, 1993). The objective of upholding the currency's internal and external value, like the maintenance of price stability, in effect derives directly, in a certain respect, from a modern central bank's basic guarantee to keep money markets functioning smoothly. Seen in this respect, the delayed development of the Bank of France and the Bank of Spain is obvious and calls for historical analysis.

The first step is to enquire about the actual concept of 'modernity' as applied to a note-issuing bank. An essentially historical process, modernization, by its very nature, comprises various and changing elements. It is typical of economic theory today to condemn as archaic the concepts once held to be modern. In this sense, the function of lender of last resort, given theoretical form in Great Britain in the last third of the nineteenth century, has not always and not everywhere been the universal indicator of a note-issuing bank's modernity.

Immediately after the Second World War, for example, the French economist François Perroux proposed a definition of a modern central bank's function which allowed the problem of modernization to be explained in a very different light: he contrasted the old model of private and passive bank of issue with the modern one of public and active central bank (Perroux, 1945: 485–98). This development, Perroux explained, reflected the schematic transition from an economy globally driven by market mechanisms to a production method dominated by state preferences and state controls. The role of the bank of issue was no longer the traditional one of reacting to the spontaneous and anonymous needs of trade. Once modernized, it was to become on the contrary, 'the centre of control and administration of money and credit'. Distinguishing 'pathological inflation' from 'productive inflation', Perroux no longer gave a modern bank of issue the strictly 'financial' task of guaranteeing the metallic value of money, but instead the 'economic' responsibility of creating, by a veritable 'draft on the future', 'the manoeuvring space needed to generate a volume of investment judged desirable'. François Perroux's analyses, which were formulated in the spring of 1945, several months before the nationalization of the Bank of France, led to a new view of the historical problem of a central bank's modernization.

The history of central banks in the twentieth century, at least in France and Spain, and certainly also in Italy, is thus rooted in the existence of different and partly contradictory conceptions of the *modernity* of a bank of issue. To some extent, this is what studying the apparent French and Spanish time-lag is essentially about. It involves examining what were, at various times in their respective histories, the objectives and instruments of the Bank of France and the Bank of Spain. How did the global structure of their balance sheets and, more precisely, the composition of their portfolios develop? What operations, in particular, were permitted to them by their successive statutes? Are these developments also discernible in the changes in their administrative organization? Finally, one could examine how the two banks themselves conceived their role, by looking, for example, at the Research Departments which have come into being during the twentieth century.

All these questions constitute an internal analysis of the modernization of a central bank. They have historical relevance only insofar as they concern the more general development of the financial, economic and even political environment. Four external conditions can therefore be defined *a priori*:

1. The degree of integration into the mechanisms and rules of the international monetary system: to what extent were the attempts at monetary cooperation between central banks able to influence their

modernization according to a unique model based, for example, on maintaining convertibility and preserving monetary stability.

2. The structure of the national banking system: the functions of a central bank clearly depend on the development of the banking system in its entirety, on its openness to competition, and thus on the degree of risk which is typical of it. The development of the function of lender of last resort, for example, derives quite naturally from this.
3. The nature of the institutional and practical relations between central bank and Treasury: is it possible to define historically a relationship between the central bank's level of autonomy – or, on the contrary, of its integration into the state – and the modernization of its tasks?
4. Finally, the importance of the human factor must be mentioned. After all, the process of transformation in the role of a bank of issue is closely linked with the personalities of the people in charge of it, with their theoretical make-up, their career profiles, and with their social or ideological beliefs.

All these aspects invite us to ask the question of the modernization of the Bank of France or the Bank of Spain in an essentially historical perspective. An attempt will therefore be made to propose a chronology of the slow modernization of the two institutions during the twentieth century, varying the different possible indicators of their eventual modernity or, on the contrary, of their relative slowness to modernize. In this respect, the comparative approach seems the most promising, as it should also contribute by pinpointing the differences in pace and environment which for a long time distinguished and possibly also assimilated the French and Spanish banks of issue within the scope of a model that could be qualified as 'latin'.

The Bank of France

For a long time, the Bank of France occupied a special position among the banks of issue of the industrialized nations. In effect, it seems to have fulfilled the functions of a modern central bank later than others in the twentieth century (Plessis, 1995: 9–19). 'In truth,' wrote Jean Bouvier in 1973, 'the lack of understanding of the exact role of the Bank of France in the monetary and economic system was a permanent phenomenon which does not seem to have ended until after the Second World War. Neither monetary nor state authorities really took account – or then only with a considerable time lag – of changes imposed upon the note-issuing bank by changes in its monetary and economic environment' (Bouvier, 1973: 155). This analysis explicitly echoes numerous criticisms made in a number of quarters before the war in connection with the role of the bank of issue and which emphasized the need for its modernization.[1]

But the subject of the Bank of France's late development is surely, by definition, essentially historical. On the eve of the First World War, the modernity of the bank had taken the form of a continuous and deliberate reinforcement of the Bank of issue's commercial functions at the expense of its role as 'bank of banks'. It must therefore be stressed that, at the start of the twentieth century, the bank of issue's modernity still consisted primarily, in its governors' eyes, in a broadening of its basically commercial banking functions, at a time when the Bank of England, since the 1870s, had at least completed the adjustment to its function as lender of last resort.[2]

Above all, therefore, a study of the modernization of the Bank of France in the twentieth century raises the crucial question of the yardstick for a bank of issue's modernity. Is it just a question of measuring the lag by comparison with a foreign model which could be, as was apparently the case up to the end of the 1950s, the Bank of England, and then, more recently, Germany's *Bundesbank*? Or would it be necessary – a very ambitious enterprise – to try to relate the effective mission of the central bank to the global conditions of the economy in a given period? In practice, taking as the hypothesis the distinction established by Perroux in 1945, an attempt will be made here to examine the possibly contradictory forms taken historically by the modernization of the Bank of France, from 1914, as a function of the development of its capacity to impose a systemic policy, whatever its purpose, be it stability or expansion, financial or economic.

In this light, it seems that the process of modernization of the Bank of France in the twentieth century can be studied at three specific points in its history. The first is from 1926 to 1930, over the brief phase starting with the stabilization of the *franc*, in which the Bank, under the leadership of Emile Moreau, clearly played an active part, and ending with France's slide into depression. The second covers the years from 1936 to 1945, being the period of the gradual nationalization of the bank of issue. Finally, the third concerns the turning point from 1969 to 1973, under Governor Wormser, which took the Bank into the most recent phase of its history. The bank law of 4 August 1993 still seems in many respects to belong to this phase, subject to the final opening of the archives for this period.

The turning point of 1926–29

The nomination of Emile Moreau as Governor of the Bank of France on 26 June 1926 was the start of a new era for the bank of issue. This period, interrupted by the Great Depression in the 1930s, was a first attempt to equip the Bank of France with the instruments of a modern central bank. Emile Moreau himself testified to new ambitions guiding the policy of the Bank of France between 1926 and 1930. 'I attended to big questions,' he stressed, 'I didn't look at all, or only very little, at the smaller matters.'[3] In effect, in his view, 'the bank of issue does not have, as its principal role, the job of discounting. It is a very important question, it is a matter of controlling the market, because its impact is the stabilization of the currency – not only on the inside, but also in relation to international money. It is my firm belief. I have always governed the Bank of France from this perspective, and it runs counter to many established ideas in France.' The consequence accordingly was the need to suppress the entire commercial character of the bank of issue: 'The central bank,' he added, 'should not have branches, should not need to make money, should only have to regulate what concerns the market.' The change in conception was total. The period from 1926 to 1930 thus marked an important stage in the Bank of France's evolution towards the functions of a modern central bank.

A key element behind this development was played by the thoughts and deeds of Pierre Quesnay. Recruited by Moreau in June 1926, and very soon after appointed Head of Research at the Bank, he stayed in this post until 1930 when he left to become the first Director General of the Bank for International Settlements. Quesnay applied with great determination his brilliant knowledge of monetary phenomena and his experience on the Financial Committee of the SDN (Société des Nations) in an effort to modernize the Bank. He expressed his views in particular detail, in June 1928, in an internal memorandum some time before the legal stabilization of the franc. Monetary stabilization was, in his eyes, just the first stage in a global reform of the French financial system in its fundamental adjustment to the new monetary conditions which had emerged since the War. The Bank of France, in his opinion, had the heavy burden of conceiving and organizing the modernization of the French banking system and, firstly, its own modernization: 'To have control over money in circulation, to be able at all times to reduce its commitment sufficiently to lower the volume of lending, to regulate the capital market, to counteract a general inflationary tendency on the stock market or in prices, these are the bank of issue's main tasks today, beyond the job of protecting the currency' (Quesnay, 1928). A surprisingly modern programme at that time! It recognized that the traditional policy of discounting, which had led the Bank to multiply its branches throughout the territory, was a thing of the past. 'This phase in the history of lending,' Quesnay said clearly, 'is over today.'

The changes since the end of the First World War in the structure of the Bank's assets reflected this evolution extremely well, he said, and at the same time required the bank of issue to be given new means of intervention. Especially enlightening is the development of the relative weight of the Bank's commercial portfolio between 1892 and 1928 compared with the total portfolio held at the same time by the four leading deposit banks (Table 2.1).

Table 2.1 Commercial portfolios of the Bank of France and other leading French banks, 1892–1928 (millions of constant *francs*)

	1892	1913	1928
Mean value of the Bank of France's commercial portfolio	550	1 655	2 345
Mean value of the commercial portfolio of the top four deposit banks	899	3 509	18 186
Ratio	60%	47%	12%

Source: Quesnay (1928: 34).

The fall in the relative weight of the Bank's commercial portfolio from the end of the nineteenth century also reduced the effective management of the discount rate which, as Quesnay underlined in 1928, 'no longer allowed the credit volume to be influenced'. The Bank therefore had to have a means of direct intervention, 'capable of ensuring the Bank's control of the money market' (Quesnay, 1928: 13). From 7 August 1926, for the first time in its history, the Bank of France was able to intervene on the foreign exchange market inasmuch as Moreau undertook to give the Bank a true foreign exchange service. In fact, from the end of 1926, the Bank's foreign exchange portfolio, as is well known, did not cease to grow, reaching a peak volume of 36.5 billion *francs* in June 1928 (Bouvier, 1984; and Sicsic and Villeneuve, 1993). This development, immediately after legal stabilization, gave the monetary authorities, at least in theory, room for manoeuvre capable of allowing them, through the purchase or sale of foreign exchange for *francs*, to carry out their function as 'money market regulator'. But the sale of foreign exchange with the aim of reducing the amounts available in *francs* to the public entailed the risk of achieving the opposite effect by raising the *franc* exchange rate to the gold import point, ultimately causing the Bank to issue new notes against the imported gold. The persistence of certain gold standard mechanisms after the First World War was an initial obstacle to achieving the bank of issue's objectives. But an even bigger one was the strong weight of the Treasury on the money market in France.

From 1926, the analyses done by the research department at the Bank of France had explicitly shown that the main obstacle to the adoption by the bank of issue of an open market policy, based on the example of the Bank of England, lay in the role played by the Treasury on the money markets since the war: 'Contrary to what is happening in all countries where the bank of issue ensures the functioning of the money market,' said Pierre Ricard, of the research department, in September 1926, 'the Bank of France has practically no immediate influence on the various segments of the market: demand deposits, securities market, foreign exchange markets' (Ricard, 1926). This impotence of the Bank, already present before 1914, Ricard continued, 'was accentuated by the deposit and discount bank role, which the State Treasury was called upon to play.' This distortion of the Treasury's role was reflected in the unprecedented inflation of public debt, notably the debt outstanding from 1914. 'There, we touch upon the basic vice of the French monetary régime at the time', wrote Quesnay in November 1926 (Quesnay, 1926). The freedom of banks and persons to open current accounts with the Treasury and the issuance of public securities at rates below market were clearly at the root of 'the disorganization of the market'. This situation, aggravated by the fact that in France 'the tendency of the state is always to take money', made it impossible to standardize the rate of interest and, with that, for the bank of issue to take any action to regulate the market.

At any rate, it was these considerations and not, at that time, 'the fear of controlled money' (Sicsic and Villeneuve, 1993: 35), which prevented the Bank of France from crossing the Rubicon from 1928 and initiating the start of an open market policy. If the Bank of France did not become a modern central bank at the end of the 1920s, like other banks of issue at that time, it was due less to a persistent theoretical conservatism on the part of its leaders than to the objective constraints typical of the money markets in France at that time. As Quesnay stressed, 'possessing negotiable assets would not be enough to make the Bank of France a central bank. The market would have to be organized in such a way that it is forced to have recourse to the Bank' (Quesnay, 1928: 14). The weight of the Treasury, the diversity of public-sector debt instruments, the absence of true discount houses – equivalent to the discount houses of the City of London – despite the creation, on the initiative of the Bank of France, of the Compagnie Parisienne de Réescompte in 1928

– were fundamentally counter to any real control of the money market by the bank of issue. This structural impediment was compounded from 1926 to 1933 by a more cyclical factor: the persistent abundance of money on the short-term capital market in Paris, due both to repatriation of French companies' funds placed at short term in London and to international speculation on the *franc* revaluation. This situation was clearly the main reason why modernization projects developed at the Bank of France were held up between 1926 and 1930.

The Bank on the defensive (1930–35)

From 1930 to 1935, Bank of France policy was totally dominated by the defence of the Poincaré *franc's* gold parity in the tight corset of a gold standard system reduced from 1933 to the mere gold block.[4] In this perspective, the Bank retired to its traditional operations. This explains why the direct discount peaked in 1934, representing up to 55 per cent of the Bank's portfolio, albeit at a time when its global volume was strongly depressed by the general slowdown in business activity (Netter, 1994: 403). The result was keener competition between the bank of issue and the commercial banks. In this context, the Bank of France had to endure much criticism. It had passively accepted the banking crisis in 1930–32, even provoking the collapse of regional banks perceived as potential competitors; in particular, it had, as a liberal reaction, refused to intervene on the money markets, and hence to influence the movement of interest rates, thereby suppressing any recovery in productive capital investment.[5] Without entering into an historical debate which would call for new research, the fact of the Bank's reticence towards any policy of monetary intervention during this entire period can certainly be stressed. It coincided with the appointment to the Research Department of Robert Lacour-Gayet, who remained in this key post until his demission when the Popular Front came to power.

Robert Lacour-Gayet, who was financial attaché in New York from 1924 to early 1930, was a privileged witness to the perverse effects of the Federal Reserve Board's monetary policy in that period and to the outbreak of the American financial crisis in 1929. He concealed neither his liberal convictions nor his attachment to the regime of the gold standard. To him, intervention by the note-issuing bank was anathema to the extent that it ultimately impeded the free play of the market, particularly the automatic mechanisms of the gold standard. His total condemnation of the open market derived in essence from the same postulate. From 1932, as the Director of Research, he had clearly expressed his position in response to criticism, especially from across the Channel, of the Bank of France, which was reproached for sterilizing the gold which had returned to the Paris centre when the monetary stabilization process was initiated. 'Certain authors,' wrote Lacour-Gayet, 'thought that this inflow of gold could have been held up if the Bank of France, instead of contenting itself with managing the official discount rate, had deliberately undertaken operations on the free market ... but it is easy to show that for the Bank there was no way of creating francs in correct monetary conditions' (Lacour-Gayet, 1932). Adoption of an open market policy, according to Lacour-Gayet, would have led to 'indiscriminate dispersion of securities and a serious disturbance of market equilibrium'. That was the main criticism of the open market, which was seen primarily as 'manipulation of the market, a set of technical devices impeding the proper working of the gold standard'. The bank of issue therefore had no authority to intervene on the 'free market' where its action would have been considered, rightly for the author of the note, 'as an inadmissible irritation for the management of the private banks'.

These conceptions developed by research at the bank of issue make it easier to understand why the reforms implemented between 1926 and 1930 did not go far enough: the constraints of business activity were compounded by the radical modification of the theoretical options available to the Bank's management.[6] The arrival of the Popular Front, the personnel changes it caused in the Bank's management, and also the reforms that accompanied it led ultimately once again to a shift in the bank of issue's position.

Political reform of the Bank and modernization of its tasks (1936–37)

The reform of the Bank of France in July 1936, following the Popular Front's electoral victory, germinated in the current of thought initiated at the beginning of the 1930s. This had its roots in central planning circles, and then, more broadly, in socialist and syndicalist ranks (Margairaz, 1991). The reform of the bank of issue was reflected more globally in a 'nationalization of credit' programme clearly formulated in the CGT (*Confédération Générale du Travail*) plan of 1935 under the influence of syndicalists such as Léon Jouhaux, Achille Dauphin-Meunier and Francis Delaisi. Some time before the elections of April 1936, the contents of the reform were set out precisely by the Socialist André Philip, appointed Minister of Finance in 1946, at a time when the future statutes of the recently nationalized bank were being discussed. He affirmed, before the war, 'the necessity of a central bank with the job of creating the monetary circulation and of directing the country's capital investment policy' (Margairaz, 1991: 236). This objective referred back to an explicit will to modernize the functions of the bank of issue. Vincent Auriol, Minister of Finance in the first Popular Front government, formulated this clearly in the course of the senate discussion on the legislative project involving reform of the organization of the Bank of France: 'What we wanted was to adapt this organization to modern circumstances, to contemporary economic life' (*Journal Officiel*, 1936: 809). In the spirit of the legislators of 1936, this adaptation was to permit the bank of issue to be 'in a position to control and guide the distribution of credit in the country' (*Journal Officiel*, 1936: 807). The more limited contents of the law of 25 July 1936, which for the moment only assumed an essentially political dimension with the suppression from the managing board of the *régents*, the privileged representatives of the 200 largest shareholders of the Bank (Dromer, 1978: 229), should not, however, hide the reality of the debate, renewed as from this time, concerning the necessary modernization of the bank of issue. The official adoption of the open market principle on 17 June 1938 has its origin here.

From November 1936, following the reform of the Bank of France, the staff of Vincent Auriol, Minister of Finance in the Blum government, undertook to put back on the agenda the issue of what the central bank's tasks and modes of action actually were. Thus, the project of the Budgetary Law of 1937 set forth an arrangement seeking to 'create for the bank of issue the effective scope to carry out open-market policy operations'.[7] It appeared once again that modification of the Bank's role included the possibility of a control over the money market. Seen in this way, the project explicitly upheld the modernization efforts made in 1926–30: 'This decision,' the text effectively underlined, 'is inspired by interests identical to those subscribed by the authors of the 1928 monetary reform. As in 1928, the object of the Bank's operations, of which the Bank alone will appreciate the opportunity, is to influence the volume of credit and to keep control of the monetary circulation.'[8] An internal note from the Bank of France, unfortunately unsigned, commented on the reform project in somewhat favourable but still prudent terms: 'it is an experience which the Bank of France is proposing to undertake. If this article is adopted by parliament, the bank of issue will henceforth be empowered – just like the Bank of England, the Federal Reserve Board of New York, the *Reichsbank* and as the Bank of the Netherlands will shortly be – to conduct an open market policy.'[9] The British model, as in 1928, seems at this date to have been decisive: 'The bank of issue has the intention of using this faculty in the sense of selling and buying public securities. It will thus conform to the principles currently applied by the Bank of England.'[10] These express precautions can be understood all the better inasmuch as the government of Léon Blum was at that time confronted by growing Treasury difficulties aggravating the suspicion that intervention by the Bank in the money markets would ultimately create inflation for the benefit of the Treasury. The note of November 1936 had stressed this risk: 'The change which may be made to the statute to the Bank of France must not be interpreted as the early sign of a policy of inflation or indirect financial aid to the state.'[11] Behind the question of the modernization of the task of the central bank there arose, once again, the problem never truly solved of the financial links between the Bank and the Treasury. If the announcement in February 1937 of 'the pause' in the programme of reform, then the fall of the Blum Ministry in June, did not permit for the time being the open market project to become reality, it was still the first government of the popular front that reopened the door to the necessary reform of the operations of the bank of issue, of which the law of 25 July 1936 was simply the first stage, not the conclusion.

The attempt at an open market policy: a decisive step (1938–40)

The historical importance of the decree of 17 June 1938 authorizing the bank to negotiate public securities and bank acceptances on the market for its own account 'with a view to influencing the volume of credit and regulating the money market' (Netter, 1994: 610) poses a delicate problem of interpretation.[12] Was this a decisive step in the process of modernization of the bank of issue, giving it at last an instrument to manage credit or, as a number of contemporaries saw it at the time, a simple expedient intended to finance in an occult manner the growing needs of the Treasury facing an increasingly heavy burden of rearmament? This was, for example, the sense of the reservations expressed by the magazine *Banque* following the adoption of the open market: was not the 'true design' of the decree of 17 June to 'obtain for the state new financial facilities' and to 'realize a systematic expansion of credit to meet the requirements of the Treasury' (Desbois, 1938: 401–2). From the opposite direction, André Philip, who in 1935–36 had been one of the authors of the credit nationalization project foreseen by the Popular Front, underlined the extent to which the decree of 17 June 1938 could inaugurate 'a new monetary policy' and 'give a decisive orientation to our economic life' (Philip, 1938): 'Modern monetary technique', open market policy was to be 'placed in the service of a constructive economic policy' and finally permit, along the lines of the United States of the New Deal, a solution to the problem of the inadequacy of credit which alone explained the duration of the economic depression in France. The Socialist Deputy regretted moreover on this occasion that the Popular Front in power had not been able to implement this necessary reform to the system of lending: 'It must be recognized,' he confessed, 'that at this moment we have not had the financial policy of our social policy.' Such were the terms of the debate in the summer of 1938. They reveal precisely the ambivalent character of the introduction of the open market in France in that period, at the same time as underlining, once again, the historical features of the slow process of modernization of the Bank of France: were its objectives basically 'financial' or 'economic'? For Alfred Pose, writing at the beginning of the 1940s, there was no doubt that the reform of June 1938 had reflected 'objectives far less economic than financial.' The action taken by the public authorities came from a desire to ensure that Treasury bills had 'a large and smooth market' (Pose, 1942: 745, 754).[13] Could there be a clearer explanation of the historical significance of the introduction of the open market in France? A first response is the development of the position 'negotiable securities bought in France', which appeared for the first time in the Bank's balance sheet on 30 June 1938.

It is clear from this development that, judging by the difference in the item of 30 days' advances on public securities, introduced in 1935, the progression of which peaked immediately,[14] the Bank's operation on the money market underwent a real development from the autumn of 1938. This even exceeded the value of the traditional commercial portfolio on 31 August 1939. It is the development of their ratio which, even more than the development in current francs, allows one to measure the major innovation introduced in the Bank's operations by the statutory introduction of the open market in 1938: the ratio between the two items clearly reflects the transition from passive behaviour on the part of the bank of issue, automatically reacting to the needs for central money expressed by economic agents, to an active policy of intervention, through purchases and sales of securities on the money market. The daily fluctuations prove this, 'ending', to use the famous image coined by Warburg, 'with the bank of issue being more of a hammer than an anvil'. If one admits as a criterion of a central bank's modernity its capacity to intervene actively on money markets, then one can date precisely from 31 August 1939 the moment when the Bank of France became a modern bank of issue. This attempt at dating, which is necessarily artificial if one tries to pinpoint the chronology of a long-term phenomenon, nevertheless raises more questions than it answers.

It is certainly not unimportant that the item corresponding to the securities bought by the Bank on the money market exceeded in value the portfolio of discounted securities at the very moment when France entered the Second World War. The correlation between the growing financial needs of the state, confronted with the burdens of the war, and the development of the open market operations, is quite evident. But

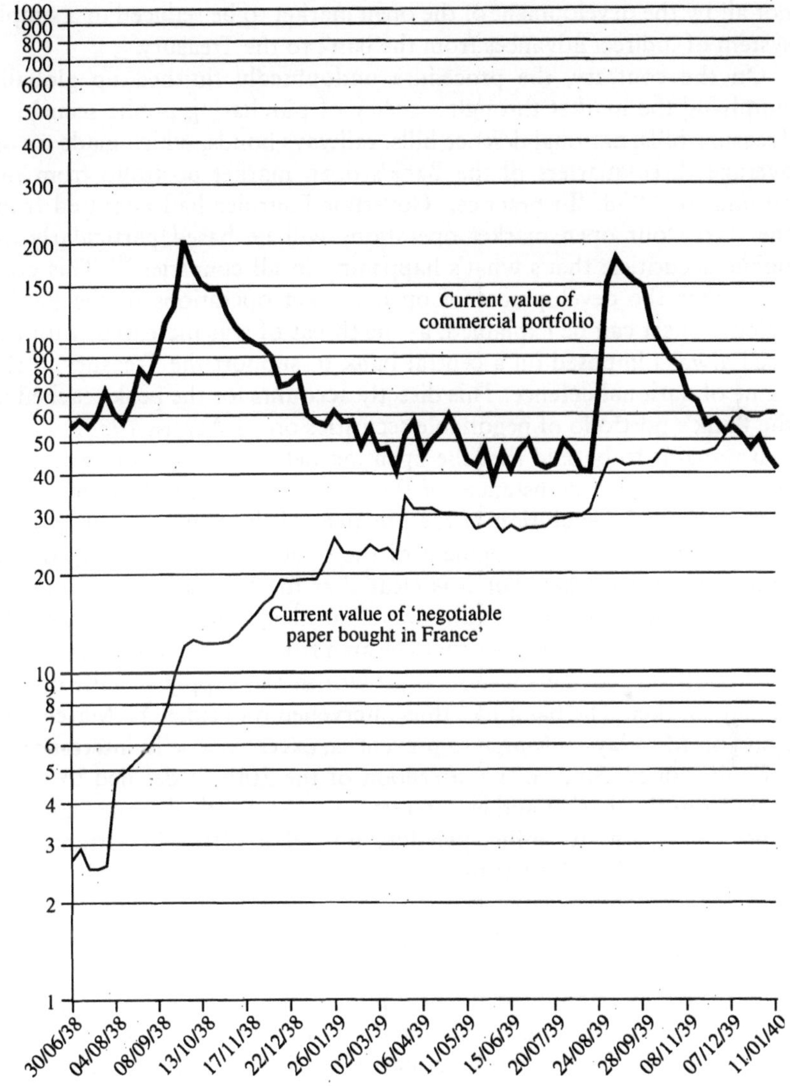

2.1 Comparative development of commercial and open market portfolios of the Bank of France from June 1938 to January 1940 (million current *francs*; semi-logarithmic scale)

Source: Weekly balance sheets of the Bank of France.

from the records of the deliberations of the Managing Board of the Bank in this period, it appears that this correlation is complex and does not allow the development of the open market to be reduced to a simple system of indirect advances from the bank to the Treasury.

On the contrary, the procedure undoubtedly finished up globally supplying the market through a policy of purchasing public securities, Treasury bills, national defence bills, railways bonds, which made up on average three-quarters of the Bank's open market portfolio from the autumn of 1938. 'In practice,' Governor Fournier had admitted from the start, 'our open market operations will be based particularly on public securities; that's what's happening in all countries.'[15] This confirms that the development of open market operations in the Bank's balance sheet can be explained, as the threat of war increased, with the need always imposed on a central bank to support the Treasury in the name of national defence. This directly accounts for the peak reached in the Bank's portfolio of negotiable securities on 31 August 1939.

It remains to be said that the open market experience, stimulated by the exceptional circumstances of the march to war, marked an important stage in the evolution of the practices of the Bank of France, and, beyond that, in the development of the structure and mentality of the French money market. For it is clear that the Bank's interventions on the market were not always one-way. Fournier demonstrated this on 23 March 1939, when the news that German troops had entered Prague on 15 March fuelled the substantial growth in the supply of bills on the money market. The bank had thus intervened on Friday 17 March and again on Monday 20 March to prevent an excessive rise in interest rates for call money. But, on the afternoon of the 20th, it decided to withdraw from the market and let interest rates rise a little, by one-eighth of a per cent, so as to 'inflict penalties on sellers'. 'It is important,' the Governor concluded, 'that the market should get into the habit of self-discipline. I don't want people who have bought bills to hold them in quiet times and then rush to drop them on the Bank as soon as the slightest cloud appears.'[16] An unquestionable modernity, which on the eve of the war established the new principles in the role of the central bank on the short-term money market and which, in many respects, anticipated the forms that the policy of the Bank of France adopted in full from the end of the 1960s. The Second World War, therefore, contributed here as in many areas to accelerating and realizing developments which had originated, but had not ended, in the years between the wars. But the period of occupation was also an occasion to adjust the function of the French money market and to reinforce there the role of the central bank (Cauboué, 1955), whose control over the entire banking system was also established by the law of 13 June 1941 (Andrieu,

1990: 201). All these developments did not end, however, until the second half of the twentieth century.

Learning the rules of a central bank (1945–73)

The nationalization of the bank of issue in 1945 was, in the opinion of Wilfrid Baumgartner, its Governor from 1949, 'a matter of natural logic'.[17] It was, in fact, the end of the current of thought which began with the constitution of the Popular Front and led to the nationalization of credit. It ended in 1944–45, at a time when the new constraints imposed by the reconstruction and modernization of the French economy helped to give precise meaning to the modernization of the financial system. As Pose wrote, from 1942 onwards the central bank had the main task of being the 'regulator of economic activity. The currency in the service of the economy, that is the objective currently proposed to the banks of issue' (Pose, 1942: 744, 746). It must be emphasized here that the nationalization of the capital of the bank of issue in December 1945, as had already been the case at the time of the July 1936 reform, did not lead immediately to radical redefinition of its tasks. It was only in January 1973 that the Bank finally received new statutes.[18] The reasons for the delay with the new definition of the bank's mission are easily summarized. They range, on the one side, from the opposition of successive governors of the bank of issue, Emmanuel Monick, then Wilfrid Baumgartner, to any formal amendment to the Bank's statutes for as long as, in their view, the economic situation remained exceptional and required 'the currency to be not deliberately, but implicitly sacrificed to the economy'.[19] The development of the bank of issue's mobilization of medium-term debt instruments from the end of 1944 and until the middle of the 1960s illustrates without any doubt the reality of monetary dirigism, implying on the part of the central bank a control of credit which was at once quantitative and qualitative. The creation, at the heart of the Bank's organization, of a general management of credit and the development of an instrument to centralize banking risks are to be seen in this perspective. But the delay can also be explained by the fact that, unlike before the war, the banking system then remained constantly 'in the bank', strictly subordinated to the dual constraint of the floors of public securities and the discount ceilings instituted in 1948. This system, which remained in place until 1967, helped to render pointless, and thus to hold up the development of an active policy of the bank of issue on a monetary market which was, as it were, non-existent. The particular and complex nature of the relations established after the war between Bank and state also makes it clear, at the final count, why upholding the status quo could appear desirable from the point of view both of the Bank and Treasury, inasmuch as it permitted reciprocal flexibility at a time when the public deficit was chronic (Feiertag, 1993: 361–83). Adoption of the 1973 statutes put a definitive end to this transitional phase and re-opened in France the question of modernization of the bank of issue.

The reform of the Bank of France at the beginning of 1973 under Governor Olivier Wormser was a decisive stage in the process of modernization of the bank of issue in the twentieth century. It appears in many respects to be the outcome of the efforts made at the end of the 1920s, interrupted by the long parenthesis of crisis and war. The Act of 3 January 1973 thus stipulated that the Bank's 'general task was to protect the currency and credit', and also 'the proper functioning of the banking system'.[20] This put an explicit end to all truly commercial activities of the bank of issue, which thus officially became at this time 'the bank of banks'. Direct discounting, reduced to very little since 1945, was consequently suppressed. Moreover, from July 1971, the Bank's management resolved for the first time the closure of 27 of the Bank's branches, the number of which had been unchanged since 1926, thereby initiating a reduction which has continued to the present day. In particular, the new statutes of 1973 decisively modified the nature of the Bank's operations. Discounting activities no longer appeared to be the bank of issue's principal aim. Discounting was regarded as just one of several instruments used by the Bank 'to achieve monetary policy objectives'.[21] In return, the Bank was formally given the faculty of operating freely on the market, by the purchase, sale or purchase subject to repurchase agreements, 'at the Governor's initiative' and under conditions determined by its General Council.[22] These dispositions apparently constituted the end of a long process which was partly rooted in projects born in the Bank at the time of stabilization of the *franc* in 1926–28. But they were also the result of a more recent development which began at the end of the 1960s.

In a famous report written in collaboration with Robert Marjolin and Jean Sadrin before his nomination as head of the bank of issue in April 1969, Olivier Wormser formulated the need for and details of a French financial reform. The MSW report, *On the monetary market and credit terms*, demonstrated in effect, unambiguously, 'the need for an overall reform' of the financial system, based on the 'organization of a money market in which, under the surveillance of the Bank of France, overall equilibrium will emerge in the finances of financial institutions' (Marjolin, Sandrin and Wormser, 1969).

In reality, it is clear from the balance sheets of the bank of issue that its money market actions developed notably from the beginning of 1966, when a period of exceptional prosperity in the banking system came to an end. This was directly explicable by the strong development of the eurodollar market from 1959 and by the return to external convertibility of European currencies. But it was only when Wormser was installed as head of the Bank, in April 1969, that the movement began which in less than three years led to the absolute primacy of interventions on the money market and to the quasi-suppression in the assets of the Bank of the traditional discount portfolio. The development of the ratio between the current value of the item of negotiable securities and that of the discount portfolio is once again particularly illustrative: it rose from 104 to 270 per cent between March to July 1969, reached 300 per cent at the end of 1970, and stood at 654 per cent in January 1971. Over the same period, the value in constant francs of the portfolio of negotiable securities held by the Bank doubled. (It increased fourfold between April 1969 and December 1973.) The decision taken at the beginning of 1971, on the Governor's initiative, to let the money market interest rate fall below the official discount rate was decisive for this development. This new orientation in the Bank's policy led to a decrease in operating income in the course of 1971 on a scale that the Governor himself considered 'very substantial'. He was referring in effect to a fall of 20 per cent compared with 1970. He explained it was 'due to a decrease in the volume of bills presented following the change in monetary policy, i.e. when the money market interest rate fell below the discount rate.'[23] This development justified the decision, then taken to reduce operating costs, to close 27 offices which, in effect, lost their main *raison d'être* with the short-term extinction of discount operations. In modifying the character of the Bank's operations, it was the bank of issue's overall role which was placed in question. Beyond the generalization of the open market policy, Olivier Wormser, like Pierre Quesnay in 1928, knew that what was really at stake was the Bank's capacity to modernize.

The elaboration of new statutes from the end of 1971 was part of this ambition. 'The body of texts ruling the Bank of France,' said the Governor in Council at the end of April 1972, 'is complex and archaic. But an institution like the Bank of France must, from time to time, make an effort to review its own workings in order to change so as not to be bypassed by overall development.'[24] This modernization of the statutes, to quote the word used by the Governor, referred explicitly to the model of other central banks: 'We do not want to turn the Bank of France into a bank of issue with a very individual charter which would distinguish it from other central banks, notably those of the other countries of the European Economic Community.'[25] It therefore seems that the modernization of the Bank of France at the beginning of 1973 was embedded more generally in the process of building up Europe. It is not uninteresting to note that, in the spirit of the people at the Bank's helm, it was linked to the still distant, at that time, prospect of possible monetary unification of the Community, which seemed to anticipate the signing in Basle, in 1971, of the agreements creating the European monetary snake.

The reform of January 1973 was therefore a decisive stage in the slow history of the modernization of the Bank of France in the twentieth century. It is the outcome of a development which began just after the First World War. At the end of this process, lasting more than half a century, only the question of the relations between Bank and state was left unanswered by the law of 3 January 1973. (Bouvier, 1987: 23–33). It was, in a sense, resolved by the law of 4 August 1993 nominating the Governor for five years and thus guaranteeing the independence of the bank of issue in the spirit of the Treaty of Maastricht.

At the end of this development, it appears that, in the course of the twentieth century, the Bank of France completed its transformation into a modern central bank which matched the model of most European central banks. But the end of this process was not clear from the outset, and the modernization of the bank of issue was the product of various and sometimes contrary conceptions of a central bank's mission. The Bank of France evolved more slowly than other central banks, which had gained effective control over the entire financial system earlier than was possible in France. Having remained for a long time on the borderline between private business and the public sector, it was faced until well into this century by the dual need to ensure a balanced operating account and at the same time to satisfy the financial demands of the state, the importance of which expanded continuously until very recently. This fundamental ambivalence of the French bank of issue is undoubtedly one of the main reasons for the historic delay in its evolution. The history of the Bank of Spain in the twentieth century can shed light on this analysis as a neighbouring example, but at a different pace due to different economic and political developments peculiar to each of the two countries.

The Bank of Spain

In 1929, Sir Ernest H. Harvey, deputy governor of the Bank of England, stated before the Macmillan Committee what were, or ought to be, the responsibilities of a central bank. Harvey indicated that its principal mission was to maintain the stability of the currency. Other obligations included the issue of legal money, undertaking the duties of cashier of the Government and, of course, Bagehot's dictum of lender of last resort.

The history of European central banks demonstrates that undertaking such functions, especially playing an active role in monetary policy, is a difficult and slow process. It can also be argued that for a private commercial bank, it may be easier to acquire the features predicated for a central bank (that is to say, an institution capable of performing the four tasks mentioned by Harvey) when all, or some, of the following conditions are present.

First, what could be called the 'external exposure'. The learning process is facilitated if the central bank is well linked to other institutions of its kind, and if it has a close relationship with the international monetary system. Therefore, those central banks that participated in the Latin Monetary Union and in the gold standard system, and, in consequence, were forced to look after convertibility and currency stability, learnt to comply with their responsibilities as monetary authorities better than those other banks that remained detached from international financial networks.

The degree of openness of the economy and the structure of the national banking system, as well as its level of competitiveness, are also important elements in the acquisition of the required expertise to become an effective central bank. An institution that operates within a closed and regulated environment hardly has the opportunity to perform as a central bank; competition brings risk into economic affairs and offers good chances for central bankers to acquire knowledge of how to act as lenders of last resort.

In the learning process the type of relationship between the bank of issue and the Treasury is of the utmost importance. Those central bankers that, by statutes or for any other reason, enjoyed more autonomy, learnt quickly and became better bankers. On the contrary, if the central bank is just a mere extension of the Treasury under its direct control, it may never have the chance to perform its duty as monetary authority, since its main mission would be essentially reduced to providing finance to the public sector.

The fourth condition is what may be termed the significance of the human factor. Central banking is also a question of character. The members that belong to the board have to have the desire to be and to act as central bankers. This means that the role of the persons in charge of the institutions is crucial to understanding the development of the bank towards the assumption, or otherwise, of its duties as monetary authority. To a certain extent, the quality of the institution and its power to influence events rest on the character of who is in its command.

The final condition is rather an instrumental one. It may be argued that to perform the duties of a central bank adequately, properly defined legal texts may not be of any significance. None the less, it is also true that poorly drafted texts do not help in paving the way towards the transformation of old credit institutions into banks with monetary responsibilities.

None of the above conditions have been present in Spain until very recently. External economic (and political) exposure has been very limited or non-existent. Spanish central bankers did not participate in the gold standard system before or after 1914, and hence they never had the chance to play, or to fool, the rules of the game. The degree of openness of the Spanish economy as well as its degree of competitiveness is certainly smaller than that of other Western European economies. Furthermore, the links of the Bank of Spain with the Treasury have surpassed all reasonable limits and, with a few exceptions, the men in charge of its management have been individuals with serious technical shortcomings: politicians and major shareholders, usually aristocrats rather than businessmen, whose knowledge of the Spanish economy and of the complexities of a modern monetary system have been extremely limited. Successive governors, appointed by the Ministers of Finance, have only remained in their post for short periods of time as they have changed as the political administrations have changed. Finally, the legal texts that have regulated both the Bank and the entire banking system cannot be praised; rather, Spanish banking acts have lacked rigour and precision.

A brief account of the role of the Bank of Spain in the nineteenth century

The origin of the Bank of Spain harks back to 1782, and its inception, like that of many other European central banks, was related to the financial needs of the state. The Bank was born to rescue the Treasury, and this would remain its main historical mission in the following two hundred years.[26]

After 1829 the Bank assumed its first task as a central bank when it became the state's cashier, taking charge of some Treasury operations, such as budgetary expenditures and revenues. Later, in 1874, it was entrusted with the monopoly of bank note issue for the entire country. The assumption of the remaining central bank's goals, that of lender of last resort and monetary management, would have to wait, however, until the end of the following century.[27]

Between 1874 and the outbreak of the First World War, the Bank of Spain played two distinct roles. First, it gave permanent support to the failing finances of the Government, in need of resources to balance the budget. The Treasury was always 'in the Bank', assistance was provided by continuous advances, never repaid, and by direct purchases of public debt, which the Bank maintained in its portfolio. Second, the Bank remained, in its nature and operations, a commercial institution; with a monopoly on note-issuing it experienced a considerable territorial expansion, opening branches all over the country and competing successfully against other commercial banks. By 1900 the Bank of Spain was the largest credit institution of the country, its influence unchallenged, and holding nearly 70 per cent of the total assets of the combined credit system.[28]

The suspension of currency convertibility in 1883 left the *peseta* off the gold standard and, hence, the Bank of Spain was discharged of the historical mission performed by other European central institutions: to keep currency convertibility (Martín Aceña, 1994). But far from causing any distress to shareholders and members of the board of directors, the non-adherence to the gold standard was received with relief, since it meant that the Bank, with no commitment to defend the *peseta* exchange rate, felt free to orientate its credit and discount policy regardless of the balance of payments situation and independently of the evolution of the currency. Its primary concern, as that of any other private company, was to maximize profits. The responsibility for the fluctuations in the value of the currency was transferred to the Ministry of Finance, but here officials were far more concerned with the budget than with the fate of the *peseta*. During those years, the total quantity of bank notes in circulation expanded substantially, both as the result of increases in credit to the non-banking private sector and as a consequence of public deficits covered with new issues of government debt that found their way into the portfolio of the Bank.

After 1900, the Treasury made successful efforts to balance the budget and cancelled its outstanding debt with the Bank. Different projects were drafted in order to cut the link between the Bank and the Treasury. Furthermore, the Government wanted the Bank of Spain to accept fully its monetary responsibilities as a bank of issue. The classic idea of what a central bank ought to be gained ground within the Ministry of Finance. It was thought that the time had arrived for the Bank of Spain to play an active role in the defence of the stability of the currency. Between 1902 and 1912, Parliament discussed a string of projects aimed at introducing the gold standard, with full redemption of bank notes. It was made explicit in all of them that the Bank of Spain should play a leading part in the future. None the less, this vision was never shared by officials at the Bank. In their view, the monopoly of issue was the mere result of a temporary and mutually beneficial contract between the state and the Bank, by which the latter had received a privilege in exchange for a promise to finance the government when needed, but with no additional obligations. In consequence, the projects never won the support of the Bank, which resisted a change in the *status quo*. The Bank simply had no desire to assume any duties in addition to providing cash to the economy and/or to the Treasury. For the Bank the value of the *peseta* was a matter for the monetary authorities but they did not consider themselves a party to such an enterprise.

Table 2.2 examines the balance sheet of the Bank of Spain during the second part of the nineteenth century and the first decade of the twentieth century. Under the heading of Treasury assets are included both loans and advances as well as the public debt in the portfolio of the Bank. It is apparent that until 1900 the financing of the Treasury absorbed more than half of the total resources of the Spanish central bank and that private domestic assets represented a relatively small portion of the total outstanding credit of the Bank of Spain. At the most, discounts and loans to the bank and non-bank private sector reached 30 per cent in 1890, although these items remained usually below such a figure until the turn of the century. When the government balanced the budget after the Cuban war, the Bank of Spain reinforced its financial relationship with the commercial and the industrial sectors of the economy; this shift is reflected in Table 2.2 which shows that, by 1910, the volume of Treasury assets had declined while the credit to the private domestic sector had clearly increased.

Table 2.2 Bank of Spain: selected assets, 1860–1905, in per cent

	Treasury assets	Private domestic assets	Other
1860	50	22	28
1865	69	12	19
1870	52	10	38
1875	50	11	39
1880	41	17	42
1885	57	25	18
1890	51	30	19
1895	50	15	35
1900	57	11	32
1905	31	25	44

Source: Anes (1974): tables III-2, III-9 and III-21.

The Bank of Spain in the twentieth century: the inter-war period[29]

Between the wars, the evolution of the Bank of Spain towards a central bank model developed under the influence of two conflicting forces. On one side was the Ministry of Finance which, as we have seen, desired that the institution become an authentic bankers' bank and share the responsibilities of monetary policy. On the other side was the Bank itself, little interested in modifying the *status quo*.

The modernization party desired a transformation of the Bank of Spain towards the model provided by the Bank of England. With such an idea in mind, in 1921 the Government approved a Banking Law to restructure the entire banking system and place the Bank of Spain at its centre. It also sought to increase the control of the state over the institution. The authorities believed that some of the post-war economic difficulties could have been avoided had the Bank behaved as a real lender of last resort. Furthermore, they were convinced that until then the Bank had only performed one of the functions predicated for an institution of issue, that of government's banker, but had neglected the other two (lender of last resort and monetary management).

To correct some of the past practices, the law limited the amount of advances that the Treasury could obtain from the Bank and fixed the quantity of bank notes in circulation (at the time, 5000 million *pesetas*) – an issue over and above that limit required government approval. In order to strengthen the links between the banking community and the Bank of Spain, the law forced the latter to give preferential treatment to credit institutions. In particular, it established that banks and savings organizations could discount paper at preferential rates. Finally, although the act did not forbid the Bank of Spain to operate with the non-banking private sector, it set a ceiling on the outstanding amount of private securities in its portfolio. Nevertheless, a close examination of the law shows that it left many other matters undefined. Although the intention of the Ministry of Finance was to transform the Bank of Spain into a real central bank, scrutiny of its different articles proves that it overlooked important matters. The criteria to regulate the quantity of money were left undefined and it was not clear whose was the final decision to change the discount rate. The Bank was entrusted with some monetary duties, but the Treasury kept the initiative in the case of exchange rate policy.

The law of 1921 also increased the control of the state within the Bank. In addition to appointing the Governor, the new act allowed the Minister of Finance to appoint three members to the Board of Directors, in representation of the so-called 'general interests of the country'. The Bank tried to resist what it considered to be a serious interference in the internal affairs of a private institution and a loss of autonomy. The case was taken to the *Cortes* (parliament) while the law was under discussion, in an attempt to avoid its approval, but the project passed as it had been submitted by the government. The appointment of these new members to the Board was important not only because it reinforced the power of the Governor and the control of the Treasury, but also because it introduced an element of modernization: the persons named to occupy the seats on the Board were reputed economic experts and had worked for the Treasury for many years. They were cognisant of the tasks performed by other central banks, and certainly favoured a swift transformation of the Bank of Spain. Furthermore, in policy matters they shared the views of the Treasury: currency stability and, if feasible, an early adoption of the gold standard.

The stabilization of the *peseta* in the late 1920s is a clear example of the differences between the Treasury and the Bank. After 1928, the Spanish authorities tried to follow the way taken by the *franc* and the *lira* which, after some hesitation, were stabilized and linked to gold. They also wanted to establish full convertibility and a swift adoption of the gold standard. Although consultation with the Bank was minimal, the Treasury counted on its support. In this case it meant basically to be able to use its rather large metallic reserves to defend the exchange rate of the *peseta*, if needed. From the outset, the Bank made it clear that it disliked the operation, arguing that before any formal stabilization the budget should be balanced. Despite the Bank's lack of support, the Treasury went ahead with its plan. When later in 1929 and 1930 the *peseta* came under pressure and the Ministry of Finance sought the help of the Bank, it refused to collaborate and rejected any suggestion to commit its gold reserves to defend the exchange rate. It also opposed a rise in the discount rate to introduce some measure of monetary restriction. In order to avoid a clash, the Treasury decided to establish an independent stabilization fund to intervene in the exchange market; the endowment of the fund came out of foreign credits obtained in Paris, since once again the Bank of Spain refused to lend its gold reserves for the operations. However, in less than three months the fund had exhausted its resources without achieving its goal.

In 1931 the socialist Minister of Finance of the recently formed first Republican government reformed the 1921 law. His main intention was to strengthen the control over the Bank, declaring that he wanted to subordinate the Bank of Spain to the state. The result was the transference of nearly all monetary responsibilities to the Treasury, and discharging the Bank of its monetary duties. In this, the Ministry of Finance disregarded the recommendations enshrined in two reports prepared for the Spanish authorities by François Quesnay and Charles

Rist, two well-known French monetary experts. Both argued in favour of full autonomy for the Bank and advised that the Bank of Spain, like any other bank of issue, should be provided with adequate monetary instruments and powers to conduct whatever monetary policy was decided by the government.

There was, however, a significant advance in the internal organization of the Bank. In 1930 a small but quite active research office was established, directed by two prestigious economists. Until the eve of the civil war, in July 1936, the research office conducted two important tasks. First, it produced a series of reports about the Spanish economy, with special attention to monetary events and with recommendations for monetary policy. A number of studies on the international financial situation were written as well as a much-quoted study examining the impact of the world depression on the Spanish economy. Many of these reports reached the Board and, on some occasions, they were discussed at length. The second type of work undertaken by the research department was the collection of monetary statistics. For instance, they produced the first Spanish balance of payment figures for the period 1930–34. The Bank was also the source of much of the data included in the series of statistical volumes published by the League of Nations.

The evolution of the Bank's assets during this period can be observed in Table 2.3. The most remarkable feature is the reduction of Treasury assets after 1920. The explanation rests on a change of the strategy to finance the budget deficit. Instead of using the traditional mechanism of direct advances, the Treasury issued short- and long-term debt which were taken by both the financial and non-financial sector and could be automatically monetized. In fact, part of the increase in private domestic assets hides the continuing role of the Bank as an institution to finance the government. The other interesting feature of the table is the

Table 2.3 Bank of Spain: selected assets, 1910–35, as percentage of total

	Foreign assets	Treasury assets	Private domestic assets	Other
1910	14.4	47.2	24.3	14.1
1915	25.4	48.9	22.8	2.9
1920	41.3	28.6	27.0	3.1
1925	25.9	15.2	34.5	24.4
1930	16.0	17.4	30.5	36.1
1935	16.4	19.0	30.0	34.6

Source: Martín Aceña (1995) and Bank of Spain, *Memorias* (1910–35).

sharp rise of foreign assets, mainly gold, that took place during the war years. This development was a consequence of the large current account surpluses on the Spanish balance of payments.

The Bank of Spain in the twentieth century: From 1940 to the law of autonomy of 1994

During the civil war the Bank of Spain was divided into two distinct political entities: one under the Republican side and the other under the administration of Franco. However, the two institutions played the same role: providing resources to finance the war. Thereafter, from 1940 to 1959, followed the blackest years in the history of the Bank, since more than ever it was subordinated to the scrutiny and control of the Ministry of Finance.[30]

A new law in 1946, which superseded that of 1921, established the new relationship between the government and the Bank. It reduced the autonomy and the monetary powers of the latter. The law did not nationalize the institution but it strictly regulated all its operations and functions. With regard to domestic monetary policy, all responsibilities were taken by the Treasury, while the management of the exchange rate was transferred to the 'Spanish Foreign Currency Institute', a newly created body within the Commerce department. As a consequence, the two sides of monetary policy were split. In the following years, this arrangement would cause an apparent lack of coordination between the two government departments with monetary responsibilities. The law of 1946 meant a step backwards in the autonomy of the Bank and in its painful process of conversion into a truly central institution. Without a mission, or rather with the only mission being to finance the Treasury, the Bank of Spain hibernated until the end of the 1950s.

Easy and cheap money was a characteristic of the 1940s and 1950s. Domestic monetary management resulted in the creation of unlimited amounts of liquid resources at the lowest possible interest rate. The Treasury financed the budget by issuing public debt which was automatically monetized in the Bank. Furthermore, the issue of debt by a significant number of newly created government agencies could also be used as collateral to obtain advances from the Bank. The consequence of this unorthodox behaviour was a rampant inflation that reached two digits for most of the period. On the other hand, exchange controls were tight and the *peseta* was set at an unprecedented and grossly overvalued rate. Exports were highly penalized and imports subjected to administrative controls. Between 1940 and 1950 the Spanish economy stagnated and regulations and controls caused a considerable misallocation of resources. After 1953 foreign aid was made available due to the Treaty signed with the USA. Nevertheless, by the end of the decade all foreign reserves had been exhausted and the economy was heading dangerously for a standstill.

Until the nationalization of the Bank of Spain in 1962, two opposite groups coexisted within the Board of Directors. On one side, and led by the governor, sat the members appointed by the government; the other side was composed by the members who represented private capital. The records of the meetings of the Board reveal that there were sharp discrepancies between the two groups. The private members of the Board continuously challenged the other party. Firstly they complained that the Board was not allowed to discuss monetary matters, or questions that they considered significant to a central bank, such as changes in the discount and rediscount rates. Secondly, they also complained that the concerns and rights of the Bank as a commercial credit institution were not taken into account, with negative consequences for the shareholders. The so-called 'government's delegation' performed the role of an intermediary, by translating to the Board the orders and instructions coming from the Treasury. After 1946 monetary discussions entirely disappeared from the weekly meetings of the Board and if such subjects were raised they were immediately blocked by the government's delegation. Although the economists of the research office sent their papers and reports to the Board, as before the war, only on a few occasions, when their content was considered 'not sensitive', were they distributed. In sum, never before in all its history had the Bank been emptier of autonomy and power than during these years.

The time for an active monetary policy came with the preparation in 1959 of the so-called stabilization programme. Earlier, a reshuffle in the government had also brought about some changes within the administration of the Bank, with the substitution of some of the members of the 'government's delegation'. The new deputy governor wanted to create an atmosphere of collaboration and permitted the return of monetary policy discussions to the meetings of the Board; special attention was given to the many critical reports drafted in the research department, where a capable professor of economics was appointed as its director.

The Bank of Spain played an important part in the stabilization programme, despite its lack of practice and of suitable instruments. The implementation of the plan provided the Bank with the opportunity to regain a certain autonomy and to be able to play a relatively independent role. Bank officials were in charge of the negotiations with the IMF and the World Bank, when the Spanish authorities turned to both institutions to obtain cooperation and financial help. The Bank, together with a few open-minded officials at the Treasury and at the Commerce department, was able to persuade the rest of the

Government and especially Franco of the need for a sharp devaluation of the *peseta*.

The stabilization programme brought to the fore the shortcomings and limitations of the Bank of Spain as an efficient body to implement monetary policy. Despite the success of the plan, the deficiencies of the institutional framework became apparent, especially the lack of instruments and competencies of the central bank. Nevertheless, no major reforms were introduced until the end of 1962, when the Bank was eventually nationalized. When the Minister of Finance defended in the *Cortes* the new legislation, he repeated almost the same words pronounced by his predecessor in 1921. He reminded his audience of the 'long and historical role of the Bank of Spain as the institution of issue and as the banker of the State', but recognized that it had neither become yet a real bankers' bank, nor the centre of the monetary system, or the body responsible for the value of the *peseta*. But in spite of the intentions of the government, the law was faulty on many accounts. The Bank received little autonomy, if any. The relationships between the Bank and Treasury remained undefined, and the latter maintained wide powers not only in relation to the definition of monetary goals but also to daily monetary management. Furthermore, exchange rate policy remained outside the scope of the Bank and there were no major improvements with regard to monetary instruments. In fact, it could be said that the only mission left to the Bank was the supervision of the credit system. In sum, the 1962 law nationalized the Bank of Spain but it neither laid any foundations to solve the many technical problems of monetary control, nor transferred to the Bank the responsibility for monetary management. On the contrary, the Bank remained under the strict surveillance of the Treasury.

During the 1960s monetary policy again played a passive role. The budget was balanced for most of the period and the quantity of money accommodated the needs of the economy. Interest rates were kept low to facilitate private investment. In Treasury circles and elsewhere in the government, officials argued that a central bank's mission ought to be to provide financing to the economy; for many, the Bank constituted a powerful instrument to propel economic growth. Only in a few cases, such as in 1967–68 when an acute balance of payments difficulty arose, was monetary policy called upon to sort out the problems by temporarily raising interest rates.[31]

It is necessary to wait until the early 1970s to see new developments in monetary management, when the international economic crisis severely hit the Spanish economy. Then, the need for efficient monetary control provided the Bank with another opportunity to gain a few more degrees of autonomy. After 1970 the Bank began to manipulate the discount rate without the interference of the Treasury, a variety of legal cash and liquidity ratios were introduced and some limited open market operations were also conducted. Eventually, in 1973, the Bank was able to regain full control of exchange rate policy. Thereafter the Bank of Spain has been slowly moving towards a definite, and irreversible, transformation into a modern central bank. However, full autonomy had not been reached until the last reforms of June 1994, carried out in order to comply with the provisions of the Maastricht Treaty.[32]

Notes

1. See Dauphin-Meunier (1942: t.II, 738ff).
2. See Sayers (1976: 37ff) and F. Capie, (1995), 'Banking in Europe in the Nineteenth Century: The Role of the Central Bank', working paper presented at the seminar of the OFCE, Paris, 16 February 1995, p. 2.
3. Hearing of Émile Moreau, Honorary Governor of the Bank of France, 23 March 1931, before the Parliamentary Inquiry Commission on the Oustric affair, *Bulletin des Commissions*, no. 92, 2 April 1931, p. 3933.
4. See Eichengreen (1995: 67ff) and Mouré (1995: 341–62).
5. See Plessis (1995), and Hautcoeur (1990).
6. It is very important in this context to note that in the margins of many of the notes produced by Pierre Quesnay between 1926 and 1929, the archives of the 'direction des études' have kept the handwritten comments written by Robert Lacour-Gayet which were intended to refute, point by point, the reform propositions of his predecessor.
7. *Projet de loi d'open market policy, exposé des motifs*, November 1936, ABF, 7e I 225, boite 35.
8. Ibid., p. 2.
9. Note sur le projet autorisant la Banque de France à pratiquer une politique d'open market, direction des Études économiques, 7 November 1936, 6 p.dactyl., Archive de la Banque de France, 7e I 225, boite 35.
10. Ibid., p. 3.
11. Ibid., p. 1.
12. See Mouré (1991, ch. 4: 120–55).
13. This opinion is taken up by Bouvier (1973: 159).
14. See Guenser (1938: 300 sqq).
15. *Procès Verbaux du Conseil Général de la Banque de France* (PVCG = deliberations of the Managing Board of the Bank of France), meeting on 7 July 1938.
16. *Idem.*
17. *La Banque de France, tradition et progrès*, 1955, p. 15.
18. O. Feiertag (1998), *Wilfrid Baumgartner, les finances de l'Etat et l'économie de la Nation, biographie d'un financier public (1902–1978)*, Paris, CHEFF-Imprimerie Nationale, unpublished PhD thesis, University of Nanterre, 1995.
19. W. Baumgartner (1951), *Problèmes financiers et monétaires*, conference on 21 February 1951 at the Institut d'Études Politiques, Archives W. Baumgartner, 2BA5, Dr8.

20. *Loi no. 73–7 du 2 janvier 1973 sur la Banque de France*, article 1er.
21. Ibid., art. 24.
22. Ibid., articles 27 et 28.
23. PVCG, meeting on 27 January 1972.
24. PVCG, meeting on 27 April 1972.
25. Ibid.
26. For the early history of the Bank of Spain see P. Tedde de Lorca (1982), *El Banco de San Carlos (1782–1829)*, Madrid, Alianza Editorial.
27. For the history of the Bank of Spain during the twentieth century see Anes (1974) and Tortella (1970).
28. For an overview of the Spanish financial system see Martín Aceña (1987 and 1995).
29. This section is based on P. Martín Aceña (1984), *La política monetaria en España, 1919–1935*, Madrid, Instituto de Estudios Fiscales; and also Tortella (1970).
30. The best account of monetary policy for the years 1940–59 is still J. Sardá Dexeus (1970).
31. For monetary policy during the 1960s and the 1970s, see Rojo (1963) and also Rojo and Pérez (1977). A excellent analysis of the process of money creation is in Poveda (1973).
32. For the latest development in Spanish monetary policy, Servicio de Estudios del Banco de España (1997).

References

Andrieu, C. (1990), *La banque sous l'Occupation, paradoxes de l'histoire d'une profession*, Paris, Presses de la FNSP.

Anes, R. (1974), 'El Banco de España, 1874–1914: Un banco nacional', in Tortella, G. and Schwartz, P. (eds), *La banca española en la restauración*, Madrid, Banco de España.

Banco de España (1910–35), *Memorias*, Madrid.

Bouvier, J. (1973), *Un siècle de banque française*, Paris, Hachette.

Bouvier, J. (1984), 'À propos de la stratégie d'encaisses (or et devises) de la Banque de France de juin 1928 à l'été 1932', *Bulletin de l'Institut d'histoire économique et sociale*, no. 13.

Bouvier, J. (1987), 'Les relations entre l'État et la Banque de France depuis les années 1950', *Vingtième Siècle, revue d'histoire.*

Capie, F. et al. (1994), *The Development of Central Banking. The Tercentenary Symposium of the Bank of England*, Cambridge, Cambridge University Press.

Cauboué, P. (1955), 'Le marché monétaire français', *Moneta e Credito*, no. 32, Rome.

Collins, M. (ed.) (1993), *Central Banking in History*, Elgar, Hants/Vermont.

Dauphin-Meunier, A. (1942), *La Banque de France*, Paris, PUF.

de Lorca, P. Tedde (1982), *El Banco de San Carlos (1782–1829)*, Madrid, Alianza Editorial.

Desbois, J. (1938), 'L'extension des attributions de la Banque de France et le marché libre', *Banque*.

Dexeus, J. Sardá (1970), 'El Banco de España, 1931–1962', in *El Banco de España. Una historia económica*, Madrid, Banco de España.

Dromer, L. (1978), *La réforme de la Banque de France du 24 juillet 1936*, unpublished dissertation, Université de Paris I, Jean Bouvier -dir.

Eichengreen, B. (1995), *Golden Fetters: The Gold Standard and the Great Depression, 1919–1939*, Oxford, Oxford University Press.

Feiertag, O. (1993), 'Les pouvoirs de la Banque de France et de son gouverneur sous la IVe République', in *Du franc Poincaré à l'écu*, Paris, CHEFF.

Guenser, G. (1938), *Le Marché monétaire français et son contrôle par la Banque de France*, Paris, Librairie du Recueil Sirey.

Hautcoeur, P. (1990), 'La Banque de France et la crise bancaire de 1930–1932', *Études et Documents*, no. 2, pp. 295–313.

Journal Officiel de la République française (JO) (1936), Vincent Auriol in the Senate, at the 2nd meeting on 23 July 1936.

Journal Officiel de la République française (JO) (1936), Report by Abel Gardey submitted in the name of the Senate Finance Commission on 23 July 1936.

Lacour-Gayet, R. (1932), *La politique d'intervention sur le marché libre*, note by Robert Lacour-Gayet, 24 October 1932, dactyl., Archive de la Banque de France (ABF), 7ème 1 225 boite 35.

Margairaz, M. (1991), *L'État, les finances et l'économie, histoire d'une conversion, 1932–1952*, Paris, CHEFF.

Marjolin, R., Sandrin, J. and Wormser, O. (1969), *Rapport sur le marché monétaire et les conditions de crédit*, Paris, La Documentation française.

Martín-Aceña, P. (1987), 'Development and modernization of the financial system, 1844–1935', in Sánchez-Albornoz, N. (ed.), *The Economic Modernization of Spain, 1830–1930*, New York, New York University Press.

Martín-Aceña, P. (1994), 'Spain during the classical gold standard, 1880–1914', in Bordo, M. and Capie, F. (eds), *Monetary Regimes in Transition*, Cambridge, Cambridge University Press.

Martín-Aceña, P. (1995), 'Spanish banking in the inter-war period', in Charles H. Feinstein (ed.), *Banking, Currency and Finance in Europe between the Wars*, Oxford, Clarendon Press.

Mouré, K. (1991), *Managing the Franc Poincaré, Economic Understanding and Political Constraint in French Monetary Policy, 1928–1936*, Cambridge University Press, Cambridge.

Mouré, K. (1995), 'Le chef d'orchestre invisible et le son de la cloche officiel: the Bank of France and the Campaign Against Devaluation, 1935–1936', *French History*, 9 (3).

Netter, M. (1994), *Histoire de la Banque de France entre les deux guerres*, Paris, published by the author.

Perroux, F. (1945), 'Les Banques d'Émission et l'État', *Revue d'Economie Politique*, vol. 1/IV.

Philip, A. (1938), 'L'open market', *Marianne*, 13 July.

Plessis, A. (1995), 'The Bank of France from the early twentieth century to the 1950s', in Cassis, Y. et al. (eds), *The Evolution of Financial Institutions and Markets in Twentieth-Century Europe*, Scolar Press, Aldershot.

Plessis, A. (1995), 'La Banque de France' in *Les Banques en Europe de l'ouest de 1920 à nos jours*, Comité pour l'Histoire Économique et Financière de la France (CHEFF), pp. 273–81.

Pose, A. (1942), *La monnaie et ses institutions, histoire, théorie et technique*, Paris, PUF.

Poveda, R. (1973), *La creación de dinero en España, 1956–1970*, Madrid, Instituto de Estudios Fiscales.

Quesnay, P. (1926), *Contrôle du marché monétaire*, note by P. Quesnay, November 1926, Archives de la Banque de France (ABF), 4é 5512H, boite 6.

Quesnay, P. (1928), *Moyens d'action de la Banque de France sur le marché*, Direction des études, Bank of France (ABF), 7ème 1 225, boite 35.

Ricard, P. (1926), *La Banque de France et le marché monétaire*, note by P. Ricard, 23 September 1926, Direction des études, Bank of France, (ABF), 4é 5512H, boite 6.

Rojo, L.A (1963), 'La política monetaria', in *El desarrollo económico de España*, Madrid, Revista de Occidente.

Rojo, L.A. and Pérez, J. (1977), *La política monetaria en España: Objetivos e instrumentos*, Madrid, Banco de España.

Sayers, R.S. (1976), *The Bank of England, 1891–1994*, Cambridge, Cambridge University Press.

Servicio de Estudios del Banco de España (1997), *La política monetaria y la inflación en España*, Madrid, Alianza Editorial.

Sicsic P. and Villeneuve, B. (1993), 'L'afflux d'or en France de 1928 à 1934', in *Du franc Poincaré à l'écu*, Paris, CHEFF.

Tortella, G. (1970), 'El Banco de España entre 1829 y 1929. La formación de un banco central', in *El Banco de España. Una historia económica*, Madrid, Banco de España.

CHAPTER THREE

Post-war Central Banking Reform: A German–Japanese Comparison

Carl-L. Holtfrerich and Toru Iwami

Introduction: purpose of the German–Japanese comparison

Two nations defeated by the Allied Powers, both with currencies ruined by government expenditure excesses due to the war effort, and with central bank portfolios loaded with relatively worthless government paper, lend themselves to a comparison of post-1945 central banking reform. It is true that the sovereignty of the German Reich had completely vanished with Germany's unconditional surrender and the country was partitioned among the Allies, while the Japanese state remained intact and the country remained united under American occupation. But as the Americans, due to their financial strength, also played the leading role among the three occupying powers of West Germany, it is especially useful to compare the aims and results of American banking policies in Japan and Germany under partly equal and partly different conditions. Especially in the financial and economic field, there were cases in which even the persons responsible for planning and executing policies in Germany and Japan were identical. Joseph M. Dodge first served as financial adviser to the American military government in Germany and was later sent with a similar function to Japan. The same is true for William H. Draper, who was General Clay's economic adviser in Germany and later also served in Japan.

Such a comparison enhances the chances of success in attributing causes to observed developments in central banking policies. Did American policy plans fail, because the outbreak of the Cold War changed US policy priorities, because German or Japanese politicians opposed US policy objectives or resisted the implementation of such policies, or because the US was meeting with opposition from its Allies in Germany? It is these sort of questions that this chapter can help to answer. The international comparison, as always, reduces the difference between the number of variables and equations.

The institutional setup of the central banking system up to 1945

Germany

When the *Reichsbank* – the Prussian Bank bought from Prussia by the newly founded Reich – came into existence on 1 January 1876, it was a centralized institution in Berlin with subsidiaries all over Germany.[1] The owners of the *Reichsbank* were private stockholders. Their annual General Assembly elected a 15-member Central Committee, which closely monitored monetary policies and performed advisory functions, especially in credit policy matters and in the appointment of members of the Directorate. The *Reichsbank* was not yet exclusively a 'bank of banks'; it also did business with non-bank enterprises, especially from the manufacturing and agricultural sector. Until 1922 it was not independent of the government, but was directly subordinate to the Reich's Chancellor who was explicitly designated the head of the *Reichsbank* in the Banking Act of 1875. The Directorate of the *Reichsbank* and its president, all civil servants of the Reich appointed for lifetime tenure by the Emperor, were merely executive organs. Somewhat typically for central banks in the pre-First World War period, the *Reichsbank* displayed a mixed status between private ownership and government control.

Although the Bank was a centralized Reich institution, the states had retained some rights. The federal chamber of parliament, the *Bundesrat*, which represented the different states of Germany, nominated the *Reichsbank* president and the members of the Directorate. It also appointed three out of four members of the supervisory body, the *Kuratorium*, which was automatically chaired by the Chancellor himself.

As long as the *Reichsbank* was obligated by law to keep one third of its note circulation covered essentially by gold, the Reich government could hardly interfere in monetary policies and never exploited the printing press. This changed when the gold cover requirement was lifted with the outbreak of the First World War, in August 1914. From then on the Reich government had practically unlimited access to the printing press of the *Reichsbank* with the familiar inflationary and hyperinflationary consequences during the war and post-war period until November 1923.

An important legal change in the *Reichsbank* status *vis-à-vis* the government came about on 26 May 1922. On the demand of the Allies as a condition for a moratorium on reparation payments, the Autonomy Act became law in Germany. The Reich's Chancellor ceased to be the head of the *Reichsbank* and the *Reichsbank* could decide on monetary policy by itself. None the less, the supervisory body, the

Kuratorium with the Reich's Chancellor as its Chairman, remained in place. The procedure of appointing the Bank's President and the other members of the Directorate was also changed. From then on, the Bank's President could be nominated by the *Reichsrat* (as the second chamber of parliament representing the states was called in the Weimar Republic) and be appointed by the Reich's President only after the expert opinion of the Central Committee and of the Directorate had been heard. The Directorate members were co-opted, that is nominated by the Directorate and – with the consent of the *Reichsrat* – appointed by the Reich's President after the opinion of the Central Committee had been heard.

The Allies had hoped that more *Reichsbank* independence from the government would stop the inflationary process in Germany. Instead the *Reichsbank*, which previously had criticized the government for its budget deficits and had pointed to their inflationary consequences, did not resist the government's demand for monetizing the progressively growing deficits. By starting to discount commercial bills on a big scale besides treasury bills, it opened the floodgate for Germany's famous hyperinflation that began in June 1922. Hjalmar Schacht, *Reichsbank* president from the end of 1923 to 1930 and again from 1933 to 1939, explained this by arguing that on account of the unfortunate foreign policy situation of Germany, the *Reichsbank* lacked the will to restrict the Reich to its own financial means (Schacht, 1927: 117). One of the responsible members of the Bank's Directorate, Karl Friedrich, stated shortly after the event that, at the time, the situation did not allow the full utilization of the *Reichsbank*'s legal autonomy. The question of what would happen if the Bank simply refused its credit to the Reich had been examined and answered to the effect that the denial of credit most probably would have had much worse economic and political consequences than the monetary implications of further credits to the government (Friedrich, 1923/24: 342). The case demonstrates that central bank independence might be a necessary, but is not a sufficient condition for providing stable monetary conditions.

Karl Helfferich, who was favoured by the *Reichsbank* Directorate as the successor to Rudolph Havenstein as president of the Bank when the latter had conveniently died just at the end of hyperinflation in November 1923, also published his view of the issue. In a judgment typical of conservative and nationalist circles, he pointed out that the Autonomy Act had not been a voluntary action by German legislative authorities, but 'the execution of a dictate' by the Allies. He nevertheless approved of the change arguing that in the new republican-parliamentary system the Bank needed protection from interference by partisan and non-expert governments (Helfferich, 1921/22: 215–17). Others opposed the

Bank's autonomy on the grounds that it was alien to the German tradition (Singer, 1922: 734–35).

As part of the Dawes Plan Reparation Treaty between Germany and the Allies of 1924, the old *Reichsbank* of 1875/76 was put on a new legal footing. The structure of the 1924 banking law and of the new *Reichsbank* resembled that of 1875. The main difference was that the 1924 banking law stipulated the independence of the Bank *vis-à-vis* the government. The Directorate was given the final say in shaping credit policies. The *Reichsbank* was merely obliged to report to the government on its credit policies and not to support the overall economic policy of the government, as the Bundesbank is obliged to do today. Even in matters of appointing the Directorate and its President, the Reich's authority was much reduced. The *Reichsbank* President and the ordinary members of the Directorate were to be elected by the newly created General Council that consisted of seven German and seven foreign members. It succeeded the *Kuratorium* through which the Reich had previously supervised the Bank. The German members of the General Council were elected by the private owners of the Bank, represented in the General Assembly, which had been in existence since 1876. The only influence that the Reich retained was the Reich's President's right to veto the appointment of an elected *Reichsbank* President twice. The third time around, however, the Reich's President was obliged to carry out the appointment.

The lifetime tenure for the members and President of the Directorate was removed. Directorate members were appointed for twelve years, and they had to resign at the age of sixty-five. The President was appointed for four years. Re-election and revocation at any time of members or the President of the Directorate by the General Council were possible. The Central Committee, elected by the General Assembly, was retained as an advisory body.

A completely new institution was the Commissioner for the Note Issue who had to be a foreigner. He was to ensure that the bank note circulation was managed according to the law, in other words that inflation would not be repeated. With the same purpose in mind, Article 25 strictly limited the Reich's access to the *Reichsbank*'s credit to a total of 100 million *Reichsmarks* and to a three-month term at most. At the end of each business year the Reich was not allowed to have an outstanding *Reichsbank* credit at all.

In this way, the *Reichsbank* was completely cut loose from the German government. Instead, it was subjected to influence by foreign agents, albeit legally to a lesser degree than during its subordination to the Reich's Chancellor from 1876 to 1922. But the *Reichsbank* and the foreign agents were operating under the same rules, those of the newly established gold-exchange standard: the *Reichsbank* was obliged to cover its note circulation by at least 40 per cent in gold and foreign exchange instead of the 33.3 per cent gold coverage requirement before the First World War. The remaining 60 per cent were allowed to be covered by qualified commercial bills and checks.

Another revision of the 1924 banking law that followed the acceptance of the Young Plan in 1930 eliminated the control foreigners had exercised over the *Reichsbank*. The position of the Commissioner for the Note Issue was abolished. The General Council consisted of German members only, thus strengthening the influence of the Bank's private owners. At the same time, however, the Reich's President was given the ultimate right to veto the appointment or the revocation of members of the *Reichsbank*'s Directorate and of its President. This strengthening of the powers of the Reich's President, in fact, amounted to a strengthening of the government's role, because his decision had to be countersigned by the Chancellor or the cabinet member in charge. In addition, the Bank was allowed to accept treasury bonds on collateral for lombard credits, thus opening for the Reich an indirect path to the Bank's credit.

While the Bank's independence of the government had been strengthened under the Banking Act of 1924, its room for manoeuvre had been curtailed by subjecting it to the rules of the gold-exchange standard and by establishing foreign supervision to ensure that those rules would be guarded. When foreign supervision was terminated in 1930 after the acceptance of the Young Plan, full legal convertibility of the German currency was introduced also for Germans, already having been introduced for foreigners in 1924. This strengthened the gold-exchange standard's grip on the conduct of German monetary policy. After the financial crisis in the summer of 1931, however, the *Reichsbank* failed to meet the 40 per cent coverage requirement. Foreign exchange control was then introduced in Germany. Thus, the Bank's dependence on the rules of the gold exchange standard again weakened.

Throughout this post-inflation period, Germany's central bank enjoyed a freedom of action *vis-à-vis* the government that it had never had (or used from May 1922 to November 1923) before and that it would never retrieve. It was a period of extreme tension between the government and the Bank (Müller, 1973). The *Reichsbank* even used its power to dictate fiscal-restraint legislation to the government. Its pressure contributed to the instability of Weimar governments and to the rather low prestige that the Weimar Republic enjoyed in public.

During the Nazi period (1933–45), the *Reichsbank* was gradually subjected to total control by the Reich, for the principle of division of power is alien to a totalitarian state. Furthermore, the Nazi government needed complete subordination of the central bank in support of its war effort.

The Banking Act of 27 October 1933 again revised the banking law of 1924. The General Council, through which the private owners of the Bank had exercised an important degree of control over the *Reichsbank*, was abolished. The Bank's President was to be appointed by the Reich's President, after hearing the opinion of the Bank's Directorate. The Directorate members were to be nominated by the Bank's President, but appointed by the Reich's President. In addition, the right to revoke Directorate members or the Bank's President was transferred from the General Council to the Reich's President alone.

The *Reichsbank* was empowered to trade in the open market in treasury and regular bonds without any limitation. This not only meant the introduction of a new instrument of monetary policy, the open market policy, but also easier access to the Bank's credit for the Reich. The *Reichsbank* was authorized to fall short of the 40 per cent coverage requirement, subject to majority decisions by the Directorate and the Central Committee.

The next legal change came about on 30 January 1937, this time by a simple declaration of the *Führer* in the Reichstag that the Reich had resumed unlimited sovereignty over the *Reichsbank*. It is not a coincidence that it took place on the fourth anniversary of the Nazis' seizure of power. This declaration was the final breach of Germany's international obligations from the Treaty of Versailles, in particular those that concerned the *Reichsbank* and still provided for a participation of the Bank for International Settlements (BIS) in changes of the German central banking law. The Reich's government, not the *Reichstag*, passed a law accordingly on 10 February 1937. It stipulated, similarly to the law of 1875, that the *Reichsbank* Directorate administered the Bank, but that it was subordinated to the *Führer* and Reich's Chancellor.

The final reform came about when, shortly before the Second World War, the Reich's government passed the Banking Act of 15 June 1939. The Bank was now totally subordinated to the Nazis' policy aims and to the *Führer*. The introduction to the Act stated that the Bank was subjected to the Reich's unlimited sovereignty and that it was obliged to support the realization of aims set by the Nazi leadership within its field of functions, 'the safeguarding of the value of the German currency' being mentioned as the Bank's prime duty.

The Bank's Directorate was subjected to instruction and supervision by the *Führer* and Reich's Chancellor. The Directorate merely administered the Bank. Its decisions were no longer taken by majority vote, but by the Bank's President alone. The *Führer* was given the exclusive right to appoint and revoke the Bank's President and the members of the Directorate. The Bank's private owners retained their General Assembly, but were left powerless. The Central Committee was abolished and substituted by an advisory council with members chosen by the Bank's President alone.

In addition to bonds the Bank was from now on allowed to trade in treasury bills, the total amount of which was left to a decision by the *Führer*. All minimum coverage requirements for the *Reichsbank*'s note issue were dropped. Gold and foreign exchange reserves should only suffice to clear accounts in international transactions and to safeguard the external value of the German currency. Whatever portion of the note issue was not covered by gold or foreign exchange, could be covered by commercial bills and checks, the Reich's treasury bills, bonds and lombard credits on daily notice. Thus, the *Führer* had attained total control of the *Reichsbank* and an unlimited access to its credit.

In January 1939 *Reichsbank* President H. Schacht and his Directorate had protested the ongoing use of the printing press by the Nazi government to finance the massive expenditures for armaments. Although Schacht had helped to pave the Nazis' way to power, he and other members of the Directorate were immediately dismissed by the *Führer* and replaced by politically more streamlined and at the same time less expert figures. During the war from September 1939 to May 1945, the *Reichsbank* never resisted any government demands for credit.

Japan

The Bank of Japan (hereafter BOJ) was established in June 1882 as a joint-stock company, modelled after the Belgian National Bank. The Finance Minister, Masayoshi Matsukata, accepted advice from Leon Say, the French Finance Minister, to follow the Belgian example because of its relatively recent establishment in 1850. However, why the model of the German *Reichsbank*, even more recently established in 1876, was not chosen is still a puzzle. Yoshino has guessed that the strong governmental control over the Belgian central bank attracted Matsukata's attention (Yoshino, 1962: 116).

Indeed, the BOJ's dependence on the government was quite evident from the beginning. As in the Belgian case, the government had the power to authorize any revision of the Bank's Article and the Governor was to be nominated by the Emperor. But half of the BOJ's stock capital was owned by the government, while the Belgian counterpart had solely private stockholders. Moreover, the BOJ Law showed such expressions as the 'control', 'authorization' and 'approval' by the government more frequently than the Belgian case (BOJ, 1982, 186–8). In this sense, the Japanese government had traditionally a stronger power over its central bank.

Matsukata was faced with an inflationary situation and pursued a deflationary policy. He drastically contracted the inconvertible government currency that had been issued during the Seinan War (a large-scale rebellion of the former *Samurais*) from the peak of 139 million *yen* in 1878 to 88 million *yen* in 1885. The consumer price index rose *circa* 26 per cent between 1879 and 1881, and then fell *circa* 32 per cent between 1881 and 1886.[2] The foundation of a central bank to issue bank notes convertible into specie was expected to be the final act of his monetary reform. However, the statutes of the BOJ Act did not include a clear rule for its note issue. Because the inflation was not yet completely under control, the government had to permit the circulation of inconvertible currencies (not only government paper currency, but notes issued by commercial banks as well) at least for a while, even after the foundation of the BOJ in 1882.

The convertibility of the BOJ notes took effect only in May 1885. The amended Convertible Note Act of 1888 finally stipulated a limit for the BOJ's note issue: the maximum was equal to the BOJ's specie reserves plus a fiduciary amount (70 million *yen* plus allowance when necessary, with tax payments and permission by the Finance Minister). Nevertheless, the circulation of the inconvertible currencies continued for a few more decades, being overtaken by that of the BOJ notes only in 1889 and terminated finally in 1899.[3] From its beginning, the BOJ was expected to do business as a commercial bank, mainly to rediscount bills for private banks. During the initial decades, commercial bills constituted less than half of its assets and most of them were held as collateral for long-term loans. The BOJ simultaneously worked as a government's bank, administering the Exchequer. This business led to the building of a nationwide network of correspondence contracts with 90 banks (122 offices), of which those without business on behalf of the Exchequer were only 21 banks (23 offices), in 1887 (BOJ, 1982: 331).

Although the New Currency Act of 1871 determined the Japanese monetary standard to be based on gold, it worked in fact as a bimetallic standard of gold and silver, because East Asian countries traditionally traded with silver currencies and accordingly the Japanese government had accumulated silver species. The indemnity of the Chino-Japanese War enabled Japan to adopt the gold standard in 1897 with gold purchased in London. This is similar to the episode in Germany when the gold standard was introduced with the indemnity of the Prussian–French War. The BOJ did not strictly change money supply in accordance with its gold reserves, however, because the *Zaigai Seika* (specie and foreign exchange held abroad), which was initially introduced in 1896 and continued to exist from 1904 onwards, worked as a cushion when the balance of trade registered large deficits, and hence gold would otherwise have flowed out of Japan.

From the outbreak of the Russo-Japanese War in 1904, the BOJ credit was largely supplied to the government mainly through monetizing government bonds to finance growing military and colonial expenditures, nationalizing private railways, building post and telecommunication networks and urban engineering. The share of the government stood at more than 50 per cent of the total BOJ credit until 1911 (Itoh, 1987).

During the First World War, Japan enjoyed a windfall demand for her exports and recorded the highest level of current account surplus (more than 10 per cent of GNP) in her modern economic history.[4] Since the United States and other industrial countries suspended gold exports, Japan followed suit in September 1917, despite a large surplus in her balance of payments.

There was no drastic change in the BOJ organization after the war, because Japan, having joined the Allies, did not need to pay an indemnity and did not experience hyperinflation as did Germany. Although Japan tried to resume the freedom of gold exports and re-establish the gold standard through the 1920s, financial crises in 1920 and 1927 and the earthquake around Tokyo in 1923 prevented these efforts. The most important task for the BOJ in this period was its lender of last resort function, namely to assist financial institutions in difficulties by providing emergency credit.

Foreign reserves accumulated during the First World War and held abroad enabled Japan to neutralize, at least temporarily, the effects of the balance of trade deficits on its money supply. In January 1930, after a considerable delay compared with other industrial countries, the gold standard was reintroduced in Japan at the pre-war parity, but it was suspended again in December 1931.

Shortly thereafter, the maximum limit of the BOJ's fiduciary note issue was extended from 120 million to 1 billion *yen*, in July 1932, up to 1.7 billion in April 1938, and again up to 2.2 billion in April 1939. These repeated measures corresponded to a policy of monetizing government bonds which financed the increased scale of military spending. The expanded money supply was one of the factors which contributed to a rapid recovery from the Depression in Japan.[5]

In addition, a new BOJ Law was enacted in May 1942, following the German *Reichsbankgesetz* of 1939, and simultaneously the previous acts dealing with the BOJ and its note issue were removed. The principle of being 'a commercial bank' since its foundation had become increasingly inconsistent with the growing needs of the war finance. The economic management of Nazi Germany seemed to be successful at that time, and attracted popularity not only among government officials but also academic circles. As a result of its duty 'to accomplish solely the national purpose' (Article 2 of the Law), the monetary authority became subject to a strict governmental control, for example, over changes in the bank rate and its note issues. In particular, articles 42 and 43 established an overall supervising authority of the Finance Minister over the BOJ. The Governor was to be nominated by the Government (Article 16) and could be dismissed whenever he failed to observe the orders of the Finance Minister (Article 47).

Like the *Reichsbank*, the BOJ played a very important role in financing the war economy, in particular during the Pacific War. Firstly, the Temporal Fund Adjustment Law (*Rinji Shikin-Chosei Ho*) of 1937 stipulated that the total financial funds should be primarily allocated to war-related manufacturing. Banks, forced to finance these firms, participated in loan syndicates. While the Industrial Bank of Japan (IBJ, *Nippon Kogyo Ginko*) initially organized these loan syndicates, the BOJ took over this task later after the National Financial Control Association (*Zenkoku Kinyu Toseikai*) was founded and the new BOJ Law was enacted.

Secondly, the BOJ monetized 60–80 per cent of the government bonds, which naturally created a potential source of inflation. The bonds purchased by the BOJ were to be subsequently sold to the public. Insofar as the central bank succeeded in reselling the bonds in the open market, the government's deficit spending should not have been so much of a worry. In fact, the BOJ, in association with the government, promoted a campaign to increase saving of the private sector in order to resell government bonds. Although *circa* 97 per cent of the government bonds were resold to the public between 1942 and 1945, the BOJ simultaneously supplied loans against these bonds as collateral. Therefore, the successful bond sales did not put a brake on the growing money supply.

Thirdly, the Bank was obliged to expand its credit to military industries, through rediscounting commercial bills either accepted by the IBJ and/or guaranteed by the government, and through lending to the Wartime Finance Bank (*Senji Kinyu Kinko*) and the IBJ (Teranishi, 1993: 158–61 and Yoshino, 1962: 491–4).

In this way, the BOJ gave up its responsibility for price stabilization. According to the wholesale price index of the BOJ, the price of all commodities almost doubled between 1941 and 1945. Cash in circulation increased from 5.4 billion *yen* at the beginning of 1941 to 58.9 billion *yen* in August 1945, while M3 rose from 17.3 billion *yen* to 100.3 billion *yen* during the same period. Due to this experience of losing monetary control, independence from the government was expected to become an indispensable part of the whole financial reform after the war.

The post-war reform goals and banking reform failures of the Allies

Germany

The famous controversy within the American administration and with the British over the Morgenthau Plan and over occupation policy in general was ignited in September 1944, when Treasury Secretary Henry J. Morgenthau, Jr managed to persuade President F.D. Roosevelt to officially endorse his plan to turn post-war Germany into a partitioned and de-industrialized agrarian nation.[6] Within the American administration, three departments were involved in this controversy: the Treasury Department with its Morgenthau Plan; the State Department, under Cordell Hull, which favoured a long-term economic and political re-integration of Germany into the community of democratic and peaceful nations; and the War Department, under Henry L. Stimson, which demanded a pragmatic approach to occupying Germany that should address the specific problems of military government there. The final version of the American occupation directive for Germany, JCS 1067, was completed and sent to General Eisenhower in mid-May 1945. Truman had succeeded Roosevelt about four weeks earlier and both the State Department and the War Department had regained much of the political influence over German policy that they had lost to Morgenthau, due to his close personal contact with the president, at the summit meeting of Roosevelt and Churchill in Quebec in September 1944. Finally, in early July 1945, Morgenthau resigned in protest over the fact that he was not appointed to the American delegation attending the Potsdam Conference, which took place from 17 July to 2 August 1945.

JCS 1067 constituted the official foundation for American occupation policy, until a new more constructive occupation directive, JCS 1779, was prepared by General Clay, the head of the American military government in Germany (OMGUS), and was sent to him officially from Washington, DC, on 15 July 1947, that is after the announcement of the Truman Doctrine on 12 March 1947 that marked the beginning of the Cold War. According to JCS 1067, OMGUS was to take no responsibility for stabilizing the German economy. In anticipation of the decisions of the Potsdam Conference, JCS 1067 placed the authority over banking policy in the hands of the Allied Control Council, the four-powers government for all of Germany established at Potsdam. In practical terms this meant that a banking policy reflecting only American viewpoints could not be executed by the American military government, not even in its own occupation zone. The Potsdam Agreement represented the second comprehensive agreement of the Americans with the British, following CCS 551 of April 1944, on common guidelines for occupation policy in Germany. It was to be the first and only understanding on occupation directives reached at the tripartite level with the Soviets.

The Potsdam Agreement provided for the decentralization of the political structure, meaning the federalization of Germany, similar to the federal structure of the US. At the same time, the Agreement included provisions for 'Germany as a whole', for which the Allied Control Council was put in charge. German unity was emphasized especially for the economy: 'During the period of occupation Germany shall be treated as a single economic unit.' With regard to financial policy, 'currency and banking, national taxation and customs' were specifically listed as the areas in which the Control Council was given responsibility to determine a common policy. Yet at the same time a common decentralization policy for the German economy, to be applied also to banking, was agreed upon as an economic pendent to political federalism. It was considered necessary to prevent a concentrated German economy from ever supporting aggressive militarism in Germany again. 'At the earliest practicable date, the German economy shall be decentralized for the purpose of eliminating the present excessive concentration of economic power as exemplified in particular by cartels, syndicates, trusts and other monopolistic arrangements', according to the Potsdam Agreement.

The Soviet military government had acted on these principles even before the Potsdam Agreement. Upon taking control of Berlin the Soviets closed all banks 'temporarily', which in the case of private banks, including the head offices of the big banks, later turned out to be forever. In Berlin the *Reichsbank* and its branches were transformed into the new Berlin City Bank (*Berliner Stadtbank*) and as such were permitted to reopen, as were the Savings Bank of Berlin (*Sparkasse der Stadt Berlin*) and its branches. As to the Soviet occupation zone, where the banks had also been closed, the supreme commander of the Soviet military administration, Marshall Shukow, ordered on 23 July 1945 that new banks and savings institutions in public ownership be established at the province, *Länder*, city and communal levels. The Soviets not only decentralized, as their and the American interpretation of the Potsdam Agreement demanded, but they also socialized the banking system, a point on which the Potsdam Agreement was mute and on which the Western Allies disagreed with the Soviets. But it has been argued that the closure of the old credit institutions and the creation of the new ones were motivated less by the ideological aim of quickly nationalizing the economy in the Soviet occupation zone than by a pragmatic goal: by confiscating currency and simultaneously stripping the private bank customers of their claims to currency, the occupation authorities intended to increase the purchasing power of their confiscated *Reichsmark* holdings and ensure that a greater percentage of the demand for goods and services from German production could be paid for with the newly issued occupation currency, the 'Allied military mark', which was legal tender like the *Reichsmark*.[7] The Soviets were in a position to issue the occupation currency in unlimited amounts because they had demanded and eventually been given duplicates of the plates (Ziemke, 1975: 60). Unlike the Western Allies, they had objected to having the Allied military marks printed solely in Washington, DC, on behalf of all four powers, starting in the spring of 1944. The complementary effects of this step in 1944 and the closure of the banks in the Soviet zone in 1945 enhanced the ability of the Soviets in the post-war period to place massive demands on the German national product simply, quickly and without any control from their Western Allies. Since the Soviet Union had suffered most from the war in comparison with its Allies, and since its zone proved to be the most costly to occupy, the behaviour of the Soviets in the banking issue is understandable from economic and financial perspectives that transcend ideological considerations (Deckers, 1974: 25–7).

The Soviet side retreated into its ideological shell only after it became increasingly clear in the years that followed that the Western powers were neither going to fulfil the great expectations of the Soviets for resource transfers from Western Germany to both the Soviet zone and the USSR itself, nor willing to pay any price to ensure that Germany was treated as a single economic unit.

The American military government likewise saw the *Reichsbank* and the big banks as 'excessively concentrated'. By August 1945, it had not yet decided at what level the *Reichsbank* and the other big banks should be decentralized. When General Clay arrived in Europe in April 1945, he discovered that his Finance Division was being run by Bernard Bernstein, a close colleague of Treasury Secretary Henry Morgenthau. Bernstein had surrounded himself with other colleagues from the Treasury Department in Washington who also favoured the type of Carthaginian peace that Morgenthau envisioned for Germany, or, as the *Wall Street Journal* once criticized, preferred revenge over reconstruction (Clay, 1950: 19; Schwarz, 1980: 99). Throughout America a general debate ensued as to whether a policy of repression or rehabilitation could best ensure that Germany remained peaceful in the future (Gaddis, 1972: 96). Clay's ambivalent position arose from his evaluation of the directive JCS 1067 shortly after his arrival in Europe: 'We were shocked – not at its punitive provisions but at its failure to grasp the realities of the financial and economic conditions which confronted us' (Clay, 1950: 18). Clay was speaking not only for himself, but also for his new financial adviser Lewis Douglas, an insurance entrepreneur who also served on the board of directors of General Motors (Horstmann, 1991:

54). Douglas labelled the authors of the directive as 'economic idiots' and added: 'It makes no sense to forbid the most skilled workers in Europe from producing as much as they can for a continent which is desperately short of everything' (Murphy, 1964: 308). Clay appointed Douglas as Bernstein's supervisor and then sent Douglas back to Washington immediately, where he was able to have several smaller modifications made to the directive by early May. Two months later, however, Douglas resigned out of frustration with the final version of JCS 1067.

Like the entire community of American big business, the two other top advisers Clay had brought with him from America were vehemently opposed to the Morgenthau policy: William H. Draper from the banking establishment Dillon, Read & Co., New York, as economic adviser, and Robert Murphy from the State Department as political adviser. These two men used what leeway for interpretation there was to make constructive use of the occupation directive. Draper later went to Japan to apply recipes for industrial transformation similar to his policies in Germany (Berghahn, 1995: 71). In October 1945, 'Morgenthau's man' Bernstein resigned from the military government after Clay had stripped him of much of his authority by making Bernstein chief of the new 'Division of Investigation of Cartels and External Assets' and by appointing a man of Clay's choice from Washington to succeed Douglas in heading the Finance Division in September 1945. This new top adviser was the respected banker Joseph M. Dodge, chairman of the board of Detroit Bank and Trust Co. and president of the American Bankers Association. He was also sent to Japan later on. Until he was succeeded in Germany by his deputy Jack Bennett on 1 June 1946, Dodge was the American decisive in conceptualizing the reorganization of the banking business, currency relations and financial structures in West Germany.

Starting in June 1945, before Douglas left his post, the financial experts in the American military government were divided into two camps, each camp supporting a different plan for the decentralization of the *Reichsbank* and the big banks. The plan that best concurred with Douglas's own ideas called for a decentralization of the *Reichsbank* at the level of the occupation zones. The *Reichsbank* chief office in Frankfurt was to become the central bank of the American zone and to assume the supervision of the banks in that zone. The second plan mirrored Bernstein's vision of decentralization on a *Land* basis in conjunction with the American plans for creating a federal, *Land*-oriented political order in Germany (Horstmann, 1991: 58–9). In both cases, the decentralization of the big banks was not stated explicitly, but the practical application of these plans to big banks was implied by the analogy of the situation.

Following the Potsdam Agreement, some financial experts of the American military government even developed a plan that provided for a central bank for all of the zones, and for the continued existence of the big banks with new head offices to replace the closed ones in Berlin. Such a design corresponded to their interpretation of the commitment made at Potsdam to treat Germany as a single economic unit, especially in the areas of currency and banking. In the experts' opinion, such a structure would also facilitate greater economic and administrative efficiency.[8]

Shortly after he took office, in late September 1945, Dodge chose the plan he preferred. Surprisingly, the plan he chose was the one based on Bernstein's concept of decentralizing the banking system at the *Länder* level, while his staff favoured the model of zonal decentralization (Horstmann, 1991: 61–2). At most, he was willing to concede the creation of an inter-*Länder* Bank Council that would coordinate the Land Central Banks in the American zone. Dodge was determined to subordinate the creation of a new banking system to the political goal of federalization decided upon at Potsdam. Another influence on Dodge's decision was the 'home model': in the United States banking was decentralized at the level of the individual states, except for the US Federal Reserve system. It operated on the basis of 12 Federal Reserve banks, each in districts superimposed on the state banking system.[9] Dodge was also borrowing from this 'home model' when he proposed to dismantle the universal banking system in favour of a division of labour among banks, so to speak, in which banks would do business either in long-term securities (investment banks), or in short-term deposits and credit (commercial banks). He also wanted to ban the use of supervisory board positions to interlock industrial and banking directorates.

The Dodge Plan provided for the decentralization of the German banking system and of bank supervision to the *Land* level in order to destroy the financial monopoly of the *Reichsbank* and the big banks. A central bank was to be established in each of the federal states. These were not the legal successors of the old *Reichsbank*, whose head office, like those of the big banks, in Berlin had been closed by the Soviet occupation authorities. But they were authorized to take over the *Reichsbank*'s assets and liabilities in each respective *Land*. They were not authorized to issue currency, but entitled to regulate the existing currency and credit in each *Land*. They were designed to serve as reserve centres and as lender of last resort for the commercial banks and savings institutions. They were to function as bankers' banks and as the fiscal agent for the respective *Land* government. In contrast to the *Reichsbank* they would not be permitted to do business with the non-bank private sector. They had to provide for clearing arrangements with the other central banks. The big banks were to be decentralized accordingly. The *Reichsbank* and the central offices of the big banks were to be legally eliminated (Loehr, 1952: 9–11).

In late October 1945, Joseph Dodge submitted his decentralization plan to the Allied Control Council for discussion in its Finance Directorate. It was taken up on 6 November 1945.

Only the British opposed the American proposals. They considered an efficient, even centralized banking system to be the prerequisite for a rapid revival of the German economy. The British zone was dependent on this much more than were the Soviet, American or French zones. The Ruhr valley was the industrial heart of Europe, and the recommencement of coal shipments was considered essential for the revival of industry in the neighbouring countries as well. It was for this reason that the British national budget had been burdened after the end of the war with large subsidies which were needed just to commence the mining of Ruhr coal again. The British zone was also the most densely populated and therefore least able to feed itself. So another heavy burden to the British national budget was the food it imported into its occupation zone.[10] There was only one solution to this dilemma for financially crippled Great Britain: the German economy had to be revived to the extent that its industrial exports earned the foreign currency needed to finance the importation of foodstuffs and the subsidization of coal mining as long as coal prices were regulated.

There was another factor influencing British banking policy. The British banking system itself was similar to the German one in that its structure was also centralized, within both the central and the commercial banking system. The British system was similar to the American banking structure only in that commercial banks were separate from investment banks. Therefore, in contrast to the Soviets, the Americans and the French, the British refrained from morally condemning a centralized banking system as having been the support system of the National Socialist war machine. The liabilities of German banks to the British that had arisen from the Standstill Agreements of the inter-war period provided another strong motive for the British desire to retain as centralized a banking structure as possible in Germany.

The British member of the Finance Directorate, S.P. Chambers, argued against the Dodge Plan by pointing out that a unified central and commercial banking system would be more efficient and would correspond to the Potsdam Agreement to treat Germany as a single economic unit. Furthermore, a system of big banks with a network of branch operations could not evolve into a dangerous concentration of economic power if controlled by the military governments. On the contrary, a centralized banking system would aid the Allies in implementing their plans for monetary and credit policy. Such a system would be less susceptible to crisis and would prevent any possibility of creating local monopolies.

While the Americans were preparing the implementation of their decentralization proposals in their own occupation zone, the British acted in the opposite direction. After the British military government had officially ordered, in September 1945, the big banks to establish a directing office in Hamburg for their banking operations in the British occupation zone as a whole (which the Deutsche Bank and the Commerzbank had already done) it ordered, on 24 November 1945, that a *Reichsbank* chief office for the British zone, that is for several states, be set up in the existing branch office of the *Reichsbank* in Hamburg. In contrast, in mid-December 1945, the American military government instructed the *Länder* governments in its zone to prepare to set up Land Central Banks.

Discussions in the Finance Directorate of the Allied Control Council continued to meet with British opposition. By April 1946, Dodge felt compelled to propose a compromise in order to find a solution to the stand-off that had developed. He proposed establishing a *Länder* Union Bank that would act as a central bank for all four zones placed above the Land Central Banks. This bank would coordinate the measures needed to treat Germany as a single economic unit, namely the fundamental decisions on monetary and credit policy, and the balancing of the financial requirements of the German economy: that is, the savings–investment relations between surplus and deficit areas, reparations, foreign trade and reconstruction. The organization of the bank would also be mirrored by its functions: it was proposed to create a department for issuing bank notes, a separate one for the usual banking business, a department of reconstruction finance, and one for exports and imports.[11]

The British reacted favourably to this concession by agreeing to the decentralization of the big banks and to bank supervision on a *Land* basis, to the creation of Land Central Banks in place of the *Reichsbank*, and to the liquidation of the head offices of the big banks and the *Reichsbank* in Berlin. The Soviets and the French rejected the idea of a *Länder* Union Bank because they felt it would be a far too centralized institution; yet the British refused to back down on their demand for the creation of some sort of supra-zonal institution such as the *Länder* Union Bank.

Before Dodge resigned and his colleague Jack Bennett took over the Finance Division in June 1946 (until May 1949), Dodge proposed yet another compromise in May, featuring a 12–member *Länder* Central Bank Commission, which would comprise three Land Central Bank presidents from each zone who would be appointed by the respective military governments. All decisions made by this commission would first have to be approved by an Allied Banking Board, which would be made up of one representative each from the four military governments.

This proposal became the basis for an agreement in the Banking Committee of the Finance Directorate on 21 June 1946, to decentralize the banks on a *Land* basis, including the liquidation of the *Reichsbank* and the big banks' head offices in Berlin.[12] Yet a month later, as the Finance Directorate itself met to deliberate on the plan proposed by its Banking Committee, only the three Western powers were still willing to agree to it. At the meeting held on 24 July 1946, the Soviets now rejected this proposal because it would not truly break up the power of the German 'monopolies' in the banking sector. Instead, they recommended a solution that would have corresponded to the practice in the Soviet zone, where – except for the cooperatives – the only credit institutions still permitted to operate were state-owned.

As a result, the issue of socialization was introduced into the talks alongside that of decentralization. The inflexibility of the Soviet position in the negotiations was certainly related to the failure of the second conference of the Council of Foreign Ministers in Paris on 12 July 1946; this council had been created by the Potsdam Agreement. The other factor was the concurrent announcement of the US Secretary of State, James F. Byrnes, that if it became impossible to consolidate the zones in order to administer them as a single economic unit, this step would be taken – and indeed the USA and Great Britain did agree on 5 September 1946, to create what would become the so-called Bizone (Weber and Jahn, 1973: 15–18). After the Soviets refused to treat Germany as an economic unit according to the Anglo-American interpretation of the Potsdam Agreement, and after they then proved only to be interested in free reparation transfers from the Western zones, Clay had all such transfers from the US to the Soviet zone stopped in early May 1946.[13]

Due to the irreconcilable differences that had arisen in the Finance Directorate, the policy decision was handed up to the Coordinating Committee,[14] the next highest political authority at the four-power level; from there it was finally passed on to the Allied Control Council itself, where all attempts to arrive at an agreement among the Allies finally failed on 21 October 1946.[15] As a result, the job of restructuring the banking system once again reverted to the commanders-in-chief of the respective zones.

Japan

In accordance with the occupation policy in Germany, General Douglas MacArthur, the Supreme Commander of the Allied Powers (hereafter

SCAP),[16] aimed at reforming the Japanese economy with the objectives of 'demilitarization and democratization' which would not allow the country's military capabilities to be reconstructed. An important difference from the German case lies in the fact that, despite the use of the name 'Allied Powers', Japan was actually occupied by the United States alone and that the Occupation Powers did not directly govern but only indirectly controlled the policies of the Japanese government. In other words, the Japanese side maintained a limited degree of freedom to resist orders from SCAP.

Post-war economic reforms included the break-up of such 'feudalistic' systems as the *Zaibatsu* conglomerates and the landowner–tenant relationship, on the one hand, and the creation of democratically legitimized trade unions and collective wage bargaining, on the other hand. The reformists within the Economic and Scientific Section (ESS) of SCAP worked on the assumption that the shortage of effective demand in pre-war Japan had led to the aggressive drive for export markets coupled with growing militarism. As the reform policy began to bear fruit, private domestic consumption would be expected to rise and lead to economic growth and a higher level of employment. But officially, the US side did not regard it as its responsibility to repair and stabilize the Japanese economy.

However, once the East–West confrontation had developed momentum and had eventually led to the Cold War, as symbolized in East Asia by the foundation of the People's Democratic Republic of Korea in August 1948 and subsequently the People's Republic of China in October 1949, the aim of the occupation policy turned to the reconstruction of the Japanese economy. The rehabilitated economy would reduce the expenses of the economic assistance programme called GARIOA (Government Account for Relief in Occupied Area) and EROA (Economic Rehabilitation Account in Occupied Area), and hence the burden on the US tax-payers, while it would also secure the material basis for the US military engagement in East Asia. Already in October 1947, SCAP had produced a report on the 'Possibility of a Balanced Japanese Economy', and in November 1948, its revised version, 'Program for a Self-Supporting Japanese Economy', was published. In December 1948, following up these requests from Tokyo, Washington ordered nine principles for economic stabilization.[17]

According to the Ministry of Finance (MOF, 1976: 333), the focus of the occupation policy turned to the reconstruction of the Japanese economy when George F. Kennan, Policy Planning Staff of the State Department, and William H. Draper, Under-Secretary of the US Army, visited Japan and met with MacArthur in March 1948 (Tsutsui, 1988: 59–60; MOF, 1982: 517–18). Draper stood firmly against the strict application of the anti-monopoly policy to the banking industry, and is said to have drafted the principles for Economic Stabilization (MOF, 1976: 330). His position symbolized the changing course of the US occupation policy.

The nine principles included a balanced budget with expenditure cuts and increased taxes; deficit financing to be restricted to reconstruction; stabilization of prices and wages; control of foreign exchange and trade; promotion of industrial production and exports; and efficient food allocation. These principles reflected a compromise between the interventionists, in other words 'New Dealers' in Tokyo and conservative liberals in Washington. The latter finally gained the upper hand in shaping Japanese economic policy when President Truman sent Joseph Dodge, a bank president from Detroit, as a fiscal and monetary adviser to SCAP, in February 1949.

Dodge, while heading the financial department of the US military government in Occupied Germany, had prepared a report for the currency reform in the Western Zone of Germany (Hamada and Kasuya, 1993: 174). He pursued a stabilization policy in accordance with the liberals' tendency within the debate over the nine principles and ignored both the Japanese government and SCAP's desire for a mild course of stabilization. His policy, named the Dodge Line, was characterized by a balanced budget, coupled with suspending the Reconstruction Finance Bank (RFB: *Fukko Kinyu Kinko*) credit and introducing the single exchange rate parity of 360 *yen*/dollar. The single exchange rate was a very important step toward the stabilization of prices, because Japanese exports had been undervalued and imports overvalued, while differentials between the official prices in *yen* and the international prices had been subsidized by the Special Trade Financial Account (*Boeki-kinyu Tokubetsu Kaikei*). The BOJ had financed the deficits of this account.

Recently economists of the younger generation have tended to stress the continuity from the war economy rather than the discontinuity brought about by the economic reforms during the occupation.[18] Although it is outside the scope of this chapter to assess this new interpretation of the post-war economic history of Japan, the financial sector is a good example with which to evaluate the above argument, as the following remarks reveal.

Taking account of the financial institutions' active participation in the war economy, SCAP naturally intended to implement radical reforms to the Japanese financial system. As early as September 1945, the most fundamental measure of post-war financial reforms took place: closing central and colonial banks in the former colonies Taiwan and Korea, as well as those institutions specialized in war finance, the Wartime Finance Bank for example. Other financial institutions which had engaged in more or less nationalistic objectives were either closed or reformed. In December 1946, the Yokohama Specie Bank, which specialized in international finance, was closed and eventually transformed into a private foreign exchange bank – the Bank of Tokyo – because formerly it had extended its business into issuing military scrip in occupied territories and had financed military operations in China.

The big banks within the four *Zaibatsu* concerns (Mitsui, Mitsubishi, Sumitomo and Yasuda) became targets of economic democratization and antitrust policy, as the report of the State-War Mission (March 1946) clearly stated. It is important to note, however, that while the *Zaibatsu* conglomerates were partly broken up, the leading banks within them were not partitioned.[19] These banks were not allowed to retain their traditional *Zaibatsu* names, however. Mitsui remained as the Teikoku Bank, when its partner Dai-ichi Bank became separated in October 1948. Mitsubishi, Sumitomo and Yasuda were simultaneously obliged to change their names, to Chiyoda, Osaka and Fuji, respectively (Tamaki, 1994: 190).

After the compensation payments for wartime financing were terminated in the second half of 1946, those banks which had lent to military industries recorded large-scale bad loans. At the end of March 1946, three quarters of total bank lending was related to war finance, while its share stood still higher in the case of big banks (Tamaki, 1994: 182). In this situation, most financial institutions were too weak to accept radical restructuring.

The BOJ was also opposed to the break-up of the big banks on the grounds that such a measure would disturb the reconstruction of the economy (BOJ, 1985: 283). SCAP determined, shortly after the Antitrust Committee issued its final report in July 1948, that the Antitrust Law (the Law against Excessive Concentration of Economic Power) would not be applied to banks. The reasons officially stated were that the *Zaibatsu* had already lost control over their banks since banking stocks had been taken over by the Holding Company Liquidation Commission, and that the banking industry would be strictly supervised by the Fair Trade Commission and the newly prepared Financial Business Law. The fact is, however, that it was consideration for the undercapitalized state of banks and the demand for funds of major industries which determined the policy (MOF, 1982: 528 and Tsutsui, 1988: 64).

Until 1948 SCAP did not announce clear ideas on financial reform in Japan, except for a discussion of breaking up big banks. In March 1948, Clifford E. Cagle, a senior analyst of the US Federal Reserve Board (FRB) sent as an adviser for the ESS, proposed to the ESS Finance Division an overall programme of banking legislation. This proposal was drafted, in a sense, in order to stand against the idea of partitioning the big banks which had been advocated by the Antitrust and Cartel Division. The essence of this memorandum was repeated again in May and proposed as a New Banking Law in August of the same year. The new Law included the idea of a Banking Board, which will be discussed in the next section.

Following the principle of this law, SCAP advised the Ministry of Finance (MOF) to close semi-public banks which specialized in long-term business. For the administrators from the United States, where banks engaged in short-term business and long-term credit operations were left to the capital market, those 'special banks' issuing finance bonds and providing long-term credit were hard to accept. In addition, their activities within the war economy, in particular the case of the IBJ, had been examined with critical eyes.

The IBJ, the Mortgage Bank of Japan (*Nippon Kangyo Ginko*), and the Hokkaido Colonial Bank (*Takushoku Ginko*) were subsequently all privatized, but allowed to subsist. The Mortgage Bank and the Hokkaido Colonial Bank were re-chartered in 1948 as 'ordinary' commercial banks, while the IBJ retained its privilege to issue finance bonds and was later reorganized as a most powerful, private institution for long-term credit.

As the US reform plan was initially aimed at the 'democratization' of the economy, little attention was paid to the efficient working of the whole financial system. The American principle of commercial banking, coupled with long-term fund-raising in the capital market, did not take account of the situation in which the post-war Japanese financial system was rooted. Due to runaway inflation, private financial assets had almost completely lost their real value, and hence the capital market operated well below its normal capacity under stable conditions.

Although SCAP initially stood firmly against specialized public financial institutions, long-term credit for capital accumulation could not be provided by private banks alone. Therefore, despite initial objections from the US side, public financial institutions were established after the deflation under the Dodge Line came to an end, for example the Export Bank of Japan (December 1950) and the Development Bank of Japan (March 1951). Moreover, the Long-term Bank Law (June 1952) legalized the business of private banks in long-term credit.

Japan's financial sector was largely shielded from the mainstream of post-war economic reforms because first, the Japanese side (both the government and the financial sector) strongly resisted proposals from the US side, and second, SCAP gradually changed its aims to prefer the efficient reconstruction of the Japanese economy over the original 'democratic' reform ideas, particularly after the Chinese communists took power in 1949.

Results of central banking and currency reforms and of monetary policy performance

West Germany

Parallel to his suprazonal banking decentralization proposals to the Allied Control Council, Dodge had ordered the *Länder* in the US zone, in mid-December 1945, to pass their own legislation to decentralize not only the big banks but also the *Reichsbank*, by establishing Land Central Banks. While the decentralization of the big banks was resisted not only by the banks themselves, but by almost all the German politicians involved, the *Länder* of the US zone came to cooperate with OMGUS on the Land Central Bank issue. They recognized that their political influence would grow once Land Central Banks had been established at the expense of the *Reichsbank*. After the failure of an agreement on a common banking policy in the Allied Control Council in October 1946 and before the *Länder* in the US zone were equipped with parliaments in late 1946, which would have had to deliberate on a law on Land Central Banks, each of the *Land* governments issued an identical Land Central Bank law at the request of OMGUS. The Land Central Banks in the US zone were thus opened for business in early 1947. The French military government followed suit and issued 'Ordinance No. 78 on the Liquidation of the *Reichsbank* and the Establishment of Land Central Banks' on 18 February 1947, in which the *Länder* of the French zone were required to establish these institutions by 1 March 1947.

The British, however, resisted the American decentralization policy again. Even before OMGUS issued Military Government Law No. 57 on 5 May 1947, to override German resistance and implement the decentralization of the big banks in addition to the *Reichsbank* in the US zone, Charles A. Gunston, the expert on Germany at the Bank of England, was pleased to note on 17 January 1947 that the British military government had not also implemented this 'lunatic idea of the American Dodge'.[20] For a long time, the British did not give in to the pressure by OMGUS to decentralize banking in the British zone. They were on the side of an almost unanimous German opinion on this issue. The American decentralization scheme for the big banks was evaluated as being completely unsuitable for the German system of banking, as was emphasized in reports submitted on 27 November 1946, and again on 29–30 April 1947, by the finance committee of the *Zonenbeirat* (Zonal Advisory Council), a body of German citizens appointed by the British military government.

Although in principle the British Finance Division shared this view fully, in practice it wanted to remain politically more flexible in dealing with the Americans. This was necessary since both the agreement on the founding of the Bizone of 5 September 1946 and the Potsdam Agreement had explicitly specified finance, and thus the banking system, as one of the political areas in which the policy of the occupation powers was to be uniform. The banking issue was deliberated in a banking subcommittee of the Bipartite Finance Committee/Panel, which was composed of the heads of the Finance Divisions in the British and American military governments, and to which was also assigned a *Gemeinsamer Deutscher Finanzrat* (Joint German Council on Finance) with its subcommittee, 'Money and Credit'.

In return for their willingness to federalize the *Reichsbank* structure and to decentralize the big banks in their zone accordingly, the British not only demanded a bizonal budget, which would commit the Americans to sharing the heavy financial burden of subsidizing the British zone, but also asked that a type of bizonal central bank be established in order to centrally direct monetary and credit policy. The British had been advocating such a central bank for quite some time in the negotiations on the institutional framework of the Bizone since October 1946. Following the announcement of the Marshall Plan in June 1947, they also wanted American cooperation in establishing a Reconstruction Loan Corporation for the purpose of financing industrial reconstruction, especially in the Ruhr region, through long-term credit from outside their zone.

Sir Eric Coates, who succeeded Chambers as head of the finance division in June 1947, presented this package of demands to his American counterpart, Jack Bennett, in late August 1947, nearly six weeks after the American decentralization policy, also for banking, had been explicitly spelled out in the new occupation directive JCS 1779 issued by Washington on 15 July 1947. Although this directive acknowledged more than its predecessors the necessity of making reconstruction a priority over revenge, the British pushed for more. Bennett, whom the British did not think highly of and considered obstinate and doctrinaire,[21] balked at the idea of creating a bizonal institution with the functions of a central bank. At most he was willing to concede the setting up of a coordination office above the Land Central Banks of the Bizone, so that the responsibility and decision-making power in monetary and credit policy would actually remain decentralized at the *Länder* level.

However, Clay wished to reach a compromise with the British quickly and was now convinced himself that a central bank was a prerequisite to bringing urgently needed economic stabilization to the Bizone. On 16 September 1947, he took up the matter with Washington,[22] and on 3 October 1947, he received the go-ahead to set up a central bank, the

Länder Union Bank. This model of the *Bank deutscher Länder*, the forerunner of the *Bundesbank*, had already been under discussion at the four-power level. The 'doctrinaire' Jack Bennett was forced to relent.

The British now convinced the Americans that a bizonal central bank should be headed by a board of managers with a president or general managing director. From this would later evolve the Directorate of the *Bank deutscher Länder*, later the *Bundesbank*. The board of managers was to carry out the decisions on monetary and credit policy made by the board of directors, the later Central Bank Council (*Zentralbankrat*). This body was composed exclusively of the presidents of the Land Central Banks, as the Americans had originally proposed, and functioned independently of any instructions by the governments, similarly to the Board of Governors of the Federal Reserve system and unlike the Bank of England since 1945.

The *Bank deutscher Länder* was established on 1 March 1948, by both military governments of the Bizone.[23] The new legal residence of the Bank became Frankfurt. At the same time, the Allied Bank Commission was also formed, comprising the heads of the finance divisions of the military governments and later of the High Commissioners. This new commission had veto power over the decisions made by the bodies of the *Bank deutscher Länder*.[24] France, which wanted to support currency reform in the three Western zones, integrated its three Land Central Banks into the new central bank and joined the Allied Bank Commission by issuing Ordinance No. 155a of the French military government on 19 June 1948, retroactively to 25 March 1948. The founding of this central bank made it possible to implement currency reform in the Western zones on 20 June 1948.

The further demand of the British for a suprazonal reconstruction credit institution was also accepted by the Americans. But it was only after the currency reform that several drafts for legislation were drawn up in the Bizonal Finance Administration and the Economic Administration. The final version became the Reconstruction Loan Corporation Act (*Gesetz über die Kreditanstalt für Wiederaufbau*) and went into effect on 5 November 1948.

Currency reform and monetary policy performance Once the *Bank deutscher Länder* had been founded and the French zone had been retroactively integrated on 19 June 1948 into the British–American agreement concerning this bank, everything was set for the long-discussed and well-planned currency reform in the three Western zones. The very next day, on 20 June 1948, the three Western military governments enacted identical legislation for the immediate introduction of the currency reform so long awaited by the population and business.

The Western Allies had attempted one last time in early 1948 to implement such reform in conjunction with the Soviets, but these efforts had failed.[25] This came as no surprise to C.A. Gunston, who had commented on 15 January 1948 that the government experts in London were all aware that quadripartite currency reform was not realistic. 'The problem is how to offer it to the Russians in such a way that the Russians will reject it without putting us in the wrong.'[26]

The Soviets reacted to the currency reform in the West by implementing their own currency reform in the Soviet occupation zone and all of Berlin three days later, on 23 June 1948. They first introduced a makeshift currency known as the Coupon Mark (*Klebemark*); due to the lack of new bills, coupons were simply glued on to the old *Reichsmark*, devaluing these at a ratio of 10:1 in East German *marks*. Every individual could exchange up to 70 RM into the new currency at a ratio of 1:1. Savings deposits in savings banks and other institutions were exchanged at the rate of 1:1 for the first 100 RM; at a ratio of 5:1 for the next 900 RM; and at 1:10 for amounts above this and for any other bank liabilities and debts.

This step forced the three Western sectors of Berlin to introduce, a day later, the new *Deutsche Mark*, the currency in circulation in the Western occupation zones, so that the city would not lose its economic connections to the Western zones, or sacrifice its economic and political future to the Soviets (Wolff, 1991). Because so many people still travelled back and forth between East and West Berlin, the East German *mark* continued to be treated as legal tender to a limited extent in the Western sectors of Berlin at an exchange rate of 1:1 with the *Deutsche Mark* until 20 March 1949, but only for items under price control, such as foodstuffs and rent, for taxes and other fiscal charges, as well as for fees for postal services, public transportation, electricity and gas. Otherwise, the rate of exchange for the new East German currency sank quickly against the *Deutsche Mark* in the following months to a rate of 4:1.

These developments sealed the fate of Germany as a partitioned land, at least as far as currency was concerned. The Soviets immediately reacted to the currency reform in West Berlin by blockading all access routes (streets and waterways) and by cutting off the electrical supply to West Berlin. Not until the airlift to West Berlin had gone on long enough to convince the Soviets that the Allies were determined to support West Berlin and its connections to the West did they end this blockade on 12 May 1949. The Soviets also reacted to the currency reform introduced in West Berlin by leaving the *Kommandatura*, the four-power administration governing the city, on 1 July 1948. After this, the political tensions within the joint municipal administration of

Greater Berlin grew worse. Municipal elections could only be held in the Western sectors in December 1948. The new City Assembly for the Western sectors elected Ernst Reuter as mayor. By then the municipal administration had already been partitioned, and it had been decided to establish the Free University in West Berlin in September 1948 as a result of the Communist interference in the freedom of research and teaching at the traditional Humboldt University in East Berlin.

On 20 June 1948, two laws were enacted in the Western zones, the Currency Act and the Currency Issue Act. The former legislation defined the new legal tender, the *Deutsche Mark*, regulated the process of turning in and registering the old currency, and stipulated the initial allotment for individuals (*Kopfgeld*), businesses (*Geschäftsbeträge*) and the public sector. Individuals received 40 DM per head at first and were permitted to exchange another 20 DM at a rate of 1:1 two months later. Businesses were equipped with 60 DM per employed person. Public sector institutions received funds in DM which in principle amounted to the prospective outlays for one month, while the German railways and postal service were allotted half a month's outlays. Although the original intent had been to link currency reform immediately to an equalization of war burdens, so imperative for social reasons, this was not done. It was merely stipulated in the preamble of the Currency Act that German legislative bodies were 'assigned the pressing task of regulating the equalization of war burdens by 31 December 1948'.[27] However, provisional legislation was not enacted until August 1949 and the final Equalization of War Burdens Act not until July 1952.

In the Currency Issue Act, the issue of bank notes and coins was regulated through the *Bank deutscher Länder*. For the first time a German central bank was delegated authority in determining minimum reserve requirements. The most important legislation in the currency reform package was the Currency Conversion Act of 27 June 1949 and the numerous ordinances issued afterwards to implement it. In order to reduce the excess money supply that had resulted from financing the war, and thereby make the level of prices set by control correspond to fair market prices, monetary assets were generally converted at a rate of 1 DM for 10 RM. To prevent prices from plummeting, a conversion ratio of 1:1 was set for regularly recurring obligations, such as wages and salaries, rental payments and retirement pensions, as well as liabilities resulting from purchase and work contracts, disputes between companies, and in family matters and inheritance cases.

As it was, deposits at banks (including savings banks), into which cash had to be placed in order to be converted, had an even lower rate than the 10 per cent prescribed for other financial assets. All *Reichsmark* liabilities between banks were cancelled and declared void. Deposits of non-banks were credited at a rate of 1 DM for 10 RM, but the depositor only had free access to half of this; the other half was deposited in a blocked account, known as a *Festkonto*. On 4 October 1948, both the Fourth Currency Reform Act *(Viertes Gesetz zur Neuordnung des Geldwesens)* in the Bizone and the corresponding ordinance of the military government in the French zone went into effect. These stipulated that 70 per cent of the deposits on each *Festkonto* were to be voided, 10 per cent were to be transferred into medium-term and long-term securities, and 20 per cent were to be released. Thus only 6 per cent of *Reichsmark* cash and deposits at the banks were directly accessible in *Deutsche Marks*, and 93.5 per cent of the *Reichsmark* deposits were lost completely.[28]

This discrimination against liquid assets in the form of cash and bank deposits resulted in part from the disproportionate losses which banks (and insurance companies) incurred because one stipulation of the Currency Conversion Act declared the liabilities of the Reich, including the *Reichsbahn* (State Railways), the *Reichspost* (Postal Service) and the *Reichsbank*, to be null and void (para. 14). Since these outstanding debts of the Reich represented the major portion of the assets of credit institutions (and insurance firms), these financial businesses would have gone bankrupt had they not been granted somewhat equivalent financial relief. On the liability side of their balance sheet, relief came in the form of the reduced conversion rate of 6.5 per cent mentioned above. On the assets side these financial businesses also received some compensation: 15 per cent of their *Deutsche Mark* demand deposits and 7.5 per cent of their savings and time deposits were credited to them on giro accounts by the Land Central Banks. The Land Central Banks also credited them the full amount of the *Geschäftsbeträge*, that is, the initial allotment in *Deutsche Marks* that the banks had paid out or credited to businesses.

If these credited funds and their other assets were still not sufficient to secure a 'suitable equity capital' and cover the converted liabilities, the banks were granted so-called equalization claims against the public sector at 3 per cent interest from the *Länder*. However, para. 28 of the Currency Conversion Act prohibited budget deficits in the public sector. In order not to overburden the public sector from the very start with debts incurred through such equalization claims, a significant proportion of the losses suffered by the banks as a result of the nullification of Reich debts was passed on specifically to the depositors at the banks by granting a currency conversion rate of only 6.5 per cent at most instead of the formal 10 per cent.

The Fourth Currency Reform Act of 4 October 1948 must also be considered in connection with the inflationary trend that followed currency reform. This trend was easier to spot than that of the earlier period of suppressed inflation because Ludwig Erhard, who was at the time director of the Economics Administration and later became Federal Economics Minister, ordered the decontrol of most prices in tandem with an end to rationing on most markets. Erhard had been given the authority to take such action by the Bizonal parliament, comprising the Economic Council and the *Länderrat*, in the *Gesetz über Leitsätze für die Bewirtschaftung und Preispolitik nach der Geldreform* (Act on Guidelines for Rationing and Price Policy following Currency Reform) passed on 24 June 1948.

The price increases that occurred during that summer may therefore have been an important reason why, on 4 October 1948, the military governments passed the Fourth Currency Reform Act, which greatly diminished the purchasing power on the *Festkontos* of the banks. In order to combat inflation further, the Bizonal Administration prohibited profiteering by enacting laws that went into effect on 7 October 1948 and 28 January 1949 (Stucken, 1964: 209). In late October 1948, the *Bank deutscher Länder* placed restrictions on credit, which were gradually lifted once prices began to stabilize in late May 1949. In the meantime, wage controls had been lifted by law on 3 November 1948. The fact that aid from the Marshall Plan began to arrive during this critical period helped stabilize the situation (Buchheim, 1993: 69–83).

Decisions made in connection with currency reform also simplified foreign business relations. On 1 May 1948, the exchange rate for 1 RM was uniformly set at 0.30 US dollars. Subsequently this rate was also valid for the *Deutsche Mark*. Step by step, this exchange rate replaced a multitude of differing settlement rates in foreign trade that had been used by the Joint Foreign Exchange Agency (JFEA) and the Joint Export–Import Agency (JEIA) of the Bizone.[29] Due to the dollar gap, foreign exchange controls had to be continued, of course.[30]

Japan

SCAP initially regarded the BOJ as the focus of financial reform, due to its central role in financing the war. Even before Japan finally surrendered to the Allied Powers, the US War Department prepared guidelines for the 'Control and Use of the Bank of Japan' in August 1945. They included such proposals as dismissing members of the executive board, issuing new *yen* and suspending the use of the foreign exchange reserves. These guidelines actually influenced the subsequent US policy to a certain extent (MOF, 1976: 47–53).[31]

However, in October 1945, the Japanese government took the initiative in setting up a provisional committee for reforming the BOJ, with the intention of avoiding the intervention of SCAP. According to the BOJ (BOJ, 1985: 268), the central bank insisted, within this committee, on its neutrality and independence from the government, which the MOF did not want to accept. Subsequently, the first Council of the Financial Institutions (CFI: *Kinyu Seido Chosakai*) under the MOF proposed a plan in January 1946, largely similar to the above committee, to reform the BOJ and establish the Finance Agency (*Kinyucho*). This agency, to be managed jointly by the MOF and BOJ, was supposed to deal with national financial needs and to control fund allocation as a whole.

In November 1947, the second CFI proposed instead a Currency and Credit Committee. It was to design and conduct an overall monetary and credit policy, with a membership consisting of the BOJ Governor, the Ministers of Finance and of the Economic Stabilization Agency (ESA: *Keizai Antei Honbu*), and representatives from financial and other industries. The BOJ was supposed to obey the policy designed by the Committee and to function solely as a note-issue bank. It is interesting to note that this idea was similar to the 'Banking Board' later proposed by SCAP.

The issue at stake concerning central banking reform was whether the money supply should be determined within, or outside the MOF. In fact, the Currency-Issue Council was established in December 1947. The Japanese government initially intended to define its task as merely giving advice to the Finance Minister on the maximum limit of the currency issue, since under the Law of 1942 the BOJ Governor was deprived of the power to decide on this.

But later, in accordance with a requirement of SCAP, its task was changed from advising to deciding upon the money supply. This Council did not function well, however, because the extent of the money supply could not be determined independently of fiscal needs (Kato, 1974: 335–6 and BOJ, 1985: 136ff). In particular, during the years of post-war inflation, government deficits were the main reason for printing money. The wholesale price index (WPI) of all commodities stood at 4.6 in 1946, 13.8 in 1947, 36.5 in 1948 and 59.7 in 1949, as against 1.0 in 1945.

After the reform plans from the Japanese side had been announced but had eventually failed except for the Currency-Issue Council, the ESS submitted to the Japanese government in August 1948 'an informal memorandum' on the overall revision of the banking structure. The term 'informal' was applied because it had not yet been authorized by the War Department in Washington. The Banking Board proposed in this memorandum would be distinct from the BOJ and independent from the MOF. It would be in charge of the monetary and credit policy and the supervision of all financial institutions. The BOJ would be reorganized as a Reserve Bank of Japan and charged only with implementing the policy determined by the Board. All private banks would be obliged to participate in the Reserve Bank System. Naturally, this plan was based on a federalist idea with the American Federal Reserve Board in mind. But the Board would be empowered with far more responsibilities than the Finance Agency proposed by the Japanese side and even than the FRB in the United States, in the sense that the chairman would be placed in the Cabinet and that this organ would function as a sole supervising authority over the whole financial system (Tsutsui, 1988: 78 and Muto, 1991).

The Japanese counterpart for the reform negotiation was the troika of the MOF, the BOJ and the ESA. The Japanese side resisted the US proposals on the ground that a Board independent from the MOF was not only unpractical, because public finance and central banking were closely interrelated, but also needless since the BOJ had been in charge of monitoring and controlling financial institutions (BOJ, 1985: 288). Thus, resistance to the Board united potentially conflicting interests between the MOF and the BOJ. Moreover, because Japan was a small country compared to the United States and was not divided up by Occupation Powers like Germany, this idea turned out to be unrealistic in the end.

The War Department in Washington eventually opposed the idea of the Banking Board in October 1948. The reason was that a radical reform of the financial system, including the establishment of a Board, would hamper an effective rehabilitation of the economy. As Draper repeatedly stated, Washington preferred stabilization to reform. Cagle responded in November that the Banking Board was a prerequisite for economic stabilization, since a powerful and permanent monetary agency independent from politics would constitute an indispensable element to control inflation. The main difference in opinion was whether to give more power to the BOJ, or to set up a new organ outside the central bank. SCAP had been worried about the one-man control, by Hisato Ichimada (the Governor of the BOJ from June 1946 to December 1954), which had resulted in a permissive stance toward inflation. His influence in the financial community was powerful enough to invoke a comparison with the Pope in the Vatican.

At the end of 1948, the Chief of the ESS-Finance Division finally achieved a compromise: a Policy Control Board within the framework of the BOJ.[32] The transformation of the Board from an outside organization to an insider of the BOJ was promoted by Ichimada's strong opposition to the initial idea of the Banking Board, according to his own memoirs. But other changes that had also taken place in the intervening period, and which would have had some bearing on events, were the announcement of the nine principles and the appointment of Dodge. In March and April 1949 Dodge met Ichimada in order to exchange opinions over the financial reform. Ichimada finally agreed with the proposal of the Policy Board which would remain within the BOJ (Muto, 1985a and 1985b and BOJ, 1985: 295–301).

The Policy Board, established in June 1949, is a rare example of a financial reform idea of SCAP that bore fruit. The members of the Board consisted of the Governor of the BOJ, representatives from the MOF and the ESA, local and city banks, as well as from agriculture, industry and commerce. Nevertheless, it remained in fact a 'sleeping board', because the principles of the BOJ Law remained intact. The Board has been chaired by the Governor of the BOJ ever since.

The history of central banking reform in Japan reveals the continuity of such strong ties between the BOJ and the government that even SCAP could not substantially modify them. It is remarkable that the BOJ Law of 1942 constitutes the legal framework of Japanese central banking to the present day. Accordingly, its independence from the government has been largely restricted.

Currency reform and monetary policy performance Inflation shortly after the war was highly accelerated in Japan. At the end of the war, total financial assets amounted to no less than 500 billion *yen*, while GNP in 1944 and the national wealth at the end of the war are estimated at only 74.5 billion *yen* and 189 billion *yen*, respectively. This wide gap between potential purchasing power on the one hand, and the national product and wealth on the other, led to a highly inflationary pressure. The stock of BOJ notes circulating with the public increased from 30.3 billion *yen* (mid-April) to 55.4 billion *yen* (year-end of 1945). Consumer prices in the black market, in particular, skyrocketed; they were 37 times as high as the official prices at the end of 1945 (BOJ, 1985: vol. 4, 5–15 and Toyo Keizai Shimposha, 1980: 520).

Compensation payments for wartime financing were the main cause of government deficits, which were monetized by the BOJ. Deposit accounts at banks were kept open for withdrawals. As early as November 1945, the Finance Minister announced a scheme for introducing the new *yen* and for a new tax on property and wartime profits. This announcement brought about large-scale deposit withdrawals and subsequent purchases of real values. The government had no other option but to take immediate action in such a critical situation, action which naturally included a currency reform.

The emergency financial measures and the ordinance to deposit BOJ notes in February 1946 determined that the old *yen* would cease to be legal tender. Those who held old *yen* were obliged to deposit them in closed accounts at financial institutions. Depositors were allowed to withdraw only 300 *yen* per household head and 100 *yen* per additional family member, in new *yen* notes. Moreover, firms were allowed to pay business expenses in new *yen*, and governmental payments also provided cash to the public. Accordingly, the money supply by the BOJ statistically did not contract on a regular basis, although the urgent task for the monetary authority was to control the post-war inflation. In 1946, the BOJ note issue declined from a peak of 62 billion *yen* (mid-February) to 15 billion *yen* (mid-March), thereafter it increased to 23 billion (end of March), 64 billion (end of September) and 93 billion (end of December) (BOJ, 1985: 44–5; 77–8).

The reconstruction of the economy and price stabilization were not separate issues. The former, expanding the supply of goods, helped to fight inflation from the supply side.[33] The well-known reconstruction policy, named Priority Production System, was based on the priority allocation of funds, to which the BOJ contributed through controlling the fund allocation, directly and indirectly.[34] In this sense, the role of the BOJ did not decline even after the war.

The BOJ contributed directly, in the sense that it implemented the Rules of Funds Supply (*Kinyu-kikan Shikin Yuzu-junsoku*) from March 1947, which induced financial institutions to provide credit to key industries, such as coal-mining, iron and steel, fertilizers, electric power, and also to invest in government bonds. The Temporal Fund Adjustment Law during the war was the forerunner of this system. Moreover, the BOJ organized loan syndicates of banks. From January 1947 to April 1950, the BOJ took the leadership for 5964 syndicates which put together 315 billion *yen* in total. Those loans are estimated to correspond to *circa* ten per cent of total bank lending during this period.

The BOJ contributed indirectly through making bills issued by the above industries eligible for collateral at the BOJ and thus lowering borrowing cost. After negotiations with the Japanese government, SCAP approved the idea of the Reconstruction Finance Bank (RFB), probably because of its resemblance to the US Reconstruction Finance Company (MOF, 1976: 624–5). The RFB was established in January 1947 and was mainly financed through the BOJ purchasing 71 per cent of the finance bonds issued by this institution during the period 1946–48. The RFB, for its part, supplied funds largely to the key industries for the sake of economic reconstruction.

The BOJ thus assisted key industries in the post-war years. The question is whether this enlarged role was promoted by, or realized despite, SCAP policy. Since the measures outlined above had been experimented with during the war – purchasing the RFB bonds was, in its essence, similar to monetizing government bonds – we can conclude that the continuity of the system worked in favour of reconstructing the Japanese economy. Indeed, these active commitments of the BOJ generated an inflationary tendency, and therefore the ESS considered it a most important task to establish the 'Banking Board' outside the Bank. The reason SCAP permitted such a continuity of the BOJ role from the war period can be attributed to the same circumstances as those that determined the whole financial reform package.

As already stated above, currency reform in Japan had been undertaken almost three years before the stabilization policy named after Dodge was introduced. Inflation did not disappear even after the currency reform, however. The annual average of WPI stood at 7.9 in 1948 and 13.0 in 1949, as against 1.0 in 1946.

From March 1949 onward, the Japanese economy encountered a severe deflationary pressure under the Dodge Line. The WPI in the free market actually declined 16 per cent between 1949 and 1950. The government tried to relax the credit supply through a so-called disinflation policy, providing an increased amount of public funds, postal savings for example, to firms in difficulty. The BOJ credit constituted an important part of this policy. It rediscounted foreign trade bills and assisted long-term financial institutions with funds of lower cost. The provision of public funds paved the way for the Fiscal Loan and Investment Programme (FLIP) in later years. The outbreak of the Korean War in June 1950 finally ended the deflationary tendency. As the Korean War boom disappeared, the Currency-Issue Council was abolished, simultaneously with the ESA, in July 1952, and thereafter the MOF regained the power to decide the maximum limit of the BOJ note issues.

Results of the German–Japanese comparison

Central banking in Japan displayed a number of similarities to its German counterpart up to 1945. More precisely, Japanese policy makers learned and followed the German experience quite often in pre-1945 monetary history. However, post-war history shows differences rather than similarities.

In retrospect, US policy during the Occupation left little impact on Japan's central banking or whole financial system. One reason is that these reform plans were unrealistic. The federalist idea of organizing the central bank was based on the historical characteristic of the US economy, whereas the BOJ was established as early as 1882 and had constituted an integral part of economic policy. Any policy aimed at dissolving the historical background would inevitably encounter a strong resistance.[35]

While the same reason could be applied to Germany, the outcome of central banking reform there was quite different. The difference resulted from the fact that Occupation policy was indirect and milder in Japan, in the sense that the country maintained a unified central government under the Occupation. It is worth remembering, however, that while the German *Reichsbank* had enjoyed an independent status from the government after 1924, the BOJ had had no such experience in the inter-war years. It is an irony of history that although Japan did not suffer from a hyperinflation after the First World War, as Germany did, this circumstance also meant that the BOJ Act did not need to be modified, which in the long run disfavoured the independence of the Japanese central bank.

However unrealistic the reform plan would have been, if SCAP and Washington had maintained a firm and consistent stance the outcome of the financial reforms in Japan might have been different from the situation we have reviewed above. The Cold War and the subsequent 'reverse course' of Occupation policy were in this respect important factors, and the divided opinions within the US camp allowed the Japanese opposition to disturb the actual implementation of the reform.

In contrast in West Germany, American Occupation policy left an imprint on the central banking system that is still evident today. Its federal structure, following the home model of the US, still constitutes the basis of the *Bundesbank*, although not quite to the same degree as during the existence of its forerunner, the *Bank deutscher Länder*, from 1948 to 1957. Its centralized elements were created over the original opposition of OMGUS largely thanks to the insistence of the British Occupation authorities, whose concern for the economic efficiency of the financial sector prevailed over the original American intent to give a higher priority to the political goal of democratization through federalization, also of the financial structure, than to economic efficiency. In contrast to Japan, German politicians had relatively little influence on the central banking reform. As no central German government existed before the Federal Republic was founded in September 1949, German politicians mainly voiced the interest of the *Länder* that they represented and thus in principle were not unfavourable to American federalist tendencies.

The differences of opinion within the US Administration and Occupation authorities early on had helped Japanese central government politicians to preserve the traditional centralized banking structure of the BOJ and the big banks, although there was no British Ally involved. But Cold War developments, as well as the election of a business-minded Republican majority in the Congress in November 1948, not only softened the American will to impose their home-model solutions on occupied Japan, but also contributed to the basic shift of American Occupation policy in Germany from far-reaching ideological reform goals to pragmatic and cooperative solutions. The difference to Japan in banking policies was only that the American decisions to abolish the old centralized *Reichsbank* and to decentralize the German central banking structure (and the big banks) had already been taken and executed in Germany by the time the Cold War and a Republican majority in Congress had changed the American stance. For Japan these developments still came in time to preserve the big banks when a decision on their future structure became due in the autumn of 1948, and to preserve the traditional role of the BOJ when Joseph Dodge arrived in 1949 to shape his financial reform programme.

Notes

1. This section is based on Holtfrerich (1988: 107–39).
2. The statistics for currencies and the consumer price index for Japan are from Asakura and Nishiyama (1974) and Ohkawa et al. (1967), respectively, unless otherwise stated.
3. For the pre-war history of the BOJ, see BOJ (1982; 1984) and Yoshino (1962).
4. Even the largest surplus of the current account in the 1980s amounted to only *circa* 4 per cent of GNP.
5. How the suspension of the gold standard contributed to the recovery from the depression is described in Iwami, Okazaki and Yoshikawa (1995).
6. This section is based on Holtfrerich (1995: 402–14).
7. Deckers (1974: 26–7). The Americans estimated the monthly issue of military notes by the Soviets in 1945 to be 1 billion RM. See Gottlieb (1956/57: 398–417).
8. National Archives, Washington, DC (NA), RG 260 (OMGUS), FINAD. Records Relating to Financial Institution Policy 1945–49, Box 153, Folder: Potsdam Agreement. Memorandum dated 5 September 1945, 'Implementation of the Potsdam Agreement' by Major E.C. Ophuls, Financial Institution Section of the Financial Branch, G-5 Division, USFET. The three concepts for restructuring the German banking system mentioned here were also noted in a historical report on 'Financial Institutions – SHAEF Period' from 29 August 1945. NA, RG 260 (OMGUS), FINAD. Records Relating to Financial Institution Policy 1945–49, Box 131, Folder: Administration of Military Government in the US Zone in Germany, July 1945.
9. For more on the impact of the 'home model' on American banking policy in Germany, see Loehr (1952: 124–6).
10. In 1946, exports from the British zone earned a total of $145 million, as opposed to $350 million spent on imported goods, of which $291 million went for the importation of food alone. Historical Archive of the Deutsche Bundesbank (HADBB), Monatsberichte der Reichsbankleitstelle Hamburg, No. 11 (for April 1947).

11. NA, RG 260 (OMGUS), FINAD. Records Relating to Financial Institution Policy 1945–49, Box 135, Folder: Banking Committee – Elimination of Excessive Concentration of Economic Power in Banking. DFIN/P(46)39, 5 April 1946, Paper Submitted by US Member: 'Proposal for a New Länder Union Bank'. Also located in Bank of England Archive (BEA), OV 34/11.
12. The paper that the representatives of the four powers agreed upon is filed under the reference number DFIN/BC/MEMO(46)15. It is located in NA, RG 260 (OMGUS), FINAD. Records Relating to Financial Institution Policy 1945–49, Box 135, Folder: Banking Committee – Elimination of Excessive Concentration of Economic Power in Banking. See also the minutes of the meeting of the Finance Directorate on 24 July 1946, ibid., Box 144, Folder: Elimination of Power of Banks, etc. A reconstruction of the events and all of the important documents can also be found in BEA, OV 34/11 and 34/12.
13. Latour and Vogelsang (1973: 158–60); Krieger (1987: 139–43).
14. The papers presented to this committee contained the proposals unanimously passed by the Banking Committee and a notation of the differences that arose in the Finance Directorate. See NA, RG 260 (OMGUS), Allied Control Authority, Finance Directorate (DFIN), Box 342, specifically DFIN/Memo (46)161, 30 September 1946, with DFIN/Memo (46)130 (2nd Revise) as supplement [identical with DFIN/BC/MEMO (46)15].
15. These failed attempts at reaching a common banking policy are described in detail in Appendix B of DFIN/BC/MEMO (47)1 'Subject: Banking', in BEA, OV 34/13.
16. The abbreviation, SCAP, is used below as the central organ of the Occupation Powers, which was also called GHQ (General Headquarters).
17. For the general trend of the occupation policy, see Nakamura (1979).
18. See papers in Teranishi and Kosai (1993) and Okazaki and Okuno (1993).
19. Tsutsui (1988: 42ff). For the financial reform as a whole, see Kato (1974), Tsutsui (1988) and MOF (1976; 1983).
20. Memorandum by C. Gunston of 17 January 1947, 'Reichsbank chief office in Hamburg', Bank of England Archive (BEA), OV 34/13.
21. Ibid., p. 134. For more on the British arguments in the controversy with the US military government during the establishment of the *Bank deutscher Länder*, see BEA, OB 34/90.
22. Telegram quoted in Smith (1974: 429–31).
23. Law No. 60 of the American military government and Ordinance No. 129 of the British. For the history leading up to its founding, see Horstmann (1990: 202–18). Horstmann (1989: 135–54).
24. Wandel (1980: 81). A more detailed account of the policies of the Allied Bank Commission can be found in Loehr (1952: 21–40).
25. The reasons for this are presented in Graml (1985: 203–7). Brackmann (1993: 239–43).
26. Memorandum from Gunston 'Germany: Financial Reform', 15 January 1948, to Sir O.E. Niemeyer and Mr Siepmann, BEA, OV 34/19. This file contains other interesting details on the preparation phase of currency reform. See also Möller (1961), and Möller (1976: 433–83). For the more recent discussion of the political impact of currency reform on stability and growth and of the significant German contribution to shaping this reform, see the numerous articles by C. Buchheim and R. Klump, including

those in Fischer (1989: 391–422); Klump (1989); Brackmann (1993). Several documents showing the influence of German experts on shaping currency reform, e.g. the final report of the 'Konklave in Rothwesten' and two memoranda of Bernard, President of the Central Bank Council about meetings with the military governors, are located in Historisches Archiv der Deutschen Bank, Frankfurt/M. (HADB), file: Währungsreform 1948. There is more on currency reform in HADB, RWB, 7.

27. Langen (1948: 5). The technical details of currency reform are to be found here and also in Stucken (1964: 201–8).
28. On the discussion within the Allied Bank Commission about these quotas, see Loehr (1952: 24–6).
29. Letter from the Allied Bank Commission ABC/DIR(48)12, June 1948, BEA, OV 34/228, with which this authority was transferred to the *Bank deutscher Länder*. See also Buchheim (1990: 62–3).
30. The currency reform and its consequences, as well as the reasons for the continuing dollar gap, were described with impressive clarity by Abs (1950: 481–8).
31. For more details of the central banking reforms, see BOJ (1985), MOF (1983) and Muto (1984, 1985, 1991).
32. Almost simultaneously, the MOF, associated with the BOJ, submitted a proposal for a Finance Industry Law in December 1948.
33. For problems during the inflation, see Hamada and Kasuya (1993).
34. Teranishi (1993: 169–70); for more details, see Okazaki (1996).
35. Kato (1974: 347–48). Tsutsui (1988: 118) states that 'In general, the Americans' grand reform proposals were inherently weak and superficial, founded on questionable assumptions and characterized by an essentially ethnocentric orientation'.

References

Abs, Hermann J. (1950), 'The structure of the Western German monetary system', *Economic Journal*, 80.

Asakura, Kokichi and Nishiyama, C. (1974), *Nihon Keizai no Kaheiteki Bunseki (Monetary Analysis of Japanese Economy) 1868–1970*, Sobunsha.

BOJ (Bank of Japan) (1982), (1984), (1985), *Nippon Ginko Hyakunenshi, (Centennial History of the Bank of Japan)*, vols 1, 4 and 5, Tokyo.

Berghahn, Volker (1995), 'West German reconstruction and American industrial culture, 1945–1960', in Reiner, Pommerin (ed.), *The American Impact on Post-war Germany*, Providence, RI, Berghahn Books.

Brackmann, Michael (1993), *Vom totalen Krieg zum Wirtschaftswunder. Die Vorgeschichte der westdeutschen Währungsreform 1948*, Essen, Klartext.

Buchheim, Christoph (1990), *Die Wiedereingliederung Westdeutschlands in die Weltwirtschaft 1945–1958*, Munich, Oldenbourg.

Buchheim, Christoph (1993), 'Marshall Plan and currency reform', in Diefendorf, Jeffrey et al. (eds), *American Policy and the Reconstruction of West Germany, 1945–1955*, Cambridge, Cambridge University Press.

Clay, Lucius D. (1950), *Decisions in Germany*, New York, Doubleday.

Deckers, Josef (1974), *Die Transformation des Bankensystems in der sowjetischen Besatzungszone/DDR*, Berlin, Duncker und Humblot.

Fischer, Wolfram (ed.) (1989), *Währungsreform und Soziale Marktwirtschaft. Erfahrungen und Perspektiven nach 40 Jahren*, Berlin, Duncker und Humbolt.

Friedrich, Karl (1923/24), 'Vom alten zum neuen Bankgesetz', in *Bank-Archiv*, vol. 23.

Gaddis, John Lewis (1972), *The United States and the Origins of the Cold War 1941–1947*, New York/London, Columbia University Press.

Gottlieb, Manuel (1956/57), 'Failure of quadripartite monetary reform 1945–1947', *Finanzarchiv*, 17.

Graml, Hermann (1985), *Die Alliierten und die Teilung Deutschlands. Konflikte und Entscheidungen 1941–1948*, Frankfurt/Main, Fischer-Taschenbuch-Verlag.

Hamada, Koichi and Kasuya, M. (1993), 'The reconstruction and stabilization of the postwar Japanese economy: possible lessons for Eastern Europe?', in Dornbusch, Rudiger et al. (eds), *Postwar Economic Reconstruction and Lessons for the East Today*, Cambridge, MA, MIT Press.

Helfferich, Karl (1921/22), 'Die Autonomie der *Reichsbank*', in *Bank-Archiv*, vol. 21.

Holtfrerich, Carl-L. (1988), 'Relations between monetary authorities and governmental institutions: The case of Germany from the 19th century to the present', in Gianni Toniolo (ed.), *Central Banks' Independence in Historical Perspective*, Berlin/New York, de Gruyter.

Holtfrerich, Carl-L. (1995), 'Die Deutsche Bank 1945–1957: war, military rule and reconstruction', in Gall, Lothar et al., *The Deutsche Bank 1870–1995*, London Weidenfeld & Nicolson.

Horstmann, Theo (1989), 'Kontinuität und Wandel im deutschen Notenbanksystem. Die Bank deutscher Länder als Ergebnis alliierter Besatzungspolitik nach dem Zweiten Weltkrieg', in Pirker, Theo (ed.), *Autonomie und Kontrolle. Beiträge zur Soziologie des Finanz- und Steuerstaates*, Berlin, Schelzky & Jeep.

Horstmann, Theo (1990), 'Die Entstehung der Bank deutscher Länder als geldpolitische Lenkungsinstanz in der Bundesrepublik Deutschland', in Riese, Hajo and Spahn, Heinz-Peter (eds), *Geldpolitik und ökonomische Entwicklung. Ein Symposion*, Regensburg, Transfer-Verlag.

Horstmann, Theo (1991), *Die Alliierten und die deutschen Grossbanken. Bankenpolitik nach dem Zweiten Weltkrieg in Westdeutschland*, Bonn, Bouvier.

Itoh, Masanao (1987), 'Nichiro-Sengo no Nippon Kinhoni-sei to Chuo-Ginko Seisaku (Japan's gold standard and central banking after the Russo-Japanese War)', in Koji Fujise and Akihiko Yoshioka (eds), *Kokusai Kinhoni-sei to Chuo-Ginko Seisaku (International Gold Standard and Central Banking)*, University of Nagoya Press.

Iwami, Toru, Tetsuji Okazaki and Hiroshi Yoshikawa (1998), 'The Great Depression: why so short and "mild"?', in Dick, Trevor J.O. (ed.), *Business Cycles since 1820: New International Perspectives from Historical Evidence*, Cheltenham, Elgar.

Kato, Toshihiko (1974), 'Kinyu Seido Kaikaku (Reforming financial institutions)', in *Sengo Kaikaku (Post-war Reforms), vol. 7 Keizai Kaikaku (Economic Reforms)*, University of Tokyo Press.

Klump, Rainer (ed.) (1989), *40 Jahre Deutsche Mark. Die politische und ökonomische Bedeutung der westdeutschen Währungsreform von 1948*, Wiesbaden, Steiner.

Krieger, Wolfgang (1987), *General Lucins D. Clay und die amerikanische Deutschlandpolitik 1945–1949*, Stuttgart, Klett-Cotta.

Langen, Eugen (1948), *Die neuen Währungsgesetze*, Essen, West-Verlag.

Latour, Conrad F. and Vogelsang, Thilo (1973), *Okkupation und Wiederaufbau. Die Tätigkeit der Militärregierung in der amerikanischen Besatzungszone Deutschlands 1944–1947*, Stuttgart, Dt. Verlags-Anstalt.

Loehr, Rodney (1952), *The West German Banking System*, Washington, DC, Government Printing Office.

Ministry of Finance (MOF) (1976), (1982), (1983), *Showa Zaiseishi* (The Fiscal History of the Showa Era), vols 2, 12 and 13, Tokyo, Toyo Keizai Shimposha.

Möller, Hans (ed.) (1961), *Zur Vorgeschichte der Deutschen Mark. Die Währungsreformpläne 1945–1948*, Tübingen, Mohr.

Möller, Hans (1976), 'Die westdeutsche Währungsreform 1948', in Deutsche Bundesbank (ed.), *Währung und Wirtschaft in Deutschland 1876–1985*, Frankfurt a.M., Knapp.

Müller, Helmut (1973), *Die Zentralbank – eine Nebenregierung: Reichsbankpräsident Hjalmar Schacht als Politiker der Weimarer Republik*, Opladen, Westdeutscher Verlag.

Murphy, Robert (1964), *Diplomat Among Warriors*, New York, Doubleday.

Muto, Masa-aki (1984), 'Banking Board Secchi Koso' (The idea of establishing the Banking Board), *Soka-Keiei Ronshu*, vol. 9.

Muto, Masa-aki (1985a, b), 'The idea of Policy Board', 'Founding the Policy Board', *Soka-Keiei Ronshu*, vol. 10.

Muto, Masa-aki (1991), 'Banking Board Secchi Koso Sairon' (The idea of establishing the Banking Board revisited), *Soka-Keiei Ronshu*, vol. 16.

Nakamura, Takafusa (1979), 'SCAP to Nippon' (SCAP and Japan), in Nakamura, T. (ed.), *Senryo-ki Nippon no Keizai to Seiji* (Economy and Politics in Occupied Japan), University of Tokyo Press.

Ohkawa, Kazushi et al. (1967), *Estimates of Long-Term Economic Statistics of Japan since 1868* (LTES), 8 Prices, Tokyo, Toyo Keizai Shimpo.

Okazaki, Tetsuji (1996), 'Sengo Keizai Fukkoki no Kinyu Sistemu to Nippon Ginko Yushi-assen' (Japanese financial system in the postwar economic recovery and the role of loan mediation by the BOJ), *Keizaigaku Ronshu, University of Tokyo*, 61 (4).

Okazaki, Tetsuji and Masahiro Okuno (1993), *Gendai Nihon Keizai Sistutemu no Genryu* (The Origins of the Contemporary Japanese Economic System), Tokyo, Nippon Keizai Shimbun-sha.

Schacht, Hjalmar (1927), *The Stabilization of the Mark*, London, Allen & Unwin.

Schwarz, Hans-Peter (1980), *Vom Reich zur Bundesrepublik. Deutschland im Widerstreit der außenpolitischen Konzeptionen in den Jahren der Besatzungsherrschaft 1945–1949*, 2nd edn, Stuttgart: Klett-Cotta.

Singer, Kurt (1922), 'Die Autonomie der *Reichsbank*', in *Wirtschaftsdienst*, vol. 7.

Smith, Jean Edward (ed.) (1974), *The Papers of General Lucius D. Clay*, Bloomington, IN, Indiana University Press.

Stucken, Rudolf (1964), *Deutsche Geld- und Kreditpolitik 1914 bis 1963*, 3rd edn, Tübingen, Mohr.

Tamaki, Norio (1994), 'The American "democratization" of Japanese banking 1859–1959' in Checkland, O., Nishimura, S. and Tamaki, N. (eds), *Pacific Banking 1859–1959*, London, Macmillan.

Teranishi, Juro (1993), 'Financial sector reform after the war', in Teranishi, J. and Kosai, Y. (eds), *The Japanese Experience of Economic Reforms*, London, Macmillan Press.

Toyo Keizai Shimposha (1980), *Showa Kokusei Sohran* (Ge), (The National Census of the Showa Era, vol. 2), Tokyo, Toyo Keizai Shimposha.

Tsutsui, William M. (1988), *Banking Policy in Japan: American Efforts at Reform during the Occupation*, London, Routledge.

Wandel, Eckhard (1980), *Die Entstehung der Bank deutscher Länder und die deutsche Währungsreform 1948*, Frankfurt a.M., Knapp.

Weber, Werner and Werner, Jahn (1973), *Synopse zur Deutschlandpolitik 1941 bis 1973*, Göttingen, Schwartz.
Wolff, Michael W. (1991), *Die Währungsreform in Berlin 1948/49*, Berlin/New York, de Gruyter.
Yoshino, Toshihiko (1962), *Nippon Ginko Seidokaikaku-shi* (History of the BOJ Reform), Tokyo, University of Tokyo Press.
Ziemke, Earl F. (1975), *The US Army in the Occupation of Germany, 1944–1946*, Washington, DC, Center of Military History, US Army.

CHAPTER FOUR

Central Banking in Sweden and Finland in the Twentieth Century[1]

Tarmo Haavisto and Lars Jonung

The present central banks of Sweden, the *Riksbank*, and of Finland, *Suomen Pankki*, emerged as a result of a long process. The functions defining a modern central bank such as being a monopoly note issuer, a lender of last resort and a framer of monetary policy evolved slowly over time in Sweden and Finland. Central banking in the two countries displays great similarities, primarily due to an influence from British as well as continental central banking in the nineteenth and twentieth centuries.

As a background to this account, the history of central banking in Sweden and Finland up to 1914 is first described. This year signals the beginning of the end of the gold standard, thus paving the way for a variety of monetary experiments. The chapter then focuses on the policies pursued by the central banks in the inter-war and post-Second World War periods and demonstrates how they were influenced by changing policy preferences and political circumstances. The chapter deals first with Sweden, then Finland.[2]

Central banking in Sweden

The Swedish central bank, the *Riksbank*, is commonly regarded as the world's oldest central bank although it did not accept the functions of a modern central bank until the early part of the twentieth century. It was initially founded as a private bank in 1657 by Johan Palmstruch. Due to financial problems, the private bank was taken over and reorganized by Parliament in 1668. A unique feature of the Swedish central bank is that it has remained the Bank of Parliament since its establishment.

Central banking prior to 1914[3]

The experience of the Palmstruch bank made Parliament aware of the risk of over-issue. The convertibility of the deposits of the Bank – and eventually of its notes – into specie was announced as the prime objective of the Bank when it was set up as the Bank of Parliament. The first paragraph of the Bank's charter of 1668 gave strong guarantees of convertibility and, over the centuries, the legal guarantees for convertibility were extended. As a consequence of repeated failures to maintain convertibility, such guarantees were even put into the constitution of 1809 and remained in force well into the twentieth century.

In spite of these legal rules, the Bank was forced to abandon convertibility a number of times, primarily due to wartime events. The financing of military expenditures during wars could not be carried out through ordinary taxes or lending through capital markets. Lending from the Bank became, in several war episodes, the ultimate way of financing government expenditures.

In this way, Sweden became the first country to experiment on a frequent basis with paper standards. This is demonstrated in Table 4.1 which displays suspensions and resumptions of convertibility, that is the

Table 4.1 Monetary arrangements in Sweden, 1668–1995

Type of exchange rate regime	Period
Fixed exchange rate (copper)	1668–1709
Flexible exchange rate (paper)	1709–1719
Fixed exchange rate (copper)	1719–1745
Flexible exchange rate (paper)	1745–1776
Fixed exchange rate (silver)	1776–1788
Flexible exchange rate (paper)	1789–1803
Fixed exchange rate (silver)	1803–1809
Flexible exchange rate (paper)	1809–1834
Fixed exchange rate (silver)	1834–1873
Fixed exchange rate (gold)	1873–1914
Flexible exchange rate (paper)	1914–1924
Fixed exchange rate (gold)	1924–1931
Flexible exchange rate (paper)	1931–1951
Fixed exchange rate (gold-dollar standard)	1951–1972
Semi-fixed/semi-flexible exchange rates	1972–1992
Flexible exchange rate (paper)	1992–

Note: The exchange rate system 1972–92 encompassed a number of different experiments. Sweden was a member of the European monetary arrangement called the 'snake' until 1977. The *krona* was tied to a currency basket from then on. In May 1991 the *krona* was tied unilaterally to the ECU. From November 1992 the *krona* has been floating.

changes between specie standards and paper standards, between 1668 and 1995. The specie standard was upheld between 1668 and 1709. However, at the news of the Swedish defeat at the Battle of Poltava in present-day Ukraine, in 1709, the Bank was closed, not to open again until 1719. Convertibility was abolished in 1745 as a result of Bank financing of a war with Russia and providing domestic subsidies to various industries. In 1777 a silver specie standard was established.

A paper standard was soon reintroduced as a result of a new war with Russia in 1789. The Bank managed to maintain its independence, however. To circumvent it, the King ordered the National Debt Office, established in 1789, to issue notes. These notes soon replaced Bank notes – demonstrating that an independent central bank is not a sufficient condition for preventing high inflation.

A new silver standard was adopted in 1803, lasting for only six years until Sweden was pulled into a new war with Russia in 1809; a silver standard was not re-established until 1834. In 1873 Sweden switched from a silver to a gold standard which lasted until 1914. The years 1834–1914 were thus the longest period of an uninterrupted specie standard.

The Swedish financial system developed rapidly in the second half of the nineteenth century. One important element of this process was the rise of note-issuing private banks. They soon turned into successful competitors to the note issue of the *Riksbank*. Public and political debate on monetary matters concerned primarily the note issue of the private banks which was resented strongly by many groups. The private note-issue was protected and supported by the executive power against opposition from Parliament which owned the *Riksbank*. In addition to note issuing, there was a similar development in deposit banking. The commercial banking system displayed remarkable growth from the middle of the nineteenth century till the outbreak of the First World War.[4]

The *Riksbank* gradually evolved into a central bank during the pre-1914 gold standard, much influenced by British practices. It learnt the techniques of monetary management primarily from the behaviour of the Bank of England.[5] The *Riksbank* was granted a monopoly of the issuance of bank notes by legislation in 1897. At the same time, it functioned as a clearing house for the commercial banks and engaged in lending to commercial banks by rediscounting. The Bank also phased out its deposit activities. In the crisis of 1907 the *Riksbank* performed a lender of last resort function.

During the specie standard of 1834–1914 the independence of the *Riksbank* was not an issue of debate. The main objective of the Bank during this period was to maintain the convertibility of the *krona*, the new currency unit introduced when Sweden joined the gold standard in

1873. The role of the *Riksbank* changed dramatically with the outbreak of the First World War.

The policy of the Riksbank 1914–31

Sweden moved to a *de facto* paper standard in August 1914 when the *Riksbank* took the unconstitutional step of suspending the gold standard.[6] During the war years the *Riksbank* experimented with several policies. There was a rapid rise in the money stock and in the price level during 1914–20. A heated debate on monetary issues ensued, with the *Riksbank*'s inability to check inflation being a prime target of criticism by Swedish economists. Knut Wicksell, David Davidson, Gustav Cassel, Eli Heckscher and even the young Bertil Ohlin took part in this exchange of opinion. For the first time the governor of the central bank, Victor Moll, became engaged in public discussion on the proper conduct of monetary policy. He argued that the Bank was unable to arrest the rise in the price level. Most economists, however, were of the opposite opinion: a rise in the discount rate of the Bank would hold back inflation.

After the war, the Bank decided upon a return to the gold standard, the first European bank to do so, at the pre-war parity rate to the dollar, first *de facto* in 1922 and then *de jure* in 1924. Most economists were initially in favour of a return to gold at the pre-war rate, that is at the dollar parity rate of 1914. The deflationary experience associated with an extremely high unemployment rate in 1920–22, however, undermined the credibility and acceptance of the gold standard. The economics profession became sceptical of the workings of the gold standard and this paved the way for the monetary programme of 1931.

The inter-war gold standard turned out to be short-lived. When the Bank of England was forced off gold in September 1931, the *Riksbank* followed a week later. The main reason was that the foreign exchange reserves were depleted and the *Riksbank* was unable to obtain any loans from New York, London or Paris.

The policy of the Riksbank 1931–51

On leaving gold in 1931, a monetary programme of price stabilization inspired by Knut Wicksell's theoretical work was adopted by the *Riksbank* and the government. The aim of the *Riksbank* was given as to 'preserve the domestic purchasing power of the *krona* using all available means'. This was a true central bank innovation. The *Riksbank* became the first central bank openly to declare price stability as the target of its policy. The monetary programme of 1931 remained the official basis for Swedish monetary policy in the 1930s.[7]

The Bank lacked knowledge, however, of how to manage a price stabilization programme. Confidentially, a questionnaire was sent to Sweden's most prominent monetary economists at that time, Gustav Cassel, David Davidson and Eli Heckscher, dealing with a large number of issues. The *Riksbank* asked for an immediate reply. The answers became available within two weeks. They gave the Bank clear guidance on a large number of issues and probably influenced the Bank's subsequent policy. A consumer price index was constructed and collected on a weekly basis by the *Riksbank* to use in the implementation of the new monetary programme.

The depreciation that accompanied the decision to leave the gold standard in September 1931 had favourable effects on the performance of the Swedish economy by partially isolating it from the world deflation. During the Kreuger crisis in March 1932, the Bank accepted the role as lender of last resort to the commercial banking system, thus contributing to financial stability.

In the summer of 1933 the *Riksbank* decided at its own initiative to peg the *krona* to the British pound. The pegged rate was in force until the outbreak of the Second World War and, as long as British inflation remained at a low level, the pound pegging was consistent with the programme of price stabilization. However, the pound pegging of the 1930s indicates that the *Riksbank* still had a propensity to adhere to fixed exchange rates.

Ivar Rooth was appointed governor of the *Riksbank* in 1929. Although his position was weakened by the fall of the gold standard in 1931 and the Kreuger crash in 1932, he was not replaced by the new Social Democratic government that came into power in 1932. The *Riksbank* actually remained independent from direct government influence throughout the 1930s although there was an early acceptance of ideas in Sweden concerning more expansionary stabilization policies. These ideas stemmed from the work of a group of young economists later dubbed the Stockholm School. Parliament also made requests for a 'reflation' in the spring of 1932, that is, it asked for a rise in the wholesale price which was not to be accompanied by a rise in the consumer price index. To some extent the *Riksbank* followed this recommendation, at least for a brief period.

The Second World War marks a watershed in Swedish economic policies. It closed Sweden off from the world economy. As an isolated neutral country surrounded by belligerent states, this opened the doors for far-reaching domestic controls. During the Second World War wages, rents and prices were thoroughly regulated by various government agencies. Monetary policy became integrated into the system of controls. The rate of interest was kept at a low and stable level, making ground for the post-Second World War policy of low interest rates.

At the end of the war a new monetary programme, initially prepared by a group of experts, was announced by the government and Parliament. The programme set up three goals for the *Riksbank*: a stable level of interest rates, a stable price level and a stable exchange rate, without any explicit ranking between the three goals. The programme was much influenced by the experience of the deflation after the First World War. Prices could be allowed to fall as a result of improved productivity, that is David Davidson's norm was replacing that of Knut Wicksell. This programme is to date the most recent fully-fledged monetary plan adopted by Parliament as 'owner' of the *Riksbank*.

Events after the end of the Second World War soon demonstrated the inconsistencies of the monetary programme. Sweden experienced a burst of inflation in 1947 and 1948 when the economy was opened up to world markets again and, as a result, the *Riksbank* asked for restrictions on imports. There was upward pressure on the level of interest rates when commercial banks started to dispose of their large holdings of government bonds that they had accumulated during the Second World War.

Meanwhile, a split developed within the Board of the *Riksbank* owing to the request of the governor, Ivar Rooth, for a rise in the level of interest rates. He was opposed by the Social Democrats on the Board and by the Minister of Finance, Ernst Wigforss. Eventually, in the fall of 1948, Ivar Rooth resigned, leaving his post in protest. This was a unique step for Sweden: Rooth remains to this day the only governor who has left after a conflict about the conduct of monetary policy in modern times.

Ivar Rooth was replaced by Klas Böök (governor 1948–51). A most important decision during his term of office was the devaluation of the *krona* in 1949 when Sweden followed the European devaluation relative to the US dollar. The *krona* thereafter kept a fixed rate against the dollar until the early 1970s.

The regulatory regime of the Riksbank 1951–82

The boom associated with the Korean War contributed to the end of the bond price support programme that had been in effect since the end of the Second World War. In December 1950 the *Riksbank* decided to raise the discount rate. The government requested new techniques of monetary controls that could hold down the rate of interest below the market level. In Autumn 1951, Parliament passed new legislation that encompassed direct controls on lending and deposit rates and the *Riksbank* used this piece of legislation to bargain for 'voluntary agreements' with the commercial banks concerning the allocation of bank loans and the rates charged by banks.

A new policy regime was thus introduced in the early 1950s based on a non-market approach. It lasted for about 35 years. The main goal of the *Riksbank* during this long episode was to maintain low rates of interest, in particular subsidizing the investment activities of the housing sector and the public sector at the expense of other sectors. For this purpose, new monetary instruments were introduced and used, such as liquidity ratios and lending ceilings, primarily aimed at the commercial banking system. It was relatively easy to control the latter because it was highly centralized and dominated by a few large banks. The complete financial system became the subject of close supervision and regulation and financial innovations were actively prevented, Sweden following in this respect the general West European pattern of monetary policies.

The monthly meetings between the *Riksbank* and various representatives from financial institutions were a central feature of the system of selective credit market regulations. The meetings between the managers of the commercial banks and the *Riksbank* were the most important. They started in the early 1950s and remained an important forum until the deregulation process in the 1980s eliminated their policy role. Here 'open mouth operations' replaced open market operations. At the beginning of the meeting, the assets and liabilities of the commercial banking system as well as of every commercial bank were reported and often commented on. The governor of the *Riksbank* could criticize and threaten commercial banks that did not follow the spirit of the *Riksbank*'s policy. He could also give suggestions and recommendations to commercial bankers present at the meeting. The protocols from the meetings were distributed to the management of all commercial banks.[8]

The price stability goal of the post-war monetary programme was gradually ignored, as can be seen in Figure 4.1. Inflation increased from a low average level in the 1950s to a high one in the 1970s and 1980s. A fixed exchange rate for the *krona*, that is convertibility, was maintained until the breakdown of the Bretton Woods system in the early 1970s, while capital and exchange controls remained stronger than in most other OECD countries during this period.

The demise of the Bretton Woods system and the oil price increases following the OPEC I crisis changed Swedish stabilization policies. The Swedish government initiated an expansionary fiscal policy of 'bridging over' during the OPEC I crisis. This policy was not successful as Swedish exports declined and a trade and a budget deficit arose. The *Riksbank* devalued the *krona* in 1976 and twice in 1977 as a result of the policy of fiscal accommodation during OPEC I. As a consequence of OPEC II

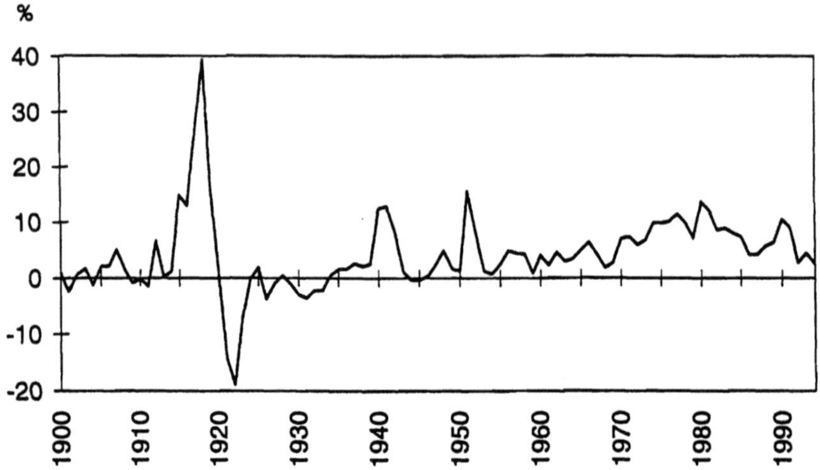

4.1 The rate of inflation in Sweden, 1900–94, in per cent

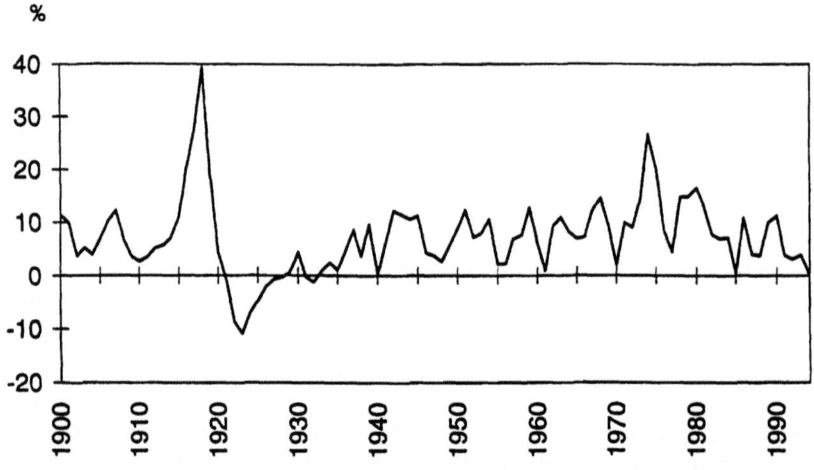

4.2 Annual growth in the money stock in Sweden, 1900–94, in per cent

a new devaluation was carried out in August 1981. The devaluations of 1976–81 came about in cooperation between the *Riksbank* and the government. The fiscal and monetary accommodation in the 1970s was accompanied by a rise in the inflation rate and by high growth in the money supply, as can be seen in Figures 4.1 and 4.2.

From soft to hard krona *policy to inflation targeting cum deregulation 1982–95*

The Social Democratic party returned to power after the parliamentary election in September 1982. The first step of the new government was to devalue the Swedish currency by 16 per cent – initially the plan called for a 20 per cent devaluation. The devaluation of 1982 was decided by the new government while still in opposition and forced upon the *Riksbank*. This event should be regarded as indicating that the *Riksbank* at that time was considered as the servant of the political majority.

This 'offensive' devaluation came to influence monetary thinking in the 1980s and 1990s, though the 'super-devaluation' was eventually regarded as a large overshooting. There is much to suggest that the Swedish currency was close to an equilibrium rate in the fall of 1982. The nominal devaluation of 1982 was not combined with a real devaluation, that is a switch of expenditures from the public (non-tradables) to the private sector (tradables). Instead, structural (supply side) measures were postponed until the end of the 1980s.

In the 1980s the *Riksbank* was actively pushing for deregulation. Several forces were driving the Bank. The effectiveness of the old system of regulation was being eroded by intermediation outside the controlled 'organized' financial system. The rapid development of financial technologies made it difficult for the *Riksbank* to influence financial flows by non-market-oriented controls. A new generation of policy-makers was entering the Ministry of Finance and the *Riksbank*, who were more positive towards the workings of well-functioning financial markets than the older generations. As the rest of the world was deregulating, it became more difficult for Sweden to stand apart.[9]

Deregulation peaked in the second half of the 1980s. An important deregulatory step was taken in November 1985 when the *Riksbank* abolished existing quantitative restrictions on the volume of commercial bank lending. The outcome was a rapid rise in bank lending when households and firms, previously rationed, expanded their borrowing. The expansion in the volume of credit fuelled a swift rise in the price of assets such as stocks and real estate. In 1988–89 unemployment was around 1.5 per cent. The economy was booming. These years were designated as the period of 'overheating'.

The *Riksbank* did not raise its discount rate out of fear of causing an inflow of capital that would aggravate the boom. In 1989, the last remnants of exchange controls were eliminated. Swedish private individuals and firms became free to invest outside Sweden and immediately started to do so.

Swedish economists in the mid-1980s became highly critical of the soft *krona* policy, that is, the policy of devaluations in 1976–82. It was blamed for the slow growth and high inflation of the Swedish economy. They suggested a move from a soft to a hard currency strategy and the government, the opposition parties and the *Riksbank* accepted the hard currency option – at least rhetorically.

The main objective of the *Riksbank* after the devaluation of 1982 was to turn the *krona* into a hard currency. Actually, there was some discussion of tying the *krona* to the *D-mark* in late 1982. A fixed exchange rate became the main goal: the devaluation of 1982 was to be regarded as the last one. However, this policy failed eventually when the boom of the late 1980s was followed by a bust in the early 1990s.

The Swedish economy peaked in 1990. The asset price inflation of the late 1980s was followed by an asset price deflation with real rates of interest rising sharply and inducing households and business to reduce current expenditures and increase financial savings. The stock market and the real estate market plummeted. The budget deficit exhibited an explosive rise. By 1992 the Swedish economy was in the most severe recession since the 1930s.[10]

In May 1991 the *krona* was tied unilaterally to the ECU.[11] As events unfolded, this step implied a minor but unexpected appreciation of the *krona*. After the 'No' vote in the Danish Maastricht referendum, the *krona* came under increasing speculative pressure. In September 1992, the *Riksbank* carried out a stubborn defence of the *krona*, using for a short time overnight rates of 500 per cent but the attempt to switch from a soft to a hard *krona* failed. In November 1992, the *Riksbank* was forced to let the *krona* float.

In January 1993 the Bank announced an inflation target. Starting from January 1995 the aim of the Bank is to hold the rate of consumer price inflation at 2 per cent per year plus/minus one percentage point. It is too early to tell how successful the inflation targeting of the *Riksbank* will be. So far it appears to have worked well. The Swedish inflation rate has remained close to the targeted level, actually rather below than above it, thus contributing to enhanced credibility for the programme.

The independence of the Riksbank

As long as Sweden adhered to a specie standard, that is to the gold standard, the independence of the *Riksbank* was not an issue. Monetary policies were designed to maintain full convertibility of the *krona*. The room for monetary politics was minimal under this institutional arrangement. Monetary policy was thus not a part of the political process. In the 1930s, following the fall of the gold standard, the independence of the Bank became a subject of discussion among economists, initially, however, with no consequences for the legal framework of the Bank.

In the post-Second World War period the relationship between the *Riksbank* and the government, and thus the independence of the *Riksbank*, changed character twice. First, with the advent of the regulation of the financial markets, the political system was given an opportunity to influence the allocation and the price of credit flows within the Swedish economy through the *Riksbank*. The *Riksbank* felt obliged by political pressure to maintain interest rates below the market clearing level. In this process it became subordinated to the Ministry of Finance. The *Riksbank*, at least judging from some statements by one of its governors in the 1950s, did not appreciate this role. It wanted to remain free from pressure by the Ministry of Finance.

Second, as a consequence of the financial deregulation in the 1980s, the *Riksbank* gradually gained a more independent position towards the Ministry of Finance. The goal of the *Riksbank* became solely to maintain a fixed rate for the *krona*, abdicating from the role of directly controlling interest rates and the flow of credit.

The Social Democratic party ruled Sweden from the election of 1932 until the election of 1976. The dominance of this party meant eventually an increase of the power of the political system over the framing of monetary policies and thus over the *Riksbank*. As a socialist party it was highly critical of the workings of private commercial banking and a private financial system. Nationalization of commercial banks was a regular demand at the party conferences until recent times.

Ivar Rooth's exit in 1948 as governor of the *Riksbank* signalled the rising influence of the Social Democratic government over the framing of *Riksbank* policies. The executive power controlled the Bank through the appointment of the governor and of the chairman of the Board of the *Riksbank*. The Board was composed of members of the Parliament reflecting the political balance in Parliament. The majority party or parties thus held a majority on the Board as well. The chairman of the Board was as a rule the under-secretary at the Ministry of Finance.

After Ivar Rooth's departure the Social Democrats as the ruling party controlled the governorship until 1976. This meant a break with a past during which new governors, as a rule, had experience gained in positions in the financial system. The Social Democrats appointed governors, often with a background in Social Democratic politics. Still, this could not prevent a major clash between the *Riksbank* and the government in 1957. The Board of the Bank raised the discount rate without first informing the government, that is the Minister of Finance. This step caused a major political reaction and debate about the independence of the Bank. The chairman of the Board, actually a

Social Democrat, was forced to leave, to be replaced by another Social Democrat.

The power of the Minister of Finance over the *Riksbank* can also be seen from a series of interviews of former policy makers within the *Riksbank*. These interviews bring out the close contacts between the *Riksbank* and the Ministry of Finance, with the *Riksbank* consistently asking for tighter fiscal policies and the Minister of Finance asking for lower rates of interest, that is for low discount rates, or at least no hikes (Jonung, 1996). It is clear from these interviews that the *Riksbank* felt pressure from the Ministry of Finance concerning the conduct of its policy and was ready to listen to the arguments of the Minister. On the other hand, monetary policies during this period were geared towards maintaining a fixed exchange rate for the *krona* which reduced the room for discretionary measures not consistent with external balance.

The term of office for the governor of the *Riksbank* coincided with the election period. Thus, after every election to Parliament, the government had the opportunity to appoint a new governor of the *Riksbank*. In 1976 the Social Democratic party lost an election for the first time in the post-war period. The new government tried to convince the governor of the Bank, a former Social Democratic minister, to remain in office. However, at the request of the leadership of the Social Democrats he resigned. When the Social Democrats returned to power in 1982, they replaced the governor with Bengt Dennis, one of their own.

The term of office of the governor of the *Riksbank* was changed in 1989 in such a way that it did not coincide with the elections to Parliament.[12] This meant that after the election of 1991 when the Social Democrats were again forced out of office, Bengt Dennis remained as governor of the *Riksbank*. He left in 1994 to be replaced by Urban Bäckström, a former conservative under-secretary at the Ministry of Finance, an appointment of the non-socialist government.

After the victory of the Social Democrats in the election of 1994, there was some uncertainty about the position of governor Bäckström. It turned out that he stayed in office. This should be regarded as a step towards a more independent *Riksbank*, although the debate about the relationship between the *Riksbank* and the government continues. There is still a highly sceptical attitude, in particular among union representatives, towards an independent *Riksbank*.

Swedish economists, influenced by the inflationary experience of the 1970s and 1980s, as well as by international developments, have been arguing for a more independent *Riksbank* in order to create an incentive structure less prone towards inflation. This view has gained support primarily among the non-socialist parties. It led to reforms of the legislation concerning the *Riksbank* in the late 1980s. Additional legislation to increase the independence of the Bank has been put forward in the 1990s to adjust Swedish central bank legislation to the European pattern in case Sweden wanted to join EMU.

Without doubt the Bank is now more independent from the executive than earlier in the post-Second World War period. The Board has fewer members taken from Parliament. The chairman of the Board is no longer directly associated with the Ministry of Finance. The present chairman is openly arguing for more independence. It is an irony that the push for an independent *Riksbank* is motivated by some proponents by Sweden's membership in the EMU. Before abolishing the world's oldest central bank, it is necessary first to make it independent from the executive power.

Is there an election pattern in the policy of the Riksbank?

The concept of central bank independence is a complicated one. One aspect concerns the room for short-run manipulations of monetary measures. An independent central bank is not supposed to engage in such activities. Considering the strong position of the Ministry of Finance towards the *Riksbank* in the post-Second World War period, there are reasons to suspect that the behaviour of the *Riksbank* was influenced in a systematic way by the timing of elections to Parliament.

This issue has recently been studied by testing several reaction functions of the *Riksbank* including a dummy variable for parliamentary elections (Frennberg and Jonung, 1996). These tests do not lend support to there being a consistent election pattern. However, in some cases it cannot be ruled out that the *Riksbank* was influenced by an upcoming election.

The *Riksbank* thus appears to have been independent in a short-run stabilization policy perspective. In the long run, however, it has been forced to carry out the policy of low rates of interest and selective credit and capital controls. The lack of an election pattern in monetary policies is thus not inconsistent with the view that the Bank had been the long-term servant of the Ministry of Finance prior to the financial deregulation of the 1980s. Once the financial markets were deregulated, however, the *Riksbank* no longer had the ability to control the level of interest rates and the allocation of credit. Instead, the policy of the Bank now requires the existence of well-functioning financial markets. This suggests that the independence of the *Riksbank* relative to the Ministry of Finance has been fostered by the development of efficient capital markets.

Central banking in Finland

Historical background

Finland and Sweden share a long common history. Finland was joined to Sweden from the twelfth century, until it was annexed to the Russian Empire, in 1809, as a result of the Napoleonic wars. During the nineteenth century, Finland was an autonomous grand duchy of the Russian Tsar. During this period, until 1917, when Finland declared its independence, the old Swedish constitution, as well as fundamental parts of Finland's legal, administrative and religious institutions that were in force under Swedish rule, remained intact. The autonomy of Finland was reinforced by the maintenance by the Finnish central bank of its own currency, the *markka*. Fiscal policy, economic legislation and the state finances remained under the control of the Finns.

The first precursor of the Bank of Finland, called *Åbo Diskontoverk*, was in operation between 1806–1808. As a result of the Napoleonic Wars and the separation of Finland and Sweden, the *Åbo Diskontoverk* was dissolved and was later, in 1811–12, succeeded by the *Vaiheitus-, Laina- ja Depositioni-Contori Suomen Suuren-Ruhtinanmaasa* (the Exchange, Loan and Deposit Office of Finland). This precursor of the Bank of Finland had little resemblance to a modern central bank. It did not conduct monetary policy, nor did it regulate or support the banking system. It did not even have the right to issue its own notes.[13]

In the first half of nineteenth century two different currencies were circulating in parallel in Finland. The Swedish currency, which had been traditionally used in Finland before 1809, circulated at least until the 1840s in large amounts. The second currency was the *rouble*, which was introduced after Finland was annexed by the Russian Tsar in 1809. The first notes denominated in the Finnish currency, the *markka*, were issued by the Bank of Finland in 1860. Initially the value of the Finnish *markka* was directly tied to Russian paper money. In 1866, the Finnish monetary system was separated from the Russian *rouble*, when the *markka* was put on the silver standard. The Finnish silver standard lasted for 11 years from 1866 to 1877. After Denmark, Germany, Norway and Sweden had adopted the gold standard in the early 1870s, the Bank of Finland wanted to follow suit. This transition of the *markka* to gold implied a further separation of the Finnish monetary system from the *rouble* system. Finland adhered to the gold standard during 1878–1914, that is for 36 years.

During the next 36 years, Finland experienced several monetary arrangements: 1914–26, the First World War paper standard; 1926–31, the inter-war gold standard; 1931–32, the inter-war paper standard;

Table 4.2 Exchange rate regimes of the Finnish *markka*

Period	Regime	Value
1865–1877	Silver standard	Fixed, 1 FIM = 4.44987 grams of silver
1878–1915	Gold standard	Fixed, 1 FIM = 2.9032 grams of gold
1915–1925	Paper standard	Floating
1926–1931	Gold standard	Fixed, 100 FIM = 3.7894 grams of gold
1931–1932	Paper standard	Floating
1933–1939	Sterling	Fixed, £1 = 227 FIM
1939–1949	Dollar	Floating (in 1939: $1 = 49.35 FIM)
1949–1971	Bretton Woods	Fixed, devaluations 1949: $1 = 231 FIM 1957: $1 = 320 FIM 1967: $1 = 4.20 FIM*
1971–92	Paper standard 1971–91: Pegged to a trade-weighted currency index 1991–92: Pegged to the ECU	Fixed (pegged) devaluations 1977–78: 18% 1982: 10% 1991: 12%
1992–	Paper standard	Floating

* Currency reform in 1963: 100 FIM (old) = 1 FIM (new).

Source: Elonen (1992) and Autio (1992).

1933–38, the pound standard; 1939–50, the Second World War paper standard (see Table 4.2). Although the monetary system in force changed several times during this period, monetary thought and policy were greatly influenced by the experience of the classical gold standard. In 1948, Finland became a member of the IMF and the par value of *markka* was confirmed three years later in 1951. Finland participated in the dollar gold standard until the collapse of the Bretton Woods system in 1971. Since 1972, the Finnish currency has been a paper currency and from 1973 until the early 1990s the foreign value of the *markka* was pegged against a basket of currencies most important to Finland's foreign trade.

The regulation of financial markets has been of great importance for the structure of banking in Finland and has constituted a principal instrument of monetary policy. Consequently, this section will examine the regulation system in some detail and offer a chronological overview of the history of regulated money in Finland.

Historically, the structure of Finnish capital markets has had four cornerstones: (1) the central bank, the Bank of Finland, as a 'market maker', (2) large deposit banks, (3) isolation relative to foreign capital, and (4) regulation of the domestic actors. The Bank of Finland has been heavily involved in all these fields that characterize the Finnish financial system and, thus, the history of money and banking in Finland is, to a large extent, the history of the Bank of Finland.

The legal framework

From 1809 to 1917, a period in which Finland was a Grand Duchy of the Russian tsar, many of the old Swedish laws and constitutions from the former Swedish rule remained in force.[14] When the precursor of the Bank of Finland, *Vaiheitus-, Laina- ja Depositioni-Contori Suomen Suuren-Ruhtinanmaasa,* was established by an act of the Tsar, in 1811, the estates of the realm in Finland expressed a wish that this bank could be established in the Swedish manner as the Bank of the Diet. However, the Russian Tsar decided not to take any notice of these wishes and the bank came to be controlled by the Russian Crown and the Finnish government, known as the Senate. The Board of Governors had three members, the senior member of whom was the Chairman of the bank. Until 1840 the main purpose of this bank was to carry out a currency reform through which the Swedish currency would be replaced by the Russian *rouble.*

Prior to 1840 the currency system in Finland was rather chaotic; both Swedish and Russian species as well as Swedish and Russian notes circulated. The paper *roubles* issued by the precursor of the Bank of Finland were of minor importance. In 1840, after both Russia (1839) and Sweden (1834) went on silver, monetary conditions improved. A currency reform was put in force and the authorities finally succeeded in replacing the Swedish currency by the silver-*rouble*, which was now issued by the Bank of Finland.

During this period, the Bank of Finland introduced several activities which appeared important for the subsequent development of the Finnish payment system. New branches were established in the countryside and new contacts with foreign banks were established (St Petersburg and Hamburg). Although the Bank of Finland was still the only commercial bank in the country, important steps were taken for its subsequent role as the Finnish central bank. From 1840, the Bank of Finland had responsibility for the functioning of the Finnish payment system, but with regard to monetary policy the Bank was subordinated to the economic department of the Finnish Senate, that is the government.

The direct tie between the Finnish and Russian *rouble* became fatal during the Crimean War of 1854–56. When the Russian *rouble* went off the silver standard, Finland had to follow suit and returned to a paper standard. In 1860, the Finnish government succeeded in getting the Tsar's approval for a new monetary unit in Finland: the *markka* divided into a hundred *pennies*. The Finnish *markka* remained tied to the Russian *rouble* with an exchange rate of four *markka* to one silver *rouble*. The heavy fluctuations of the Russian *rouble* delayed the adoption of the silver standard, and it was not until 1865 that the Finnish government placed the *markka* on silver.[15] According to the 1865 monetary reform, both the new silver-*markka* and, within certain limits, the silver-*rouble*, were to be the only means of payments in Finland. This reform separated the Finnish monetary system from the unstable Russian *rouble*.

Parallel to the currency reform, another important reform was undertaken. Under a decree of 1867, the Bank of Finland was placed under the control and supervision of the Finnish parliament. A Parliamentary Supervisory Board was instituted, composed of one member of each of the estates, the chairman of which could directly control the Bank and the central bank policy in Finland. The Governor of the Bank was still appointed by the Tsar, but the Board of Management was supervised by the parliamentary board. This system, whereby the Governor of the Bank is appointed by the head of the state while the supervisory board is appointed by Parliament, is still in force.

A further step in separating the Finnish currency system from the Russian system occurred in 1877–78, when Finland adopted the gold standard. While Finland went onto gold, the monetary instability in Russia prevented the *rouble* from doing the same and thus it was possible for the Finnish authorities to liberate the *markka* from its remaining ties to the *rouble* as a parallel currency. It was the first time when the characteristic features of Finnish central banking were fulfilled: (1) the central bank was under the supervision of the Parliament (the estates), (2) central bank policy was outlined by the Parliamentary Board, and (3) monetary policy was defined primarily in terms of the external value of the *markka*, the gold value of the *markka*.

The decree of 1867 was successively modified in 1875, 1878 and 1890. The main changes occurred in 1875, when the role of the Bank of Finland as monetary authority and bankers' bank was accentuated by a decree which stated that 'the object of the Bank of Finland is to maintain a stable and secure monetary system, and to assist and facilitate the circulation of money in Finland'. Furthermore, the government's monetary transactions were removed from the Bank of Finland to a new authority, the State Treasury. The other modifications did not imply any fundamental changes in the rules and regulations of central banking: these modifications included changes in the conditions of the note issue, the number of members in the management board, ceasing the payment of interest on deposits and so on.

Two major banking laws essentially shaped the bank system before the First World War. The first one dates from 1866 and the second from 1886. The first banking law was established only some years after the first commercial bank, *Suomen Yhdyspankki*, was founded in 1861–62. It regulated the minimum size of the capital stock, the share of foreign participation, reserve fund requirements and the right of note issue. Furthermore, the banks were placed under the supervision of the government and the supervisory authority had the right to investigate banks at any time.

The regulations applying to the minimum capital stock and to the commercial bank note issue were significant factors governing the development of the Finnish banking structure. The capital requirement was so high that it was difficult to meet it out of local funds. Accordingly, the minimum capital stock requirement contributed to the development of a commercial banking structure that consisted of a few, relatively large banks with country-wide operation. The commercial bank notes did not circulate in any large amounts during the period of this banking law. The main reasons for this were partly the limits on the total volume of note issue and partly the high face value of the notes.

The banking law of 1886 eased capital requirements and accordingly removed the restriction to establishing smaller provincial banks. The result was that many smaller banks were established after 1886, mainly in Helsinki. However, the banking structure remained the same with the dominance of a few, nation-wide banks. One other major change was that the right of note issue for commercial banks disappeared as a result of the 1886 law and the earlier *de facto* central bank monopoly on note issue was now confirmed by legislation.

After independence in 1917, the formal standing of the Bank of Finland was confirmed by the constitution of Finland. According to the constitution (Constitution Act 1919 and Parliamentary Act 1928), the Bank of Finland 'operates under the guarantee and care of Parliament and is supervised by the Parliamentary Supervisory Board'. The Governor and the members of the Board of Management were appointed by the President of the Republic for an indefinite period of time. Furthermore, the constitution stated that 'parliament decides on the disposal of profits of the Bank according to the needs of the State'. Under the Currency Act (1926, 1962), the bank has the exclusive right to issue notes.

The environment of central banking has changed several times during the past decades. The most recent changes are the deregulation of interest rates, the liberalization of capital movements and international integration. However, the legislation of the Bank has not required any major changes. It appears that although the relationship between the financial markets and the central bank has experienced remarkable changes, those changes have not required any fundamental changes in the rules of monetary policy decision making, which have remained more or less the same during the twentieth century.

The Bank of Finland has a high degree of independence from the government. The Parliamentary Supervisory Board has mainly supervisory duties but also monetary decision-making authority in certain key matters such as the conditions for foreign and central bank borrowing. The Board of Management decides all matters which have not been expressly entrusted to the Supervisory Board: interventions on the money and foreign exchange markets, interest rates on overnight loans, minimum reserve requirements and foreign exchange regulations.

The only monetary decision directly made by the government is the fixing (or the changing of the limits of fluctuations) of the external value of the *markka*. The government can either approve or reject a proposal on these matters made by the Parliamentary Supervisory Board upon the recommendation of the Board of Management. The Finnish Parliament, in turn, participates in monetary policy through legislation and through the selection of the members of the Parliamentary Supervisory Board. This selection is based on relative party representation in parliament, which implies that the coalition making up the government also has a majority on the Supervisory Board.

The members of the Management Board are highly independent of the government and as long as a major part of monetary decision making is vested in the Board, the position of the central bank will remain strong.

The early stage of central banking in Finland

In 1857/58 an 'active' interest rate policy was applied by the Bank of Finland for the first time (Pipping, 1961: 295–6; Pipping, 1969: 146–7). Since 1840 (the starting year for the discounting of bills), the discount rate had been constant at four per cent. In 1858, with the aim to reduce the foreign trade deficit, the discount rate was increased in stages and regulations were applied to both foreign currency and central bank credits. Also, after the recession of the 1870s, the Bank of Finland decided upon an active interest rate policy to stimulate the domestic economy.

These observations are of very exceptional phenomena and they should not be interpreted as a confirmation of the Bank of Finland's position as a modern central bank. During the entire nineteenth century, the Bank of Finland acted more as a commercial bank than as an institution with responsibility to carry out discretionary monetary management. Its role as a government-supported commercial bank[16] was accentuated in 1859 when the bank was allowed to hold deposits from the public.

The role of the Bank of Finland as a central bank emerged very slowly during the late nineteenth century. The public deposit holdings with the Bank of Finland ceased in 1875 and the rediscounting of the bills of other commercial banks started gradually as early as the 1870s. But the use of the discount window only became more extensive during the 1890s.[17] The rediscount rate seems to have been the same as the minimum discount rate applied by the banks. The degree to which the banks used the discount window is not known before 1890, but the significance of this form of central bank borrowing increased during the 1890s. The smaller banks particularly used borrowing from the central bank as a regular channel to finance their activity.

The rediscounting of bills at the central bank increased rapidly and in 1907 the central bank placed quantitative limits on this kind of borrowing. The ceiling was expressed as a specific amount for certain banks. If the limit was exceeded, a higher discount rate was charged. Depending on the quality of bills, the maximum was a one per cent penalty charge.

To sum up, in the latter part of the nineteenth century certain measures were taken by the Bank of Finland which could be characterized as typical central bank policy measures (for example, rediscounting bills, 'active' interest rate policy and control of credit facilities). However, this picture is ambiguous and Rossi claims that the Board of Governors of the Bank of Finland was unaware of the principles of interest rate policy as late as during the First World War (Rossi, 1951). As a result, the discount rate policy was seen as an instrument to compete with the commercial banks for customers rather than as a part of the interest rate policy to maintain economic balance.

The aftermath of the First World War

After the outbreak of war, both Finland and Sweden were exposed to large economic shocks that pushed them off the gold standard. Both eventually returned to gold: Sweden in 1924, as the first country in Europe, and Finland in 1925. However, the routes taken by these two countries differed sharply. Sweden went back to gold at the pre-war parity after a rapid deflation. Finland returned to gold at the going rate. The macroeconomic consequences of these two strategies were quite different. Sweden suffered from deflation and the international post-war contraction, while Finland was more or less unaffected.[18]

In early 1921, the international depression seriously threatened the Finnish export industry and led to a deterioration of the trade balance.[19] The Finnish currency depreciated on the international currency market and the Bank of Finland decided not to support it in this situation. One reason, beside the low level of foreign reserves, was that the depreciation was one way of affecting the activity level in the economy. At this time, an increase in the discount rate was not seen as an effective measure against a weakened trade balance. To reduce the import surplus, the Supervisory Board recommended rationing credits for import purposes.

The Finnish currency was heavily depreciated at the end of 1921, the foreign deficit was eliminated in 1922 and money market conditions were eased. However, this favourable movement in market conditions (combined with an abandonment of the inflation economy) did not result in a lower interest rate level. In 1923/24, increased central bank lending to the public was discussed as one means of reducing interest rates. The new Governor of the Bank of Finland, Risto Ryti, considered discount policy to be an unsatisfactory method of influencing the level of interest rates. In order to improve the influence of the central bank over interest rates, he proposed for instance that central bank credit should be made available to export industries.

The political pressure to lower the rate of interest remained massive and both the Bank of Finland and the commercial banks were held responsible for the high interest rates. In 1925, the Bank of Finland lowered the discount rate twice, yet the commercial rates did not follow the discount rate. In this situation, the commercial banks agreed on a common reduction of deposit and loan rates at the end of October 1925. Two months later, after an initiative from the central bank, the central organizations of savings banks and co-op banks recommended to their member banks not to apply higher deposit rates than 7.5 per cent (the highest deposit rates in commercial banks were set at 7.25 per cent). However, the member banks did not, in general, follow this recommendation.

The low interest rate policy during the inter-war period

The return to the gold standard in 1926 was seen as a fundamental step towards a more stable monetary system. The public associated the high interest rate levels of the early 1920s with the turbulence of economic life during those years. Thus, it was expected that a return to the pre-war gold system would also restore the pre-war interest rate level.

When the interest rate remained at a high level, the monetary authorities and the banking sector as a whole were seen as responsible for this. Political pressure on the authorities increased. In the contemporary debate, a main reason for the high level of interest rates was the stiff competition between the different banks, which led to upward pressure on the interest rates paid on deposits. At the initiative of the Bank of Finland in 1926, negotiations were started in order to reach an agreement between the banks that would ease the competition between these institutions. The negotiations, in June 1926, resulted in recommendations to local savings banks and co-op banks to lower their deposit rates and to reduce the spread between deposit rates and loans rates. However, in January 1927, about 60 per cent of savings banks still continued with 8 per cent deposit rates, and the small savings banks as well as co-op banks argued that they, as the 'savers' banks', had a responsibility to the public to pay deposit rates as high as possible.

The discount rate of the central bank was lowered three times during 1927, from 7.5 per cent in March 1927 to 6.0 per cent in November of the same year. To increase the pressure on commercial banks to lower their rates, the central bank raised its own lending to the public and announced that the conditions for central bank borrowing by the banks would be tightened. Nevertheless, while the discount rate fell by 1.5 percentage points, the level of interest rates fell by only about 0.5 percentage points.

At the end of 1927, the Finnish economy experienced a speculative boom. Following a sharp deterioration of the trade balance and an alarming decline in the central bank's currency reserves, the Bank of Finland was finally forced to raise the discount rate. This signalled the breakdown of the 'low interest rate policy' and opened the way for the banking institutions to raise their interest rates again.

By late 1930, it had become apparent that if the banking institutions could not reach an interest rate agreement that would cover all banks, legislation would have to be used to lower interest rates. Against such threats, a new 'voluntary' interest rate agreement came into force in July 1931. This established the highest interest rate that could be charged on deposits, with all banks being covered by the new agreement. Banks were classified into three categories and the agreement determined the highest interest rate for each category. An interest rate committee was established in order to set the actual interest rates and to see that the agreement was followed by all banks. From 1931, the banking sector in Finland thus was gradually transformed into a cartel. This development had consequences for interest rate policy as, in such an environment, it became easier to manage the market rate of interest by means of the central bank borrowing rate. The interest rate agreement was later completed in 1952, 1953 and 1955 in order to unify the interest rates on all kinds of time deposits. In 1963, all demand deposits were also regulated by such agreements between banks.

The discount rate of four per cent remained unchanged between 1934 and 1947, while even the market rate seems to have remained stable. During those 13 years, the largest commercial banks only changed their deposit rates on one occasion, in 1936/37.

1950–90: the prosperity and termination of regulated money

Two main arguments for regulation may be distinguished. The first one is that there was political pressure on the Bank of Finland to maintain low levels of interest. In the 1930s, this was done in order to ease the burden of the depression. Subsequently, in the 1950s and 1960s, it was carried out again to encourage economic growth. The second reason is associated with the global crash of the financial sector in the 1930s. Though Finland managed the worldwide financial crash relatively well, confidence in the operation of financial markets was shaken and hence the speculative character of the financial markets has been used as a motive for the regulation and control of the financial sector.

The Second World War inflicted serious damage on Finland. Almost 100 000 lives were lost, a large part of the capital stock was destroyed and 12 per cent of the territory was annexed by the Soviet Union. Meanwhile, war reparations to the Soviet Union and the need for resettlement were a heavy burden on the nation. Finland decided to finance the reconstruction of the economy by using domestic funds.[20] The role of the government sector became very pronounced. The government was not only responsible for fiscal policy, but also for the allocation of major investments. Furthermore, a large part of total savings was generated by the public surplus.

Thus, we may conclude that the regulation which was started in the 1920s and 1930s, as a result of political necessity, and continued in the 1940s, as a result of convenience, was well suited to the reconstruction of the country after the Second World War. However, in the 1950s, the regulatory system was not removed when the economic circumstances became more normal again. Instead, the regulatory system was completed during this decade and remained in force for more than two decades thereafter until the early 1980s. Deregulation was therefore delayed by almost 20 years compared to many other European countries and even some years compared to the other Nordic countries.

It is surprising to see how simple the system was. On the other hand, we must recognize the primitive nature of the financial system in

Finland at that time. The bond and equity markets were both unsophisticated and small. A major part of savings was carried out either in the form of banking deposits (private sector) or in the form of budget surplus (public sector). The lack of foreign banks and foreign financial investment of any kind made the system easy to regulate.

After the Second World War, the interest rate policy of the Bank of Finland was focused mainly on discount rate changes. Through these changes, the central bank announced its intentions regarding the level of interest rates, in other words they were signals to the market of 'desirable' changes in the behaviour of the other financial actors. Although this method of control of the market rate has worked rather well when the level of interest rates has been rising, the central bank has been forced to 'negotiate' with the other banks in order to secure downward movements of interest rates.

In 1947, the discount window system was introduced when the Bank of Finland set quotas on the rediscount credit of the other banks. At that time, the other banks' borrowing at the central bank was rather limited and direct central bank loans both to the public sector and to firms were still extensive. The post-war discount window system based on a differential interest rate schedule was completed in 1951, when the penal charge on borrowing in excess of the quota was introduced. Although, this system was modified several times during the 1950s and 1960s, the basic structure remained the same.

A significant change in central bank financing occurred for the first time in 1975, when the call money market was opened. The quotas declined in importance since fluctuations in bank liquidity were now evened out in the call money market. Central bank borrowing remained the major source of bank liquidity and, accordingly, the actions of the banks in the money market reflected their position *vis-à-vis* the central bank. A limit was placed on the average monthly amount by which any bank could exceed its net overall overdraft, that is central bank borrowing plus borrowing from other commercial banks. If a bank exceeded this limit, it would be punished in the form of 'progressively stricter scrutiny by the central bank'.

Although the importance of the call market increased during the late 1970s, it was not until 1983 that the most important regulations were relaxed. The system of granting quotas for central bank finance was abolished and the call money rate became the marginal cost of central bank borrowing. Even more important was the revision of the lending rate regulations. This revision was one step in the deregulation process and the banks were now allowed to transfer some of their funding costs in unregulated markets to their lending rates. Thus, the first steps toward market-oriented interest rates were taken.

The breakdown of the regulatory system first started after the rapid development of financial innovations in international markets during the 1970s. This revealed the allocative inefficiency of the existing regulatory system combined with the problems of controlling the capital flows in a more open international financial system. The regulatory system never actually collapsed but rather was blown away by the winds of change in international financial markets.

The exchange rate systems since 1900

The main macroeconomic target of the Finnish central bank policy has historically been a stable external value of the *markka*. This target has been formulated in terms of silver, gold, sterling, US-dollar or a basket of foreign currencies.

The suspensions of the gold standard in 1915 and 1931 were both due to external shocks; in the first case due to the outbreak of the First World War and, in the second, due to the world-wide recession which caused the UK, the main trading partner of Finland, to suspend the gold standard. Subsequently, the abandonment of a fixed exchange rate has as a rule been related to a continuous appreciation of the real exchange rate when the domestic inflation rate has exceeded the inflation rate of the main trading partners.

Finland made a major change in its exchange rate system in the autumn of 1992 when its currency was forced off the fixed exchange rate. Finland has had a floating exchange rate since then as well as an inflation target as a guide for its monetary policy. Here Finland was apparently inspired by Sweden's move towards inflation targeting.

Figures 4.3 and 4.4 display the inflation rate and money stock growth in Finland between 1900 and 1994. The secular pattern of the former is similar to that of other Nordic countries. It can be divided into two distinct periods which are separated by the Second World War. The pre-Second World War period includes one inflation 'peak', namely the heavy inflation during the First World War. The significant difference relative to the pre-1939 period is that after the Second World War the price level has never declined. Rather, the latter has been a time of rapid monetary expansion in which the annual growth rate has fluctuated around 10 percentage points.

Foreign currency controls after the Second World War

Before the Second World War, the Finnish exchange markets had been completely free and open.[21] In 1939, currency controls were introduced with regard to foreign investment in Finnish equities. Subsequently, a

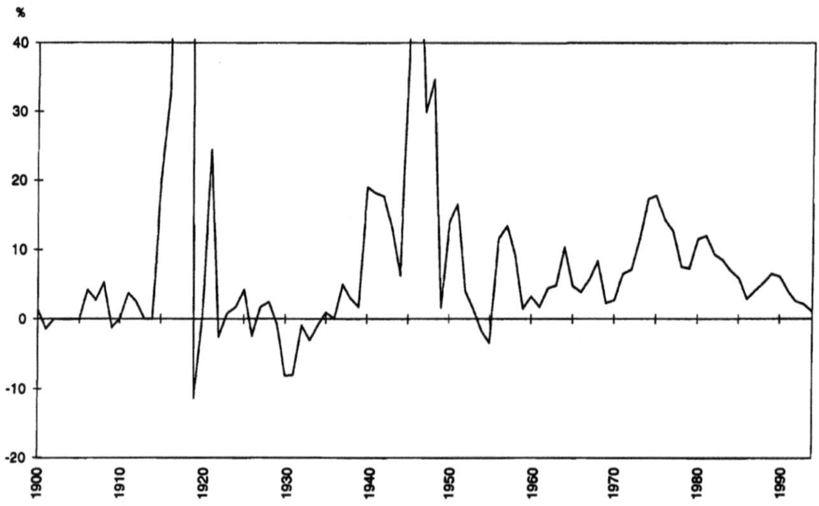

4.3 The rate of inflation in Finland, 1900–94, in per cent

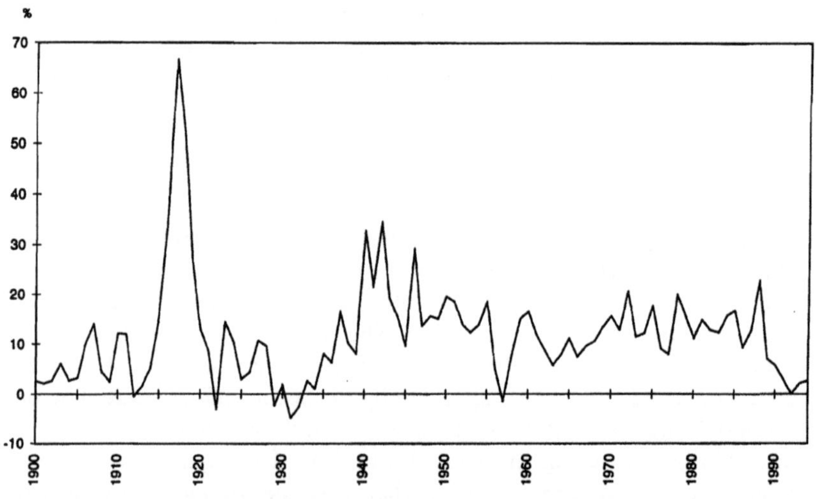

4.4 Annual growth in the money stock of Finland, 1900–94, in per cent

more general currency regulation was introduced and all trade in foreign exchange was licensed. During 1940–41, the foreign exchange regulations were successively extended to cover all foreign payments.

Immediately after the war, currency regulation became a part of the reconstruction of the Finnish economy. The chronic trade balance was the main argument used to maintain the regulations. The 1948 and

1959 Exchange Control Acts rendered permanent the regulatory system introduced during the Second World War.[22]

The growth of foreign trade with western countries during the 1950s and 1960s together with a gradually more liberal trade regime were the major factors underlying the internationalization of the Finnish economy. In 1957, foreign trade was opened up and, after this reform, liberalized trade came to cover about 80 per cent of the value of imports. However, trade liberalization was not accompanied by a deregulation of capital movements. Only short-term capital flows related to financing foreign trade were allowed along with trade in securities on the Helsinki Stock Exchange.

Exchange rate legislation was reformed in 1959 and again in 1972. Changes in the regulatory system were intended to facilitate foreign trade and the short-term credits associated with foreign trade. In the 1960s trade-related transactions became free. However, most capital transactions were still subject to the authorization of the Bank of Finland and the Finns were not allowed to make portfolio investments abroad.

The liberalization of capital movements in Finland occurred during the 1980s. As pointed out above, the observed increased degree of openness during the earlier periods is mainly an optical illusion since it is explained by the rapid expansion of foreign trade. However, the increase in foreign borrowing was a new feature of the 1970s; the foreign debt expanded rapidly and loans were now taken on the commercial Euromarket, instead of via loan negotiations with international organizations, as had previously been the case.

In 1980, the Bank of Finland left the foreign exchange markets and the forward rate was subsequently determined by market forces. Banks were able to use both foreign currency denominated deposits and credits to cover their forward positions. For the domestic banks, this reform was of a great importance. Foreign capital markets became a complement to central bank borrowing and the forward exchange rate reflected changes in money market conditions.

The Foreign Exchange Act of 1986 still maintained the Bank of Finland's exchange control power, especially the control of capital movements and restrictions on portfolio investments. The Bank was granted wider-ranging powers to regulate foreign exchange with the aim of avoiding volatility coming from abroad. There was thus a policy which can be described as a step-by-step dismantling of the controls, although particularly in the case of the liberalization of portfolio investments this has been subject to extensive caution.

During the 1990s the dismantling of exchange control continued. The usefulness of exchange control as a policy instrument has decreased as a result of the global integration of the capital markets. However, the Bank of Finland's exchange control powers are still maintained by law. The main argument is the concern over disturbances caused by speculation or other uncertainties related to the integrated markets. Thus, attitudes regarding foreign exchange controls have switched. During the 1950s and 1960s, exchange control was a fundamental part of the governmental programme aimed at encouraging economic growth based on domestic investment. Today the Finnish authorities leave capital allocation to market forces.

The process of financial deregulation in Finland displays great similarities with that of Sweden. In both countries financial deregulation was accompanied by a boom and bust period with significant macroeconomic consequences. At present, the two countries have followed almost exactly the same macroeconomic course over the past ten years.[23] Indeed, the great resemblance between the Swedish and Finnish economies has inspired some economists to suggest a monetary union between the two countries as an alternative to membership in the EMU (Jonung and Sjöholm, 1996).

Summary

This account has demonstrated striking similarities between central banking in Sweden and Finland. The central banks in the two countries emerged gradually over time. The functions defining a modern central bank, such as having a monopoly of the issue of notes, accepting the role of lender of last resort and conducting monetary policy were established in the late nineteenth century and early twentieth century, roughly at the same time in the two countries. Here the two central banks followed more or less the general European pattern of central banking. There was a considerable influence on the financial and monetary systems from the United Kingdom and from Germany.

The breakdown of the gold standard initiated by the outbreak of the First World War allowed for different monetary policy strategies in the two countries. Sweden chose to return to the gold standard in 1922 at the pre-war parity rate. Finland went back to gold a few years later at a devalued rate. The Bank of Sweden did not regulate interest rates in the inter-war period. The Bank of Finland, however, tried in the 1920s to control domestic interest rates, subject to strong political pressure.

Both countries pursued a policy of low interest rates in the post-Second World War period when the central banks achieved far-reaching controls over the activities of the banking system. The aim of this policy was to increase economic growth and subsidize sectors according to political priorities. The regulation of domestic financial markets rested ultimately on tight exchange controls.

The non-market-oriented control of capital markets represented a shift in the balance of power between the central bank and the political system. Monetary policy became an integral element of stabilization and growth policies during the Bretton Woods period. The decision by the governor of the Bank of Sweden to resign in protest in 1948 marks this shift in the balance of power in Sweden. For about forty years, from the end of the 1940s till the end of the 1980s, the *Riksbank* was clearly influenced by the Ministry of Finance.

This loss of independence occurred in parallel with the disappearance of freely functioning financial markets. The emergence of a more independent *Riksbank* took place during the process of financial deregulation. It seems safe to conclude that 'free' capital markets are a prerequisite for central bank independence. Financial openness has allowed both central banks to enjoy greater independence from the executive power as well as facilitating the process towards independence.

Financial deregulation took place in Sweden and Finland later than in other OECD countries. In the early 1990s this process was associated with severe financial crises threatening to wipe out large parts of the financial sector and consequently forcing government measures to prop up the solvency of the banking system. The crises are of an identical nature in the two countries, as in both cases the budget deficit exploded and unemployment rose to an unprecedented level where it still remains.

The two countries have a history of frequent devaluations in the past 20 years. Both were outside the ERM mechanism and were forced to leave a fixed rate in the early 1990s. The Swedish and Finnish central banks are now trying to establish credibility for their currencies by a policy of low inflation and so far seem to have succeeded. Both countries presently maintain inflation targets adopted after the floating of their currencies. Both have been preparing to join the EMU, a step which will ultimately imply the end of the Bank of Sweden and the Bank of Finland as central banks.

Notes

1. We gratefully acknowledge constructive comments from Krister Andersson, Forest Capie, Bengt Dennis, Klas Fregert, Carl-Göran Lemne and Jaime Reis.
2. There is a recent interest in the evolution of central banking. See for example Capie et al. (1994), Goodhart (1988) and Toniolo (1988).
3. This section builds upon Fregert and Jonung (1996).

4. Larsson and Lindgren (1993) examine the rise of the commercial banking system. Jonung (1986) describes the history of private bank notes.
5. See Jonung (1984) for an account of the policy of the *Riksbank* during the classical gold standard.
6. As a result of the unconstitutional step of the *Riksbank* to abandon the gold standard in 1914, an escape clause was written into the constitution in 1915 allowing the Bank to suspend gold convertibility in an emergency. See Fregert and Jonung (1996). The policy of the Riksbank in the 1930s is covered by Jonung (1979).
7. The abandonment of the gold standard in 1931 was regarded as a temporary step. Every year until 1974 Parliament took a decision to prolong the suspension of the gold standard in order to maintain the legal base of the paper standard.
8. The protocols from the monthly meetings between the *Riksbank* and the commercial banks for the period 1956–73 are analysed by Jonung (1993a).
9. See Jonung (1993b) for an account of the driving forces behind the deregulation process.
10. Monetary and fiscal policies during the boom and bust episode are described in Jonung and Stymne (1996).
11. This step was taken at the initiative of the *Riksbank* after the consent of the government.
12. The term of office for the governor of the *Riksbank* is now five years, while the political electoral cycle is four years.
13. This historical background is carefully described in various monographs on the history of the Bank of Finland, see e.g. Pipping (1961, 1969) and Schybergson (1914) regarding the history of central banking in the nineteenth century, but also Aaku (1957), Lefgren (1975), Korpisaari (1920) and Kuusterä (1989), who provide descriptions of early banking in Finland.
14. In fact, the Tsar became subordinate to a Swedish constitution in Finland. The autocrat of Russia could not enact new laws or change existing ones without the approval of the Finnish Diet. The Tsar had, however, the right to issue decrees in matters which were not ruled by these laws.
15. The economic conditions to implement this monetary reform were the worst one can imagine. Beginning in 1862, there was a change in the climate with unusually long and severe winters. In 1867/68, Finland suffered the last famine in Western Europe. Thus, the introduction of the silver-*markka* was criticized in the contemporary debate, since it restricted those opportunities the authorities had to reduce the heavy burden of crop failure. The question was whether silver should be used to back up the new currency or to import foreign grain. Silver was used to back up the currency.
16. See Goodhart (1988: 88). The author distinguishes between government-sponsored commercial banks, i.e. the early stage with note issuing government banks, and modern central banks. In the Finnish case, as in Sweden, this transition occured successively.
17. For details see, Korpisaari (1920: 221), Thesleff (1909: 68), and Schybergson (1914: 247).
18. See Haavisto and Jonung (1995) for a comparison of economic policies and economic developments in Finland and Sweden during the period 1914–39.

19. Currency regulations were abolished during the autumn of 1920 and foreign trade was deregulated in April 1921. See Rossi (1951: 142–3).
20. Finland decided to stay outside the Marshall Aid programme that was a decisive stimulus to recovery in most other Western European countries.
21. Finland was one of a few European countries with a free foreign exchange market for most of the 1930s. On the other hand, most of the foreign trade was in terms of bilateral trade and, thus, the corresponding payments were effected by means of clearing arrangements.
22. For a comprehensive, chronological list of exchange control measures in Finland, see Lehto-Sinisalo (1992).
23. For an account see Jonung, Stymne and Söderström (1996).

References

Aaku, Eero (1957), *Suomen Liikepankit 1862–1955*, unpublished.

Aaltonen, A. et al. (1994), *Monetary Policy in Finland*, Bank of Finland Series A:92, Helsinki.

Autio, Jaakko (1992), *Valuuttakurssit Suomessa 1864, Katsaus ja tilastosarjat*, Bank of Finland Discussion Papers, Helsinki.

Capie, F., et al. (1994), *The Future of Central Banking. The Tercentenary Symposium of the Bank of England*, Cambridge, Cambridge University Press.

Elonen, Heikki E. (1992), 'Suomen Pankin lyhyt historiikki', in Ikonen, Autio and Elonen (eds), *Suomen Pankki ja 1930–luvun lama*, Bank of Finland Series A:85, Helsinki.

Fregert, K. and Jonung, L. (1996), 'Inflation and switches between specie and paper standards in Sweden 1668–1931. A public finance interpretation', *Scottish Journal of Political Economy.*

Frennberg, P. and Jonung, L. (1996), *Has the Riksbank Been Governed by Electoral Tactics?*, mimeo, Stockholm School of Economics.

Goodhart, C. (1988), *The Evolution of Central Banks*, Cambridge, MA, The MIT Press.

Haavisto, T. and Jonung, L. (1995), 'Off gold and back again: Finnish and Swedish monetary policies 1914–1925', in Feinstein, C. (ed.), *Banking, Currency, and Finance in Europe between the Wars*, Oxford, Clarendon Press.

Hörngren, L. and Lindberg, H. (1994), 'The struggle to turn the Swedish *krona* into a hard currency', in Åkerholm, J. and Giovannini, A., *Exchange Rate Policies in the Nordic Countries*, London, CEPR.

Jonung, L. (1979), 'Knut Wicksell's norm of price stabilization and Swedish monetary policy in the 1930s', *Journal of Monetary Economics*, (4).

Jonung, L. (1984), 'Swedish experience under the classical gold standard 1873–1914', in Bordo, M. and Schwartz, A. (eds), *The Classical Gold Standard in Retrospective*, University of Chicago Press/NBER.

Jonung, L. (1986), *Private Bank Notes in Sweden 1832–1902*, mimeo, Stockholm School of Economics.

Jonung, L. (1993a), 'Riksbanken i regleringsekonomin. Mötena mellan riksbanken och affärsbankerna 1956–1973' (The *Riksbank* in the regulated economy. Meetings between the *Riksbank* and the commercial banks 1956–1973), in Werin, L. (ed.), *Från räntereglering till inflationsnorm. Det finansiella systemet och Riksbankens politik 1945–1990*, Kristianstad, SNS förlag.

Jonung, L. (1993b), 'The rise and fall of credit controls: the case of Sweden 1939–89', in Bordo, M. and Capie, F. (eds), *Monetary Regimes in Transition*, Cambridge, Cambridge University Press.

Jonung, L. (1996), *The Decision-Makers' Views on Riksbank Policy. An Interview Study*, mimeo, Stockholm School of Economics.

Jonung, L. and Stymne, J. (1996), 'The great regime shift. Asset markets and economic activity in Sweden, 1985–93', in Capie, F. and Wood, G. (eds), *Credit Crunches and the Real Economy*, London, Macmillan.

Jonung, L., Stymne, J. and Söderström, H. (1996), 'Depression in the North – boom and bust in Sweden and Finland, 1985–93', *Finnish Economic Papers*, 9 (1).

Jonung. L. and Sjöholm, F. (1996), 'Bör Finland och Sverige bilda en valutaunion?'(Should Finland and Sweden form a currency union?), *Ekonomiska samfundets tidskrift*, no. 3–4.

Korpisaari, Paavo (1920), *Suomen Pankit*. Taloustieteellisiä tutkimuksia XXV, Porvoo.

Kuusterä, Antti (1989), *Valtion sijoitustoiminta pääomamarkkinoiden murroksessa 1859–1919*, Helsinki.

Larsson, M. and Lindgren, H. (1992), 'The political economy of banking: retail banking and corporate finance in Sweden, 1850–1939', in Cassis, Y. (ed.), *Finance and Financiers in European History*, Cambridge, Cambridge University Press.

Lefgren, J. (1975), *Banking in the Early Industrialization of Finland, 1860–1914*, PhD Dissertation, University of Utah.

Lehto-Sinisalo, Päivikki (1992), *The History of Exchange Control in Finland*, Working paper, Bank of Finland, 3/92, Helsinki.

Pipping, Hugo E. (1961), *Från pappersrubel till guldmark, Finlands Bank 1811–1877*, Helsinki.

Pipping, Hugo E. (1969), *I guldmyntfotens hägn, Finlands Bank 1878–1914*, Helsinki.

Rossi, Reino (1951), *Suomen pankin korkopolitiikka vuosina 1914–1938*, Institute of Economic Research, Series B:12, Bank of Finland, Helsinki.

Schybergson, Emil (1914), *Finland's Bank 1811–1911*, Helsinki.
Svensson, L. (1995), 'The Swedish experience of inflation targets', in Leiderman, L. and Svensson, L. (eds), *Inflation Targets*, London, CEPR.
Thesleff, Rolf (1909), *Den finska penningmarknaden 1879–1903*, Ekonomisk undersökning, Helsinki.
Toniolo, G. (ed.) (1988), *Central Banks' Independence in Historical Perspective*, de Gruyter, Berlin.

CHAPTER FIVE

The Bank of Portugal's First Century: From 1846 to the Second World War

Jaime Reis

Introduction

The history of the Bank of Portugal has developed 'back to front', that is, the further back, the clearer the picture; the closer to us, the dimmer it becomes. As a result of the way in which research on the subject has developed, we know a good deal about its foundation and its early decades up to the First World War, a good deal less about the inter-war period, and, characteristically, very little about the last fifty years. For this reason, the following paper, which is intended simply to introduce the history of this institution, concentrates on roughly the first century of the Bank of Portugal's existence only.

The general framework for this account is the excellent outline of central bank history since the earliest times which Capie, Goodhart, Fischer and Schnadt (1994) have drawn in the 1994 volume for the Bank of England celebrations on 'The Future of Central Banking', a narrative with which the Bank of Portugal's first hundred years broadly conform.[1] Taking it as our reference, this chapter begins by dealing with the efforts to secure currency stability during Portugal's gold standard period, between 1854 and 1891, and how, surprisingly, the Bank succeeded, with relatively small reserves while using its discount rate sparingly. The second topic is the Bank's role as lender of last resort, which seems to have started in the mid-1870s. It merits attention because the Bank of Portugal was prepared to help the system as a whole but, occasionally, also to assist individual banks covertly, a behaviour which raises the perennial issues both of motives and moral hazard. A third classic feature of central banking history is, of course, that of independence. Here the noteworthy features are that the Bank, comparatively speaking, was initially quite independent. When it was subjected to restriction, after 1888, it still succeeded in keeping much of its autonomy until 1914, when it finally lost some of this independence in common with its counterparts in Europe. As far as the inter-war period is concerned, there are two issues which stand out. One has to do with the difficulties encountered by the Salazar government in fulfilling its desire to create a modern central bank, during a time when Portugal abandoned the gold standard and chose to follow sterling. The second resides in the conjunction of rapidly rising reserves during the 1930s, with the structural weakness of the domestic financial market, which caused this policy to be beset by contradictions.

Ensuring currency stability under the gold standard

From the time of its foundation in 1846, in the midst of a formidable monetary crisis, maintaining the convertibility of its notes was one of the two overriding objectives of the Bank of Portugal (Reis, 1996). The other was, of course, making a profit for its shareholders. For almost forty years, the former was achieved with complete success – there was only one suspension, for a few days, in 1876. And as happened elsewhere in Europe, changes in the short-term interest rate were the main instruments of intervention against the impact of external and internal drains, although various 'gold devices' were also used from time to time as an alternative.[2] From at least as early as the mid-1860s, the directors of the Bank understood perfectly well how important it was to raise their interest rate in order to protect reserves, when gold flowed out of the country in dangerous proportions. As they explained to the government on the first of such occasions, in September 1864, 'when capital is dear in England or France, it has to be so in Portugal also because when money is free to move, it will flow like a liquid in communicating vases, to where the level is lowest'.[3] Despite this belief, and although Portugal was as exposed as any to external shocks associated with international trade and capital movements, by comparison with most countries, this instrument was rarely used, as can be seen from Table 5.1. The main reason was not that the Bank of Portugal preferred it this way, but that it could only alter its rate by means of a governmental decree and, out of motives of both political and financial expediency, governments made this difficult to obtain.

The fact that the Bank of Portugal was able nevertheless to maintain convertibility for such a long time, under these constraints, is even more puzzling if we consider three other potentially destabilizing circumstances. In the first place, Portugal was a primary product exporter on the periphery of Europe, with a high dependence on the British market. The gold standard literature tells us that for such economies, in the nineteenth century, long-run convertibility was a hard goal to attain.

Table 5.1 Average number of yearly interest rate changes by central banks, 1871–90

Central bank	Average number of yearly interest rate changes
Bank of England	8.8
Reichsbank	3.6
Bank of Denmark	3.6
Bank of Norway	1.9
Bank of France	1.4
Bank of Portugal	1.3
Bank of Sweden	1.0

Source: Henriksen and Kaergård (1995: 98–9) and Bank of Portugal Historical Archives.

Secondly, given the comparatively rudimentary nature of its financial system, one might expect some difficulty for a 'proto-central bank' in enforcing its discount rate on the home market, whenever, for reasons of stability, this became necessary. The third issue has to do with the relation between the size of the central bank's reserves and the frequency with which it might have to use rate changes in order to ensure liquidity and therefore currency convertibility. As Capie et al. point out, 'there was a well-known trade-off between having more volatile short term interest rates and maintaining a larger gold reserve, with the UK at one end of this spectrum and France at the other (and Germany in the middle)' (Capie et al., 1994: 11). The Bank of Portugal fits awkwardly into this picture because paradoxically its discount rate was not at all volatile and yet its reserve ratio, which was not subject to any legal prescription, was low by contemporary standards. The average overall, for the period 1870–90, was 30.6 per cent and on a yearly basis, as Table 5.2 shows, not only did it rarely reach the 33 per cent mark of Palmer's rule but was often well below it. Looking at the monthly data, the conclusion is even more striking. During the 1880s, for instance, the reserve ratio was below 25 per cent for a total of 20 months, that is, one sixth of the time. As Table 5.3 suggests, this was low compared to the figures for other Continental central banks. In other words, the Bank of Portugal tended to be 'English' in terms of its reserve position, and 'French' in terms of its discount rate behaviour.

That the Bank of Portugal was able to weather the shocks to the monetary system over such a long time, notwithstanding these adversities, can be explained by three further aspects of the situation. In the first place, Portugal was not a particularly open economy. Its ratio of

Table 5.2 Bank of Portugal: monetary policy instruments, 1870–90

Year	Interest rate changes	No. months/year of gold imports	Reserve ratio (%)
1870	1	4	28
1871	0	9	25
1872	0	6	26
1873	0	7	24
1874	0	4	23
1875	0	7	20
1876	2	2	36
1877	3	3	34
1878	1	9	25
1879	2	1	30
1880	2	6	30
1881	1	6	32
1882	2	6	28
1883	4	8	30
1884	3	7	31
1885	0	8	30
1886	2	12	23
1887	0	11	32
1888	0	8	55
1889	0	12	41
1890	5	10	39

Note: The reserve ratio is the mean of the monthly figures of gold reserves divided by the means of the monthly figures for deposits plus notes in circulation.

Source: Bank of Portugal Historical Archives.

exports to gross domestic product was one of the lowest in Europe, was certainly far lower than that of major Latin American countries and was not exposed to severe destabilizing fluctuations on this account, in spite of its primary product exporting orientation. Moreover, during the entire period it was in receipt of a growing flow of emigrant remittances from Brazil. This helped not only to close its current account deficit but even enabled it to be a net importer of gold for most of the years under consideration. There is also evidence that invisible flows generally compensated adverse movements in the trade balance. Thus the Bank of Portugal's task in dealing with gold drains appears to have been less exacting than one might have supposed.

Table 5.3 Reserve ratios of some European central banks, 1870–90

Year	Bk. France*	*Reichsbank*	Bk. Norway	Bk. Denmark
1870	99	xx	xx	42
1875	62	56**	xx	54
1880	85	61	xx	56
1885	74	61	64	56
1890	80	60	69	62

Notes: * = not including deposits.
** = the year is 1876.
xx = not available.

Source: Conant (1969) and Johansen (1985).

Secondly, it must be noted that when it was used, the discount rate was a very effective instrument. In all of the 28 instances in which it was changed, only one or two days lapsed before the other banks followed suit by raising or dropping their own discount rates by the same amount as the Bank of Portugal. This proves an exception to Gallarotti's recent statement that 'central banks generally followed rather than led market rates in their economies' (Gallarotti, 1995: 82). The ease of the Bank in obtaining the compliance of the financial sector was simply a result of its very considerable market power and this it owed to its dominant size in the financial system. Any bank which failed to raise its rate at the same time would suffer a rush of customers and would be put in the uncomfortable, not to say dangerous position of having to turn them away.

If the discount rate was scarcely used, it still remains to explain how the Bank of Portugal managed to withstand all the small liquidity shocks it was subjected to from time to time, while retaining the public's confidence and managing to convert its notes freely into gold. The use of so-called 'gold devices' is a part of the answer. Another may have been the large size of the denomination of the notes which were therefore held predominantly by substantial merchants and financiers, whose behaviour was apt to be less volatile and who could be persuaded, up to a point, not to seek conversion into gold when there was a drain on reserves. What really made the difference, however, was the availability to the Bank of Portugal of what one might call an informal 'international lender of last resort facility'. This does not mean the occasional international cooperation between the great central banks of Europe, particularly from the 1890s on, which is well known and the subject of current debate (Flandreau, 1997). Nor does it refer to the occasional episodes of borrowing gold on the market of which some of the smaller central banks were the protagonists and which were recently identified by Gallarotti (Gallarotti, 1995: 80–81). Rather it has to do with very long standing arrangements which the Bank of Portugal had with two or three bankers in London and Paris to allow it credits totalling half a million sterling or more for this purpose. With these, it could draw bills on foreign markets when the local market was short; or acquire gold coin in London, to be shipped to Lisbon, to restock depleted gold reserves (sovereigns were legal tender in Portugal). These operations were always short term, though generally renewable and they carried the going commercial rate in London or Paris, which at critical times could be high. They were guaranteed by values deposited at these bankers and also by the impeccable reputation the Bank enjoyed internationally. The ready availability of credits such as these was no doubt encouraged by the knowledge that ultimately the Bank enjoyed the support of the Portuguese government in these matters. It was also helped by the fact that Portugal's needs were so small as to not be felt by the international money market.

One can gauge the importance of this facility to the Bank of Portugal's efforts to stabilize the currency by the number of times it resorted to importing gold from London in order to smooth out its liquidity position without having recourse to discount rate changes. As we can see from Table 5.2 (col. 3), between 1870 and 1890 such imports were made in more than half the months of the period considered. The quantitative impact of this on reserves can hardly have been insignificant. If these gold imports had not taken place, on many occasions the reserve ratio would have dropped below the 30 per cent level that bankers generally considered desirable and which the official balance sheet was able to show thanks to these reinforcements. These were generally short-term difficulties, which tended to go away with the return of confidence to the market or with the arrival of a ship from Brazil bearing commercial paper on London. Therefore, the repayment of these debts normally did not constitute a problem and did not require further intervention. Only if they persisted, would the Bank then act more vigorously and seek a rise in the discount rate. This finding, which accounts for how stability could be achieved on such slender reserves, by no means contradicts Eichengreen's conclusion that the central banks of small countries had no access to the developing international cooperation among core countries of the late gold standard period (Eichengreen, 1995). Quite the contrary, since the Bank of Portugal had no formal relations with the Banks of England, France or the *Reichsbank*. It suggests, however, that perhaps other central banks are not the best place to look for signs of international cooperation at this time.

The Bank of Portugal as lender of last resort

By the end of the nineteenth century, the lender of last resort function appears to have been accepted in some form by several European central banks although, according to Capie et al., there was still much uncertainty as to the degree of commitment to it (Capie et al., 1994: 65). Some central banks had already tried their hand at it in moments of acute market distress in the 1870s and 1880s and the Bank of Portugal was one of them. In 1876, it provided assistance to a large number of commercial banks throughout the country, for the first time in its history, in the aftermath of a strong bout of speculation. The funds for this came from London and from the Portuguese Treasury and the system recovered successfully, though at the cost of some mortality. Several aspects of this episode are worth noting here. First of all, it must be pointed out that the Bank of Portugal could hardly have been more precocious in taking on the role of lender of last resort since a banking system with a plurality of institutions was only coming into existence in the late 1860s and could hardly have experienced a crisis sooner. The perception the Bank's directors had of the event is a second topic of interest. On the one hand, the board was firm in its acceptance that the privileges which the institution enjoyed, its dominant market position and its long history were together sufficient to justify the expectation that the Bank would be 'the supreme and reliable resource which all can rely upon in moments of hardship, during a crisis, to vanquish their difficulties and ward off the dangers of an imminent storm' (*Relatório*, 1876: 2). On the other hand, besides a sense of obligation to the community, there was clearly also a selfish reason: to prevent the downfall of any significant bank from becoming contagious and obliging the Bank of Portugal to take even more costly defensive action. Thus the directors further explained, in 1876, that they had assisted the other banks because 'the state of our reserves rendered the situation too dangerous for the Bank of Portugal, in the event of a disaster befalling any of the large Lisbon banks' (*Relatório*, 1876: 10).

According to Capie et al.'s rather rigorous definition, an attitude like this disqualifies such interventions from being treated as genuine lender of last resort actions because profit considerations are not overridden by the concern to ensure the system's stability (Capie et al., 1994: 156). If, however, one considers the matter from the point of view of the consequences, instead of the motives, that is systemic stability, then one might want to argue that what should count for the definition is the readiness to be a lender of last resort, even if for selfish reasons. This would mean that we could speak of a lender of last resort function emerging much earlier than the beginning of the twentieth century, even while central banks were still heavily engaged in competitive commercial activity. This would be particularly true of countries like Portugal, where precisely because of the central bank's profit motive and because of its dominant size, it had a large vested interest in preventing the occurrence of crises and this made it act like the central bank it had not yet become.

Finally, there are the questions of 'discretion vs rules' and moral hazard raised by the fact that during this and other crises the Bank did not lend 'blind' to the market. Instead of providing liquidity to any institution that could afford the price, it assisted individual banks directly, according to its own judgement as to their solidity. Moreover, both before and after 1876 and outside moments of general crisis, it engaged sporadically but fairly frequently in rendering assistance to certain large banks, to ensure that their passing difficulties did not go too far and threaten others. The data in Table 5.4 documents this second category of efforts and shows that almost every year one or two of these institutions were helped to the tune of £30 000–50 000. Little is known about these interventions, as they were carried out with the utmost discretion, but again the motive was clearly entirely selfish: to prevent the difficulties of a large bank from spreading and requiring an even greater sacrifice from the Bank of Portugal. Again, was this genuine lender of last resort behaviour or was it an invitation instead for banks to behave rashly, with destabilizing consequences? According to the definition of Capie and Wood inspired by the classics, it was the latter since the lender of last resort function requires the central bank only to ensure that there is not an excessive contraction of the money stock by supplying the whole of the market with liquidity (Capie and Wood, 1995: 215). When one considers the actions of the Bank of Portugal in 1876, it is far from evident, however, that they were all that far removed from Bagehot's principles. The aim of the latter was to ensure the survival of the institutions which were in a good condition and leave 'unsound people', as he called them, to sink. This is precisely what the Bank did in 1876. It bailed out only those that it considered 'serious banks' and turned down the others without a shade of regret, which meant that they failed. In a small economy like the Portuguese one, where the financial system was modest in scale, the problem of information, which was at the root of Bagehot's concern about the Bank of England lending 'blind' to the market in a crisis, did not exist. The Bank of Portugal's directors knew well which were the sound banks that ought to be helped, and which ones were not. On the other hand, it is true that this was also a situation where several banks were 'too big to fail' and at times a risk of moral hazard may have been incurred. It should be noted, however, that the Bank could be ruthless even with the

Table 5.4 Advances by the Bank of Portugal to other banks, 1873–87

Year	Bank	Amount in *contos*
1873	B. Nacional Ultramarino	200
1874	B. Nacional Ultramarino	760
1875	B. Lusitano	100
1875	B. Lisboa e Açores	50
1877	B. Lusitano	60
1878	Credito Predial	49
1878	B. Nacional Ultramarino	50
1879	B. Lusitano	100
1880	B. Lisboa e Açores	100
1881	xx	0
1882	B. Lisboa e Açores	200
1882	B. Lusitano	170
1882	B. Insulano	40
1883	B. Comercial Lisboa	225
1883	B. Aliança	225
1884	B. Lisbonense	7
1884	B. Lisboa e Açores	100
1884	B. Lusitano	49
1885	xx	0
1886	xx	0
1887	B. Comercial Lisboa	300
1887	B. Nacional Ultramarino	120

Notes: 1 *conto* = £220 sterling approximately.
Detailed data for 1876 has not been provided here because the number of banks assisted during the crisis is too large.
xx : no intervention found.

Source: Bank of Portugal Historical Archives.

heavyweights whose behaviour became too risky, the best example being the Banco Lusitano, one of Lisbon's largest, which was allowed to go under in 1891.

Central banking under inconvertibility: 1891–1914

The 1891 crisis was a major watershed, which arrested certain trends in the development of the Bank of Portugal as a central bank, but not others. The gold standard was permanently replaced by an inconvertible currency. The Bank was obliged to become a major creditor to the Treasury by monetizing a substantial part of the public deficit. Many banks failed because this time, through sheer lack of resources, the Bank of Portugal was unable to be the lender of last resort that was needed. The use of the discount rate as an instrument to stabilize the currency, which was now floating, was entirely abandoned for the next 23 years, until 1914. The main reason was that it was thought that in a prevalently gold standard world, the only way to restore convertibility in Portugal was to contract the supply of notes and increase the gold reserve to their appropriate levels. Both of these depended primarily on the government's, not the Bank's will, hence the retreat from the more active monetary policy stance of earlier times.

By contrast, the lender of last resort function, in both the systemic and the individual versions, seems to have become more important, with both the government and the Bank showing a greater keenness for intervention when they saw trouble, although the Bank's competition with the other banks, if anything, increased relative to the pre-1891 period. There are several reasons for this accrued protagonism. The first was the increased public pressure on the central bank to fulfil its public duty in view of the fact that, as a result of being able to increase the note issue substantially without the extra cost of larger reserves, it was now in receipt of larger profits than ever. The second was that owing to the weakening of the joint stock bank sector after the 1891 crisis, the position of the Bank of Portugal had become even more dominant and therefore its interest in keeping the credit market stable was commensurably greater. On the other hand, since it no longer controlled the market's behaviour through the discount rate, it is likely that some banks may have overextended themselves more than before and consequently found themselves in trouble more often. Finally, in the politically and socially more unstable situation of these years, the public implications of cyclical downturns in the economy were amplified. The need to ward off criticism for its lack of intervention may have become stronger and it became prudent for the Bank of Portugal to do more to assist large enterprises and even whole sectors in trouble.

In this context, central bank independence is an issue that naturally presents itself. Before the 1890s, the Bank of Portugal enjoyed considerable autonomy by current European standards. In statutory terms, none of its directors or its officers was appointed by the government and it had no obligation to share its profits. There was no limit on the note issue, nor was there any minimum ratio of reserves to sight liabilities. Loans to the state required the prior approval of a public meeting of the shareholders, the scrutiny of whom could be quite a powerful deterrent for any government. The reality very much mirrored this description.

The Bank was never forced to allocate a large part of its assets to public loans and at no time did the note issue become tied to the government's financial needs. Its profits were substantial and were freely distributed to its shareholders. There may have been occasional official pressures to act as lender of last resort but, as we have seen, usually this was so much in the Bank's own interest that it is best to describe it as a work of partnership rather than as a relation of subordination. And although one must recognize that it was not free to change its discount rate, even then the government, no matter how reluctant, eventually gave in because the Bank had ways of retaliating, such as rationing credit to its customers, which always produced a strong public outcry in business circles.

During the pre-war inconvertibility period, it is not clear whether or not the independence of the central bank diminished. On paper, a new balance appears to have been struck under the contract signed in 1887: a government-appointed Governor and Secretary-General were placed on the board to try and control it. Profit sharing was introduced while, in compensation, the Bank was given complete discretion to alter its discount rate, providing the profits thereof were shared. In practice, however, the exceptional circumstances of the period significantly altered its statutory relation to the state. The Bank failed to make use of its new freedom with the discount rate. At the same time, it was given no option but to engage heavily in monetizing the debt during the 1890s, something it disliked intensely, as it meant delaying the return of convertibility. On the other hand, in all its many conflicts with the authorities, the record shows that governors, in spite of their political origins, generally sided with the directors and the shareholders and in the end the Bank got its way, even in important matters. The weakness of most governments during this period and the powerful interest group which the shareholders had come to represent were an important reason for this. One of the consequences was that, after 1897, no more large loans tied to the note issue were made to the Treasury. Another was that none of the several governmental attempts to alter the Bank's statutes in the direction of reducing its autonomy was successful. Moreover, the lender of last resort actions which were carried out were those which the Bank approved of, not the ones which, out of political motives, governments wanted.

The inter-war period

The war and its aftermath, up to the stabilization of the mid-1920s, dramatically reduced the Bank of Portugal's status as a central bank.

Most of its assets were absorbed as Treasury loans and the note issue became entirely a function of the government's financial needs. As a consequence, it had to withdraw to a large extent from the market and completely lost its earlier informal influence over the other banks. It is hardly surprising that these, for example, were able now to set their interest rates quite freely, when one considers that the Bank of Portugal's share of total bank credit shrank from 32 per cent, in 1913, to 8 per cent, in 1924 (Reis, 1995). Likewise, although it continued to consider itself under the obligation to rediscount for banks in difficulties, its lender of last resort function became a shadow of its former self, as the available resources were now too scarce to enable it to carry out significant rescue operations, particularly during the severe bank crises of the first half of the 1920s. This situation persisted right down to 1931, in spite of a banking law in 1925 which sought, for the first time, to make it into a central bank by formally entrusting it to be the regulator of the financial sector while obliging it to forsake its commercial role.

The 1930s were shaped by two circumstances: the international crisis and the policies followed by the recently empowered Salazar government. The latter, which were being forged already in the late 1920s, were to restore the gold standard and to make the Bank of Portugal a proper, modern central bank, while leaving it in private hands. Both measures were put into effect in 1931, but the gold standard was abandoned a few months later and Portugal opted to join the sterling area soon after. On the other hand, the legal dispositions regarding the Bank of Portugal's new role remained in force. Essentially, they attempted to consecrate and rationalize the central bank functions which had already been developing for some decades, as we have seen. The Bank was given the right to set interest rate ceilings for the other credit institutions, as well as to determine the supply of high-powered money, its general remit being to maintain the external value of the *escudo* and to regulate the price and the quantity of global credit available to the economy in harmony with this objective. By a combination of the revaluation of reserves with the repayment of a large part of the Treasury's debts, it was supplied with sufficient funds to enable it to intervene effectively again through the rediscount mechanism and thus to become truly a banker's bank once more.

In two respects, these reforms represented a significant break with the past. One was that these central bank functions were now to be exercised by virtue of a legal empowerment and no longer as a practice which had emerged gradually as a result of the necessity felt for it by the system as a whole and by the Bank in particular. The other is that no longer were these functions to be exercised with the autonomy of former times, a trend which has been noted for other countries (Caesar, 1995). For one thing, the Bank was expected now to coordinate its actions with those of the Ministry of Finance and other relevant bodies. This meant, for example, that its discount rate policy had to be in line with that of the government which was to keep it as low as possible, and therefore not always that which the regulator of the banking system would have wanted. For another, within the Bank, all decisions pertaining to these functions were placed in the hands of a newly established Committee for Stabilisation, which was composed half by government-appointed officials and half by officials elected by the shareholders, with the government-appointed Governor enjoying the casting vote. This increased subordination was not agreeable to the Bank and produced repeated friction with the authorities, a possible consequence of which, for example, was the latter's refusal, for the entire period 1936–57, to appoint a Governor.

Leaving aside formal aspects, it is hard to say whether, in purely functional terms, the Bank of Portugal became much more of a central bank during the 1930s than it had before, during the time it did not enjoy officially that designation. The doubt arises because of the limitations to the exercise of this role which it encountered as a result largely of contradictions with other policies followed by Salazar in the realms of money and finance. To begin with, it had no practical authority over the activities of the state-owned savings bank, the *Caixa Geral de Depósitos* (CGD), which Salazar had decided to transform into a major player in the supply of financial services, particularly in long-term credit to agriculture and industry. By 1939, the CGD was holding 40 per cent of all bank assets. In the second place, the Bank was given a subsidiary role only in the salvage and reconstruction of banks in difficulties as a result of the crisis, as well as in the decision as to which to help and which to wind up. These operations were primarily carried out by the Ministry of Finance, sometimes employing funds provided by the Bank. Thirdly, all prudential regulation of the banking sector was put into the hands of an Inspectorate of the same Ministry, which meant that the Bank of Portugal was left with little say in matters such as capital requirements, permitted credit operations, liquidity ratios, standards of management and the licensing of branches or new banks.

The functions of lender of last resort and of regulator of the money market via the discount rate were hampered by two further difficulties, this time of a more structural nature. One was the continuation of the traditional conflict between being a lender of last resort and continuing to compete commercially with the other banks. To make it an effective central bank, Salazar felt that the Bank of Portugal must have a 'dominant position'. The difficulty was that to do so it must be allowed to engage in business so as to employ profitably its substantial resources and regain its former influence over the financial system, and therefore its commercial role could not be restricted too much. Besides, the market was still not strong enough that it could do without the direct credit of such a large institution. This was particularly so in the provinces but also in Lisbon and Oporto and, consequently, although some restrictions were imposed on its direct discounting activities in order to allow other banks to recover business, it continued to expand and by 1939 its bill portfolio was 12 per cent higher than it had been at the beginning of the decade.

Paradoxically, the second structural feature has to do with Portugal's success in weathering the 1931 crisis and the ensuing depression. An important consequence of its newly won political and economic credibility was a consistently favourable balance of payments, due to capital inflows and receipts from tourism, leading to a steady growth of reserves. These increased by 84 per cent over the decade. In this climate, joint stock banks felt able and optimistic enough to increase their creation of money also, through deposit expansion. Since this was not stopped, the money multiplier increased from 1.8 to 2.4 in the same period and M1 practically doubled in just the eight years before 1939. The banks thus found themselves flush with money and were able to become increasingly independent of the Bank of Portugal's rediscount facility, the volume of which fell all through the decade. By 1939, it had reached 20 per cent of what it had been in 1930. Since the Bank had not been given the power to impose reserve ratios, could only set a ceiling but not a minimum on interest rates, and had no possibility of using open market operations, it had no way of preventing its grip over the banks from becoming increasingly tenuous. Even though it claimed that by withdrawing or contracting its rediscount it could influence their credit practices, it was forced nevertheless to admit publicly that monetary abundance had allowed 'the commercial banks to continue to do without the rediscount facility or any other forms of credit from the bank of issue' (Bank of Portugal's Annual Report, 1939: 50).

We do not know the extent to which the monetary policy of the 1930s mirrored the views of the Bank of Portugal itself and we may wonder whether it was completely in favour of it, even though it was its official executor. On the other hand, there is no doubt that to lower interest rates drastically and to provide sufficient liquidity to satisfy the growth needs of the economy was an integral part of the overall aims of the government. In this respect, Portugal apparently followed a British policy line rather than a French one, which is hardly surprising, given its trade partnership with the UK and its adherence to the sterling bloc (Eichengreen, 1995: 111–12). Besides leaving gold in 1931, it acted flexibly in regulating monetary supply and did not attempt to play according to 'the rules of the game'. Had the rules of the 1931 law,

Table 5.5 Bank of Portugal: note issue and reserve 'sterilization', 1931–39

Year	Reserves 1	Note issue 2	Maximum issue permitted by law 3	'Sterilization' index 4
1931	966	2 062	2 486	0.17
1932	1 177	2 001	2 667	0.25
1933	1 097	1 989	2 637	0.24
1934	1 359	2 137	2 899	0.26
1935	1 401	2 205	2 941	0.25
1936	1 523	2 257	3 043	0.26
1937	1 541	2 224	3 082	0.28
1938	1 616	2 279	3 119	0.27
1939	1 789	2 550	3 120	0.18

Note: Values in columns 1 to 3 are in thousands of *contos*. During this period, 1 *conto* = £9 sterling approximately. Calculations for the maximum permitted circulation are based on the 1931 Bank of Portugal law which stipulated that up to 2.2 million *contos* the note issue could be covered by 30 per cent of gold or gold-backed assets, and that above this limit it had to be backed 100 per cent by gold. The 'sterilization' index is the percentage of this maximum issue which was not made use of by the Bank.

Source: Valério (1983).

which reformed the Bank, prevailed over discretion, with the steady rise in reserves, monetary expansion would have had to go much further. But, as can be seen from Table 5.5, the Bank 'sterilized' some of these reserve gains and kept the monetary base consistently at three quarters of its maximum legally permitted level. In this sense, one could say that, in money terms, the Bank of Portugal was as restrictive as the circumstances permitted but this was never enough to restore the power it had enjoyed over the banking system in the days when it was not called a central bank and was not in the thrall of governments.

Conclusion

The study of the Bank of Portugal's first century of existence highlights two important features of its past which may find interesting parallels in the history of other central banks, as further research is carried out.

One is that long before 1914, a combination of market, political and institutional circumstances could drive a privileged bank of issue into behaviour which already suggested quite clearly the contours of some of the most essential modern central bank functions. The other is that law and regulation are an essential component of any analysis of central bank history but not a sufficient basis from which to draw conclusions. In this perspective, the Bank of Portugal provides a striking illustration of how appearances can be illusory. This is brought home to us by how much less of a central bank it appears to have been during the 1930s compared with earlier periods, when officially it was not committed to such a role but felt such commitment as a necessity created by the place it had built for itself in the Portuguese financial system.

Notes

1. A comprehensive study of the Bank of Portugal up to 1914 is in preparation, the first volume having been published as Reis (1996). For studies which cover part of the twentieth century, see Mata and Valério (1982) and Valério (1996).
2. The instruments of monetary policy used by early central banks, that is during the nineteenth century, are fully discussed in Bloomfield (1958).
3. *Parecer ácerca das Exigências do Governo do Estado para que o Banco de Portugal Ceda dos seus Privilégios* (1865), Lisboa, p. 16.

References

Bloomfield, A.I. (1958), *Monetary Policy under the International Gold Standard, 1880–1914*, New York.

Caesar, Rolf (1995), 'Central banks and governments: issues, traditions, lessons', *Financial History Review*, 2.

Capie, F., Goodhart, C., Fischer, S. and Schnadt, N. (eds) (1994), *The Future of Central Banking. The Tercentenary Symposium of the Bank of England,* Cambridge.

Capie, F. and Wood, G. (1995), 'A European lender of last resort? Some lessons from history', in Jaime Reis (ed.), *International Monetary Systems in Historical Perspective*, Houndmills and London.

Conant, C.A. (1969), *A History of Modern Banks of Issue*, New York.

Eichengreen, Barry (1995), 'Central bank cooperation and exchange rate commitments: the classical and interwar gold standards compared', *Financial History Review*, 2.

Flandreau, Marc (1997), 'Central bank cooperation in historical perspective: a sceptical view', *Economic History Review*, L.

Gallarotti, Giulio M. (1995), *The Anatomy of an International Monetary Regime: The Classical Gold Standard, 1880–1914*, New York and Oxford.

Henriksen, Ingrid and Kaergård, Niels (1995), 'The Scandinavian currency union 1875–1914', in Jaime Reis (ed.), *International Monetary Systems in Historical Perspective*, Houndmills and London.

Johansen, Hans Christian (1985), *Dansk Økonomisk Statistik*, Copenhagen.

Mata, Eugénia and Valério, Nuno (1982), 'O Banco de Portugal, Único Banco Emissor (1891–1931)', *Revista de História Económica e Social*, 23.

Reis, Jaime (1995), 'Portuguese banking in the inter-war period', in Charles Feinstein (ed.), *Banking, Currency and Finance in Europe between the Wars*, Oxford.

Reis, Jaime (1996), *O Banco de Portugal das Origens a 1914. Antecedentes, Fundação, Consolidação 1821–1857*, Lisboa.

Relatório da Direcção do Banco de Portugal Apresentado à Assembleia Geral dos Accionistas na Sessão Extraordinária de 29 de Agosto de 1876 (1876), Lisboa.

Valério, Nuno (1983), *A Moeda em Portugal 1913–1947*, Lisboa.

Valério, Nuno (1996), 'O Banco de Portugal, banco central privado 1931–1974', in *Ensaios de Homenagem a Manuel Jacinto Nunes*, Lisboa.

CHAPTER SIX

The Bank of Italy from its Foundation to the 1950s: Institutional Aspects

Cosma Onorio Gelsomino

Foreword

The Bank of Italy occupies a special position in the Italian institutional panorama. The stability of its leadership (it has had only nine Governors since it was founded just over a hundred years ago), together with the solidity of its technical and administrative structures, has made it into one of Italy's so-called 'strong' institutions. This strength neither owes anything to chance nor does it derive exclusively from the legal framework in which the Bank operates, but is the fruit of its history, which, albeit marked by difficulties, setbacks and outright crises, has consolidated its position with respect to economic agents and governmental authorities.

It is therefore of interest to examine some of the key moments of this history, drawing in part on studies that have recently been published in the Bank's historical series. Inevitably, such an examination has to be delimited as regards both the years and the aspects covered and this paper is therefore restricted to the years between the foundation of the Bank and the end of the 1950s, the period in which the Bank established its role at the centre of Italy's financial system. Furthermore, the focus is mainly on the development of the institutional framework within which the Bank operated, with a division into sub-periods based on the adoption of legislation bearing on its activities. Accordingly, rather than an analysis of the Bank's policies, which will only be touched on in passing, the chapter seeks to provide a concise description of the set of objectives, constraints and instruments embodied in the written and unwritten rules that governed its action.

From the creation of the Bank of Italy to the First World War

What are the key features of the institutional framework within which the Bank of Italy operated in the twenty years before the outbreak of the First World War?[1]

The foundation of the Bank of Italy in 1893 was part of the reorganization of the Italian banking and monetary system made necessary by the state of near collapse that had been reached at the beginning of the 1890s. Of the six pre-existing banks of issue, one (*Banca Romana*) was dissolved and three (*Banca Nazionale nel Regno d'Italia*, *Banca Nazionale Toscana* and *Banca Toscana di Credito*) were merged into the new bank. All the banks of issue had been heavily involved in the speculative boom and in the following bust of the early 1890s. Their assets were immobilized in long-term credit of uncertain quality, mostly in favour of building firms, and in real estate, and their capital was deeply eroded. The new institution thus inherited a heavy burden at its birth, which took place in the middle of a major economic, financial and political crisis. Moreover, the risks of the liquidation of the *Banca Romana* were transferred to the Bank of Italy in October 1894, a few months after the beginning of operation. One commentator referred to the Bank as a 'new economic and monetary abortion'[2] and many expected the Bank to have a short and blighted existence.

The fundamental task for the Bank in its early years was thus to free itself from the problems inherited from the past, primarily by clearing the dead wood from its balance sheet and restoring a capital base befitting its position as the country's leading bank of issue. Achieving this objective called above all for a long period of sound administration: a task that was carried out behind the scenes, but which none the less made a decisive contribution to the vitality and prestige of the new institution. In the words of Einaudi, 'it was the masterpiece of Stringher [...] and Miraglia [...] to have succeeded, through long years of prudent administration, shrewd disposals and strict economy, in putting the past to rights.'[3] By the second half of the first decade of this century, the process of rehabilitation could be considered completed: the non-performing assets had been liquidated, the reserves built up to a high level in relation to the note issue and the exchange rate of the *lira* brought back close to parity.

The reorganization of the Italian monetary and credit system in the 1890s had another more far-reaching objective, however: to create a set of rules and institutions that would put the Italian currency on a sounder footing and prevent the repetition of events such as those that had brought the country to the verge of economic and financial collapse. In many respects, the outcome of the codification that was undertaken, part of which is still in force today, was a compromise between the special conditions present in Italy and the trends that had emerged in the more advanced countries with regard to their banks of issue. It was none the less a 'forward-looking' compromise that, rather than crystallize the Italian situation, sought to foster progress. This can be seen in the solution adopted for the question as to whether there should be a single bank of issue or several. The Bank of Italy was created first and foremost in response to events within the Italian monetary system, but the resulting concentration of nearly three-quarters of the note issue in the hands of one bank brought Italy closer into line with the tendency to have a single issuer that had come to prevail in the other leading European countries.[4]

In the period from the Bank's foundation to the outbreak of the First World War, the fundamental reference point for monetary debates and measures (in both the institutional and the monetary management fields) was the gold standard in the various forms it took on in Europe in the last decades of the nineteenth century. In Italy, however, an important component of this system, the convertibility of bank notes into gold at a fixed rate, was lacking throughout the period under consideration, even when conditions were most favourable, in the Giolittian era. Inconvertible *de facto* from the end of the 1880s, the *lira* was officially declared to be so *de jure* soon after the Bank of Italy started operations and remained with this status until December 1927. Reference to gold none the less played a key role in Italy as stated in the report of the *Commissione economica del Ministero per la Costituente:* 'the Bank held that its duty, even with the currency inconvertible, was to defend the external value of the *lira*'.[5] The accumulation of reserves and the stability of the exchange rate were the two main yardsticks for measuring the success of the efforts to restore the country's monetary system.

In the first phase of the Bank's life the 'art of central banking' in Italy, as in the other European countries, thus consisted basically in maintaining the gold parity of bank notes. Its primary task, in other words, was to produce a means of exchange as 'good as gold', but less costly and more flexible.

To allow this task to be performed correctly and reduce the risk of the bank of issue abusing its power to create money, the law provided two main instruments: regulation of the note issue itself and regulation of the assets eligible as backing. In this respect, Italian law conformed with the tendency prevailing in Europe. In fact from the middle of the nineteenth century it was widely held that the convertibility of bank notes alone was not enough to prevent over-issuing likely to cause upheavals in economic activity and that it was necessary for the law to impose further restrictions. Naturally, the role of these restrictions was considered all the more important in countries such as Italy where bank notes were not convertible.

As regards the regulation of the note issue, Italian law was partly modelled on the provisions adopted in Germany in 1875 (apart, of course, from those concerning convertibility). The main objective was to tie the note issue to the quantity of reserves, albeit with a degree of flexibility. It was in fact possible to increase the note issue with no change in the reserves, but only within certain limits, beyond which the bank of issue was subject to severe penalties. This result was obtained by allowing the note issue with 100 per cent reserve backing[6] to be supplemented by a quota with partial backing, subject to a minimum reserve ratio of 40 per cent. Whereas the issue with 100 per cent backing did not have any legal limit, the maximum amount of the note issue with partial backing was established by law. However, where circumstances required, the banks of issue could exceed this limit, but they had to pay a progressive note-issue surtax on the excess amount.

The aim was to render the note issue sufficiently elastic, in the sense of 'the ability of paper currency both to expand and to contract'.[7] It was possible to increase the note issue for a given quantity of reserves by reducing the proportion with 100 per cent backing (as long as this proportion was greater than zero, of course) and increasing that with partial backing up to, and if necessary beyond, the limits established by law. In the latter case, however, the economic cost imposed through the penalty rates of the tax on the excess part of the note issue created an incentive to eliminate the overshoot as soon as possible. In other words, the Bank was free to vary the amount of notes it issued with a given quantity of reserves by manoeuvring the quotas with 100 per cent and 40 per cent reserve backing, but only up to a certain limit, beyond which it incurred rising costs.

As time passed, however, the penalties, which initially had been draconian, were gradually eased in order to allow the banks of issue to cope with the wide swings in the demand for money that arose in special circumstances, such as the financial crisis of 1907: the maximum rate of the tax on the note issue, which had been set at twice the discount rate in 1893–94, was reduced to 7.5 per cent in 1907 and set equal to the discount rate in 1912.

The rules governing the note issue did not apply to the part corresponding to the advances made to the Treasury, known as 'the note issue on behalf of the state', while the note issue backed by other assets was known as 'the note issue on behalf of commerce', henceforth the 'commercial note issue'. As explained below, however, the maximum amount of the advances to the Treasury, and hence of the note issue on behalf of the state, was set by the law, and thus was not at the discretion of either the Treasury or the banks of issue. Nor did the rules apply to the deposits taken by the banks of issue. As in other countries, notes were considered to be different from the other sight liabilities of the banks of issue and to require special regulation. None the less, the deposit-taking of the banks of issue was not completely free in Italy; although exempt from reserve requirements, it was subject to quantitative limits and interest rate restrictions.[8]

The other main component of the institutional system regulating the activity of the banks of issue consisted of the rules concerning the assets that were eligible as backing for the issue of bank notes. In this field too, a firmly established body of thought had developed that basically admitted two categories of asset: metallic reserves and commercial paper. By contrast, the use of claims on the Treasury, in the form of both loans and securities, was excluded or at least restricted within rigorously defined limits.

In accordance with this view, Italian legislation provided for a ceiling on the banks of issue's funding of the Treasury in the form of both securities and advances. Credit operations (discounts and advances) were also regulated with the general aim of protecting the soundness and liquidity of the banks of issue's assets. Excessively strict rules were none the less avoided. In the case of bills, for example, the criterion was purely formal (in addition to the signatures having to be good, the residual maturity had to be less than four months) and did not prevent funding transactions that were in fact different from normal bill discounting and with maturities longer than four months (through recourse to the technique of renewals). As in other countries, no restrictions were imposed on the categories of customer with which the Bank of Italy could do business. In principle, the distinguishing feature of the credit business of the banks of issue was not their counterparts (banks versus non-banks) but the financial assets they acquired (short-term bills, preferably of a commercial nature, as against accommodation bills). The banks of issue thus participated directly in the financing of the private sector, alongside and in competition with the ordinary banks. Their participation was considered a way of influencing conditions in the credit market, as well as a legitimate source of income.

One special feature of the Italian legislation concerned the intervention of the Ministry of the Treasury in setting the discount rate. This dated back to the period prior to the foundation of the Bank of Italy, having been introduced in 1866 when bank notes were declared inconvertible. The 1866 decree established that the banks of issue were not allowed to change the discount rate without ministerial approval;[9] in 1894, the Treasury Minister was empowered to promote changes. However, these provisions did not result in the Minister having exclusive power in the matter; on a number of occasions the Minister proposed a change in the discount rate but the Bank of Italy did not comply with the request.[10] Changes in the official rates thus required agreement between the government, on the one hand, and the banks of issue (in practice the Bank of Italy, which acted as the leader of the category), on the other.

The importance of the official rates was in any case markedly diminished by the introduction in 1895 of a reduced discount rate for transactions with prime customers.[11] The purpose of this measure was to allow the banks of issue to take account of the quality of the paper presented for discounting and not remain excluded from transactions with top quality customers. Similar measures were in force in the other European countries.[12] In the period up to the First World War, changes in the cost of discounting were mainly achieved by varying the proportions of transactions at the official rate and the reduced rate. The latter was modified frequently, since it was set by a ministerial decree which was initially issued quarterly, then monthly and in the end whenever necessary. The official discount rate, which was normally higher than the rates charged by banks on good quality commercial paper, was changed much less frequently, when there was no longer scope for raising the average discount rate by suspending transactions at the reduced rate.

Economic theory saw the discount rate as the principal instrument available to banks of issue in performing their task of maintaining the parity of bank notes with respect to the monetary standard. In countries where bank notes were convertible into gold, this task took the form of defending the metallic reserves: increasing the discount rate was how the bank of issue reacted to an excessive decline in the reserves. In countries with inconvertible currencies, such as Italy, it was also possible to defend the reserves by allowing the exchange rate to weaken. However, as we have seen, in spite of inconvertibility, the Bank of Italy held that its main duty was first to re-establish and then to maintain a system as close as possible to the gold standard; hence, from the turn of the century onwards the Bank sought to keep the exchange rate of the *lira* close to its par value, so that the discount rate in Italy also served primarily as a means of defending the reserves. According to many observers, its effectiveness was none the less diminished by the continuance of a degree of exchange rate variability and by the lack of a legal obligation to defend the parity, which, together with Italy's marginal role in the international financial system, resulted in changes in the discount rate having only a limited influence on capital movements. Such changes were therefore intended to defend the reserves by primarily influencing domestic conditions (control of the Bank's credit operations and of the note issue).[13]

The rehabilitation of the Italian financial system was basically accomplished during the 15 years following the creation of the Bank of Italy, with a marked acceleration from the turn of the century onwards, which resulted in the process taking less time than had originally been expected. The liquidation of the Bank's non-performing assets was completed in 1906; the reserves were built up to a high level and reached 75 per cent of the note issue in 1908; in 1903 the exchange rate of the *lira* was close to its parity and it remained stable for a number of years. The recovery of full operational freedom is testified by the successful management of the 1907 crisis, which ratified the acquisition by the Bank of Italy of the role of lender of last resort. A new legislative cycle began in the wake of this experience, aimed primarily at attenuating the rigidities of the 1893 legislation in the light of the return to normal operating conditions at the Bank of Italy.[14]

The inter-war period

The effects of the First World War

The First World War and its aftermath interrupted the strengthening of Italy's monetary system. The note issue on behalf of the state increased enormously, primarily as a result of the extraordinary advances the banks of issue granted to the Treasury. However, in contrast with what was to occur during the Second World War, the requirement that the lending of the banks of issue to the Treasury be authorized by statutory measures remained in force. In the post-war period, by contrast, it was principally the 'commercial note issue' that expanded, that is, issue based on transactions other than advances to the Treasury. This growth was fuelled by the large increase in ordinary discounts and advances and in lending connected with the banking crises that developed in this period (*Banca Italiana di Sconto* and *Banco di Roma*). The limits on the 'commercial note issue' had been raised during the war but were totally inadequate compared with the effects of inflation on nominal values both then and in the years following the war. For several years the Bank of Italy consequently exceeded the limits on a regular basis, despite the disincentive of the overshoot being taxed at a rate equal to the discount rate.

As mentioned earlier, in the period prior to the First World War, the Bank of Italy (once it had returned to normality by removing the non-performing assets from its balance sheet) had adopted two main guidelines for its action, at least in ordinary circumstances. The first, of a substantial nature, consisted in keeping the exchange rate of the *lira* as close as possible to its official parity; the second, of a formal nature, meant complying with the limits on the note issue laid down by law. In addition, its role as lender of last resort,[15] or in other words its responsibility for maintaining the stability of the Italian banking system as a whole, was recognized and the goal of fostering economic growth was accepted, provided it was compatible with the primary objectives just mentioned.

After the war neither of these two basic principles retained much validity. The earlier parity of the *lira* had become meaningless and it was far from clear when, or at what level, a credible new parity could be established. Furthermore, there were periods in which the imbalance between the internal and external values of the *lira* was so great that a rigid defence of the exchange rate would have been totally unrealistic. On the other hand, the obsolescence of the statutory limits on the money supply – clearly revealed by the fact that they were permanently exceeded by a considerable amount – prevented them from serving as a credible reference point. In the conditions of serious political and social disorder that marked the early post-war years, the Bank's primary objective became that of limiting the damage to the country's productive and banking systems until the correction of the most serious disequilibria inherited from the war (the public finances and the external debt) allowed the monetary system to be put back on a sound basis.

This period also revealed the inadequacy of the instruments available to the Bank of Italy. Basically, these consisted of the discount rate; overfunding of the Treasury's borrowing requirement; and the interest rate on deposits with the Bank.

As regards the discount rate, the war had led to the abandonment of the reduced rate. This could no longer be applied while the note issue was permanently in excess of the limits in force, both because the law prohibited it and in view of the deleterious effect it would have had on profitability, since the corresponding return would have been less than the tax on the excess note issue, which was equal to the discount rate. The abandonment of the reduced discount rate none the less diminished the flexibility of the control exercised via the cost of discounting; the ordinary discount rate remained highly sticky and at times below market rates, in contrast with the situation prevailing before the war, and in some years significantly negative in real terms. On the other hand, it proved extremely hard to establish forms of quantity control. Outright rationing (whereby credit would be denied to persons possessing eligible collateral, as opposed to the moderation that Stringher repeatedly invoked on the part of the Bank's branch managers) was not imposed until the summer of 1926, in conjunction with the policy shift that was to lead to the adoption of a parity of around 90 *lire* to the pound sterling (*quota novanta*).

The main instrument for mopping up excess liquidity was overfunding of the Treasury, that is the sale of more securities than needed to meet its borrowing requirement. Recourse was made to this instrument both during the 1920s and in the early 1930s. It was none the less subject to interference by the Treasury's debt management policy with regard to the composition of the debt and the need to reduce the interest burden.

The third instrument was the interest rate on deposits with the Bank of Italy. In 1914, the limits on the amounts of deposits the banks of issue could take were removed, together with the restrictions on the interest rates they could pay. This had created the conditions for a more systematic and a larger-scale use of such deposits for the purpose of curbing the growth in the note issue. The most striking episode in this respect occurred in 1926, when the maximum rate on deposits was raised to 5 per cent and they more than doubled.

On the other hand, the Bank made no recourse to open market operations, which the United Kingdom and the United States had begun to use systematically from the end of the war onwards. This technique was known in Italy, but it was considered inapplicable owing to the absence of a developed securities market able to absorb possibly large sales without significant price movements. Besides, the prevailing view was that the way to overcome the difficulties encountered in monetary control during the 1920s lay not so much in the search for new instruments, as in the return to a 'normal' monetary regime, analogous to that in force before the outbreak of the war. This meant re-establishing the set of incentives and constraints on the activity of the banks of issue that had permitted monetary stability to be restored and maintained in the period before the war: the anchoring of the *lira* to gold, this time on a formal basis, with the return to convertibility; the rigorous limitation of monetary financing of the Treasury; the confirmation of orthodox rules for the lending of the banks of issue, with the liquidation of the rest of the non-performing assets they had acquired since the end of the war in bank rescue operations.

Monetary reform (1926–28)

Making the *lira* convertible again was part of a general return to gold on the part of the leading European currencies that got under way in the mid-1920s. The great debate that had started at the end of the war on the reconstruction of the international monetary system appeared to have come to an end with the return to the gold standard, albeit in modified forms compared with those prevailing before the war. In Italy, the reform came on the heels of a major crisis which broke out in the summer of 1925 and was only overcome in the autumn of 1926 with the adoption of a series of drastic measures, such as the cap on the commercial note issue (which, probably for the first time, entailed a rationing of Bank of Italy discounts and advances) and the compulsory conversion of Treasury bills.[16] Italy's 'monetary restoration' led, in December 1927, to the *lira* being declared convertible at a parity which was below that prevailing before the war but which recovered part of the devaluation of the immediately preceding years (*quota novanta*).

The 1926–28 reforms were the occasion for a new burst of legislation concerning the banks of issue and the monetary system. This focused on three main aspects: the unification of the note issue in the hands of the Bank of Italy; the attribution to the latter of responsibility for the supervision of the commercial banks; and the return to convertibility. In 1928, the Bank of Italy's statutes were amended, both to bring them into line with the new legislative framework and to give the Bank an appropriate structure and organization.

In reality, the unification of the note issue did no more than adapt the law to a *de facto* situation which for a long time had seen it controlled exclusively by the Bank of Italy. The institutional standing of the Bank was none the less enhanced.

As regards supervision, the law approved in 1926 introduced the principle that all banks should be subject to special rules and to control by governmental authorities and the Bank of Italy.[17] Previously, only certain categories of bank, such as the savings banks, had been subject to ministerial supervision.

The introduction of banking supervision was an integral part of the monetary reform. As is well known, the early 1920s had been marked by major bank crises, culminating in the collapse of *Banca Italiana di Sconto* and the rescue of *Banco di Roma*. To have an idea of the order of magnitude of the problem, it is sufficient to note that Menichella estimated the losses of the Bank of Italy and the Treasury, as a result of the support of the two banks, at 2.65 billion *lire* and that the losses incurred by the depositors of *Banca Italiana di Sconto* had amounted to another billion.[18] The total losses were equal to around 3 per cent of Italy's average GDP in the years from 1922 to 1925.

There was a general consensus that the banking crises of the early 1920s and the consequent intervention of the banks of issue had made a decisive contribution to the deterioration in monetary conditions. They were seen as having caused a massive injection of liquidity that the authorities were unable to mop up with the necessary rapidity, partly owing to the lack of adequate instruments, and as having helped to undermine the note issue by tying up the assets of the banks of issue. The latter argument was considered to have considerable force. As we have seen, the classical view of the note issue required that the assets of the bank of issue should be as liquid as possible (more exactly, that they should consist exclusively of reserves and self-liquidating commercial bills). In other words, the bank of issue should have been able to reduce its total assets extremely fast. In particular, its credit operations were required to give rise to a rapid rotation of bank notes, with a sizable proportion of the outstanding stock regularly returning to the issuer. This, it was claimed, was an indispensable condition for the discount rate to be an effective instrument, since only in this way could a reduction in the *flow* of new credit produced by an increase in the discount rate rapidly reduce the *stock* of notes in circulation (the flow of notes being returned to the Bank of Italy would become larger than the outflow).

The scant effectiveness of monetary control in the years after the First World War was in fact attributed to the assets of the banks of issue having become tied up through bank rescues and advances to the Treasury. It is therefore obvious that when embarking on monetary reform the authorities should have given priority to the creation of an institutional system that would reduce the risk of new bank crises. From the monetary point of view, this was the principal function assigned to supervision. Naturally, it was intended to achieve other objectives, such as the protection of depositors (although Stringher was notably cautious in this respect)[19] and the control of the speculative banking that had been a feature of the first half of the 1920s.

The last group of measures was more directly concerned with the monetary system. In addition to those that technically restored convertibility (in the form of the gold exchange standard, whereby bank notes could be converted at the Bank of Italy's discretion into 5 kg gold bars or foreign currencies convertible into gold), it is worth mentioning the provisions concerning the note issue and those regulating the Bank's relations with the Treasury.

The distinction between notes fully and partly backed by reserves was abolished and the ceiling on the latter was removed. In its place, a reserve requirement of 40 per cent was introduced for the whole note issue and all the Bank of Italy's other sight liabilities (thus including its deposits, which had previously been exempt). Extraordinary advances to the Treasury, which had been introduced during the war, were abolished, with those outstanding being repaid out of the valuation gain on the reserves arising from the new parity of the *lira*, and a limit was set in absolute terms on ordinary advances. At the same time, the ceiling on the Bank's holdings of government securities was abolished. This was not intended to provide a means of eluding the limit on advances but simply as a technical measure to permit the transfer to the Bank of Italy of the securities owned by the *Istituto di liquidazioni*.[20] As we shall see, when the channels of monetary financing of the Treasury were formally reopened in 1936, recourse was again made to advances rather than to securities.

The reforms of the 1930s

In the early thirties, the primary objective of Italian monetary policy was to defend the gold parity of the *lira* set by the reform of 1927–28, even if this involved a considerable revaluation of the *lira* against the currencies of countries that decided to devalue and abandon the gold anchor (the United Kingdom in 1931 and the United States in 1933, followed by many others).[21] This policy was set aside towards the middle of the decade when it became clear that its cost was becoming unsustainable and that it was incompatible with the Fascists' plans for rearmament and war. However, the developments between 1934 and 1936 represented not a mere change of policy stance but rather a change of monetary regime as the key features of the 1927–28 reform were progressively overturned. In 1934, the foreign exchange monopoly was introduced, which under a gold exchange standard amounted to the *de facto* elimination of convertibility. In 1935 the requirement that the Bank of Italy hold reserves in gold and gold-backed currencies equal to at least 40 per cent of its sight liabilities was suspended. In 1936, after the Italian government devalued the *lira*, following the example of the other 'gold bloc' countries, the Treasury was given free access to Bank of Italy financing with the reintroduction of extraordinary advances, which had been abolished in 1928; in contrast with past arrangements, however, no limit was set on the amount of these advances, which were simply to be granted 'upon prior agreement between the Minister of Finance and the Governor of the Bank of Italy'.[22]

The reintroduction of extraordinary advances from the Bank of Italy to the Treasury – to which were added other avenues for central bank credit, such as the financing of special operations by the *Consorzio per Sovvenzioni su Valori Industriali* – was a particularly important measure, effectively marking the opening of a new phase. Although the Treasury at first did not abuse these facilities, from the point of view of institutional relations with the Bank of Italy their existence in itself plainly altered the monetary situation in the second half of the 1930s. In effect, the changes set up a system of 'managed money' in which the flexibility obtained by abandoning gold was primarily made to serve the requirements of the Treasury. With the rules on extraordinary advances, the state asserted its right to resort to monetary financing when and to the extent it saw fit.[23]

No doubt the change of monetary regime and the primacy assigned to the Treasury's requirements depended in part on the climate of war ushered in by Italy's Ethiopian venture. However, the transformation of the institutional framework also involved new features that reflected the general recasting of relations between the state and the economy in the late 1930s. Not even at the height of Italy's military effort during the First World War had there been such a radical revision of principles as that effected in 1936: during the Great War the advances of the banks of issue to the Treasury had continued to be subject to limits set by law, although these were repeatedly raised during the conflict and in the years immediately following it.

The institutional innovations in the monetary field in the mid-1930s were far-reaching. Yet it cannot be said that the Bank of Italy was totally excluded from the policy-making process. To be sure, its independent powers were greatly reduced: exchange rate management was completely removed from the Bank's sphere and transferred to ministerial bodies; with the institution of extraordinary advances and other forms of monetary financing of the Treasury, it lost control over the creation of monetary base; and with the introduction of preferential rates expressly intended to facilitate the placement of government securities, its room for manoeuvre with regard to official interest rates was further restricted. The Bank nevertheless retained a measure of influence through its role as advisor and technical initiator of monetary management. And it was above all in this area that Azzolini, who had been appointed Governor in 1930, played a hand. He appears to have adopted Hawtrey's view that in extraordinary circumstances such as a war 'it is not the independence of the central bank but its technical competence and insight that will gain a hearing for its protests'.[24]

The legislation enacted in 1934–36 naturally included the 1936 Banking Law (and the related amendment of the Bank of Italy's Statutes). In addition to reorganizing the whole banking system and reforming the supervision of the commercial banks, the Banking Law turned the Bank of Italy into an institution established under public law[25] and prohibited it from engaging in discount business with non-bank customers. Both these innovations, but especially the second, were opposed by the Bank.[26] Although their operational impact was relatively limited, they appear to have constituted a turning point in the Bank's institutional development, the full effects of which were to be felt after the Second World War. The transformation of the Bank into a public-law institution and the ban on discount operations with non-bank customers put the seal on its abandonment of a competitive attitude towards the other banks, which might have interfered with its pursuit of the objectives associated with its role as central bank. This was not so much because it sought to maximize its profits, an objective that had been set on one side some time before, as because its participation in commercial activities created a climate of diffidence, and sometimes of rivalry, that was detrimental to the performance of its central banking functions.

The 1936 Banking Law formally entrusted banking supervision to a governmental body, the Credit Inspectorate, set up under a Committee of Ministers chaired by the head of the government. The Inspectorate was none the less little more than a legal fiction since it was headed by the Governor of the Bank of Italy and used the Bank's structures and staff to carry out its activities. The law thus made the Bank of Italy the main operational instrument of the so-called 'management of credit' or, in other words, of the control of credit flows that potentially extended to the determination of their allocation among the different sectors of production. The Bank became a sort of operational arm of the government in the monetary and financial field. However, the consensus view of contemporary commentators and historians is that the Bank's technical approach prevailed over the political orientation of the Committee of Ministers; the 'management of credit' remained largely a dead letter and the activity of the Inspectorate was directed primarily towards banking supervision in the strict sense of the term.

The institutional reforms enacted after the Second World War

The *lira* was one of the European currencies to suffer the most in the war. Between 1938 and 1948 prices rose in Italy by a factor of around 50, wiping out the greater part of savers' financial wealth. The changes in relative prices that accompanied this inflation gave rise to serious distortions in the composition of production.[27]

On the other hand, Italy was one of the first European countries to stabilize its currency. In the autumn of 1947, after more than a year of renewed inflation, the rise in prices was halted. Immediately afterwards, the exchange rate of the *lira* against the dollar was fixed at a realistic level that allowed a rapid return to balance-of-payments equilibrium and the gradual rebuilding of the foreign currency reserves (to which American aid also contributed).

The 1947 stabilization programme has been described in innumerable publications and can be taken as given here. For the purposes of this analysis, it is important to note that the economic and financial stabilization measures were accompanied by others aimed at stabilizing, or normalizing, the institutional framework and putting an end to the period of autarchic and wartime finance that had started in the mid-1930s. The cornerstones of this institutional stabilization were: the introduction of compulsory reserves for commercial banks; the revision of the rules on Bank of Italy financing of the Treasury; the transfer to the Bank of Italy of the supervisory powers of the Credit Inspectorate; and the setting up of the *Ufficio Italiano dei Cambi* (UIC). These innovations deserve to be examined in a little more detail.

Compulsory reserves acted as the fulcrum of the 1947 stabilization programme. Recourse to a reserve requirement was not without a precedent in Italy's banking legislation. The law of 1926 had in fact set a limit of 20:1 for the ratio of deposits to own funds, beyond which banks were required to deposit the excess funds they raised in special accounts with the Bank of Italy, either in cash or in securities. However, before the war this provision had had little effect because the average value of the ratio had been well below the limit and after the war it was inapplicable, despite its having been raised from 20 to 30, because inflation had consumed banks' own funds.

Consequently, in 1947 there was the first significant application of a system of compulsory reserves geared to the amount of bank deposits. Moreover, in contrast with the 1926 provisions, those adopted in 1947 expressly sought to create a system to be used for monetary control, even though it was based on powers attributed to the monetary authorities for banking supervision purposes. Compulsory reserves represented the first technical innovation in Italy in the field of monetary control with respect to the traditional model based on the bank of issue that had been embodied in the laws enacted before the First World War. Their introduction considerably strengthened the position of the Bank of Italy *vis-à-vis* the commercial banks and increased the credibility of monetary policy.

The provisions on the financing of the Treasury were contained in laws approved on 24 December 1947 and 7 May 1948. They re-established the principle – abandoned in 1936 – that extraordinary advances from the Bank of Italy to the Treasury had to be authorized in a law. They also regulated the credit that could be granted to the Treasury by way of the overdraft on its current account with the Bank and set an annual limit on this facility equal to 15 per cent of the expenditure approved in the budget. These provisions need to be seen in the context of the more general adjustment of Italy's public finances in the post-war period. For many years, the strict interpretation of Article 81 of the Constitution, which required each new item of expenditure to be accompanied by an indication of the revenue that would finance it, provided an effective defence against the risk of inflationary financing of public expenditure.

The most important measure in the field of supervision was the law of 1947 instituting the Interministerial Committee for Credit and Savings and making the Bank of Italy responsible for the banking supervision previously performed by the Credit Inspectorate. The Credit Committee, which relied (and still relies) on the Bank of Italy for the implementation of its resolutions, was entrusted with 'the overall responsibility for supervision in matters concerning the protection of savings, the exercise of credit and foreign exchange' (Article 1). In addition to foreign exchange policy, the Committee's powers therefore covered supervision and the working of the banking system (authorization of new banks, branch networks and geographical limits on banks' operations, etc.). They did not, however, extend to monetary policy. For instance, the Credit Committee had no say in decisions concerning the official rates, which were taken by the Treasury Minister and the Governor of the Bank of Italy, or in the policy pursued by the Bank with regard to refinancing.

The creation of the *Ufficio Italiano dei Cambi* (UIC) in 1945 resulted in responsibility for implementing foreign exchange policy returning to the Bank of Italy. The UIC replaced the *Istituto Nazionale per i Cambi con l'Estero* (INCE), which had been established with close links with the Bank of Italy in 1917, but placed directly under the ministerial bodies responsible for foreign trade during the 1930s. There is documentary evidence[28] that the aim of creating the UIC was to reverse the operation effected in the 1930s and entrust exchange controls to an apolitical technical body not directly linked to the government. In the event the UIC was placed under the aegis of the Bank of Italy, which provided its capital and was made responsible for its management through the appointment of the Governor as *ex officio* Chairman.

Monetary control in the 1950s

There were no major changes in the institutional arrangements concerning the Bank of Italy during the 1950s. These were years of consolidation in which the authorities reaped the benefits of the difficult decisions taken in the aftermath of the war. A detailed analysis of the policies pursued is beyond the scope of this study, but it is worth underscoring the fact that Menichella, Governor of the Bank of Italy from 1948 to 1960, considered the maintenance of monetary stability to be an indispensable precondition for the development of the Italian economy, which called for increases in both investments and imports. In order to ensure such growth was soundly based and avoid inflationary shortcuts that in the long run would reduce the economy's growth potential, Menichella considered it was necessary for economic policy to strengthen Italians' propensity to save and the country's ability to compete abroad. Monetary policy played a decisive role in the achievement of these objectives: the defence of the monetary yardstick created conditions conducive to both increased saving and export growth in a context of exchange rate stability.

These policies made it possible to restore the external convertibility of the *lira* in 1958 and for Italy to participate in the process of European integration. The economic nationalism of the 1930s had been jettisoned, together with most of the apparatus of administrative controls on economic activity constructed during the period of autarchy.

Monetary policy operated under favourable conditions in the 1950s. These conditions were a carryover from the post-war stabilization and were propitiated by fiscal and incomes policies that were broadly consistent with monetary stability. The combined effect of the early post-war inflation and stabilization had put the economy firmly back on the rails by the turn of the 1950s: the excess liquidity in the economy at the end of the war had been absorbed; the introduction of compulsory reserves provided an effective instrument for controlling the banking system; public finances were on the mend; and the exchange rate of the *lira* had been set at a realistic and sustainable level.

Nearly all the countries of Europe emerged from the Second World War with repressed inflation owing to the imbalance between economic agents' holdings of liquidity and the level of prices and to the application of administrative controls that prevented this imbalance from translating into increases in prices (or at any rate spread their adjustment over a longer period). Italy overcame this situation by means of the inflationary flare-up of 1946–47 and the subsequent monetary stabilization. Inflation, however, not only eliminated the liquidity overhang but resulted in liquidity conditions becoming much tighter than normal. At the end of 1947, the ratio of money to GDP was half its pre-war value and only returned to its earlier level towards the end of the 1950s. Inflation also reduced enormously the value of other financial assets in real terms (especially that of government securities).

At the beginning of the 1950s, there was thus a certain shortage of liquidity in the Italian economy, as the relatively high level of short-term interest rates confirms, and, more generally, of financial assets. This situation made monetary control easier in several respects. Compared with countries where there was still repressed inflation, it was less likely that temporary problems in controlling the money supply (which none the less did arise from time to time) would have a significant effect on inflation, since they could be more easily absorbed within the general tendency for the ratio between money and GDP to return to a more normal level. Moreover, the fact that investors sought to rebuild their portfolios of government securities made it easier to fund the Treasury's borrowing requirement in the market.

Another favourable condition consisted in the renewed 'grip' of the central bank on the banking system, which had emerged from the period of inflation and stabilization much reduced in size in real terms but with a balance sheet structure that had been largely restored to normality. Notably, the ratios of loans and liquidity to deposits were back in line with those prevailing before the war. Thus, as early as 1948, Italian banks were no longer in a position to fuel an autonomous process of credit and deposit expansion by drawing on excess liquidity in their possession, nor were they able to emulate their counterparts in other countries and obtain monetary base by selling securities, the prices of which were stabilized by the central bank. Refinancing was also strictly controlled by the Bank of Italy, which applied rationing in accordance with the principle that such resources should only be used to offset seasonal shortages of liquidity. Italian banks were therefore notably dependent on the policy of the central bank even before the Korean War and continued to be so throughout the 1950s (although there were obviously moments in which monetary control posed problems).

What use did the Bank of Italy make of the opportunities offered by these favourable circumstances? Generally speaking, the monetary policy it pursued in the 1950s was marked by greater attention to the long-run effects of monetary stability than to the requirements of short-term control. As mentioned earlier, Menichella saw price stability as being important primarily because it created the environment most conducive to saving and investment and to increased Italian participation in international trade. Consistently with this view, he tended to stress the need for monetary policy to provide business with as stable and certain a framework as possible.[29]

This aversion to the risk of excessively variable monetary policy impulses associated with an overly short-term management of money and credit helps to explain the Bank's philosophy with regard to the instruments it employed. There is clear evidence that the Bank made little use of the traditional instruments of monetary control: the official rates were not changed for eight years (from 6 April 1950 to 7 June 1958), whereas in the same period they were altered twelve times in the United Kingdom, eight times in France and thirteen times in Germany; the compulsory reserve ratio remained the same from the beginning to the end of the decade;[30] and the central bank did not intervene in the open market. Factors contributing to this orientation included the limited development of Italy's money and financial markets, which resulted in a tendency to use instruments that did not work via the markets (such as the authorization of loans in excess of one-fifth of the lending bank's capital and of issues of shares and bonds, the moral suasion the

Bank of Italy applied to the leading banks and its discretionary control of refinancing).[31] Lastly, at least compared with the United Kingdom and France (but not Germany), there was the fact that the situation in Italy probably called for less intervention. This can be attributed to Italy having put its house in order earlier than the other countries by freeing itself more rapidly of the monetary and financial effects of the war and accumulating adequate reserves.

One crucial aspect of the stabilization programme was the exchange rate policy that was pursued. In contrast with what happened in 1926–27, the authorities sought to ensure that the *lira* did not appreciate excessively in relation to the domestic price level once inflation had been tamed. The aim was to establish an exchange rate that would allow the external account to be brought rapidly back into balance without having to lower domestic prices significantly (in addition, that is, to the elimination of the speculative peaks recorded in the summer of 1947, which had not yet been incorporated in incomes and values).

The adjustment of the *lira*/dollar exchange rate took place in November 1947. Since the other European countries kept their currencies overvalued with respect to the dollar until the pound sterling was devalued in 1949, Italy enjoyed nearly two years in which the *lira* was at a realistic level against the dollar and undervalued with respect to the other European currencies. These favourable circumstances, together with the reacquired control over domestic prices, explain the spectacular improvement in Italy's foreign exchange situation in the two years 1948–49.

The accumulation of reserves, to which the Marshall Plan also contributed, was an important component of Menichella's strategy. It made it possible to hold more steadily to the policy of liberalizing foreign trade, which was one of the principal factors in the modernization of the Italian economy, and to cope with adverse movements in the balance of payments without having to adopt restrictive policies of a severity that would have significantly slowed the growth of the economy. During the 1950s the competitiveness of Italian products increased owing to the greater stability of Italy's domestic prices compared with the average for the other European countries. Notwithstanding the devaluation of other currencies, such as the French *franc*, the *lira* accordingly arrived at the appointment with convertibility and the construction of the European common market in better health than it had been at the beginning of the decade.

Conclusions

Is there a single strand linking the events summarily described above? In my view, such a unifying theme can be identified in the process whereby Italy's central bank developed in a relatively backward economy. The question of the country's economic backwardness in the first 50 or 60 years of the Bank's existence is of central importance in at least two respects. On the one hand, it tended to aggravate the difficulties and obstacles the Bank of Italy had to overcome compared with those encountered by its counterparts in other countries. On the other hand, it explains the tension that existed for much of the time between reality and aspiration: the Bank appears to have been constantly seeking to implement a model that was always one or two steps ahead of conditions in the country. In short, the Bank was called upon to operate in a country committed to making the effort needed to close a wide economic gap; from the beginning its activity both contributed to and was conditioned by this effort.

Indeed, if we look at the first 60 years of the Bank's existence, we find relatively few 'normal' years: broadly speaking, the Giolittian era and the 1950s. For the rest, wars and the aftermath of wars, bank crises, depressions, inflation and monetary stabilization were more the rule than the exception. None the less, and despite the doubts about its vitality, the sapling planted in 1893 took root and developed into a landmark in the Italian institutional panorama.

The Bank's development occurred in several directions, three of which deserve to be mentioned here: the defence of the autonomy of monetary control with respect to the funding requirements of the Treasury; the evolution of its relationship with the banking system; and the strengthening of its technical and operational structures, both in terms of its ability to carry out analyses and formulate proposals and as regards the creation and use of the necessary instruments.

There were several extremely tense phases in the Bank's relations with the Treasury in connection with the preparations for and the conduct of the wars in which the country was involved. The most critical phase, as we have seen, began in the mid-1930s with the abandonment of the principle, which had been adhered to even in the most dramatic moments of the First World War, that extraordinary financing of the government had to be authorized by an act having the force of law. One of the institutional pillars erected under the stabilization programme implemented in the wake of the Second World War was the reintroduction of this principle.

The history of the Bank's relationship with the banking system is basically similar to that of the nascent central banks of other countries.

In Italy, as elsewhere, there was initially a mixture of cooperation and competition owing to the fact that the banks of issue combined the function of lender of last resort with a presence in the market alongside the commercial banks supplying services to private customers. The definitive clarification of the Bank of Italy's role came in the period between the two wars, when it was entrusted with the supervision of the commercial banks and prohibited from discounting non-bank customers' bills. This established the Bank's leadership and control functions and turned it, to use the expression current at the time, into the banker's bank.

Much of the development of the Bank's organization and operations paralleled the evolution of its functions and can be seen as both the effect of and the precondition for the assignment of new duties. Two aspects of the process are especially noteworthy. In the first place, the strengthening of the Bank's analytical capabilities in both economic and technical fields, which began in the 1930s and continued in the following decades, contributed significantly to its standing and influence. It appears as if the authority initially stemming from the personal prestige of its top management was somehow 'institutionalized' in the Bank. In the second place, the range of instruments with which to implement monetary and banking policies was extended, although the process was far from linear, with standstills and even retrenchments.

From the turn of the 1960s, a new phase opened for the Bank, in which to a great extent the problems it has been called upon to face have been different from those encountered in the first 60 years of its existence. While the distinguishing feature of the first period was the relative backwardness of the economy and all that this implied, the second saw the gap closed in many respects but has since been marked by all the problems of an advanced industrial economy with persistent fundamental disequilibria. Historical analysis of this second period is still at an early stage; the results it will produce are likely to improve our understanding of the tendencies that have been at work in these more recent decades.

Notes

1. For a discussion of the issues raised in this section, see the introduction in Bonelli (1991).
2. M. Ferraris, cited in Confalonieri (1980: 87). The quotation is from La nuova Banca d'Italia, in *Nuova Antologia*, May 1893.
3. Riflessioni in disordine sulle crisi, in *La riforma sociale* (1931: 41). Stringher headed the Bank of Italy from 1900 to 1930 and Miraglia, the *Banco di Napoli* – the second larger bank of issue – from 1897 to 1926.

4. The other two surviving banks of issue were the *Banco di Napoli* and the *Banco di Sicilia*, which were much smaller than the Bank of Italy (they accounted for about one quarter of the total note issue). Contrary to the situation prevailing before the banking reform of 1893–94, they fully accepted the leadership of the Bank of Italy. As Tito Canovai (deputy director general of the Bank from 1914 to 1921) put it, 'although we have a system of plurality of banks of issue, the agreement is so complete between them that it is not perceived that there is a plurality of banks' (National Monetary Commission, 1910: 519). To the question: 'Practically, you only have one bank as regards discount?' he answered: 'Yes. The regulations of the law are the same for the three banks and [...] the cordial relations existing between them have practically eliminated all the disadvantages arising from a plurality of banks. As the Bank of Italy is very much larger than the other two, it is in a position virtually to control the market' (pp. 523–4). The Italian system was very close to what Vera Smith called a 'residuary monopoly' in the note issue: 'A residuary monopoly denotes a case where there are a number of note issuers, but all these except one are working under narrow limitations, and this one authority is responsible for the bulk of the circulation, and is the sole bank possessing that measure of elasticity in its note issue which gives it the power to exercise control over the total amount of currency and credit available' (Smith, 1936: 148).
5. Ministero per la Costituente (1946: 53).
6. In addition to metallic reserves, those eligible included, within limits established by law, securities and bills drawn on foreign market places.
7. As writers of the period clarified, elasticity was not to be confused with extendibility. One, for instance, noted that 'Elasticity, which allows the note issue to expand and *contract* easily, is certainly a desirable quality for the note issue. But it is very different from mere *extendibility*, which is what is meant by those who call for a more elastic note issue when they really mean a larger note issue. Elasticity is the ability of paper currency both to expand and to contract. Now, the note issue, which expands without any difficulty, cannot be truly elastic, because during its expansion it does not accumulate the force required to return to its original size when the need for its expansion has passed' (G. Del Vecchio, 'I limiti della circolazione bancaria', 1912, in *Cronache della lira in pace e in guerra*, (1932: 36–7).
8. The interest rate on such deposits was not allowed to be more than one third of the discount rate and if their total exceeded certain limits, the note issue had to be reduced by three-quarters of the excess amount. These restrictions were subsequently eased, then suspended in 1914 and finally abolished in 1927–28.
9. The 1866 decree provided for the Minister of Finance to grant the necessary authorization, but this power was subsequently transferred to the Treasury Minister (see *Ricerche per la storia della Banca d'Italia*, vol. 1, Legislation appendix, Collana storica della Banca d'Italia-Contributi, Laterza, Roma-Bari, 1990).
10. One such conflict occurred in 1898. See the minutes of the meeting of the Bank of Italy's Governing Board on 22 August in Bonelli, (1991: 537–41).
11. The reduced rate could be applied in discounting bills with top quality

signatures and maturities of up to three months, provided the note issue did not exceed the limits laid down by law.

12. In 1878 the Bank of England had decided to charge customers rates in line with those prevailing in the market, while reserving its official rates, which were normally higher, to transactions with bill brokers. The *Reichsbank* had also been authorized in 1880 to charge preferential rates below its official rates. By contrast, the Bank of France only applied the official rates.
13. See Confalonieri (1980, vol. 1: 101–8), and Fanno (1933: 84–6).
14. In particular, the penalties for exceeding the limit on the note issue were made less severe and the scope for engaging in the deposit business was broadened. As mentioned earlier, in 1907 the maximum rate of the tax on the note issue was lowered from twice the discount rate to 7.5 per cent; in 1909 the limits on the amounts of deposits the banks of issue were free to take were raised and the interest rate capped at three-quarters of the rate on postal savings.
15. See the grounds on which the Bank justified its request for more flexible legislation on the note issue after the 1907 crisis in Bonelli (1991: 26–30).
16. See Cotula and Spaventa (1993: 134–7); Ripa di Meana (1993).
17. In addition to making the foundation of new banks and the opening of new branches subject to ministerial authorization (to be granted after consulting the Bank of Italy), the law imposed three fundamental restrictions: a minimum capital requirement for new banks; a maximum value for the ratio of deposits to own funds; and a ceiling on the credit that could be granted to a single customer. Generally speaking, the aim was to keep administrative interference in the management of banks to a minimum (in the Bank of Italy's annual report for 1926 Stringher wrote that 'the new legislation has avoided especially rigorous provisions so as not to hinder the free working of credit'). At the same time, however, the authorities avoided interfering with the 'model' of commercial banking that had emerged in the post-war period, notable features of which were the ownership structure, with the major banks controlling themselves, and the interlocking relationship with industrial firms.
18. Menichella (1986: 194). Menichella was one of the architects of the reorganization of the Italian banking system between the two wars and was Governor of the Bank of Italy from 1948 to 1960.
19. 'It was certainly not intended that these provisions should eliminate every danger and drawback or give depositors a firm guarantee, because such a guarantee, rather than deriving from provisions of law, should stem primarily from the ability, careful management and integrity of the persons to whom banks' destinies are entrusted.' (Banca d'Italia, *Relazione annuale sul 1926*: 71).
20. *The Istituto di liquidazioni* replaced the Special Autonomous Section of the *Consorzio per Sovvenzioni su Valori Industriali*, which had been set up in 1922 to handle the banking crises of the period (notably those of *Banca Italiana di Sconto* and *Banco di Roma*). As the institution's name indicates, the aim was to liquidate the assets remaining from the earlier interventions and certainly not to accumulate new ones. This objective had to be abandoned, however, when the crisis of the leading banks broke out in the early 1930s and in 1933 the Istituto di liquidazioni was replaced by the *Istituto per la Ricostruzione Industriale* (IRI). See Guarino and Toniolo (1993).

21. See Cotula and Spaventa (1993: 159–75).
22. Article 2 of the Ministerial Decree of 31 December 1936.
23. The documents show that the requirement of 'prior agreement' with the Governor of the Bank of Italy for the granting of advances was considered little more than a formality. According to the report of the Director General of the Treasury accompanying the measure, the Bank of Italy 'wanted to word the article so as not to give the impression that the Treasury could request supplies of bank notes at its pleasure and without limit ... Essentially, this is a formal amendment of a tactful nature, as it were, designed, as noted, to avoid giving readers of the agreement the impression that the Bank of Italy must supply bank notes in unlimited amounts at the simple request of the Treasury' ('Appunto per il Ministro delle Finanze del 29 Dicembre 1936', in Caracciolo (1992: Document no. 4.)
24. Hawtrey (1932: 268).
25. The main practical consequence of this change was that the owners of the Bank capital were restricted to saving banks, public law banks and banks of national interest, insurance and social security institutes.
26. See Gelsomino (1994).
27. At the end of 1945 price increases ranged from three or four times for some basic necessities subject to control up to 50 times or more for goods not subject to control.
28. Published in Ricossa and Tuccimei (1992).
29. In his last 'Concluding Remarks' to the Bank of Italy's shareholders' meeting, Menichella defined the monetary policy pursued in the 13 years from the post-war stabilization as 'simple in its means, frugal in its interventions and serving to confer autonomy and certainty to economic activity. Hence a stable and clearly defined framework that differed from that of other countries where, either because of the persistence of problems of excessive liquidity and public debt management or owing to a lack of foreign currency reserves, the process of liberalizing trade has been marked by stops and goes, enterprises have been, and still are, led by turns to speed up and slow down the implementation of their programmes, and individuals have been pushed first one way and then another in their consumption and saving decisions.' (Banca d'Italia, *Relazione annuale sul 1959*: 353).
30. The range of securities that could be used to meet the reserve requirement was none the less narrowed in 1953, when it was restricted to Treasury bills.
31. These instruments were supplemented by overfunding of the Treasury's borrowing requirement, especially through the issue of Treasury bonds.

References

Banca d'Italia (1926), *Relazione annuale sul 1926*.

Banca d'Italia (1959), *Relazione annuale sul 1959*.

Bonelli, F. (ed.) (1991), *La Banca d'Italia dal 1894 al 1913. Momenti della formazione di una banca centrale*, Collana storica della Banca d'Italia-Documenti, Roma-Bari, Laterza.

Caracciolo, A. (ed.) (1992), *La Banca d'Italia tra l'autarchia e la guerra 1936–1945*, Collana storica della Banca d'Italia-Documenti, Roma-Bari, Laterza.

Confalonieri, A. (1980), *Banca e industria in Italia 1894–1906*, Bologna, Il Mulino.

Cotula, F. and Spaventa, L. (eds) (1993), *La politica monetaria tra le due guerre 1919–1935*, Collana storica della Banca d'Italia-Documenti, Roma-Bari, Laterza.

Del Vecchio, G. (1932), 'I limiti della circolazione bancaria', in *Cronache della lira in pace e in guerra*, Milano-Roma, Treves.

Einaudi, L. (1931), 'Riflessioni in disordine sulle cris', in *La riforma sociale.*

Fanno, M. (1933), *Lezioni di economia e legislazione bancaria*, CEDAM, Padova.

Gelsomino, C.O. (1994), 'Da istituto di emissione a banca delle banche. Le operazioni di credito della Banca d'Italia tra le due guerre mondiali', in *Ricerche per la storia della Banca d'Italia*, V, Collana storica della Banca d'Italia-Contributi, Roma-Bari.

Guarino, G. and Toniolo, G. (eds) (1993), *La Banca d'Italia e il sistema bancario 1919–1936*, Collana storica della Banca d'Italia-Documenti, Roma-Bari, Laterza.

Hawtrey, R. (1932), *The Art of Central Banking*, Longmans, London, Green and Co.

Menichella, D. (1986), 'Il riordinamento del sistema bancario italiano del 1933–1936', in *Scritti e discorsi scelti*, Roma, Banca d'Italia.

Ministero per la Costituente (1946), *Rapporto della Commissione Economica, IV, Credito e Assicurazione*, Roma, Istituto Poligrafico dello Stato.

National Monetary Commission (1910), *Interviews on the Banking and Currency Systems of England, Scotland, France, Germany, Switzerland, and Italy*, Washington, Government Printing Office.

Ricerche per la storia della Banca d'Italia (1990), 1, Legislation appendix, Collana storica della Banca d'Italia-Contributi, Roma-Bari 1990, Laterza.

Ricossa, S. and Tuccimei, E. (eds) (1992), *La Banca d'Italia e il risanamento postbellico 1945–1948*, Collana storica della Banca d'Italia-Documenti, Roma-Bari, Laterza.

Ripa di Meana, A. (1993), *Il consolidamento del debito e la stabilizzazione Mussolini, in Ricerche per la storia della Banca d'Italia*, vol. II, Collana storica della Banca d'Italia-Contributi, Roma-Bari, Laterza.

Smith, V. (1936), *The Rationale of Central Banking*, London, P.S. King and Son.

CHAPTER SEVEN

The Emergence of National Central Banks in Central Europe after the Break-up of the Austro-Hungarian Monarchy

Aurel Schubert[1]

> Central banking is a learning process, by trial and errors and the errors of the central banks are trials for the holders of their bank notes.
>
> Bácskai (1994)

Introduction

The break-up of the Austro-Hungarian monarchy in late 1918 not only signalled the split of a political entity into several new ones, but also an end to economic and monetary union. Attempts to save the economic and monetary links were unsuccessful, as the euphoria for the newly gained independence called for the common institutions to be dismantled.[2] The new countries wanted to establish new political but also new economic institutions. Among the latter were national central banks. It took the successor states more than four years, the repeated experience of hyperinflation and foreign interventions in several of the countries to establish their own national central banks. The developments on the way to stabilization and the establishment of banks of issue show many similarities in the respective countries. The politicians in the newly formed countries had to realize that their economies were still very interdependent. In particular the developments in Austria and Hungary, but also those in Poland, showed many similarities: large fiscal imbalances, the need for central bank financing, hyperinflation, foreign financial interventions and economic stabilization with the help of the League of Nations.

The newly formed central banks were immediately subject to very difficult and challenging tests. They had to succeed and build up credibility in a very unfavourable economic environment. Their inception was marked by the dissolution of a monetary union as well as of a customs union, with all the attendant negative trade-reducing repercussions, grave economic problems, such as the legacy of a four-year-long war, and the traumatic experience of hyperinflation in Austria, Hungary and Poland.

After a brief description of the initial political, economic and monetary situation in Central Europe after the First World War, this chapter will focus on the emergence of national central banks in Austria, Hungary and Czechoslovakia. It will be shown that the process of monetary disintegration was a rather chaotic one, driven mainly by national political considerations. The process of building national central banks proved to be more difficult than anticipated, especially in an environment of very large fiscal deficits and – for Austria and Hungary – large internal as well as external imbalances. Foreign help and foreign pressure – especially via the League of Nations and its stabilization loans – played a crucial role in the emergence of the national banks of issue. But the new central banks were confronted with very fragile macroeconomic and financial situations in their respective countries and had to play a major role in the rescue and consolidation of their respective national banking systems.

The political, economic and monetary situation after the First World War

From 1867 to 1918 the Austro-Hungarian monarchy consisted of two independent states which were linked together, on the one hand, by the person of the Sovereign, and, on the other, by the administration of so-called 'common' areas, based on identical laws in both countries. In addition to these common affairs there were other common interests for which the treatment was laid down and regulated, always for a period of ten years, by laws passed in the Austrian and Hungarian Parliaments alike (Rasín, 1923: 3). Among these was the regulation of the currency.

The Austro-Hungarian Bank had been instituted as a common central bank in 1878 as the successor of the *Privilegirte Oesterreichische National-Bank* (Chartered Austrian National Bank), which 'had been established in 1816, mainly for the purpose of undertaking the withdrawal of circulation of the paper currency of the Austrian Government'(Zuckerkandl, 1911: 57). The period between 1867 and 1878 had been marked by continuing struggles to maintain the unity of the central bank and the currency. Despite Hungarian ambitions to have its own central bank, it was possible to convert the Austrian National Bank into the Austro-Hungarian Bank (*Österreichisch-Ungarische Bank*).

The Austro-Hungarian monarchy went onto a gold exchange standard in 1892 when the *krone* (crown) replaced the *gulden* as the currency with one kilogram of gold being equal to 3280 *kronen*, sometimes characterized as a 'limping gold standard', as the currency was never legally put on a gold standard and as no gold currency circulated.[3] The bank notes had to be fully covered by gold, bills of exchange, or loans against securities, but of the total cover at least 40 per cent had to be in the form of metallic reserve. The Austro-Hungarian government was entitled to require of the Austro-Hungarian Bank a 5 per cent tax for those bank notes which had been issued in excess of the required quota of metallic cover.

At the outbreak of the war, in August 1914, two amendments to the statutes of the Austro-Hungarian Bank were passed. The prohibition of granting loans to the state and the 40 per cent metallic cover requirement for the bank notes issued were suspended, as was the requirement to publish a regular (that is, weekly) statement of its position. The government authorized the Bank to ignore the prohibition to lend to the government and suspended the gold conversion. The note printing press once again became the principal source of assistance in defraying the costs of the war. 'Immediately on the outbreak of the war the management of the Bank realized that its first duty was to assist by every means in its power the States of the Monarchy, whose very existence was threatened by the war.'[4]

The resources of the Bank were drawn upon directly as well as indirectly by the Treasury. The State borrowed against Treasury bills either directly from the Bank or indirectly via private banks, which then presented these bills for rediscounting to the Austro-Hungarian Bank. In addition, the public borrowed from the Bank against war loans. As Walré de Bordes concluded: 'By the end of the War the [bank]notes represented nothing but the credit of the State: except from a legal point of view they had become Treasury notes' (Walré de Bordes, 1924: 51). In Rasín's words, 'the bank notes in circulation had ceased to be actual bank notes. Nominally they were bank notes, in reality, however, Government notes of the Austro-Hungarian Monarchy; and, considering that they were not exchangeable for gold and were forced currency, they might quite correctly be regarded as a Government bank-note debt, or as a Government forced loan, the Government, not the Bank, being the debtor, and every one who had accepted bank notes a creditor. In fact, the crippled gold standard had been replaced by an immensely inflated paper currency' (Rasín, 1923: 12).

During the war the currency had already lost a large part of its external value. By December 1918 a *gold krone* was worth 3.3

papierkronen, while they had been of equal value at the start of the military conflict.[5]

Break-up of the monarchy

On 12 November 1918, the Republic of Austria was proclaimed. The empire was split into many parts, which either became new states – the so-called successor states – or joined existing ones: Austria, Hungary, Czechoslovakia, Romania, Italy, Kingdom of the Serbs, Croats and Slovenes, as well as Poland.

The boundaries of the new Austrian republic were fixed by the Treaty of St Germain. The new Austria – 'the unhappy country which was created not by the will of its inhabitants but because the victors, having satisfied the claims of every other race of the former Austrian Empire, could find nothing better to do with German-Austrians than to force on them an undesired independence and such territory as their neighbours had no use for' (Gedye, 1931a: 547) – represented only 13 per cent of the area of the old monarchy with 13 per cent of its population; or 28 per cent of the area of pre-war Austria, with 23 per cent of its population. Austria no longer had access to the sea. More than 50 per cent of the population was rural, but most parts of the agricultural land had fallen to Hungary and Czechoslovakia, while Austria 'inherited ... a sizeable industrial endowment, but was marred by considerable and not easily remediable disproportionalities' (März and Weber, 1983: 502). Its economic structure was very unbalanced, more so than in any other of the successor states. It was hit hardest by the economic disintegration of the customs union of the monarchy and it was deprived of many of its vital sources of supply either for food or for raw materials.

The peace treaty with Hungary, signed at Trianon, reduced the area of Hungary by more than 70 per cent and the population from 20.9 to about 7.8 million (Siklos, 1994: 276).

Disintegration of the currency

Like the monarchy itself, the currency fell victim to the First World War. The monetary guidelines pursued up to then (external stability of the currency, gold cover requirements, independence of the Austro-Hungarian Bank, prohibition of state financing by the central bank, complete freedom of international payments and capital transactions) had given way to the constraints of a wartime economy, something which was reflected in the value of the *krone*. By the end of the war, its value had shrunk to one-sixteenth of its internal value in terms of the cost of living and to one-third of its external value measured in terms of the *krone*'s exchange rate on the Zurich foreign exchange market.[6]

During the first months after the disintegration of the Austro-Hungarian monarchy, the Austro-Hungarian *krone* (crown) continued to be legal tender in the new successor states of the monarchy.[7] The question of the future currency presented itself quite differently in the different parts of the former monarchy. Some parts were joined to existing states with existing currencies (for example to Italy, Romania or Serbia), others parts formed newly independent successor states and either needed new currencies or had to decide on staying in a monetary union with Austria and Hungary. And finally, Austria and Hungary would theoretically have been able to carry on with the old system.

It was the Yugoslav government that started the wave of separations in January 1919. To this end, it stamped the Austro-Hungarian bank notes in circulation within its territory. However, due to technical problems, it had to repeat the stamping process at the end of November 1919. The first successful stamping occurred in Czechoslovakia in early March 1919. This forced the Austrian government to do the same a few days later while Hungary waited another year until the peace treaty had sanctioned this practice (Table 7.1).

The Austro-Hungarian Bank considered the stampings to be infringements of its privilege to issue currency for the whole empire and therefore unlawful. It sent notes of protest to both the Czech government – on 26 February 1919 – and to the Austrian government – on 6 March 1919 (Rasín, 1923: 29ff and Kerschagl, 1920: 39). Rasín, the Minister of Finance of the new state of Czechoslovakia, justified the action with the need to put up a defence against the 'systematic destruction of the Austro-Hungarian *krone*' by the Austro-Hungarian Bank (hereafter

Table 7.1 Dates of bank note stampings

Country	Date
Yugoslavia	8–20 January 1919 and 26 November–15 December 1919
Czechoslovakia	3–9 March 1919
Austria	12–29 March 1919
Italy	April 1919
Romania	16 June–15 July 1919
Hungary	18–27 March 1920
Poland	16–26 April 1920

Source: Kerschagl (1920) and Walré de Bordes (1924: 40).

AHB). He especially criticized the fact that the AHB had made advances of 75 per cent on deposits of war loans, although the price of this security had fallen to 60 per cent and that it 'has thereby shown a total disregard alike of the interests of its shareholders and of the State' (Rasín, 1923: 30).

The purpose of the stampings was to create new national currencies and also to restrict inflation by limiting the quantity of paper money in circulation in the respective countries (Walré de Bordes, 1924: 40). Since Hungary was, except for Poland, the last of the Central European countries to implement this stamping, it had to absorb some of the notes circulating in the other successor states, causing serious problems for itself (Szapáry, 1994: 4).

Currency separation was generally characterized by two common features: the Austro-Hungarian Bank was bypassed and each state tried to shift the burden of responsibility onto its former fellow states. Throughout this chaotic dissolution process, opportunities for arbitrage and speculation arose, primarily triggered by the search for optimum conversion rates, the circumvention of new borders and the use of counterfeit stamps on bank notes. All this led to apprehension and panic on the part of the population (Schubert and Theurl, 1995a: 43). There had been absolutely no coordination or harmonization in the dissolution of the currency union. Every country as well as every individual pursued their own self-interest.

Liquidation of the Austro-Hungarian Bank

The AHB went into liquidation on 11 September 1919, the day after the signing of the Peace Treaty of St Germain. On 31 December 1919, it ceased most of its operations. On 1 January 1920, the Austro-Hungarian Bank was divided into three sections:

1. the bank in liquidation,
2. the *Oesterreichische Geschäftsführung* (Austrian section), and
3. the *Ungarische Geschäftsführung* (Hungarian section).

The Austrian section served as the temporary central bank for Austria and the Hungarian one as that for Hungary. Part of the assets and liabilities of the AHB were subsequently transferred to these sections. In August 1920, liquidators were appointed in accordance with the provisions of the Treaties of St Germain and Trianon.

Soon after the liquidation the flight from the *krone* started. According to the analysis of Sir William Goode, 'fathers of families who wanted to lay by dependable property values for their children, working men who thought of their old age, then began to set aside foreign currency'.[8] 'In some cases Austrian crowns were converted at the current rate into Swiss *francs*, Czechoslovak *crowns*, *guilders*, or dollars', as reported by Charles Rist (Walré de Bordes, 1924: 191). This shows how different the further developments of the respective currencies were in Austria and in Czechoslovakia. The Czech *crown* became a safe haven for Austrians trying to hedge against the losses caused by inflation. 'The less confidence the public felt in the future of Austria, the more it endeavoured to hoard foreign exchange at all costs and the higher soared the rates of foreign exchange' (Walré de Bordes, 1924: 191).

The emergence of national central banks: Austria

Initial conditions

In 1921 and 1922, it was the desperate situation of the Austrian state finances which was the chief cause of the public's pessimism concerning the future of the Austrian currency. The tremendous uncovered deficit of the state budget (for instance, during the second half of 1921, the government's receipts covered no more than 35.7 per cent of its expenditures) was largely due to food subsidies and was financed by placing Treasury bills with the Austrian section of the central bank in liquidation.[9] This led to continuous increases in the amount of money in circulation and resulted in hyperinflation.

'The extraordinary depreciation of the Austrian crown was at bottom a psychological development. There was a total lack of confidence. In view of the situation of the Austrian State's finances it was generally expected that the crown would continue to plunge further and further'

Table 7.2 Austria: cost of living index, 1919–23

Date	Index
January 1919	2 854
1920	4 587
1921	10 720
1922	90 215
1923	1 349 725

Note: July 1914 = 100.

Source: Kamitz (1949: 173).

Table 7.3 Exchange rate of the Swiss *franc* in Vienna, 1918–22

Date	Exchange rate
31 December 1918	322.75
1919	2 950.00
1920	10 000.00
1921	13 285.00
1922	12 395.00

Source: Kamitz (1949: 173).

(Walré de Bordes, 1924: 197). Therefore, it is no wonder that the first question which the Austrian population asked every afternoon was, 'How are the foreign exchanges moving?' or more exactly, 'What does Zurich say about the crown?' (Walré de Bordes, 1924: 197).

Intervention by the League of Nations

In 1920 the chairman of the Reparations Commission for Austria, Goode, presented a plan for the consolidation of the Austrian financial situation. In 1921 the League of Nations (LoN) sent a delegation to Vienna in order to discuss with the Austrian government ways to restore fiscal balance. The League of Nations made the creation of an independent central bank one of the prerequisites for financial help (Kamitz, 1949: 175). However, it took until October 1922 – after Dr Seipel had become Austrian Chancellor and chief negotiator and had made a desperate plea to the world to help Austria – that the loan agreement could finally be signed in Geneva. In exchange for a guaranteed loan to the amount of 650 million *gold kronen* the Austrian government pledged to balance its budget by reducing government outlays and by increasing revenues as well as establishing an independent central bank (see below). The League of Nations sent a Dutch Commissioner General, A.F. Zimmermann, to Vienna with far-reaching powers to set strict limits on the Austrian government's financial sovereignty.[10]

On 18 November 1922, the government ceased to use the central bank for budgetary financing. The value of the *krone* had already recovered before the printing press was stopped. The news of the successful negotiations had restored confidence in the currency.[11]

According to the League's plan the budget should have been balanced after two years. In fact, a balanced budget was reached after only one and a half years, as a result of much higher receipts than had been foreseen.

Table 7.4 Exchange rate between *gold krone* (gold crown) and *papierkrone* (paper crown) in Austria (*papierkronen* for one *gold krone*; end of month values), 1914–22

Date	Exchange rate
June 1914	1.01
December 1914	1.16
December 1918	3.30
December 1920	99.60
September 1921	300.81
October 1921	634.05
November 1921	1 223.19
December 1921	1 261.38
January 1922	1 780
February 1922	1 270
March 1922	1 550
April 1922	1 570
May 1922	2 100
June 1922	3 600
July 1922	7 500
August 1922	17 000
September 1922	15 100
October 1922	15 050
November 1922	14 690
December 1922	14 380
January 1922	14 500

Source: Pressburger (1966: 361).

The help of the League proved to be crucial for the successful stabilization of Austria. In 1923, Irving Fisher judged that 'there is no precedent in history to the appeal of Austria to the Society of Nations to be saved from ruin and the response which followed ... But the Austrian case affords a striking precedent for the case of Germany today' (Fisher, 1923: 80). According to Gedye 'the alternative was anarchy and dissolution'(Gedye, 1931a: 547). However, the League of Nations stabilization programme did not address the fundamental structural problems of the Austrian economy such as, for example, its unbalanced external accounts. Its persistent current account deficits had to be covered by foreign loans, the gradual selling-off of Austrian-owned shares in industrial undertakings which after the collapse of the monarchy became foreign undertakings because they were situated on the soil of successor states, and by constantly renewed short-term loans (Gedye, 1931a: 550). In addition, as Hertz concluded in his analyses, 'the new States in Central and Eastern Europe were foremost in following a policy of extreme protectionism, and in consequence Austria has been almost strangled to death' (Hertz, 1931: 558). Contemporary calculations showed that, for instance, in 1927 the average tariff in Austria was 19.2 per cent compared to 36.4 per cent in Czecholslovakia or 31.1 per cent in Hungary (Hertz, 1947: 558).[12]

Creation of the central bank

On 1 January 1923, the duties and the assets (31 billion *kronen*) of the Austrian Section (*Oesterreichische Geschäftsführung*) of the old Austro-Hungarian Bank were taken over by the newly established Austrian central bank, the *Oesterreichische Nationalbank* (OeNB; Austrian National Bank) (Compass, 1935: 261). Its establishment was based on two Federal Acts of 24 July and 14 November 1922.

From the beginning of the dictated liquidation of the Austro-Hungarian Bank it was clear that Austria would need to establish its own central bank (Pressburger, 1966: 358). The majority view was that order in the government's finances would have to be restored before a bank of issue could be established. Several plans were presented, for instance by Joseph Schumpeter, Richard Reisch and Otto Bauer. Schumpeter's plan called first for a balancing of the budget via a general increase in taxes and a wealth tax and then for the creation of a central bank that would be independent of the government but under the auspices of the provinces (*Länder*). Reisch planned to cover the budget deficit by placing bonds abroad and then creating a central bank with foreign capital, while Bauer wanted to confiscate the foreign exchange holdings of the commercial banks for budgetary purposes and then to establish a gold currency with the help of American capital (Pressburger, 1966: 359).

When Ignaz Seipel became Chancellor in May 1922, he wanted to establish a central bank immediately. In June he introduced a bill in Parliament to set up a central bank with a capital of 100 million Swiss *francs* subscribed or guaranteed by the commercial banks. The state should not have any recourse to the funds of this bank, and the bank should be required to keep the foreign value of the Austrian currency stable until payment in specie would resume. Although the law passed swiftly through the legislature and the banks were willing to subscribe or guarantee the capital of the bank, it did not yet suffice to restore confidence in the ailing currency. A further foreign currency loan would have been necessary to help finance the budget deficit and to bolster the much needed foreign exchange reserves. A desperate plea by Seipel for a loan from the British government did not receive the hoped-for positive response, but it led to the Allied Powers putting the League of Nations in charge of an investigation into the Austrian financial situation. After a dramatic appearance of Seipel before the financial committee of the League of Nations on 6 September 1922, a committee was put in charge of preparing the protocols for a loan amounting to 650 million *gold kronen* to be guaranteed by several foreign governments.[13] The decline of the *krone* immediately stopped. With the signing of the protocols the way was open for the establishment of the independent *Oesterreichische Nationalbank* (OeNB).

The new central bank was established as an independent private joint stock company with an initial share capital set at 30 million *gold kronen* and subscribed by Austrians as well as foreigners.[14] Of this amount the Austrian government subscribed 8 million *gold kronen*, of which two-fifths were paid up in gold or foreign currency (League of Nations, 1924: 90).

The OeNB took over the former Foreign Exchange Centre (*Devisenzentrale*) with its assets (66 billion *kronen*)[15] through which all foreign exchange transactions had to pass since the reintroduction of a system of rigid controls in July 1922 (Compass, 1935: 270). It ceased to be a government institution under the control of the Minister of Finance and became a body of the OeNB. However, no change was made in its powers or in its financial policy. The OeNB also took over all the foreign exchange reserves of the *Devisenzentrale*. They constituted the major part of its initial endowment of foreign exchange reserves.

The National Bank Act of 14 November 1922 (an amendment to the Banking Law of 24 July 1922), stipulated in Article 1 of the Statutes that the OeNB should 'ensure with all means at its disposal that in the period until the redemption of bank notes in specie has been regulated by law, that the value of its notes – as expressed in the rate of foreign exchange from gold standard countries with a stable currency – will at least suffer no deterioration'.

The newly created central bank was – as required by the League of Nations – largely independent of the government. Its statutes were so framed as 'to make it as independent as possible of the Government' (Walré de Bordes, 1924: 44). The government's influence was limited to the right to nominate the President of the Bank, who was then appointed by the President of the Republic.[16] In addition, the government appointed a State Commissioner who had the right to attend the meetings of the decision-making bodies of the Bank (General Meeting of the Shareholders, General Council, Executive Committee, and Board of Management) without, however, a right to vote. His role was limited to watching over the observance of the laws and regulations governing the business of the Bank.[17] He had a suspensive veto against decisions which appeared to him not to be in conformity with the laws and regulations (Sokal and Rosenberg, 1929: 121).

The practice of increasing the circulation of bank notes in order to finance the government had already ceased on 18 November 1922. The Austrian government had pledged to the Provisional Delegation of the League of Nations that it would not after that date borrow from the Bank without offering real securities (Walré de Bordes, 1924: 52). This step was of great psychological importance: the public came forward immediately with the holdings of foreign exchange which it had accumulated during the previous years of hyperinflation.

The Statutes of the OeNB prevented it from granting unsecured loans to any part of government, be it central, provincial or local, or even to the Federal Railway Administration.[18] Article 50 of the Statutes of the OeNB explicitly specified this prohibition of monetary financing of government – one of the lessons learned from the painful experience of hyperinflation.[19] In addition, for as long as the central bank's money-issuing privilege was in force the government was explicitly forbidden to issue paper money or to take any action that could hinder the bank in securing the external stability of the Austrian currency.

The Statutes defined the Austrian currency as a gold currency, but temporarily without a fixed relation to gold and without an obligation to convert paper currency into specie.[20] However, during the first five years 20 per cent of the circulating notes and the short-term liabilities of the Bank minus the debt of the government held by the Bank had to be covered by gold and foreign exchange reserves, increasing to 28 per cent and to 33.3 per cent after five and ten years, respectively.[21] In the meantime the Bank was obliged to accumulate enough reserves so that specie payment could start as soon as two requirements were fulfilled: (1) after a fixed relationship between the Austrian currency and gold had been established and (2) after the government debt had been reduced to 30 million *gold kronen*. Payments to reduce gradually the old state debt began to be made regularly, starting on 1 January 1923.

Structure of the OeNB

At the head of the Bank was the General Council (*Generalrat*) consisting of the President, appointed for a period of five years by the President of the Republic, and thirteen members elected for a similar period by the General Meeting of Shareholders. The members of the General Council chose from their midst two Vice Presidents, whose election was subject to confirmation by the Austrian government. For the composition of the General Council, the Statutes of the Bank established a very interesting and innovative rule. The following branches of economic life had to be represented on the Council by one delegate each:

1. institutions engaged in the banking business,
2. savings banks,
3. industry,
4. commerce and trade,
5. agriculture, and
6. labour.[22]

In this way all sectors of the economy were involved in monetary policy decision making. In order to strengthen the independence of the Bank *vis-à-vis* the government, federal employees, members of either house of Parliament, and members of Provincial Diets were not eligible for membership in the General Council of the Bank. Foreigners (representing foreign shareholders) could be members of the Council, but their number could not exceed four.

If an urgent decision should become necessary on any subject reserved to the General Council, an Executive Committee, consisting of the President, both Vice Presidents, the General Manager and the Assistant General Manager had the authority to take decisions provisionally. Such decisions had then to be referred to the General Council at its next meeting. The day-to-day business of the bank was run by the General Manager and the other – three to five – members of the Board of Management (*Direktorium*), all appointed by the General Council. Dr Richard Reisch – a former Minister of Finance – was appointed as the first President of the Bank and Dr Viktor Brauneis as the first General Manager.[23] Based on the agreement with the League of Nations, the Bank received a foreign advisor with very far-reaching competencies. The first such advisor was the Vice President of the Swiss National Bank, Schnyder von Wartensee.[24]

The currency during the inter-war period

The foreign exchange reserves of the OeNB rose from 1.1 billion *papierkronen* to 3.8 billion *papierkronen* in its first year, 1923, as confidence returned and the public offered its foreign exchange holdings to the Bank (Walré de Bordes, 1924: 207). At the same time the circulation of Austrian *kronen* increased from 4.1 billion to 7.1 billion, that is by nearly the same amount as foreign exchange reserves. During this first year of the existence of the OeNB, retail prices in Austria rose – despite the large increase in the money supply – by only about 18–19 per cent while wholesale prices only moved upward by 7 per cent. Thus, retail prices in December 1923 were not higher than in September 1922. Two important factors were implicated in this development after the return of confidence in the stability of the domestic currency: foreign bank notes disappeared from circulation and the velocity of circulation, which had increased strongly during hyperinflationary times, returned to more normal levels. This counterbalanced the increase in the number of Austrian bank notes in circulation.

A possible rise in the foreign value of the *krone* due to large-scale investments in Austria was undesirable and therefore not allowed to occur. The strong appreciation of the Czechoslovak *crown* in 1921 had been a warning. The OeNB therefore decided not to leave the foreign exchange market to itself, but to stabilize the rate of the *krone*. The Bank bought up all the surplus offers and so created a substantial reserve of foreign exchange. In this way the foreign exchange and gold cover of circulation was almost doubled by 1923.

The first currency chosen as an anchor for the *krone* was the Swiss *franc*. However, a few months later it was replaced by a peg to the US dollar. In this way the *krone* became 'the most stable currency in Europe in relation to the dollar, in other words to gold' (Walré de Bordes, 1924: 219). Austria adopted via the 'dollar exchange standard' a 'gold exchange standard'. In this way Austria opted for the gold exchange standard without having any sizeable gold reserves or gold coins in circulation. Out of roughly 305 million *gold kronen* of reserves at the end of 1923 only 6.5 million *gold kronen* were in physical gold. The OeNB kept the *krone* stabilized by meeting and satisfying every surplus offer or surplus demand at the fixed rate of 71 060 *kronen* to the dollar. This quotation did not vary once during the second half of 1923 earning the *krone* the nickname 'Alpendollar'. The fixed exchange rate relative to the dollar left the value of the Austrian *krone* 'to be fixed by the credit policy of the Federal Reserve Board' (Walré de Bordes, 1924: 221).

The rate of exchange and the level of reserves were of great psychological significance after the traumatic experience of hyperinflation and the concurrent collapse of the value of the *krone*. In 1924 Walré de Bordes had to conclude that despite the great success of the stabilization of the *krone* and its linking to the dollar, 'the Austrian public is still so liable to nervous panics that the mere fact that the reserve of the Bank was seen to be diminishing for some time would give rise to a belief that a fall of the crown was imminent and would cause a speculative demand for foreign exchange and a fresh flight from the crown' (Walré de Bordes, 1924: 229).

Initial successes – like the stabilization of the currency – were followed by difficult challenges, either due to speculative excesses or due to the necessary but painful re-dimensioning of the Austrian financial sector. The year 1924 brought the first major tests for the young central bank and its management. First, a public quarrel with the last Governor of the Austro-Hungarian Bank, Dr Spitzmüller, developed over the right exchange rate relative to the dollar. He argued in favour of pegging the *krone* at K 60 000 to the dollar instead of the K 71 000 chosen by the bank. He warned of incipient inflationary dangers due, in his view, to the under-valuation of the Austrian currency and the large capital inflows caused by this 'wrong' valuation. February 1924 also brought a large-scale strike of the employees of the central bank. But the most important event of the year was the collapse of the speculation against the French *franc*. During the first two months of the year a massive speculative attack on the French currency had brought its value down by about 30 per cent.[25] A joint effort by the French government in cooperation with a secret consortium consisting of J.P. Morgan Bank from New York and the French branch of the Rothschilds in support of the French currency burst the bubble. The *franc* recovered within a very short period, and many Austrians – banks as well as individuals – who had participated in this speculation suffered heavy losses.[26] The concurrent strong decline on the Viennese stock exchange compounded the losses. In order to supply the market with the necessary liquidity, the OeNB had to act as lender of last resort and discount massive amounts of bills of exchange. Many small banks and a mid-sized institution, the *Depositenbank*, collapsed, starting an unavoidable and very costly ten-year-long process of banking consolidation in Austria.

All rescue efforts for the *Depositenbank* – which included an active participation of the OeNB – could not save this institution. In order to defend the currency and the foreign exchange reserves and to discourage the excessive use of the discount window, the OeNB raised – with the explicit approval of the representatives of the League of Nations – the discount rate in two steps from 9 to 15 per cent. As one effect of this crisis, the League required Austria to install an Executive Committee (*Exekutivkomitee*) at the OeNB in order to be able to make quick decisions if required without having to convene the General Council.[27] The League of Nations also urged the rapid linking of the Austrian currency to a fixed amount of gold and the liberalization of the Austrian foreign exchange market (Pressburger, 1966: 396–7).

Following the 'recommendation' of the League of Nations, Austria moved rapidly to the introduction of a new currency, the *schilling*, with a statutory gold cover. By adopting the necessary legal basis on 20 December 1924, the *krone* was replaced by the *schilling*. The rate of exchange was fixed at 10 000 *papierkronen* to one *schilling*, which corresponded to 0.2117 grams fine gold.[28] Thus the new *schilling* was placed on a gold bullion standard, with 33 per cent cover and the suspended requirement of redemption of bank notes in specie. In this way the *schilling* was anchored in the international monetary order (that is the gold exchange standard), which had been established at the Genoa Conference of 1922.

The external value of the *schilling* remained absolutely stable until 1931. The quotation of the *schilling* in Zurich only fluctuated within the gold points. With the onset of the *Credit-Anstalt* crisis (see below) and its repercussions on government finances, the banking crisis escalated into a currency crisis and the *schilling* came under pressure.[29] During 1931 its average value fell to 99.5 per cent of the parity, during 1932 to 83 per cent and in 1933 to 78.8 per cent, the level at which it was then stabilized again (Kamitz, 1949: 182). As a consequence, on 27 April 1934, the gold stock of the OeNB was revalued in *schillings* by 28 per cent. The valuation gains were then used to contribute to the reorganization of the Austrian banking sector.

In 1936, Austria did not take part in the international round of devaluations (which included Czechoslovakia), as safeguarding the parity and thus international creditworthiness remained the prime goal of Austrian monetary policy. This strategy was perfectly in line with the economic policy paradigm of this time (Schubert and Theurl, 1995a: 46).

Banking consolidation with the help of the OeNB

Vienna had been the financial centre of the monarchy. The Viennese banks, the majority of which were universal banks, were very active in all parts of the monarchy. Before the outbreak of the First World War, the ten largest Viennese banks had more than 150 branches outside of Vienna, three quarters of them in the later successor states.

The Viennese banks had a very close link to industry, as many industrial enterprises were dependent on the banks for their capital needs. The banks owned large stockholdings and had great influence on the enterprises via their own shares as well as by exercising the voting rights of many of their customers.

The largest, the *Credit-Anstalt*, held participations in more than 100 Austrian and foreign enterprises in 1913. Its directors sat on about 120 supervisory boards. Its own shares were quoted not only at the Vienna Stock Exchange but also in Prague, Trieste, Budapest, Berlin, Augsburg, Breslau, Dresden, Frankfurt, Hamburg, Cologne, Leipzig and Munich. Later on they were also quoted in New York.

With the dissolution of the monarchy, 'the empire of the banks was doomed to failure, too' (Weber, 1995: 137). The rising political as well as economic nationalism in the successor states 'brought to an end the historical predominance of the Austrian banks in the Danube basin' (Weber, 1995: 137). The Viennese banks had to adjust to these new economic and political realities. The main question was whether they should remain active in the successor states or must restrict their field of activity to the small Austrian state. The banks decided to maintain their presence in the successor states. However, 'they never succeeded in regaining influential footholds abroad, except in a limited sense in Poland and Yugoslavia' (Weber, 1995: 138).

From the mid-1920s the consolidation of the Austrian banking sector started to gain speed. After the collapse of the speculative bubble of 1924, many banks folded or were taken over by other ones. The wave of banking consolidation and mergers among the larger Viennese banks started with the failure of the *Depositenbank* in 1924 (see above). In 1926, two important banks, the *Centralbank der deutschen Sparkassen* and the Postal Savings Bank, suffered heavy losses. In both cases the government felt compelled to guarantee the deposits in order to avoid panic. The following year two more mid-sized banks, the Union Bank and the *Verkehrsbank*, got into trouble and were taken over by the second-largest Viennese bank, the *Allgemeine Oesterreichische Boden-Credit-Anstalt* (BCA).

This wave of mergers reached its first culmination with the problems of this large bank in autumn 1929. There was no bank left to take over this ailing institution other than its fiercest competitor, the *Credit-Anstalt*, the largest of the remaining banks in Vienna. But this merger proved to be a bite too large to swallow, even for *Credit-Anstalt*.

Annus Terribilis 1931

The year 1931 was rightly termed an 'Annus Terribilis' for the world of international finance. Austria and Central Europe were right in the eye of the storm. The announcement of the collapse of *Credit-Anstalt*, 'an integral and important part of the financial structure of the world' (Toynbee, 1932: 63), in May 1931, marked the well-publicized start of the traumatic events. Heavy withdrawals of deposits, both by local depositors as well as by foreign creditors, led to large outflows of foreign exchange and to a rapid depletion of the foreign reserves of Austria. The public had reason to expect a change in the fixed parity of the currency and engaged in short-term capital transfers out of *schilling* assets. The OeNB, however, believed that the market's expectations were unfounded and consequently took steps to keep the exchange rate within the gold points. Their respective actions resulted in large-scale losses of foreign reserves for the OeNB.

The OeNB had to turn to the Bank for International Settlements (BIS) for assistance.[30] Help was granted in the form of a foreign exchange loan amounting to 100 million *schillings*, arranged in cooperation with a group of central banks while the Bank of England deposited an immediate loan of 150 million *schillings*.[31] At the request of the OeNB, the BIS appointed Dr Bruins as financial advisor to the former during the difficulties of 1931.[32]

What had happened to the largest and most prestigious bank of Central and Eastern Europe? Due to bad debts resulting from the general economic situation as well as from management errors, it had lost more than 1000 million *schillings*, an amount about seven times its equity in Austria and in the successor states. The Austrian state – with a federal budget of roughly 1800 million *schillings* – first guaranteed and then covered a large part of the liabilities and losses of the bank. The OeNB also accepted a considerable part of the costs of the rescue of this bank.[33]

In March 1933, the general banking situation became critical again and the government had to devote considerable sums to supporting the banking sector. The emergency measures taken proved adequate and the crisis was resolved with the active participation of the OeNB. Once again, the OeNB had to contribute financially to the final reconstruction of the banking sector. Over a period of about ten years it had spent 168 million *schillings* in contributions to restoring and restructuring the Austrian banking sector (Pressburger, 1966: 472).

The Austrian strategy during the 1920s and 1930s was to 'solve' the bad-assets problem of the banks by having (still) solvent banks take over the failing ones without addressing the underlying problems. As a consequence, the size of the *Credit-Anstalt* was the result of a number of take-overs – some of them more forced than voluntary – and it became not only too big to fail but also too big to be rescued. Postponing the final solution of the underlying weakness and concentrating the risks in fewer and fewer institutions was a wrong and costly approach (Schubert, 1993: 104).

The Austrian banking system had become dominated by one very large bank, with the government being its majority shareholder.[34] All the other Austrian banks, either joint stock banks or private banks, were, compared to the size of this institution, of marginal importance.

Thus, in spring 1934 the reorganization of the Austrian banking sector was finally accomplished, more than 15 years after the break-up of the empire. However, despite all the problems involved, Austria, unlike several of its neighbours such as Germany or Hungary, never had to declare bank holidays.

Table 7.5 Number of banks in Austria, 1913–35

Type of bank	1913	1919	1923	1935
Joint stock banks	27	34	76	19
Private banks	150	146	282	131

Source: März and Weber (1983: 509).

Foreign exchange controls

After the stabilization of the Austrian currency in 1922 exchange controls were slowly reduced. The Geneva Accord of 16 September 1924 demanded the complete abolition of all restrictions. Under a regulation of the Minister of Finance of 23 March 1925, the complete liberalization of the foreign exchange market was established in Austria (Compass, 1935: 270).[35]

As one of the consequences of the *Credit-Anstalt* crisis, in 1931, Austria had to resort to foreign exchange restrictions again. However, it was one of the last countries to do so.[36] It all started with Germany adopting strict exchange controls in the wake of the crisis of the *Darmstädter und Nationalbank* (Danat Bank) on 15 July 1931. Hungary was next on 17 July. Czechoslovakia followed on 2 October, after England had left the gold standard, Yugoslavia on 7 October and Austria only on 9 October 1931. Austria wanted to maintain the full gold value of the *schilling* by the imposition of these exchange controls but soon it was to break away from restrictive practices by adopting a more flexible policy, which gradually merged the official rates with those of the black market. The restrictions were then relaxed during

Table 7.6 Return to exchange controls in Central Europe

Country	Date
Hungary	17 July 1931
Czechoslovakia	2 October 1931
Yugoslavia	7 October 1931
Austria	9 October 1931
Romania	15 May 1932
Italy	26 May 1934
Poland	26 April 1936

Source: Schwarzer and Schneider (1987: 1065).

1933 and by the beginning of September 1933 the restrictions on all current commercial transactions had been removed completely. Austria thus achieved the distinction of being the first of the countries which had resorted to foreign exchange controls to remove those restrictions (Toynbee, 1935: 423).

In June 1932, the Austrian government was obliged to declare a virtual transfer moratorium and had to withhold from the account of the trustees for the Reconstruction Loan of 1923 a portion of the revenue pledged to the service the loan. Another loan agreement with the League of Nations was signed in July 1932 ('Lausanne Protocol') but not actually made available until August 1933.[37]

In the spring of 1934, the official devaluation of the *schilling* finally took place. The gold reserves of the OeNB were revalued from 1 kilogram gold equalling 4715 *schillings* to 1 kilogram gold equalling 6000 *schillings*. This rate corresponded to the market price of 128 paper *schillings* being equal to 100 gold *schillings*, involving a devaluation of the *schilling* by 22 per cent (as compared to a devaluation of about 40 per cent of the dollar or sterling). The net book profit of this revaluation of about 20.7 million *schillings* was utilized to subscribe shares of the new *Creditanstalt-Bankverein* which had emerged from the merger of *Credit-Anstalt* and *Wiener Bankverein*.

In sum, during the 1930s monetary policy was mainly guided by concepts such as stability and integration. These took precedence over the economic compatibility of the strategy pursued, because safeguarding international creditworthiness took absolute priority (Schubert and Theurl, 1995a: 41).

The emergence of national central banks: Hungary

Initial conditions

Hungary shared many of the problems Austria encountered after the dissolution of the common empire, ranging from the loss of territory, unbalanced budgets, hyperinflation, stabilization with foreign help and supervision to banking problems and foreign exchange restrictions. But Hungary did not share the famine (being a predominantly agricultural country) nor the problems deriving from having been the financial centre of the dismembered empire (Yeager, 1981: 52).

On 16 November 1918, four days after Austria was made a Republic, the Republic of Hungary was proclaimed. On 4 June 1920, Hungary signed the Peace Treaty of Trianon, which was ratified by the Hungarian Parliament on 13 November 1920. With this treaty, the area of

Hungary was reduced by roughly 70 per cent and the total population by more than 60 per cent (Siklos, 1994: 276). Given these losses of territory Hungary attempted, unsuccessfully, to regain lost territories by force.

The first years of Hungary's independence were characterized by political turmoil. In March 1919 the Bolsheviks under Béla Kun overthrew the government of Prince Károlyi. Their dictatorship lasted about four months until Romania invaded Hungary, occupied it for a few weeks and then withdrew again. But the Bolsheviks left a problem which further complicated the already difficult currency situation. They printed counterfeit bank notes, having gained access to the plates for printing 25 and 200 *kronen* Austro-Hungarian bank notes and having created falsified plates for the one- and two-*kronen* notes (Kerschagl, 1920: 31–2). In addition, they issued so-called 'white notes'. These Bolshevik-issued currencies were honoured by the subsequent government, a right-wing government led by Admiral Horty, however, only at one-fifth of their nominal value (Sargent, 1982: 57 and Kerschagl, 1920: 33). The overall amount of forged money issued during the four-month rule was estimated at 3719 million *kronen* (Kerschagl, 1920: 32).

Due to these turbulent political episodes, Hungary was – apart from Poland – the last country to stamp the notes of the Austro-Hungarian Bank, in March 1920. As a result of this time lag, Hungary was confronted with a special phenomenon. Considerable quantities of unstamped Austro-Hungarian notes remained in circulation and there was a brisk trade in them, especially in Vienna. These unstamped notes commanded a premium of up to 30 per cent as compared with the notes stamped by the Austrian government. According to Walré de Bordes, the explanation for this phenomenon was that the new Austria was regarded as the least-deserving for credit of all the successor states, so that notes stamped by other governments were believed to possess a higher value (Walré de Bordes, 1924: 41). The unstamped notes were then either presented in those states which were latest in carrying out the stamping process – like Hungary – or were furnished with forged stamps. The Hungarian stamping was – similar to the model used in Czechoslovakia – combined with a forced acceptance of government bonds. Fifty per cent of the notes presented for stamping were withheld in exchange for government bonds paying an interest rate of 4 per cent.

Structure and size of the banking system

In the Hungarian part of the dual monarchy, only one large bank had existed that could rival the large Viennese universal banks, the Hungarian

General Credit Bank (*Ungarische Allgemeine Credit-Anstalt*), which had close links to the Viennese *Credit-Anstalt*. In 1913, according to some estimates, it controlled 63 industrial companies representing about 16 per cent of the share capital of all Hungarian joint stock companies.[38]

The Vienna- and Budapest-based commercial and credit banks, however, 'formed a closely interwoven network of fundamentally universal banks and partly succeeded in continuing with their cooperation beyond the dual era' (Nötel, 1984: 139). Especially close links existed between Vienna and Budapest banks, in particular between *Credit-Anstalt* in Vienna and the Hungarian General Credit Bank, as well as between *Boden-Credit-Anstalt* in Vienna and the First Hungarian Commercial Bank of Pest (Nötel, 1984: 139). However, international links beyond the territory of the former empire were much stronger in Vienna than in Budapest. The main international partner of Budapest bankers was Vienna. As a consequence, the collapse of the international financial system influenced much more directly and importantly developments in Austria (Nötel, 1984: 144).

Just like their Austrian counterparts, Hungarian banks had a strong influence on industry, especially in the post-inflationary period.[39] As one contemporary observer remarked:

> banking establishments have controlling interest in a great number of industrial firms which allow them to yield massive controlling influence. The organizational arrangements for large-scale industry in Hungary are anyhow of a nature which subordinates them to the management of major banks. Even greater importance attaches, however, to the fact that other sectors of the economy cannot either dispense or replace banking establishments' general financial and marketing expertise or their foreign business connections (Nötel, 1984: 175).

The close cooperation between banking and industry continued in the years of stagnation and crisis and proved to be instrumental in preserving the country's industrial capacity (Nötel, 1984: 189). The links between banks and industry were actually considerably strengthened during the stages of hyperinflation and deflation (Weber, 1994: 352). The controlling influence of the banking–industrial complex over corporate industry continued to increase in all these years, up to about 60 per cent in 1938, with the greatest part concentrated in two major Hungarian banks, the Hungarian General Credit Bank and the Hungarian Commercial Bank of Pest (Nötel, 1984: 190–1).

Hungary established and developed an institution for banking control, the *Pénzintézeti Központ* (Central Corporation of Banking Companies) which was empowered to act as an official body of accounting control, as an executor in cases of bankruptcy or merger, and as an administrator of some officially financed credit schemes (Nötel, 1984: 142). In contrast, the Austrian approach to such problems remained – despite the many bank failures – mainly case-by-case, with the consequence of repeated involvement of the central bank.

One factor that played a role in the fact that the Hungarian banking system was not hit as hard as the Austrian system by the ensuing turbulence was, in addition to different business strategies followed after 1918, Hungary's somewhat better macroeconomic performance (Weber, 1994: 352).

Table 7.7 Gross domestic product for Hungary and Austria (at constant prices; annual percentage rates of change), 1925–33

Year	Hungary	Austria
1925/26	19.7	6.8
1926/27	1.4	1.6
1927/28	6.3	3.1
1928/29	6.7	4.6
1929/30	1.3	1.5
1930/31	1.8	2.8
1931/32	–5.3	–8.0
1932/33	–4.8	–10.3

Source: Nötel (1984: 200/201).

The most important feature of post-war conditions in Hungary was 'a genuine shortage of funds' (Péteri, 1995: 91). Domestic capital accumulation was very low and only recovered at a very slow pace, making the country very dependent on foreign capital. However, two of the most important traditional suppliers of capital to Budapest – Vienna and Berlin – were themselves competing for foreign (Western) capital. According to Péteri's analysis, the bulk of foreign investment in Hungary during the second half of the 1920s came from London and New York (Péteri, 1995: 92). These sources of financing were comparatively expensive and 'very choosy investors', taking mainly reliable securities of the public sector and of the urban and agricultural estate owners. Only a very limited part of the funds found its way to industry. Hungarian banks ended up importing foreign short-term funds and lending them on – mainly on a short-term basis.

Intervention by the League of Nations

It was already known before the outbreak of the First World War that '[a] separate bank of issue was as much a part of the programme of the party of independence as the separation from Austria in the matter of customs' (Zuckerkandl, 1911: 115).

In August 1921, the Hungarian Section of the Austro-Hungarian Bank was replaced – after about one and a half years of existence – by the State Note Institute.[40] This institute was under the control of the Ministry of Finance and issued its own bank notes to replace the stamped notes of the Austro-Hungarian Bank, as well as the Bolshevik bank notes. Its monetary policy was rather lax, both with respect to the government as well as the banking sector, with the institute financing a major part of the credit requirements of the Hungarian economy (Szapáry, 1994: 5). It did not follow the rather conservative monetary policy of the peacetime Austro-Hungarian Bank, but rather a legally unconstrained creation of money serving the needs of the Ministry of Finance (Magyar Nemzeti Bank, 1993: 445). Therefore, the decline in the value of the *korona* continued and inflation increased, reaching double-digit monthly rates by 1922.[41]

The substantial budget deficits of the Hungarian state – mainly due to losses at the state enterprises, subsidized food prices, civil servants' salaries and pensions, as well as large debt service payments (Yeager, 1981: 53) – were financed by borrowing from the State Note Institute and were therefore a major cause of the rapid increase in the note and deposit liabilities of the Institute (Sargent, 1982: 141). As a consequence, between January 1922 and April 1924, the price index increased by a factor of 263. The public engaged in a flight from the *korona* and attempted to secure the value of its assets by holding more stable foreign currencies. In March 1924 the rise in prices and the concurrent depreciation of the *korona* came to an abrupt halt.

Roland Hegedüs, Minister of Finance between December 1920 and August 1921, had developed a radical plan to put the government's unbalanced budget back into balance. In addition to the introduction of a comprehensive system of taxation to ensure that revenues would eventually match expenditures, his plan also included the creation of the Hungarian State Note Institute as a quasi-central bank. It issued currency but effective control over monetary policy remained with the Minister of Finance. His programme did restore confidence in the future of the currency for a while. It stemmed the flight from the *korona* and enabled the government to stop the note printing presses in March 1921. The exchange rate expressed in paper *korona* per pre-war gold *korona* improved from 2100 in January to 2030 in February and to 880 in May (Chandler, 1971: 53). In August Hegedüs resigned after parliament refused to back his planned taxation measures. As a consequence, the exchange rate worsened again to 1410 in August and then to 2100 in September.

The financial reconstruction of Hungary was finally accomplished with the intervention of the League of Nations in a way similar to the method used in Austria in 1922, but with a delay of two years.[42] Hungary experienced about the same degree of inflation as Austria. It stabilized the currency at nearly the same rate of depreciation from its pre-war gold value, and it achieved stabilization in a similar manner (Yeager, 1981: 52). As in Austria, the Hungarian government was also obligated to accept a Commissioner General responsible to the League of Nations to monitor and supervise the government's fulfilment of its commitment to fiscal and monetary reform.

Creation of the central bank

The creation of a National Bank of Hungary (NBH) was part of this stabilization programme under the auspices of the League of Nations. The creation of an independent central bank had been one of the three pillars of the stabilization plan, with the other two being strict budgetary commitments (to establish a balanced budget) and external financing (a loan of 250 million gold *korona* successfully placed in July 1924 in the UK, the US, Italy, Switzerland, the Netherlands and Sweden).

The League's outline for this new central bank, which was very similar to the one drawn up for Austria almost two years earlier, included, among other things, the total independence of the bank from the government.[43] Its entire capital should be subscribed by private shareholders.[44] Its board of directors should represent the country's economic interests (industry, trade, agriculture and finance). The Bank should not be allowed to give loans to either government, counties or municipal governments (National Bank of Hungary, 1994: 9–10). Its prime policy concern should be geared towards keeping the value of the *korona* (and later the *pengö*) stable. According to the articles of its statutes of 1924, it was the *Magyar Nemzeti Bank*'s legal duty 'to ensure by every available means that until the legal establishment of the convertibility of paper currency (bank notes) into metal, the value of notes issued, expressed in the rate of exchange of bills to countries with gold-based currencies or fixed-value currencies, should remain stable.' This requirement was almost identical with the one for the OeNB.

The legislation to establish such a central bank passed parliament on 18 April 1924. Its initial share capital was set at 30 million gold *korona* divided into 300 000 shares to be subscribed by private shareholders.[45]

In September 1925, the shares of the *Magyar Nemzeti Bank* (MNB; National Bank of Hungary) were listed on the Budapest Stock Exchange but turned out not to be very popular (National Bank of Hungary, 1994: 15). The statutory meeting of the MNB was held in the ceremonial hall of the Hungarian Academy of Sciences on 24 May 1924, while the Bank formally began to operate one month later, on 24 June 1924. It assumed the assets and liabilities of the State Note Institute and took over the functions of the foreign exchange control office, the *Devisenzentrale*, just as its Austrian counterpart had in 1923. In addition, the bank was required to hold gold reserves of the same percentages as the OeNB (rising from 20 per cent to 33.3 per cent) to back its liabilities.

Sándor Popovics, Governor of the Austro-Hungarian Bank from 1909 to 1918 and then (short-term) Hungarian Minister of Finance and later President of the Hungarian Royal State Institute of Issue, was appointed as the first President of the MNB, a post he held until his death in 1935. A foreign advisor was delegated by the League of Nations to the MNB: Harry A. Siepman, a 35-year-old English financial expert who stayed until 1926 and later became a director of the Bank of England.

At the start of its operations, the MNB had bullion reserves of 313 billion *korona*, which grew, despite Hungary's persistent current account deficit,[46] to nearly eight times that amount by the end of 1924, due to capital inflows from abroad. During 1925, the bullion reserves increased by a further 861 billion *korona* (National Bank of Hungary, 1994: 14). This provided the impetus for the introduction of a new and genuinely Hungarian currency: the *pengö*. The *korona* had been tied to the British pound – an imposed precondition for British participation in the reconstruction loan[47] – with one pound being equal to 346 000 paper *korona*. By April 1925 the *korona* was, via the pound, pegged to gold. The introduction of the *pengö* was regulated by an Act which entered into force on 21 November 1925. One *pengö* was set at 12 500 paper *korona*. One kilogram of alloyed gold was worth 4 320 *pengös* and a kilogram of refined gold 3 800 *pengös* (National Bank of Hungary, 1994: 14–15). Therefore, from 1924 to 1931, when foreign exchange controls were introduced, the Hungarian currency system was 'a *de facto* gold-exchange standard' (Péteri, 1995: 123).

As in the case of the Austrian central bank in 1924, the Statutes of the MNB were changed in 1925 in order to establish an Executive Committee as an additional decision-making body in certain urgent cases.

During 1926 the MNB was subjected to its first serious test. After a suspension of some foreign loans on which the Hungarian economy continued to be very dependent, the gold and foreign currency reserves of the MNB were depleted. The suspension of these foreign loans was a strong reminder of the dangers of Hungary's heavy dependence on foreign debt. The National Bank took measures to reduce the incentives for such capital inflows but the problem of inadequate domestic savings remained and continued to make Hungary very vulnerable during the following years.

Fiscal policy

With the help of the stabilization programme of the League of Nations the Hungarian government raised taxes and cut expenditures and so reached budget surpluses in the fiscal years 1924/25 as well as 1925/26, two years earlier than initially envisaged. At the same time, the state debt was reduced, creating a sound basis for monetary and financial stability. However, as Siklos (1994) concludes, the League of Nations reforms only accomplished an externally financed reduction in inflation, but did not correct the economic problems which led Hungary to resort to hyperinflation in the first place. Therefore, Hungary eventually repeated the experience of hyperinflation after the Second World War.

Annus Terribilis 1931

The *Credit-Anstalt* crisis of 1931 had serious consequences for Hungary culminating in July in the closure of all banks for three days and in the unexpected resignation of Count Bethlen as Prime Minister after ten years of uninterrupted tenure in that office.[48] As a result of the difficulties of the *Credit-Anstalt*, 'adverse rumours were in circulation as to the position of the Hungarian General Credit Bank. Although that bank's connections to the *Credit-Anstalt* were not so close as was generally assumed, these rumours led to the withdrawal of a certain amount of deposits and the cutting of foreign credits' (*The Banker*, August 1931: 128).

The government was forced to issue a decree guaranteeing all banking deposits, claims and debts in *pengö* to their full gold value. As *The Economist* judged at that time, 'the gold *pengö* [was] a good temporary expedient, as it [made] improbable the creation of speculative debts in the hope that they will be repaid in depreciated currency. Indeed, perhaps its most important function [was] that of checking the withdrawal of deposits from the banks, and thus counteracting inflation' (*The Economist*, 29 August 1931: 382). As far as the roots of the Hungarian crisis were concerned – the *Credit-Anstalt* collapse and the German banking troubles had only 'precipitated, but not caused' them – *The Economist* identified three reasons (*idem*): first, factors beyond Hungary's control, such as the radical change in the price level, which especially affected agricultural borrowing countries. Second, the fact that the country had lived beyond its means since 1927 and, third, defects in the banking system.

The budgetary equilibrium, which had been re-established with the help of the League of Nations' reconstruction scheme in 1924 and maintained in the following five years with great success, had given way to a heavy deficit in 1930/31.

As far as the banking sector was concerned, *The Economist* came to the clear conclusion that 'there are too many banks in Hungary and their management is too costly' (*The Economist*, 29 August 1931: 382). As a case in point, the Hungarian General Credit Bank, a former sister institution of the *Credit-Anstalt* in Vienna, ran into difficulties. The bank met the pressure by rediscounting part of its portfolio with the MNB. Between 1 May 1931 and 13 July 1931 the MNB paid gold and foreign exchange worth 40 million dollars, which exceeded the total value of its bullion and foreign currency reserves at the end of April 1931 (National Bank of Hungary, 1994: 20/21). As a consequence, the MNB needed foreign loans. After receiving a loan from the German *Reichsbank* it turned – like the OeNB before it – to the Bank for International Settlements (BIS) for a foreign currency loan in order to be able to fulfil its obligations as guarantor for the ailing commercial bank. The BIS, in cooperation with twelve central banks, among them the Federal Reserve, granted a rediscount credit amounting to 21 million dollars and 1 million pounds sterling after the MNB had lost more than 8 million pounds sterling during the first half of 1931. This was as a result of sudden withdrawals of foreign[49] – especially US and British short-term – funds (5.5 million pounds) and an increasing current account deficit (3 million pounds).[50] The BIS delegated, at the request of the MNB, Mr Henry J. Bruce as advisor to Budapest. But the operation of the central banks was judged 'unsuccessful' (Chandler, 1971: 165).

Depositors continued their run on the banks. Following the outbreak of the German banking crisis, on 14 July a banking holiday of three days was ordered to avoid insolvency and national bankruptcy. The repayment of deposits was temporarily suspended. Subsequently, the banks were ordered to make payments on a very restricted scale: 5 per cent (or a maximum of 1000 *pengös*), later 10 per cent of deposits until 17 August 1931 (*The Banker*, August 1931: 128).

On 17 July 1931, foreign exchange controls were introduced to stop capital flight and the depletion of gold and foreign exchange reserves and foreign trade was placed under state control. The trading of currencies on the stock market was suspended and all foreign exchange had to be surrendered to the MNB. The MNB invited, in accordance with the financial committee of the League of Nations, its foreign advisor, Henry J. Bruce, to make an international review of the new situation (National Bank of Hungary, 1994: 22). However, the *pengö* was not devalued, as it was judged that an inflated currency would have aggravated the problems of the country. But the Hungarian government introduced a premium system. While maintaining the official exchange rate, it paid for foreign exchange an amount in *pengös* exceeding the official rate. The MNB was put in charge of the supervision and management of the foreign exchange system (National Bank of Hungary, 1994: 24). In December 1931 a partial transfer moratorium was declared by Hungary, followed by a six-month standstill agreement in March 1932 (Bank für Internationalen Zahlungsausgleich, 1932: 14).

The economic crisis was accompanied by a political crisis: the Bethlen government, which had been successful a few months earlier at the general elections of June 1931, resigned in August 1931 and Count Gyula Károlyi followed as Prime Minister, only to be replaced by the next government as early as October 1932. At that time, in early 1933, the independence of the MNB suffered a severe blow: the Bank Act was modified to allow the government to borrow from the bank and the MNB had to give a 100 million gold *pengö* unsecured loan to the Gömbös-government.

In 1938 it finally lost its autonomy completely as it was forced to satisfy all demands for refinancing arising in the context of the so-called 'War program of Györ' (Szapáry, 1994: 8). From then on the printing of bank notes again became an important source of government finance. The State used the MNB more and more extensively to finance its military expenditure (National Bank of Hungary, 1994: 30).

The emergence of national central banks: Czechoslovakia

Initial conditions

The Czech revolution of 20 October 1918 was the final signal for the disintegration of the Austro-Hungarian monarchy (Walré de Bordes, 1924: 5). The independence of the Czechoslovak State was proclaimed by the National Committee on 28 October 1918. The Czechoslovak state adopted the Republican form of government and elected Thomas Masaryk as its first president. The frontiers of the state were only determined at the Peace Treaties of Versailles, Saint Germain and Trianon in 1920 and 1921. The new country had 13.6 million inhabitants compared to only 6.5 in Austria and it acquired about 60 per cent of the industrial capacity of Cisleithania (Bloomfield, 1984: 231).

In view of the damage done by inflation during the war, the first Minister of Finance of the new republic, Alois Rasín, considered it as a prime duty 'to obviate the continuance of inflation by means of international intervention' (Rasín, 1923: 16). In his judgement there was 'the danger that, by the continued printing of uncovered bank notes, we might descend, not only from a credit system to ready money payment, but even to a system of barter.' He did not, however, await international intervention: his goal was the establishment of an International Commission to prevent the German Imperial and the Austro-Hungarian Banks from issuing bank notes not covered by private liability, and he negotiated directly with the Austro-Hungarian Bank. In order to agree to a maintenance 'for a while' of a common currency, he required and received the right to nominate a Government Commissioner to superintend the affairs of the Bank. It was also agreed that the Bank should not be permitted to grant loans to any state, except by agreement with all successor states. No agreement was reached concerning his demand that the Bank should not be permitted to make advances on the war loans. This led him to prohibit all branches of the Austro-Hungarian Bank situated in the territory of the Czechoslovak Republic from lending on Austrian and Hungarian war loans (Rasín, 1923: 17).

On 25 February 1919, the National Assembly, in secret session, passed a law empowering the Minister of Finance to undertake the stamping of the bank notes of the Austro-Hungarian Bank circulating in the territory of Czechoslovakia by means of a stamp representing a percentage of the nominal value of the notes. It was further to withhold from circulation 50 per cent of the bank notes presented, and to declare them a government loan, irredeemable by the creditor but repayable on the part of the state at any time and carrying one per cent interest (Rasín, 1923: 25–6). The stamping was part of Rasín's concept for a reordering of Czechoslovakia's currency situation. The basic idea of this concept was an initially sudden and then more gradual revaluation of the Czechoslovak *crown* towards its pre-war value. The sudden revaluation should have been the result of a sharp reduction of the money supply. That is why half the notes presented by private agents were withheld and converted into unredeemable government obligations (Cechoslovakische Nationalbank, 1937: 40).

As some people had been expecting the dissolution of the common currency area, there had been a tendency to transport large quantities of bank notes from other parts of the former empire to Czechoslovakia in the expectation of possible capital gains (Cechoslovakische Nationalbank, 1937: 37). Therefore, the stamping had to be carried out with rapidity. On the night of 25–26 February 1919, all frontier traffic was stopped, and the entire frontier placed under military guard. The 10, 20, 50, 100 and 1000 *kronen* bank notes were stamped. The one- and two-*kronen* notes were provisionally excluded from stamping and left in circulation.[51] Postal communication with foreign countries was suspended for the period 26 February to 9 March 1919. Financial houses were not allowed to accept deposits of any kind during this period, and they were permitted to pay out deposits only with the approval of the District Commission. The desire of the public to escape the capital levy was responsible – among other reasons – for the fact that many of the notes were not presented (Walré de Bordes, 1924: 40). On 26 February 1919 the Austro-Hungarian Bank sent a telegraphic protest against the stamping of the bank notes because of the infringement of its privilege but Rasín rejected this protest (Rasín, 1923: 29).

With an ordinance on 12 May 1919, a Banking Department was established at the Ministry of Finance and a Bank Committee of independent men appointed, to which the Minister of Finance transferred his statutory powers (Rasín, 1923: 42). The Banking Department took over the entire staff of officials of the Austro-Hungarian Bank working in Czechoslovakia, where the Bank had 30 branches, and commenced to function as a bank of issue. It also took over the functions of the Czechoslovak Foreign Exchange Centre which had succeeded the Austro-Hungarian Foreign Exchange Centre (*Devisenzentrale*) in 1919. Any direct or indirect granting of credit to the government was forbidden.

In contrast to Austria and Hungary (as well as Poland), Czechoslovakia succeeded in stabilizing its currency soon after the First World War without suffering from a hyperinflation first. Thus, the Czech population was spared the worst ravages of inflation (Boross, 1984: 206). A very radical stabilization programme designed and implemented by Rasín – covering monetary as well as fiscal policy – resulted in deflation and subsequent stabilization by 1923.

As far as the exchange rate of the Czechoslovak *crown* was concerned, the initial policy was one of creating confidence by trying to avoid strong volatility of that rate. Stabilizing the *crown* at its 'natural' level corresponding to purchasing power parity was considered as the first task of monetary and exchange rate policy (Cechoslovakische Nationalbank, 1937: 188–9). In order to fulfil this difficult task, the Banking Department repeatedly had to borrow foreign exchange abroad given its low level of reserves. By the end of 1921 this policy of stabilizing the exchange rate was replaced by a policy of raising the rate, which lasted until mid-1923 and resulted in deflationary policies. The rate of exchange rose by more than 100 per cent relative to the average level of 1921. The Czechoslovak *crown* which had fallen from 35 Swiss *centimes* in May 1919 to 5.1 *centimes* in November 1921 recovered again to 19.2 *centimes* by October 1922, following the above-mentioned deflationary policies of the Czechoslovak government (Bloomfield, 1984: 228). In the judgement of Walré de Bordes, owing to speculative buying on German account, the rise of the Czechoslovak *crown*, which was initiated by Minister Rasín in 1921, 'got completely out of hand' (Walré de Bordes, 1924: 217). Thereafter, it required enormous efforts to keep the *crown* stable. From 1924, with regard to the monetary and exchange policy, a period of stabilization and consolidation started which lasted until the adoption of the gold exchange standard in 1929.

In further contrast to the Austrian and the Hungarian post-war situations, Czechoslovakia enjoyed sizeable trade and current account surpluses from 1920 on, while Austria and Hungary suffered substantial and persistent trade and current account deficits. This favourable external situation 'undoubtedly aided confidence in the economy and helped the government to check inflation' (Bloomfield, 1984: 230).

There existed confidence in the country's political and economic future, sustained by the favourable treatment which the new republic received at the hands of the Entente powers. The despair and pessimism expressed in contemporary Vienna stood in stark contrast (Bloomfield, 1984: 232). At the end of the First World War the victorious Entente powers required a new bulwark in Central Europe to block any renewed German expansionism as well as a bulwark against the Bolshevik revolution. Czechoslovakia seemed to be the most appropriate country for this among the successor states; consequently, it received favourable treatment from the Peace Treaties and this helped its later economic development (Bloomfield, 1984: 237–8).

The Czech banking system

The development of the Czech banking system in the Habsburg monarchy but also during the inter-war period differed from that of the other successor states, as even before the war the local banks managed to achieve a dominating position in the domestic or local (Bohemian, Moravian and Silesian) money markets (Teichová, 1995: 129). While the capital of the largest Viennese banks still amounted to 71.4 per cent of the total banking capital in the Austrian part of the monarchy, the share of the Czech banks in the total banking capital of Cisleithania had increased from 7.9 per cent in 1900 (four banks) to 13.3 in 1913 (13 banks), heavily concentrated on the local market. Compared to their Austrian counterparts, Czech banks were less constrained during the inter-war period. They chose a far more cautious policy and claimed lower interest rates than in Austria (Weber, 1995: 138).

The Czech universal banks were fierce competitors of the Viennese banks, especially the largest of them, the *Zivnostenská banka*. In order to gain market shares from the Viennese or Hungarian banks in the Slav parts of the dual empire, they made heavy recourse to nationalistic discourses (Teichová, 1993: 536).

During the inter-war period Czechoslovakia also managed to avoid the large-scale collapses that characterized Austrian banking. However, during the deflationary period of the early 1920s insolvencies of industrial enterprises had resulted in some banking collapses and a run on the banks. As a consequence, the banking sector had to be rescued, mainly with state help in 1924 (Cechoslovakische Nationalbank, 1937: 50). At the same time, banking supervision was strengthened. By 1925, industry had been decapitalized by the long spell of deflation and it again became very dependent on the banking sector.

Overall, the Czechoslovak banks fared far better than the Viennese ones during the 1920s and 1930s. In the judgement of Teichová, *Zivnostenská banka* pursued a much more cautious business policy with regard to loans and the accumulation of reserves than the large Viennese universal banks (Teichová, 1993: 537).

Creation of the central bank

Based on a decree of 1 April 1926 by the Czech Minister of Finance, the Czech National Bank (CNB; *Národní banka Ceskoslovenská*) started operations from that day. However, in a legal sense, it had retrospectively been in existence since 1 January 1926 (Cechoslovakische Nationalbank, 1937: 69). This means that it took Czechoslovakia three years longer than Austria and one and a half years longer than Hungary to create its own central bank. In both Austria and Hungary foreign pressure via the League of Nations had played an important role in the establishment of the bank of issue. Czechoslovakia was in a different position, as it had not required a stabilization loan from the League of Nations. The Bank was established as a joint stock company with a share capital of 405 million Czech *crowns*, split among 120 000 nominal shares. A transfer of shares required the explicit approval of the Bank Council. One third of the shares were in the hands of the government.

The CNB had the privilege, granted for a period of 15 years, of issuing bank notes on the territory of the Czechoslovak state. It was obliged to hold the external value of the *crown* stable at the level of the last two years in relation to the gold-based currencies and to hold a gold and foreign exchange cover of 25 per cent of the sum of all notes issued and short-term liabilities of the bank.[52] Thus, until November 1929, Czechoslovakia had a paper-based currency, pegged to the dollar at a rate close to 100 *crowns* = 2.9650 US dollars. In 1929, efforts to make the *crown* explicitly a gold-based currency reached their culminating point. Despite its virtual stability relative to the gold-based dollar it was not considered to be on the gold standard or the gold exchange standard. It was the creation of the Bank for International Settlements (BIS) that gave the decisive push for the decision to make the Czechoslovak *crown* formally a gold-based currency, as it was thought that only central banks with gold-based currencies would be allowed to become shareholders of this bank (Cechoslovakische Nationalbank, 1937: 194). With a law of 7 November 1929 the *crown* was put on the gold (exchange) standard with one *crown* being equal to 44.58 milligrams of gold, which implied no change in relation to the dollar. The date of the introduction of the obligation to convert bank notes into gold should have been set by governmental decree at some later point. The switch to the gold exchange standard was preceded by the full liberalization of foreign exchange transactions in late 1928 (Cechoslovakische Nationalbank, 1937: 70).

The timing of the large changes in Czechoslovakia's foreign exchange system – liberalization and gold-basing – was rather unfortunate, as these policy shifts coincided with the end of capital exports from the US and the first signs of the Great Depression. Czechoslovak foreign trade flows diminished considerably in 1929 and the country registered sizeable capital outflows. These developments increased and exacerbated the deflationary pressures, especially via a reduction in exports.

At the helm of the bank was a Governor who, as in Austria, was appointed by the President of the Republic for a period of five years, at

Table 7.8 Exchange rate of the Czech *crown* at Zurich and New York (annual averages, for 100 *crowns*), 1926–36

Date	Zurich (Swiss *francs*)	New York (dollars)
1926	15.337	2.9625
1927	15.382	2.963
1928	15.387	2.964
1929	15.359	2.9614
1930	15.294	2.965
1931	15.264	2.962
1932	15.257	2.963
1933	15.349	3.820
1934	13.138	4.248
1935	12.808	4.168
1936	13.382	4.014

Source: Cechoslovakische Nationalbank (1937: 520–21).

the recommendation of the government. He presided over the Bank Council and the Management Board of the Bank. The President of the Republic also appointed the Deputy-Governor, from a group of six elected members of the Bank Council. Dr Pospísil was appointed as the first Governor. He was followed by the former Minister of Finance, Dr Englis, in February 1934. The Bank Council consisted of ten to eleven members. Six of them were elected by the General Meeting of the Shareholders for a period of six years, three were appointed – for the same period – by the President of the Republic at the recommendation of the government. One additional member could be chosen by the Bank Council itself – with the approval of the Governor – for a period of two years.

Table 7.9 Central banks in Central Europe: dates of establishment, legal form and first presidents

Country	Date of foundation	Legal form	First president
Austria	1 January 1923	Joint stock	Reisch (1923–32)
Hungary	24 June 1924	Joint stock	Popovic (1924–35)
Czechoslovakia	1 January 1926	Joint stock	Pospísil (1926–34)

The Bank Council was in charge of monetary policy and managed all the assets of the CNB. Similar to its Austrian and Hungarian counterparts, the CNB had a narrower decision-making body, comprising the Governor and three other designated members of the Bank Council. They were allowed to take decisions in urgent cases. However, changes in the discount rate had to be submitted as soon as possible to the Bank Council for ex-post approval. In addition, they were in charge of executing all the decisions of the Bank Council.

The General Meeting of the Shareholders represented – under the chairmanship of the Governor – the shareholders' rights and interest. Only Czechoslovak citizens were allowed to participate in these meetings. A State Commissioner acted as the government's supervisory authority. He had to ensure that the CNB respected all laws and regulations. But he also had to ensure that the Bank acted in the interest of the state. These were more far-reaching powers than those of the State Commissioner at the *Oesterreichische Nationalbank*: the Czechoslovak State Commissioner was able to veto any decision of the General Meeting of Shareholders or of the Bank Council or of any other decision-making body.

At the end of 1926, the CNB had 441 employees of which only about 150 had served already in the Austro-Hungarian Bank. By 1936, this number had risen to 671, of which 81 were ex-Austro-Hungarian Bank employees (Cechoslovakische Nationalbank, 1937: 122).

Annus Terribilis 1931

The *Credit-Anstalt* crisis also had repercussions in Prague and at the end of May 1931 there were runs on two of the leading banks, the Union Bank and the Bohemian Discount and Credit Bank (*The Banker*, July 1931: 45). In comparison to their Austrian counterparts, and while not immune to the problems of the inter-war period, overall the Czech banks avoided crashes. The German banking crisis, which affected Hungary among others, left Czechoslovak banks 'unaffected' (*The Banker*, August 1931: 127). Their business policies, especially those of the largest Czech bank, the *Zivnostenská banka*, were more cautious and more farsighted than those of the great Viennese banks (Teichová, 1995: 129). At the end of the inter-war period, only 15 per cent of the total capital of all joint-stock banks in Czechoslovakia was foreign-owned, a figure far below the respective numbers for Austria or the other successor states (Teichová, 1995: 129).

Although the banks themselves stayed largely unaffected, there were considerable outflows of foreign exchange after the outbreak of the German banking crisis in July 1931. Before, the Czechoslovak National Bank had participated with more than one million US dollars in the central banking loans organized by the BIS for the *Oesterreichische Nationalbank* and the *Magyar Nemzeti Bank*. The large-scale withdrawal of short-term loans was first met by interventions of the CNB and by increases in the discount rate. On 5 August 1931, the CNB raised the rate from 4 to 5 per cent and on 22 September – the day after the gold standard was abandoned by Great Britain – to 6.5 per cent. As these changes did not stop the capital flight nor the rapid decline in foreign exchange reserves, exchange controls were reintroduced on 2 October 1931, two and a half months after Hungary had taken this step and one week before the Austrian authorities had to resort to the same measures. The controls were subsequently extended and tightened but the external value of the Czechoslovak *crown* was maintained stable until 17 February 1934, when the gold equivalent of the *crown* was reduced from 44.58 milligrams to 37.15 milligrams, that is by one-sixth.

Overall, despite its many problems and several – especially deflationary – crises, the Czech economy performed considerably better than the Austrian one during the inter-war period and this helped the country to master monetary and foreign exchange problems in a less painful way than either Austria or Hungary.

Table 7.10 Growth comparison: Austria and Czechoslovakia, 1913–37 (average compound growth rates of GNP, in per cent)

Year	Austria	Czechoslovakia
1913–29	0.3	2.7
1927–37	–1.8	–0.2

Source: A. Maddison (cited in Weber, 1995: 141).

Common trends and conclusions

The central banks of Central and Eastern Europe were the product of the upheavals created by the First World War. The emerging desire for political sovereignty included the desire for economic and monetary sovereignty. The common currency, as a strong symbol for the common empire, had to make way for national currencies. In some countries, the ambition to sever the monetary links was so strong that it did not allow for a well-planned and orchestrated dissolution of the common monetary union. The result was a rather chaotic process of monetary disintegration in the immediate post-war years.

National monies required national central banks. But the process of building up such institutions proved to be more difficult and long drawn out than anticipated. Interim solutions had to be found. The legacy of the war and the repercussions of the dissolution of the economic union created unbalanced national economies. In Austria as well as Hungary the governments were not viable financially and not able to cover their expenditures by regular tax revenues. Government deficits increased, and were monetized, leading to hyperinflation. In view of the obvious link between the monetization of such deficits and hyperinflation, the Allied governments, via the League of Nations, exerted considerable pressure to make the central banks in these countries statutorily independent of their governments (Capie et al., 1994: 28). This pressure proved to be helpful, as it was in the long-term interest of the countries concerned. With a strict stabilization programme, the Czechoslovak government managed to avoid the abyss of hyperinflation and engineered bouts of deflation instead.

The newly won economic sovereignty of the successor states was short-lived. Foreign help came at the price of foreign influence. In exchange for financial assistance, the League of Nations enforced severe adjustment programmes, supervised and enforced by foreign commissioners and advisors. The establishment of independent central banks with the main objective of maintaining the external value of the respective currencies was an integral part of these programmes.

But the financial positions in Central Europe remained fragile. The unresolved reorganization of the banking industry after the break-up of the common economic area added to the financial fragility. The notionally independent central banks could not turn a blind eye to the emerging banking problems. They had to intervene as lenders of last resort and even as shareholders of last resort. Monetary management was seriously hampered by banking problems and the same was true of fiscal policy. As the governments guaranteed the liabilities of ailing banks, banking problems became fiscal problems, which ultimately undermined the trust in the currencies. The pronounced jump in the expected present values of future government commitments led to a resurgence of inflationary expectations and therefore to a flight out of the affected currencies. Neither foreign loans given by central banks and organized by the newly established Bank for International Settlements, nor manipulations in the discount rate could stop the capital flight. In order to save the external value of their currencies, one country after the other resorted to exchange controls which they had abandoned only a few years earlier.

Even twelve years after the dissolution of the common monetary area the successor states of the Austro-Hungarian monarchy were economically more interdependent than they had expected or realized. Financial crises did not stop at new political borders. The countries and their policy makers might have heeded Schumpeter's prediction of 1919: it is easier to become politically independent than economically independent.

Notes

1. The opinions expressed are those of the author and not necessarily those of the *Oesterreichische Nationalbank*. I thank Philip Cottrell and Jaime Reis for valuable comments and Irene Sperl-Mühldorf for editorial assistance.
2. Even as late as 1919/20 some Austrian as well as Hungarian financial and political circles hoped that the common central bank would survive the break-up of the monarchy (see Magyar Nemzeti Bank, 1993: 414).
3. As Walré de Bordes (1924: 37) reports, before the war only a very small amount of gold was in circulation in Austria-Hungary. The population had been accustomed to using paper money for many years, and actually preferred it to gold. The repeated attempts of the Austro-Hungarian Bank to push gold into circulation failed completely.
4. Report of the General Council to the Extraordinary General Meeting of 19 December 1917, p. xxvi; cited in Walré de Bordes (1924: 51).

5. See Table 7.4.
6. See Table 7.4.
7. For a more detailed description of the disintegration of the currency union see Kerschagl (1920). For a recent analysis see Schubert and Theurl (1995b).
8. Address by Sir William Goode at the British Institute of International Affairs, 24 January 1922, quoted in Walré de Bordes (1924: 189).
9. The amount of Treasury bills among the assets of the central bank rose from 152 to 2558 billion *kronen* between the end of 1921 and the end of 1922 (Kamitz, 1949: 173).
10. Zimmermann's tenure as Commissioner General in Austria lasted until 30 June 1926, when the League of Nations considered the financial reconstruction of Austria as successfully accomplished.
11. The value of a *gold krone* which had reached 15 154 *papierkronen* (i.e. paper crowns) in September 1922 recovered to 14 400 by early 1923 and remained there.
12. In view of these trade problems Austria made several attempts to create special customs arrangements or even unions with neighbouring countries. In 1925, for instance, the Austrian Foreign Minister, Dr Mataja, asked Italy and Czechoslovakia to make special customs arrangements with Austria, but due to special demands from the Czechs this attempt remained unsuccessful (see Gedye, 1931a: 550). The best-known effort was the ill-fated attempt to form an Austro-German customs union in March 1931. Although seen by Austria as the first step in the cessation of tariff wars in Europe – about 21 per cent of Austrian imports came from Germany and about 16 per cent of her exports went there – and despite the emphasis by both the Austrian and the German authorities that the accession of any further country to the customs union would be welcome, it met a storm of protest, especially by France and Czechoslovakia. They regarded it as a violation of Austria's independence in the sense of the Geneva Protocols of October 1922, signed as a precondition for the League of Nations stabilization programme. In September 1931, the Permanent Court of International Justice – by eight votes to seven – gave the (advisory) opinion that the planned customs union was incompatible with the Geneva Protocols.
13. France, UK and Czechoslovakia guaranteed 24.5 per cent each, Italy 20 per cent, Belgium and Sweden 2 per cent each, and Denmark and the Netherlands 1 per cent each. In addition, Spain agreed to guarantee a tranche of the loan issued on its capital market and Switzerland granted a direct government loan.
14. Art. 5 of the Statutes of the OeNB. In light of the large inflow of foreign exchange via the LoN loan, the initially planned amount of 100 million Swiss *francs* for the capital of the bank was considered too high and reduced to 30 million *gold kronen*.
15. Half of these reserves were added to the foreign exchange reserves of the bank and half was turned over to the State Finance Authority (*Bundesfinanzverwaltung*).
16. Art. 26 of the Statutes of the OeNB.
17. Art. 45 to 47 of the Statutes of the OeNB.
18. From 1927 on the Bank was allowed to discount Treasury bills of the central government up to a maximum amount of 75 million *schillings*.

19. In 1993, with the ratification of the Treaty on European Union (Maastricht Treaty) this prohibition of monetary financing of any layer of government became part of the European Union's monetary constitution.
20. Art. 83 of the Statutes of the OeNB.
21. In the case of a higher bank note circulation, the Bank would have to pay a bank note tax (Art. 88).
22. Art. 22 of the Statutes of the OeNB.
23. Reisch was followed in 1932 by Dr Viktor Kienböck, also a former Minister of Finance. He served as President until March 1938, when the OeNB was liquidated by the Germans immediately after the occupation of Austria.
24. He served from May 1923 until May 1924 and was succeeded by Professor Anton van Gyn (June 1924 until January 1926) and Robert Charles Kay (until June 1929). The control of the League of Nations for Austria had finished on 1 July 1926 but the Austrian government had decided – at the suggestion of the Financial Committee of the LoN – to extend the tenure of the advisor of the OeNB for another three years, until 30 June 1929.
25. From 30 Swiss *francs* for 100 French *francs* in mid-December 1923, in Zurich, to about 21 on 11 March 1924.
26. An Austrian bank that profited from the collapse of speculation in the *franc* was the Austrian branch of the Rothschild imperium, S.M. Rothschild. It had received insider information from its French relative. It had been informed in advance about the intervention to support the *franc* and the exact date of the action. It is reported that its profits from this advance notice surpassed the heavy losses it had suffered during the First World War (see Cowles 1973: 210).
27. Up to this day the OeNB has kept the institution of an Executive Committee consisting of the President, the two Vice Presidents, the Chief Executive Director and the Deputy Chief Executive Director. If necessary, they are empowered to take decisions reserved for the General Council.
28. For a detailed analysis of the introduction of the *schilling* and its now more than 70-year-long history see Schubert and Theurl (1995a).
29. For a detailed analysis of the Austrian currency crisis of 1931 see Schubert (1991).
30. The *Oesterreichische Nationalbank*, the Czech National Bank and the *Magyar Nemzeti Bank* had been shareholders of the BIS since 25 June 1930 with 4000 shares each (*Bank für Internationalen Zahlungsausgleich*, 1931, Anlage I).
31. In Clarke's (1967: 186) judgement, '[b]y almost every standard, the amount of the central bank credits was too small.'
32. Dr Bruins had been commissioner of the *Reichsbank* under the Dawes Plan. For the Austrian government, the Dutchman Rost van Tonningen became the LoN advisor.
33. For an extensive study of the crisis of *Credit-Anstalt* and its repercussion on monetary and exchange rate policy in Austria, see Schubert (1991).
34. Even 65 years later the Austrian government still holds the majority of the voting shares of the *Credit-Anstalt* and the discussion about a full privatization still goes on.
35. As already mentioned above, the League of Nations had urged Austria, in 1924, to abandon all restrictions on foreign exchange transactions.

36. Austria did not formally abandon the gold standard.
37. On the basis of the Geneva Protocols of 1932, the OeNB once again received a foreign advisor.
38. See Teichová (1993: 534), citing estimates by György Ránki.
39. For a detailed account of the interrelationship between banking and industry in Hungary during the 1920s, see Péteri (1995).
40. The Hungarian Section of the AHB handed over control to the State Note Institute on 1 August 1921, but continued to keep accounts up to 31 December 1921.
41. Sargent (1982: 141) points out that the fact that neither the total amount nor the schedule of payments of reparations owed by Hungary were known for many years after the war created a serious obstacle to achieving a stable value for the currency.
42. For a detailed account of the difficult negotiations leading to the loan, see Péteri (1995).
43. Apart from the League of Nations, the Governor of the Bank of England, Montague Norman, played an important part in Hungarian stabilization and the establishment of the MNB (Bácskai, 1994: 6).
44. The choice of the form of a joint stock company was then the usual one for central banks – based on the view that this legal form defends against any undue influence of the government, even in the case that a part of the shares falls to the government (Bácskai, 1994: 10). But Bácskai classifies this view as 'an illusion'.
45. However, the Hungarian government was also initially allowed to acquire a certain amount of shares in exchange for assets, but it had to transfer those shares to private investors as soon as possible (National Bank of Hungary, 1994: 9).
46. For estimates of Hungary's balance of payments during the 1920s, see Péteri (1995: 126 and 179).
47. Péteri (1995: 108) reports a secret agreement between MNB-President Popovics and Bank of England Governor Norman stipulating the adoption of sterling as the standard of value for the Hungarian currency.
48. *The Economist* (29 August 1931: 382). For an analysis of the – possible – role of France in the resignation of Count Bethlen, see Gedye (1931b).
49. The German *Reichsbank* had also extended a five-million dollar loan (see National Bank of Hungary, 1994: 21).
50. The largest deficit item in Hungary's balance of payments was the annual payment abroad of six to seven million pounds sterling for interest, sinking funds and dividends fixed in gold currencies (*The Economist*, 29 August 1931: 382).
51. Czechoslovakia immediately ordered the printing of its own bank notes from private Czechoslovak printing works. Only the notes of the largest denomination, 5 000 Czechoslovak *crowns*, were ordered in Vienna at the printing works of the (former) Austro-Hungarian Bank. Soon afterwards, however, US printing companies were used as suppliers of bank notes until the CNB's own printing works were ready for production in 1928 (Cechoslovakische Nationalbank, 1937: 146).
52. At the start of the operations of the CNB, the cover-ratio amounted to 28 per cent (Cechoslovakische Nationalbank 1937: 191).

References

Bácskai, Tamás (1994), 'Currency reform and the establishment of the National Bank of Hungary', paper presented at the conference: *Rebuilding the financial system in Central and Eastern Europe*, Budapest, 11 November 1994.

The Banker (1931), 19(66), July.

The Banker (1931), 19(67), August.

Bank für Internationalen Zahlungausgleich (1931), *Erster Jahresbericht*, Basel.

Bank für Internationalen Zahlungausgleich (1932), *Zweiter Jahresbericht*, Basel.

Berger, Peter (1994), 'The Austrian economy, 1918–1938', in Matis, Herbert (ed.), *The Economic Development of Austria Since 1870*, Aldershot, Edward Elgar.

Bloomfield, Jonathan (1984), 'Surviving in a harsh world: trade and inflation in the Czechoslovak and Austrian Republics 1918–1926', in Feldman, G. et al. (eds), *The Experience of Inflation – International and Comparative Studies*, Berlin, Walter de Gruyter.

Bordo, Michael D. and Capie, Forrest (1994), 'Introduction', in Bordo, Michael D. and Capie, Forrest (eds), *Monetary Regimes in Transition*, Cambridge, Cambridge University Press.

Boross, Elizabeth A. (1984), 'The role of the state issuing bank in the course of inflation in Hungary between 1918 and 1924', in Feldman, G. et al. (eds), *The Experience of Inflation – International and Comparative Studies*, Berlin, Walter de Gruyter.

Capie, Forrest, Goodhart, C. and Schnadt, N. (eds) (1994), *The Development of Central Banking*, monograph prepared for the Tercentenary of the Bank of England Central Banking Symposium, 9 June 1994.

Cechoslovakische Nationalbank (1937), *Zehn Jahre Cechoslovakische Nationalbank*, Prag.

Chandler, L.V. (1971), *American Monetary Policy, 1928–1941*, New York, Harper & Row.

Clarke, Stephen V.O. (1967), *Central Bank Cooperation: 1924–31*, New York, Federal Reserve Bank of New York.

Compass (1935), *Finanzielles Jahrbuch – Band Österreich*, Vienna, Compassverlag.

Cottrell, Philip L. (1994), 'The role of the western "expert" in central European finance: Strakosch, Norman and the development of central banking from South Africa to Hungary, 1919–1924', paper presented at the conference: *Rebuilding the Financial System in Central and Eastern Europe*, Budapest, 11 November 1994.

Cowles, Virginia (1973), *Die Rothschilds – Geschichte einer Familie*, Würzburg, Ploetz.

Fisher, Irving (1923), 'Stabilization in Europe', *American Economic Review*, XIII, March.

Gedye, G.E.R. (1931a), 'The Austro-German "Bombshell"', *The Contemporary Review*, 139 (785), May.

Gedye, G.E.R. (1931b), 'France astride Middle Europe', *The Contemporary Review*, 140 (790), October.

Hertz, F.O. (1947), *The Economic Problem of the Danubian States: A Study in Economic Nationalism*, London, Gollancz.

Kamitz, Reinhard (1949), 'Die österreichische Geld- und Währungspolitik von 1848 bis 1948', in Mayer, Hans (ed.), *Hundert Jahre Oesterreichische Wirtschaftsentwicklung 1848–1948*, Wien, Springer Verlag.

Kernbauer, Hans (1991), *Währungspolitik in der Zwischenkriegszeit*, Wien, Oesterreichische Nationalbank.

Kerschagl, Richard (1920), *Die Währungstrennung in den Nationalstaaten*, Wien, Manz'sche Verlags- und Universitäts-Buchhandlung.

League of Nations (1924), *Memorandum on Central Banks, 1913 and 1918–1923*, Geneva, League of Nations.

März, Eduard and Weber, Fritz (1983), 'The antecedents of the Austrian financial crash of 1931', *Zeitschrift für Wirtschafts- und Sozialwissenschaften*, 103.Jg., Heft 5, Berlin, Duncker & Humblot.

Magyar Nemzeti Bank (1993), *A Magyar Nemzeti Bank Története I.*, Budapest, Közgazdasági és Jogi Könyvkiadó.

National Bank of Hungary (1994), *National Bank of Hungary – 70 Years of Existence (1924–1994)*, Budapest.

Nötel, Rudolf (1984), 'Money, banking and industry in interwar Austria and Hungary', *The Journal of European Economic History*, 13 (2), Special Issue.

Nurkse, Ragnar (1946), *The Course and Control of Inflation*, Geneva, League of Nations.

Péteri, György (1995), *Revolutionary Twenties*, Trondheim, University of Trondheim.

Pressburger, Siegfried (1966), *Oesterreichische Notenbank 1816–1966*, Vienna, Oesterreichische Nationalbank.

Rasín, Alois (1923), *Financial Policy of Czechoslovakia during the First Year of its History*, Oxford, The Clarendon Press.

Sargent, Thomas (1982), 'The ends of four big inflations', in Hall, R.E. (ed.), *Inflation: Causes and Effects*, Chicago, Chicago University Press.

Schubert, Aurel (1990), 'The Causes of the Austrian Currency Crisis of 1931', in Komlos, John (ed.), *Economic Development in the Habsburg Monarchy and in the Successor States*, Boulder, East European Monographs. Reprinted in Bordo, Michael (ed.) (1992), *Financial Crises*

Volume II, Hants: Edward Elgar, and in Matis, Herbert (ed.) (1994), *The Economic Development of Austria Since 1870*, Hants, Edward Elgar.

Schubert, Aurel (1991), *The Credit-Anstalt Crisis of 1931*, Cambridge, Cambridge University Press.

Schubert, Aurel (1993), 'Lessons from the *Credit-Anstalt* crisis in Austria (1931)', in OECD (ed.), *Transformation of the Banking System: Portfolio Restructuring, Privatisation and the Payment System*, Paris, OECD.

Schubert, Aurel and Theurl, T. (1995a), 'The 70-year history of the *schilling*', *Reports and Summaries*, 1/1995, Vienna, Oesterreichische Nationalbank.

Schubert, Aurel and Theurl, T. (1995b), 'Währung und Banken in den Nachfolgestaaten', in Pickl, Othmar and Metlar, R. (eds), *Zerfall und Integration*, Vienna, Bank Austria.

Schwarzer, O. and Schneider, J. (1987), 'Europäische Wechselkurse seit 1913', in Fischer, W. et al. (eds), *Handbuch der Europäischen Wirtschafts- und Sozialgeschichte*, Band 6, Stuttgart, Klett-Cotta.

Siklos, Pierre L. (1994), 'Interpreting a change in monetary policy regimes: a reappraisal of the first Hungarian hyperinflation and stabilization, 1921–28', in Bordo, Michael D. and Capie, F. (eds), *Monetary Regimes in Transition*, Cambridge, Cambridge University Press.

Sokal, Max and Rosenberg, Otto (1929), 'The banking system of Austria', in Willis, H. Parker and B.H. Beckhart (eds), *Foreign Banking Systems*, New York, Henry Holt and Co.

Stiefel, Dieter (1989), *Finanzdiplomatie und Weltwirtschaftskrise*, Frankfurt am Main, Fritz Knapp Verlag.

Szapáry, György (1994), 'The National Bank of Hungary: from cradle to manhood striving for independence', paper presented at the conference: *Rebuilding the Financial System in Central and Eastern Europe*, Budapest, 11 November 1994.

Teichová, Alice (1993), 'Kontinuität und Diskontinuität: Banken und Industrie in Mitteleuropa im 20. Jahrhundert', *Österreichische Zeitschrift für Geschichtswissenschaften*, 4.Jg., Heft 4, Vienna, Verlag für Gesellschaftskritik.

Teichová, Alice (1995), 'Commercial (universal) banking in Central Europe – from Cisleithania to the successor states', in Fase, Martin, Feldman, G. and Pohl, M. (eds), *How to Write the History of a Bank*, Frankfurt am Main, European Association for Banking History.

Toynbee, Arnold J. (1932), *Survey of International Affairs 1931*, Oxford, Oxford University Press.

Walré de Bordes, Jan van (1924), *The Austrian Crown. Its Depreciation and Stabilization*, London.

Weber, Fritz (1994), 'Universal banking in inter-war Central Europe', in Matis, Herbert (ed.), *The Economic Development of Austria Since 1870*, Hants, Edward Elgar.

Weber, Fritz (1995), 'Central European banking between 1850 and 1950', in Fase, M.M.G., Feldman, G. and Pohl, M. (eds), *How to Write the History of a Bank*, Frankfurt am Main, European Association for Banking History.

Yeager, L.B. (1981), *Experiences with Stopping Inflation*, Washington, DC, American Enterprise Institute.

Zeuceanu, Alexander (1924), *La Liquidation de la Banque d'Autriche-Hongrie*, Vienne, Imprimerie des Mechitharistes.

Zuckerkandl, R. (1911), 'The Austro-Hungarian Bank', in National Monetary Commission (ed.), *Banking in Russia, Austro-Hungary, The Netherlands and Japan*, Washington, DC, Government Printing Office.

CHAPTER EIGHT

US and Canadian Central Banking: The Triumph of Personalities over Politics?[1]

Pierre L. Siklos

> There have been three great inventions since the beginning of time: fire, the wheel and central banking.
>
> (attributed to Will Rogers)

Introduction

It is fair to say that the arrival of central banking was greeted with reluctance and scepticism in both the US and Canada. Both the Federal Reserve and the Bank of Canada were born at times when existing financial institutions seemed incapable of providing monetary stability. While there is perhaps today widespread agreement that central banks are necessary institutions, there is considerably less agreement about the limits of their authority. The experience of the last three decades has led to the perception that central banks have tended to follow the monetary policy of their governments with the resulting inflation, stagnation, or both. This experience has reinforced in the public's mind the importance of some form of price stability as a macroeconomic objective and central bankers seem to have triumphed, in the words of Paul Volcker (1994), in presenting themselves as the only guarantors of such a goal. The same realization was reached in Canada, as evidenced by the opinions of a former governor of the Bank of Canada, John Crow, in his now famous Hanson Lecture (Crow, 1988), when he declared that a central bank's sole responsibility should be the pursuit of price stability. The above considerations suggest that success at maintaining low and stable inflation rates during the late 1980s and throughout the 1990s was possible because politicians, chastened by their past excesses, gave their central banks the necessary statutory powers required to tame inflation permanently.

Friedman pointed out some time ago that actual central bank behaviour is determined more by the personalities in charge of monetary policy than by the statutory framework governing their operations (Friedman, 1962). To be sure, there are other determinants of central bank performance, such as the exchange rate regime, the nature and types of shocks which hit the economy, the degree of capital mobility, to name but three such factors. Nor can it be said that all of the personalities who headed the Federal Reserve or the Bank of Canada made their mark in equal fashion. This chapter attempts to demonstrate that a contradiction appears to exist between economic performance measures and historical descriptions of central banks and their chief executive officers (CEOs). A reading of the latter suggests that Friedman's view (articulated again more recently by, for example, Sylla, 1988 and Kettl, 1986) does not hold up as well when a time series analysis on key economic indicators is conducted. Nevertheless, personalities are important to the understanding of central banking history in the US and Canada in the following senses.

First, the weight attached to a personality's influence is a function of the institutional framework governing central bank–government relations. Second, the influence of the personality at the head of the central bank is also a function of whether he is tested either by some political conflict over the central banks' authority in the realm of monetary policy, as well as the stance of monetary policy *vis-à-vis* the stance of fiscal policy. In particular, does the central bank stand against excessively expansionary fiscal policy or is its stance rather accommodative?

The chapter is organized as follows. The next section examines, briefly, the institutional set-up of the two central banks and illustrates how informative or uninformative the statutes of these institutions are about central bank performance or the role of government interference in monetary policy. The section also provides a descriptive analysis of economic performance and a general assessment of central bank behaviour in both the US and Canada, in order to motivate the potential role of personalities and politics. The section following provides some historical examples of the role of personalities throughout the history of the two central banks. This description permits us to speculate about the issue of whether it is more fruitful to analyse central bank behaviour as a game between two players (that is, the government versus the central bank) or whether we should rely instead on the principal–agent framework where the agent (the central bank) must deal with various pressures emanating from the principal (the government). This theoretical detour serves as a useful backdrop against which to understand the apparent inconsistencies between the econometric and the historical evidence.

Needless to say, given that dozens of volumes have documented the histories of the Federal Reserve and the Bank of Canada, the objective is not to be comprehensive, indeed such a task is not feasible, but rather to illustrate the potentially far-reaching impact of some of the personalities which headed these central banks.

The chapter concludes with a summary which asks what the results and the central thesis of the chapter tell us about the recent focus on the importance attached to central bank independence.

Economic and institutional performance

Institutional make-up and rigidity in central bank laws

Both Canada and the United States possess federal forms of government with authority over financial matters constitutionally divided between the federal government and the States (US) or Provinces (Canada). Powers not specifically granted by the Constitution to the US federal government are reserved to the States. By contrast, the British North America Act of 1867 gave full authority over the financial system to the federal government in Canada but the narrow definition of banking enshrined in the first Bank Act of 1871 encouraged the development of a parallel system of banking which would become provincially regulated over time.[2] Much has been said and written about the comparative stability of the Canadian banking system in relation to the US. Some of the most important factors explaining the differences between the two systems include regulatory differences (that is, branch banking in Canada versus limited branch banking in the US), and the low threat of failure in the Canadian system (for example, see Bordo, Rockoff and Redish, 1994 and references therein).

In the US, the devastating impact of unstable banking in the late nineteenth and early twentieth centuries led to the formation of the Federal Reserve, although central banking type institutions had previously existed and failed (that is, the First and Second Banks of the United States and the National Bank Act; see, for example, Timberlake, 1993). Clearly then, the central bank as a lender of last resort represented an important consideration in the formation of the Federal Reserve.[3]

The same cannot be said to be true of the Canadian case. The MacMillan Commission, created by the Conservative government in 1933 in response to political pressure by the Liberals, advocated the creation of a central bank which would eventually remove the (profitable) note-issuing authority of the chartered banks which were regulated by the federal government. Initially, the Bank of Canada was to be privately owned but, in 1936, an election promise by the incoming Liberal government led to the effective nationalization of the young central bank. Hence, purely political influences loomed larger in the emergence of the Bank of Canada (Bordo and Redish, 1987) than in the case of the Federal Reserve. This evidence is reinforced by the fact that the agricultural crisis which helped the movement to create the Fed, and which also afflicted Canada, led the Canadian government to become the lender of last resort for a time via the Finance Act (for example, see Jamieson, 1953).

Consistent with the desire for decentralization, the lawmakers who created the Federal Reserve System put in place the kinds of checks and balances that typify the US Constitution. Initially, the regional banks, the Board of Governors in Washington and the Federal Open Market Committee (FOMC) were to perform different functions. The onset of the Great Depression changed all that and the Fed, in addition to controlling the currency in circulation and acting as a lender of last resort, began to exercise control over monetary policy.[4]

Unlike Canada, where the Bank of Canada Act enshrines the duties and limitations of central bank authority and the Bank Act accomplishes the same for banks,[5] legislation directly or indirectly influencing the Fed is far more diffuse. One need only look at the Federal Reserve Act of 1913 and the long list of amendments and laws related to banking in order to appreciate this point (Walsh, 1981). I will return to this issue below.

The diffuse nature of authority over monetary and financial policy also extends to the supervision of the banking sector. Whereas in Canada, supervision of the banking sector is not entrusted to the Bank of Canada (though there has been and continues to be some central bank involvement), the Federal Reserve, along with the Treasury, the Comptroller of the Currency and State regulators, all share part of the burden of supervising the banking system. This partial dependence was most recently in evidence with the Savings and Loan debacle (see White, 1983).

It has often been argued that the structure of the Federal Open Market Committee (FOMC) and the process by which monetary policy decisions are made generate useful information about the stance of policy (for example, Havrilesky, 1995 and references therein). The evidence using this type of analysis is, at best, mixed since there exists other evidence, at least as convincing, which suggests that FOMC chairmen get the monetary policy they wish. By contrast, in the Canadian context, authority over monetary policy is no longer the responsibility of the governor alone but is currently in the hands of a committee of senior Bank of Canada officials.[6]

Finally, there are some differences between the two central banks in regards to that elusive concept called accountability. In Siklos (1995) I define accountability as consisting of three elements:

1. Clarity and precision of the overall objectives of monetary policy.
2. The extent to which the central bank is required to formally report on its activities, and whether it is responsible or not for generating the necessary statistical information.
3. The extent to which monetary policy decisions are reported to the public.

According to these criteria, the Fed and the Bank of Canada currently fulfil the second criterion but this is only a recent occurrence in the US, where Congress has required the Fed to produce semi-annual monetary policy reports. In Canada, the monetary policy reporting device is an even more recent feature of Bank of Canada operations.[7] Since 1991, the governor[8] and the minister of finance have agreed on inflation targets, but these have not yet been enshrined in the Bank of Canada Act nor have sanctions been announced in the case of failure to meet the stated targets. In addition, of course, both central banks have published extensive annual and other reports outlining their activities and produce valuable monetary and financial data. Only the Fed publishes the minutes of its meetings on monetary policy and then only with a relatively long lag.[9]

While I have stressed the differences in the institutional setting of the two central banks, I would be remiss if I did not point out some important similarities in the financial environment in which the Fed and the Bank of Canada have operated. Importantly, the development of the two countries' financial systems has been quite similar. Econometric evidence by Bordo and Jonung (1981, 1987) and, more recently, by Siklos (1993) and Bordo, Jonung and Siklos (1997), shows that financial and institutional change has proceeded in a common fashion since the beginning of this century. This, perhaps more than the differences in central bank structures, explains the similarities in business cycle developments in the two countries (see Figure 8.1). There is another way in which the two central banks are comparable in an important respect. Remarkably, not a single aspect of the legislation governing these two central banks has changed since the 1950s, based on Cukierman's (1992) coding.[10]

Clearly, given that overall economic performance has varied a great deal since the 1950s, it would appear to be incorrect to place too much emphasis purely on central bank statutory considerations. Notice how similar the inflationary and output growth experiences of the two countries have been, according to Figure 8.1, despite two seemingly different central banks as defined by legislation. Unemployment rates too are quite similar though these became persistently higher in Canada during the 1980s. Of course, while the entire responsibility for these economic developments cannot be placed at the hands of the respective countries'

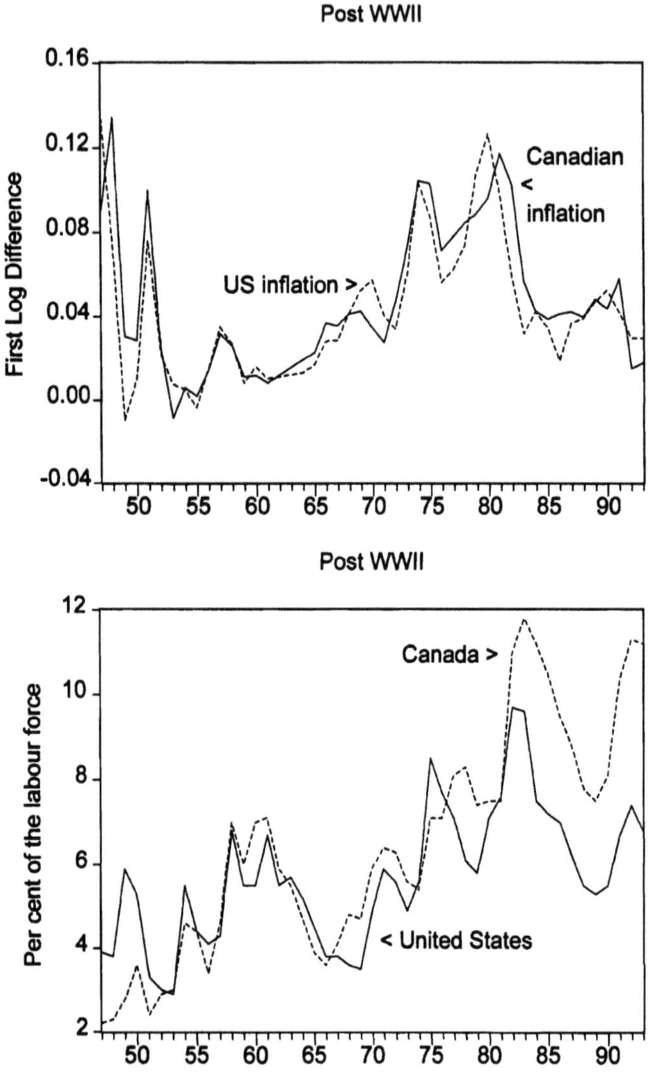

8.1 Inflation, unemployment and economic growth in the US and Canada since the Second World War

Source: All data are annual. US CPI data is from the US Bureau of the Census (1975) updated from the *Survey of Current Business*. Unemployment data are from the January 1993 Economic Report of the president and updated from the *Survey of Current Business*. Canadian data are from Urquhart and Buckley (1965), Leacy, Urquhart and Buckley (1983), and the *Bank of Canada Review*.

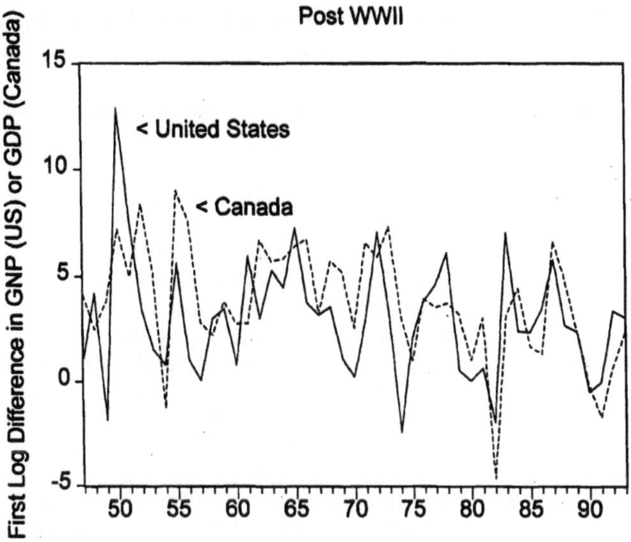

8.1 continued

central banks, they do raise doubts about the importance of central bank statutes. Moreover, the classification introduced by Cukierman omits the subtlety of central bank–government relations such as the Fed–Treasury Accord of 1951, which returned authority over interest rate setting to the Fed, or the Coyne–Rasminsky Directive in Canada (1961) which defined more precisely the mechanism by which the Federal government can interfere in the operations of monetary policy.[11] Moreover, as pointed out earlier, looking at the Federal Reserve Act in isolation can be misleading since an examination of the amendments to the Federal Reserve Act, as well as changes in laws affecting banking, and therefore the Fed to a certain extent, reveals considerable involvement by the Congress. Table 8.1 provides a selective listing of some of the legislative changes affecting the Fed over the years, while Figure 8.2 plots the frequency of legislative changes affecting the Fed in the 1914–80 period.[12] As Table 8.1 and Figure 8.2 both make clear, understanding the role and activities of the Fed requires more than just an understanding of the major piece of legislation governing its activities.

Aggregate performance indicators and their properties

Background and data I begin the exploration of US and Canadian central banking by investigating the statistical properties of key economic indicators for both countries.

Table 8.1 Significant amendments to Federal Reserve legislation

Date	Changes
23 April 1918	Complete revision
3 June 1922	Section 10
21 July 1932	Reconstruction Finance Association broadening of lending powers
22 July 1932	Creation Federal Home Loans banks
9 March 1933	Relief to emergency in banking
16 June 1934	Section 12B of Act and deposit insurance
23 August 1935	Major stability of banking system
16 August 1948	Protect economy from inflationary pressures
31 May 1960	Amendment to FDIC Act to require federal approval of mergers and consolidations of insured banks
3 March 1965	Elimination of Fed gold reserve requirement
21 February 1966	Procedures of review of bank mergers
21 September 1966	More flexible regulation of interest rates
16 October 1966	Strengthening of regulatory and supervisory functions
23 December 1969	Lower interest rates and light inflation
18 May 1971	Laws relating to the setting of interest rates
9 August 1971	Authorizing emergency loan guarantees to major business enterprises
31 March 1972	Modifying par value of the dollar
16 August 1973	Relating to the setting of interest rates
28 October 1974	Increasing protection under deposit insurance
16 November 1977	Promoting accountability of Fed
21 July 1978	Permitting audit of the Fed by the Comptroller General of the US
10 November 1978	Extending authority on interest rate setting
31 March 1980	Depository Institutions Deregulation and Monetary Control Act
15 October 1982	Garn-St Germain Act expanding power of FDIC and FSLIC (deposit insurance)
1987	Competitive Equality Banking Act – change of definition of what constitutes banking activity
1989	Financial Institutions Reform; Recovery and Enforcement Act; Changes to FDIC (deposit insurance); Abolition of FSLIC and FHLB (Federal Home Loan Board); Resolution Trust Corp established
1991	FDIC Improvements Act. Reforms in supervision of banks
1992	Futures Trading Practices Act – permits Board to set margins for derivatives
1993	NAFTA (North American Free Trade Agreement)

Source: Walsh (1981); various House and Senate documents; and Board of Governors Annual Reports (various years).

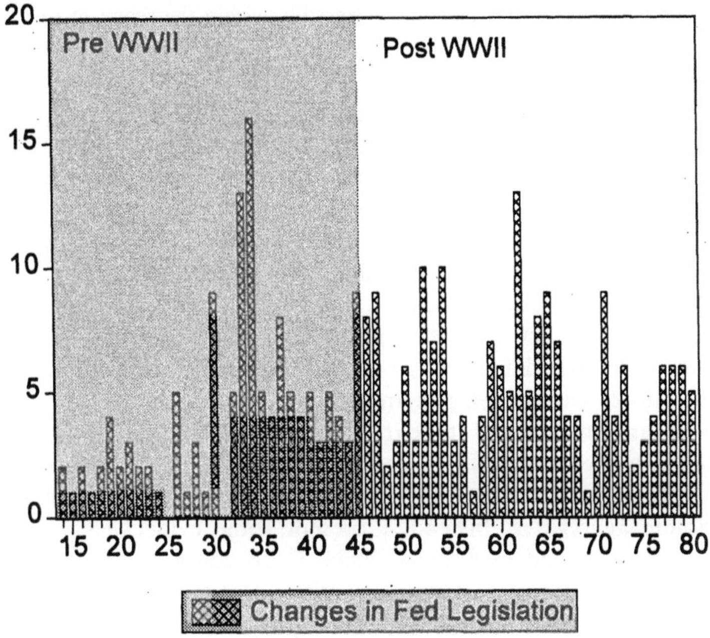

8.2 Changes in Federal Reserve and related legislation, 1914–80

Source: Compiled from information in Walsh (1981).

Because the Federal Reserve was originally created simply as a lender of last resort, to monopolize currency issue and to perform open market operations, the laws governing its operations have never clearly spelled out the *economic goals* for which it is responsible. The Preamble to the Federal Reserve Act states that the Fed is to 'furnish an elastic currency, to afford means of rediscounting commercial paper, to establish a more effective supervision of banking in the United States, ... ' (Walsh,1981: 1). Moreover, as we have seen (Table 8.1), the Fed's role has evolved over time to include a supervisory role, an anti-inflation as well as pro-economic growth role. Indeed, the novelty of the Fed system was that it was intended to serve the commercial banks and government only, as well as recognize the impact of banking and monetary policy at the regional level.

In contrast, the Preamble to the Bank of Canada Act has remained unchanged since 1934 and required the central bank

> ... to regulate credit and currency in the best interests of the economic life of the nation, to control and protect the external value of the national monetary unit and to mitigate by its influence fluctuations in the general level of production, trade, prices and

> employment, so far as may be possible within the scope of monetary action, and generally to promote the economic and financial welfare of the Dominion ... (Aufricht, 1961: 89).

To understand economic performance under central banking, five key economic indicators are briefly examined. They are: real GNP (GDP for Canada), or *y*; inflation in wholesale prices for the US (consumer prices for Canada), or *p*; the unemployment rate, or *u*; stock returns, or *s*; and government spending (as a rough proxy for fiscal policy), or *g*. Details about the data sources and definitions are provided either in Tables 8.3 and 8.4 or in the Data Appendix. Since I wish to explore the influence of central bank actions, it is desirable to have the highest possible frequency for the data.[13] However, I supplement some US and Canadian evidence with longer-run annual data.

Analysis of means and standard deviations of time series, while useful perhaps, make it difficult to ascertain the role of political, economic and institutional factors in influencing the time series behaviour of key economic aggregates. Instead, I present some evidence based on an approach suggested by Perron (1994).[14] To conserve space, however, only the statistically significant coefficients from the application of Perron's methodology are shown in Tables 8.2 and 8.3. When a moving average term is not shown it was either statistically insignificant or could not be included because the sample was split due to missing observations (see the notes to Table 8.2). Table 8.2 presents evidence for the US, while the results for Canada are in Table 8.3.

US evidence In the case of output growth, only the chairmanships of Young and Meyer, both of whom served as governors[15] before the Second World War, are significant. The impact of various Fed chairmen on inflation appears to be more significant. With the exception of the Young and Meyer's era which saw negative inflation rates, several other chairman presided over significantly higher average inflation rates. Notable by their absence are Volcker and Greenspan who, unlike their predecessors, did not produce higher or lower mean inflation rates. Turning to unemployment rates, we see again that no post-Second World War chairman had either a positive or a negative impact on average unemployment rates. Hence, if one difference emerges between pre- and post-Second World War eras it is that the Fed until 1948 was relatively more concerned with both the inflation and output (or unemployment) effects of their policies. Since 1948 only inflationary effects of Fed Chairmen can be detected.

The performance of the stock market reveals some impact throughout the Fed's history. Not surprisingly, under the governorship of Meyer and Black, average stock prices fell dramatically since their period in office coincided with the Great Depression. However, the stock market also significantly underperformed the historical average during the chairmanship of both Martin and Burns.

In the case of the fiscal policy proxy, namely the rate of change in real government expenditures, again we find significant effects throughout the Fed's history. Not surprisingly perhaps, as the Second World War was looming on the horizon, the time period during which Eccles presided over the Fed (1934–48) was one of significant expansion in fiscal policy. This was sharply reversed during McCabe's chairmanship in the years 1951–70. Both Martin and, interestingly, Volcker stand out as having presided over periods of relatively expansionary fiscal policy.

In part B of Table 8.2, the significance of electoral or partisan factors is explored. Both are measured via dummy variables which are active either around election times or around partisan changes in government. Since the literature on partisan and electoral cycles is vast, only a brief description follows. Readers are asked to consult, for example, Alesina (1988) for additional details.

In Nordhaus's (1975) seminal approach (see also MacRae, 1977), pre-election periods become the driving force for generating changes in economic activity which are meant to enhance re-election prospects. As a result, since US presidential elections are held regularly every four years, a politically motivated business cycle emerges. Economic agents in this model do not form expectations rationally.[16] This vintage of political models is generally called political business cycle (PBC) models. An alternative model posits that political parties are partisan in their application of policies (see, for example, Hibbs, 1977). This means that US Democrats or Liberals in Canada prefer lower unemployment at the expense of higher inflation prior to an election. The opposite is true of US Republicans or Canadian Conservatives. In the original exposition of this theory voters do not form expectations rationally. This is the essence of the partisan theory (PT) political business cycles.

More recently, the principle of rational expectations has been incorporated into existing macroeconomic models in which political factors also matter. Under rational expectations, voters are assumed to be forward looking, and so political business cycles can only arise due to the existence of some type of information asymmetry. For example, voters may have difficulty in distinguishing between the temporary and permanent effects of government spending on debt, thus providing governments with the opportunity to create electoral cycles despite the rationality of economic agents. Such models are usually called rational political business cycle (RPBC) models (Cukierman, 1986; Cukierman and Meltzer, 1986; Rogoff and Siebert, 1988; Rogoff, 1987). Political cycles are said to arise in part because of the uncertainty over election

Table 8.2 Summary of key indicators: US, 1914–95

Variable	Indicator	Sample	Coeff.	Std dev.
A. Personalities				
Young	*y*	Full	–5.67	4.42
Meyer	*y*		–12.12	4.80
MA(1)			–0.67	0.12
Harding	*p*		5.19	4.43
Young	*p*		–6.91	5.40
Meyer	*p*		–8.14	5.49
Black	*p*		11.48	6.32
Eccles	*p*		4.70	3.79
Burns	*p*		6.23	4.23
Miller	*p*		7.42	5.24
MA(1)			–0.90	0.05
Young	*u*		0.93	0.47
Meyer	*u*		2.45	0.52
Black	*u*		–0.84	0.62
Eccles	*u*		–0.65	0.31
MA(1)			–0.61	0.12
Meyer	*s*		–79.09	15.52
Black	*s*		–27.88	15.51
Martin	*s*		–11.53	10.25
Burns	*s*		–14.94	11.95
MA(1)			–0.99	0.0001
Crissinger	*g*		5.73	4.03
Young	*g*		7.35	4.72
Black	*g*		9.47	6.83
Eccles	*g*		10.35	3.53
McCabe	*g*		–14.07	4.76
Martin	*g*		6.16	2.78
Volcker	*g*		4.94	3.38
B. Politics				
ETMP2P	*y*	Full	2.08	0.85
ETMP2P	*y*	Pre	3.11	1.14N
MA(1)			–0.44	0.23
ETMP2P	*y*	Post	0.64	0.42
ETMP4P	*p*	Full	–1.21	0.45
MA(1)			–0.99	0.00003
ETMP4P	*p*	Pre	–0.84	1.98N
ETMP4P	*p*	Post	–0.76	0.70N
PRES	*u*	Full	0.54	0.17
MA(1)			–0.64	0.13
PRES	*u*	Pre	1.04	0.48
MA(1)			–0.65	0.28
PRES	*u*	Post	0.07	0.04
ETMP2P	*s*	Full	3.33	3.14N
ETMP2P	*s*	Pre	11.60	7.71N
ETMP2P	*s*	Post	0.71	3.51N
MA(1)			–0.50	0.31
PRES	*g*	Full	–2.14	1.77N
PRES	*g*	Pre	–1.27	0.28
MA(1)			0.99	0.0001

Table 8.2 continued

Variable	Indicator	Sample	Coeff.	Std dev.
PRES	*g*	Post	–2.27	1.66N
C. Major events				
DEPR	*y*	Full	–11.13	3.40
MA(1)			–0.40	0.18
OIL	*p*	Full	3.93	2.09
WAR	*p*	Full	–1.10	0.87
MA(1)			0.51	0.25
GOLDSTD	*u*	Full	0.51	0.20
DEPR	*u*	Full	1.92	0.38
WAR	*u*	Full	–0.81	0.21
MA(1)			–0.57	0.12
DEPR	*s*	Full	–53.62	10.91
MA(1)			0.99	0.0001
GOLDSTD	*g*	Full	–3.49	2.43
WAR	*g*		11.81	3.47
D. NBER recession				
RCESSION	*y*	Full	–8.80	1.29
	y	Pre	–15.01	2.99
	y	Post	–4.66	0.79
RCESSION	*p*	Full	–4.10	1.65
	p	Pre	–7.77	2.91
	p	Post	–0.53	1.22N
RCESSION	*u*	Full	0.01	0.01
MA(1)			0.99	0.0005
RCESSION	*u*	Pre	0.20	0.09
MA(1)			0.98	0.01
RCESSION	*u*	Post	0.05	0.02
MA(1)			0.99	0.007
RCESSION	*s*	Full	–16.67	5.34
	s	Pre	–31.85	12.22
	s	Post	–11.22	5.72
RCESSION	*g*	Full	–2.65	1.94
RCESSION	*g*	Pre	–2.88	0.71
MA(1)			0.99	0.0001
RCESSION	*g*	Post	–0.99	1.36N

Notes: Except for part B, only the statistically significant coefficients at least at the 15 per cent level are given. All regressions contain three autoregressive lags.

Column 1: The dates when the various CEOs held office are provided in Table 8.4. MA(1) represents the first order moving coefficient.

Column 2: y = real GNP; p = inflation in WPI; u = unemployment rate; s = rate of change in stock prices; g = rate of change in government purchases.

Column 3: The full sample is 01.1914–02.1995. Pre refers to pre-Second World War (01.1914–02.1939); Post refers to post-Second World War (01.1948–02.1995).

Column 5: N in part B signifies statistically insignificant coefficients.

For more detailed explanations and sources see the data appendix.

outcomes (Alesina, 1988; Alesina and Sachs, 1988). Alternatively, political parties are ideologically motivated to enact policies which redistribute income in such a way as to maximize the likelihood of re-election (Havrilesky, 1990). Such models represent the rational partisan theory (RPT) of political business cycles. (For empirical evidence in support of the above models see, for example, Alesina, 1988; Alesina and Sachs, 1988, and references therein.)

Following previous conventions, the political variables are dummy variables which take on either a value of 0 or 1, depending on the political event and its length, or are impulse dummy variables which take on values of –1, +1, or 0, again depending on the event. When pre-electoral effects on unemployment or output are thought to take place, as in the PBC model, the dummy is active anywhere from 2 to 4 quarters before the election quarter[17] and is set to zero thereafter (called ELECTB2 or ELECTB4). In the case where inflation effects are postponed, a dummy variable is active 2 to 4 quarters following the election quarter and is zero thereafter (called ELECTA2 or ELECTA4). When the pre- and post-electoral effects are assumed to be transitory, the dummies are called ETMP2 or ETMP4. Thus, for example, a pre-electoral effect on unemployment is reversed in the quarters following the election.

In the case of partisan changes the dummy variable takes the value +1, when a Republican president or Conservative prime minister (PM) is elected, and –1, when a Democratic president is elected. In the partisan view, Republicans or Conservatives prefer lower inflation to lower unemployment (higher output). By contrast, Democrats or Liberals opt for lower unemployment (higher output) over lower inflation. The impact on the goal variables can either be permanent, as in the PT model variable (called PRES), or transitory as in the RPT approach (these, however, never proved to be statistically significant).

The evidence in part B of Table 8.2 is based on the full sample, as well as pre- and post-Second World War samples (see Gordon, 1986 and Siklos, 1992). For this reason some of the electoral variables are not statistically significant but are shown in order to highlight the differences between pre- and post-Second World War data.[18]

For output, we see that electoral influences are present only after the Second World War and, on average, raise GNP growth by less than one per cent. More significantly, electoral influences do not affect inflation either in the full sample or in the separate pre- and post-Second World War samples. Moreover, as far as output growth and inflation are concerned, electoral influences are statistically more important than partisan factors, none of which proved to be statistically significant. The same result holds for stock market returns, again for the full sample as well as the separate pre- and post-Second World War samples. By contrast, partisan factors appear to be significant determinants of unemployment rates in both the pre- and post-Second World War eras though the quantitative impact of presidential partisan leanings is quantitatively small after 1947. Finally, partisan influences on fiscal policy seem to be a feature of the period before 1939 and reveal that, as expected, Republican presidents were relatively more fiscally conservative.

Part C of Table 8.2 reveals the extent to which major events such as the Great Depression, the two world wars, the gold standard and oil price shocks influenced the time series under consideration. The Depression has a significant impact (negative) on output growth, unemployment (positive) and stock returns (negative) but no independent influence on inflation. By contrast, the two oil price shocks of the 1970s significantly raise average inflation rates but no other macroeconomic variable considered is affected. Wars are seen to influence unemployment rates (negatively) and fiscal policy (positively) but neither inflation nor output growth were significantly affected. Finally, the gold exchange standard had a small positive effect on employment rates and a negative one on government spending growth, but no significant impact on inflation or output growth was detected.

I also considered for the US the impact of recessions versus expansions by using the NBER business cycle reference dates (RCESSION). Part D of Table 8.2 shows that output growth fell by more in the pre-Second World War era relative to post-1947 observations. Turning to inflation, however, recessions did not lead to lower average inflation rates after 1947; only pre-Second World War inflation rates are significantly lower during recessions, no doubt due to the presence of the gold standard. The results for the unemployment rate mirror those of output with a much larger quantitative impact of recessions on unemployment rates before 1939 than after the end of the Second World War. The same result holds for stock prices, which register smaller drops after 1947 than before 1939. Finally, government spending growth is significantly lower during recessions in the pre-Second World War era but is not significantly higher or lower after 1947.[19]

Canadian evidence The results shown in Table 8.3 follow the structure of Table 8.2. Output growth is found to be significantly higher under the Rasminsky and Thiessen governorships. Inflation is significantly higher in the Rasminsky and Bouey eras while the only unemployment rate effect shows up with Coyne's governorship. No statistically significant impact was found for governors' term of office and stock prices while average government spending is significantly higher under Coyne, Rasminsky and Bouey.

Turning to electoral and partisan influences, when the government has a majority in Parliament, both output growth and inflation as well as government spending growth are relatively lower on average. Unemployment rates are significantly lower prior to elections while a partisan

Table 8.3 Summary of key indicators: Canada, 1960–95

Variable	Indicator	Coeff.	Std dev.
A. Personalities			
Rasminsky	*y*	4.31	2.63
Thiessen		4.17	2.55
MA(1)		0.87	0.11
Rasminsky	*p*	1.97	1.45
Bouey		1.98	1.16
MA(1)		0.99	0.0001
Coyne	*u*	0.37	0.28
MA(1)		0.61	0.43
Non significant	*s*		
Coyne	*g*	8.63	5.35
Rasminsky		9.02	5.72
Bouey		5.91	4.22
B. Politics			
MAJOR	*y*	–1.83	1.17
MA(1)		0.79	0.17
MAJOR	*p*	–1.24	0.61
MA(1)		–0.93	0.03
EPRIOR	*u*	–0.65	0.39
MA(1)		0.65	0.39
DRPTB2	*s*	–14.29	7.58
MA(1)		–0.63	0.24
MAJOR	*g*	–0.80	0.26
MA(1)		0.99	0.01
C. Major events			
OILSHOK	*y*	not statistically significant	
OILSHOK	*p*	1.27	0.37
MA(1)		0.74	0.11
OILSHOK	*u*	0.03	0.01
MA(1)		1.03	0.06
OILSHOK	*s*	not statistically significant	
OILSHOK	*g*	not statistically significant	

Note: See the data appendix for sources and explanations.

change to the 'left' (that is, the election of a Liberal government) lowers mean stock returns. Given the sample period considered the oil price shock is the only major economic event considered and it is seen to have a significant positive impact on inflation and unemployment only; the other macroeconomic variables considered were not significantly affected.

Discussion The results presented so far have all been cast in terms of some assumptions about how these time series are generated and by assigning separate roles for the CEOs of the two central banks, political considerations or major economic events. Before proceeding to additional tests on the data it may be useful to step back and consider in an alternative fashion the potential for personalities, politics and economic events to impact overall economic performance. Figure 8.3 shows six plots of average inflation and output growth estimated over fixed samples of either 8 or 16 quarters and their confidence levels. For the US, these samples correspond to congressional and presidential electoral cycles, respectively, while for Canada the 16 quarter cycle corresponds approximately to electoral cycles which, of course, are not fixed in Canada. The shaded areas highlight periods when major events have taken place as well as eras for selected CEOs for both central banks.

As the overall interpretation of the results is unaffected by the window over which the means are evaluated, I shall focus on the results for the presidential cycle (the top right-hand and middle right-hand figures). If we define price stability as values for inflation which encompass zero inflation, then such periods occur rather infrequently in the Fed's history and are a fairly rare occurrence for the Bank of Canada (bottom figures). What is even more striking is the volatility of mean inflation rates, smoothed as they are, even within the period of the tenure of a single CEO. This is clearly the case for both McChesney Martin's and Greenspan's tenure at the Fed, as well as John Crow's tenure at the Bank of Canada. Clearly, even if all of these CEOs displayed a firm commitment to price stability, broadly defined other factors must clearly have come into play to explain inflation performance. It is not obvious, however, that there is a persistent or consistent electoral cycle either.

Turning to output growth, we see that positive economic growth is clearly more of a post-Second World War phenomenon for the US (or a feature of the 1960s and 1970s data for Canada). Moreover, for the US, sharp negative output growth is generally confined to the aftermath of a great event (for example, the Second World War) or the onset of some large shock (for example the Great Depression). It is also the case that output growth performance is not associated with a particular electoral cycle nor with a particular central bank CEO. Again, associating

Rolling mean inflation rates and their standard errors
(Congressional cycle)

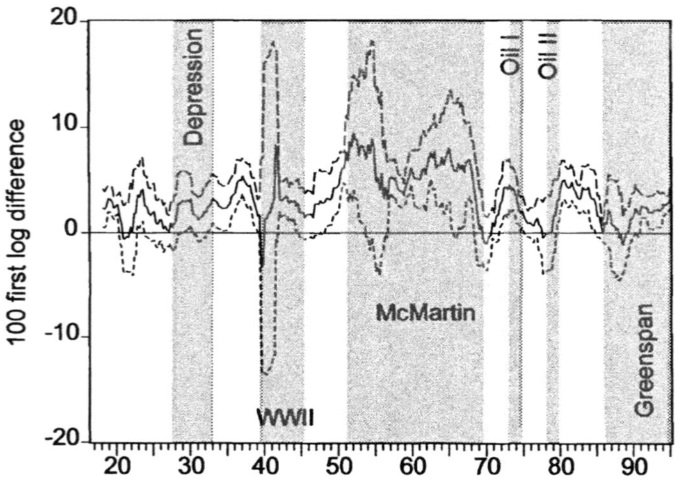

Rolling mean inflation rates and their standard errors
(Presidential cycle)

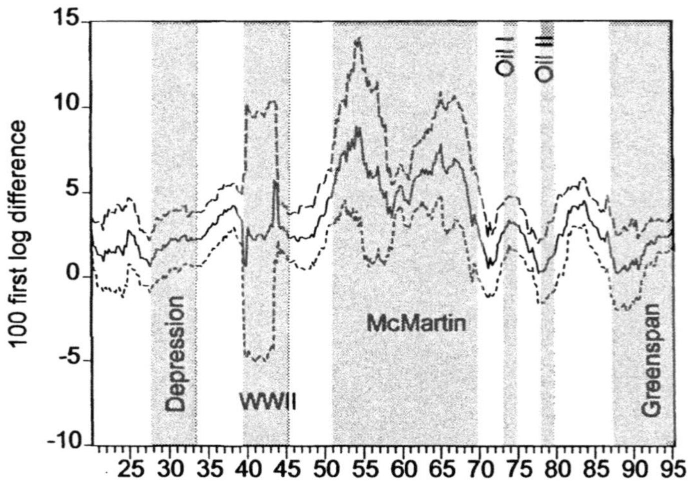

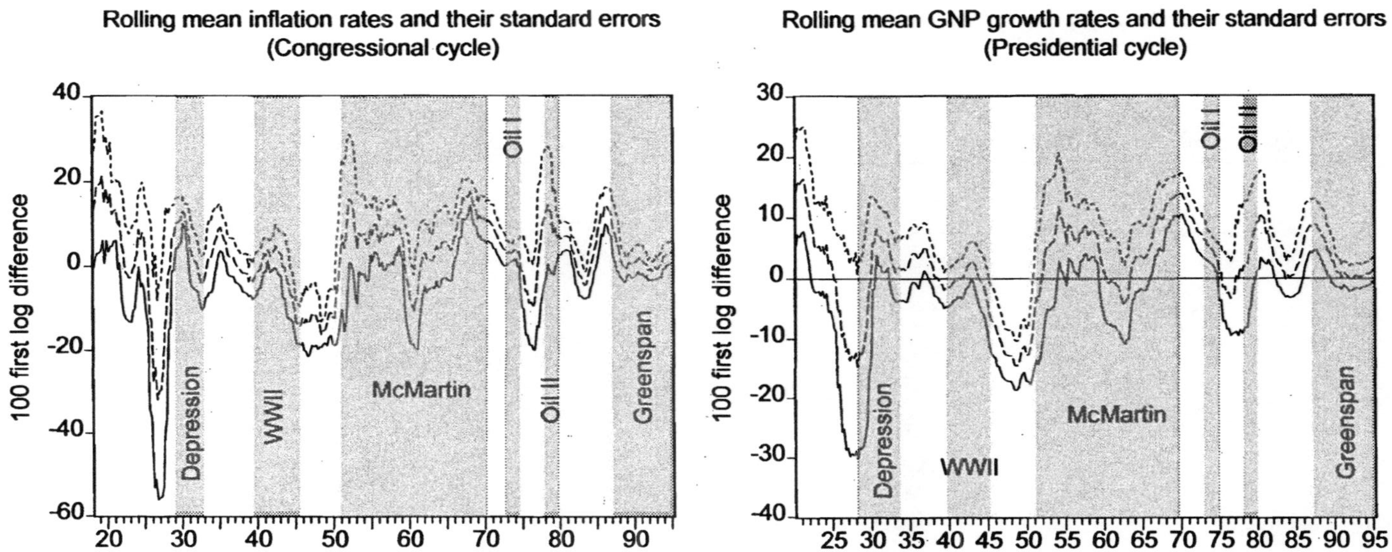

8.3 Rolling estimates of inflation and output growth for the US and Canada

Note: The results are generated by regressing inflation and output growth on a constant for a period of 8 or 16 quarters rolled over the entire available sample. For the US the sample is 1916:1–1995:2; for Canada, 1958:1–1995:2. Depression is 1928:1–1933:4; Second World War is 1939:3–1945:3; Oil I is 1973:1–1974:4; Oil II is 1978:1–1979:4. McMartin, Greenspan, Crow and Rasminsky are defined as in Table 8.4.

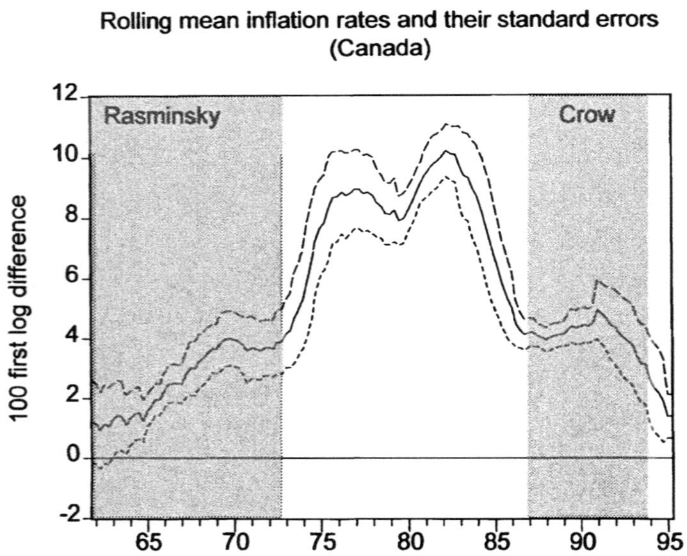

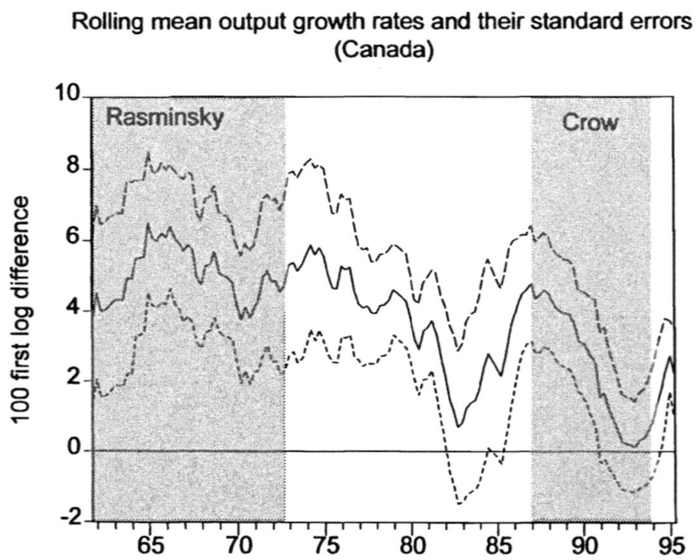

8.3 continued

economic performance with the personalities of central bankers or politics does not appear to yield unambiguous conclusions.

Personalities and politics: some highlights

Table 8.4 lists, for the Fed and the Bank of Canada, their respective CEOs since their inception. Arguments about the role and influence of central bank CEOs can be said to centre around two issues: (1) the clarity with which the statutes governing the central bank show who is authorized to conduct monetary policy; and (2) the procedures for resolving conflicts between the government and the central bank.

Table 8.4 CEOs in the US and Canada's central banks

Name	Period in office
A. Federal Reserve	
C. Hamlin	10/10/1914–09/08/1916
W.P.G. Harding	10/08/1916–09/08/1922
D.R. Crissinger	01/05/1923–15/09/1927
R.S. Young	04/10/1927–31/09/1930
E. Meyer	16/09/1930–10/05/1933
E.R. Black	09/05/1933–15/08/1934
M. Eccles	15/11/1934–31/01/1948
T.B. McCabe	15/04/1948–31/03/1951
W.M. McMartin	02/04/1951–31/01/1970
A.F. Burns	01/02/1970–31/01/1978
G.W. Miller	08/03/1978–06/08/1979
P.A. Volcker	06/08/1979–11/08/1987
A. Greenspan	11/08/1987–
B. Bank of Canada	
G.F. Towers	1934–Dec. 1954
J.E. Coyne	Jan. 1955–July 1961
L. Raminsky	Aug. 1961–Jan. 1973
G.K. Bouey	Feb. 1973–Dec. 1986
J.W. Crow	Jan. 1987–Jan. 1994
G.G. Thiessen	Jan. 1994–

Sources: Federal Reserve Bulletin, Bank of Canada and Morgan Stanley Central Bank Directory, (1995).

The US experience

Some authors have pointed out that, prior to 1935, the regionalization of the Fed built into the original Federal Reserve Act precluded any personality from dominating monetary policy. Chandler (1971, 1958), for example, argues that, as a result, the New York Fed emasculated the Federal Reserve Board and this permitted the personality of Benjamin Strong, then governor, to dominate Fed policies during the 1920s. Friedman and Schwartz (1963) concur, and they speculate that the errors which exacerbated the Great Depression might not have taken place but for the personality and influence of Benjamin Strong. On the other hand, Wheelock (1991; also see references within) shows, with equal persuasiveness, that Fed policies were consistent during the 1920s and 1930s and that a combination of faulty interpretation of economic events and common beliefs about the efficacy, or lack thereof, of monetary policy among a majority of the members of the Federal Reserve Board meant that monetary policy was consistent throughout the 1920s and 1930s. Indeed, the first twenty years of the Fed's existence was spent by the institution, and the Federal Reserve Board, defining itself and its authority. Timberlake (1993), for example, chronicles how the vagueness or lack of specificity in the Federal Reserve Act was exploited by the Board to enhance its power (also see Wicker, 1993 on this question), either via the control of discount rates or through the use of open market operations. Moreover, the first years of the Fed's existence, especially 1914–20, were spent fending off the intervention of the Secretary of the Treasury who sat as an ex-officio member of the Board (see Wicker, 1993 and Sylla, 1988).[20]

This type of interference can be said to have continued at least until the Fed–Treasury Accord of 1951 which clarified still further the functions of the Fed not specifically dealt with in the Banking Act of 1935. In fact, as Chandler remarks, Board decisions 'frequently turned on the presence or absence of the ex-officio members of the Board' (Chandler, 1971: 146).[21] About the only thing which is clear in Fed actions during the years until the Great Depression was the tenacity with which Board members held to the real bills doctrine. For example, in the 1923 Annual Report the Fed states:

> The Federal Reserve is a system of productive credit for either investment or speculative purposes. Credit in the service of agriculture, industry and trade may be described comprehensively as credit for productive use. The exclusion of the use of Federal Reserve Credit for speculative and investment purposes and its limitation to agricultural, industrial or commercial purposes thus clearly indicates the nature of the tests which are appropriate as guides in the extension of Federal Reserve credit.

From the perspective of the history of central banking, how important were the personalities of the CEOs? The Banking Act of 1935, the Fed–Treasury Accord of 1951, and the Monetary Control Act of 1980 provide convenient dividing points to ascertain spheres of influence. The six governors, as they were called then, who preceded Marriner Eccles did not generally play the role of central actors in monetary policy as have Paul Volcker or Alan Greenspan in more recent times. As noted earlier, this was partly due to the institutional set-up of the Fed which did not define lines of authority precisely but, equally importantly, owing to the belief of the Fed Board members who, more often than not, hesitated about the degree of action or inaction they should take. This attitude was fostered by political interference, especially from the likes of Senator Carter Glass, one of the framers of the Federal Reserve Board, who effectively blocked clarification of Fed objectives (Chandler, 1971). But there was also considerable ambivalence within the Fed about the desirability of a single central bank. Many, including Strong, worried that a more centralized institution would actually increase political interference. Therefore the members of the Board of Governors of the Fed, and the chair in particular, were reluctant to initiate actions or press the Fed's role in public as long as its political masters did not define that role with more precision.

It is also instructive to consider that, during the early years of its existence, when the financial system was relatively immature, the Fed was reluctant, except perhaps once, to rely on 'moral suasion' as a regular tool of monetary policy.[22] This is in contrast with the early years of the Bank of Canada when moral suasion was the dominant tool of monetary policy (see below). This too mitigated the dominance of personalities over politics in the US and, on balance, suggests that the similarity of views among the early governors of the system (and the drawing of wrong lessons from the past) did not give rise to dominant figures.[23]

Another important consideration was that Board chairmen were always appointed from the outside and, in the early years, had little training in domestic or international finance. Charles Hamlin, for example, a key Board governor and its first chairman, was a lawyer by training. Governor Harding is another case in point. As Friedman argues, 'he had a limited understanding of monetary affairs, and even less backbone' (Friedman, 1962: 234). Even Benjamin Strong and Marriner Eccles, both with experience in commercial banking, nevertheless had to learn the business of central banking on the job. Occasionally, the problem was that, in the early years of the Fed's history, the chair was able and knowledgeable but the Board was weak, at a time when the regional Feds exercised greater power. This was true of Eugene Meyer, who became governor under crisis conditions, in 1930. A further consideration was the personal and working relationship between the President of the United States and the chair of the Board of Governors of the Federal Reserve about which more is said below. Again, the contrast with the Canadian experience is striking since the deputy governor has so far always succeeded the governor of the Bank of Canada, thereby ensuring not only some continuity, but guaranteeing that considerable central banking experience would be available.

The corollary to the hypothesis about the potential importance of personalities in central banking history, outlined earlier in the paper, becomes more evident when we consider the aftermath of some of the defining events in US economic history. First, of course, is the Great Depression, the growing desire to centralize the powers of monetary policy in the hands of the Board of governors in Washington, and the greater role of fiscal policy in overall economic affairs. Both found a champion in Marriner Eccles who, as Timberlake put it, permitted the 'rule of men' to spread at the Fed (Timberlake, 1993). Indeed, Eccles was instrumental in the eventual Fed–Treasury Accord (see Hyman, 1976), which in a sense formalized the Fed's independence, and his position played a role in Truman's decision not to reappoint him in 1948 (although, significantly, he remained a Board member until 1951).

The importance of personalities is also reinforced by the fact that it is the CEO who briefs and has discussions with the President over matters of monetary policy in particular and economic policy more generally.[24] Two examples illustrate the importance of this feature of Fed operations. Hamlin, the first Board chairman,[25] feared the close connection between Eugene Meyer and both the President (Herbert Hoover) and his Secretary of the Treasury (Ogden Mills), as well as fearing his connections with the New York Fed, then by far the dominant one among the regional banks (Memoranda, 1984; Pusey, 1974).

Another example is the off-again on-again relationship between Arthur Burns and Richard Nixon during the turbulent years which saw the end of Bretton Woods, the oil price shocks and wage and price controls. It seems quite clear, according to Woolley (1984), that Burns believed he had a significant influence on Fed policies (see Wells, 1994) even though Nixon's own attitude toward Burns was either ambivalent or, occasionally hostile, again because of the influence of the Secretary of the Treasury.

But a close working relationship between a Fed chairman and a President has its drawbacks since it permits the Board Chairman, appointed by the President, to 'campaign' for reappointment.[26] It is unclear, however, whether the length of the Board Chairman's tenure can, by itself, indicate anything about the degree to which Administrations over time got the monetary policy they wanted. Apparently, in defending his record, governor Harding called attention to the fact that a different policy (that is, other than a real bills doctrine) might have led to the loss of his position (Friedman, 1962: 234). This is due perhaps to section 10 of the original Federal Reserve Act of 1913 which stipulates that, in areas where there is conflict between the Fed and the Secretary of the Treasury, the latter would prevail (see Walsh, 1981: 12). However, it is interesting to note that only one chairman exceeded the four-year term of a president (Harding) before the Second World War while after 1945, all chairmen since Eccles, with the exception of McCabe and Miller, exceeded the length of the presidential election cycle, despite controversies and disagreements with the Administration over economic policy in general and interest rate policies in particular.[27]

Recent discussions about the personalities who chaired the Federal Reserve Board have centred around Paul Volcker's term in office. He was perhaps one of the most experienced central bankers to rise to the head of the Fed, and, like some of his predecessors, was appointed at a time of crisis, this time when inflation had reached double digits by 1979 (13.17 per cent in the CPI on an annual basis). However, what distinguishes his term from that of many former office holders is that he interpreted his mandate as a signal to achieve a specific policy objective, namely a reduction in inflation, and he exploited the opportunity given to him (also see Bernanke and Mishkin, 1992). The fact that the estimates presented in the previous section do not appear to indicate Volcker's term to be 'above' average in terms of a variety of macroeconomic indicators may be due to the fact that it took some three years for inflation to come under control (thus taking up about half his term in office), and he had to contend with the Reagan deficits as well as the international debt crisis. Moreover, the failed credit control policies of 1980 and the problems caused by extensive financial deregulation and innovation also made the task of inflation reduction and the resumption of economic growth difficult to achieve. His own surprise at his selection (Volcker and Gyohten, 1992: 165), and the split in the FOMC about increases in the discount rate he initially faced, reinforced his views about why markets were cynical about the Fed and inflation, and therefore precipitated in his mind the need for some dramatic policy initiatives to break inflationary expectations.

Many of the benefits and the prestige conferred on the Fed would accrue to Volcker's successor, Alan Greenspan, appointed following Volcker's announcement that he did not wish to be a candidate for another four-year term as Fed chairman. Nevertheless, the Fed's reaction to the October 1987 stock market crash, when it provided the financial system with abundant liquidity, provided Greenspan with the opportunity to put his stamp on leadership at the Fed and to enhance both the institution's credibility and independence.[28]

This episode enabled Greenspan (and the Fed) to focus on the goal of low inflation (sometimes mistakenly referred to as price stability) as a reading of the Fed's semi-annual Monetary Reports to Congress makes abundantly clear.[29] Nevertheless, and despite several legislative attempts to do so, a formal requirement to have the Fed focus on price stability alone has yet to pass and be signed by the President possibly because the last vestiges of moral suasion practiced by the executive branch since the Fed's creation might effectively disappear. Of course, it is also unclear the extent to which the Fed itself would wish to become accountable for as Hawtrey surmised: 'If they cannot avoid taking decisions, then conformity with a few easily understood shallow empirical concepts will enable them to face criticism' (Hawtrey, 1970). More accountability would also deprive the Fed from claiming the potency of monetary policy when convenient. As Friedman put it, based on his reading of Board of Governors Annual Reports:

> In years when things are going well, the report emphasized that monetary policy is an exceedingly potent weapon and that the favorable course of events is largely the result of the skilful handling of this delicate instrument by the monetary authority. In years of depression, on the other hand, the reports emphasize that monetary policy is but one of many tools of economic policy, that its power is highly limited, and that it was only the skilful handling of such limited powers as were available that averted disaster (Friedman, 1962: 233).[30]

A less churlish view would simply argue that, as creatures of government, central banks cannot avoid for long the objectives and policies of governments in a democracy. As Paul Volcker put it, 'Central banks are human institutions. Like other institutions, how they are led and how they are staffed makes a difference for policy in both a technical sense and in the larger sense of its overall coherence' (Volcker, 1994: 22).

The Canadian experience

Canada's experience with central banking is, of course, much shorter than the Fed's but it too has undergone an evolution marked by the personalities at its head.

Graham Towers was the Bank of Canada's first and longest serving governor and was a commercial banker by profession. While he supported the concept of central bank autonomy, he also adhered to the idea that the government has final authority over the conduct of monetary policy. Given that his tenure at the Bank of Canada overlapped with the war, there naturally arose a need to finance extraordinary government expenditures during this period. Following the war, there was the problem of retiring the large accumulated debt left in its wake, although the actual technical details would be left to his successor James Coyne. Towers believed that, rather than become entirely subservient to the Treasury or initiate conflict with the Government as was the case in the US, discretion was the better part of valour. He, therefore, fully subscribed to the view of the finance minister who in 1936 indicated that 'while the Bank should resist temporary gusts of public fancy, it must in the long-run show responsiveness to public opinion and be responsible to government' (Report of the Royal Commission, 1964: 534). Moreover, the concentration of banking assets among relatively few chartered banks and the origins of the Bank of Canada as a creature of commercial banking concerns, provided the opportunity to apply the policy of moral suasion.

At the same time, the culture of the Bank, while adhering to the lender of last resort, made it very reluctant to make advances except under extreme circumstances. As the 1956 Annual Report put it, 'it is clear that the central bank cannot provide relief to disappointed borrowers ... That would simply make inflation worse' (Cairns and Binhammer, 1965: 165). Instead, the Bank argued that 'suggestions' to the chartered banks to moderate or accelerate lending, or 'discussions' with securities dealers to alter margins (the Bank of Canada had no legal authority to do so on its own) could achieve desired monetary policy objectives. This policy was effective but it also left little indication about the Bank's overall views on monetary policy. As Gordon (1961) points out, Annual Reports under Towers were uninformative and the governor made few speeches indicating the Bank's stand on monetary policy *vis-à-vis* the government.

Although the policy of moral suasion would continue well into the 1960s, the rise of James Coyne to the governorship in 1955 would usher the advent of one of the defining moments in the Bank's history. Faced with the conversion of Victory Bonds into short-term Treasury bills, the Bank was concerned that fiscal policy was too easy and that a sound monetary policy required some tightening (Annual Report of the Governor, 1959 and 1960). Faced with an election and the impact that higher short-term rates would have on the government's fiscal stance, the finance minister, Donald Fleming, prompted a crisis by criticizing the governor and the Bank's policies. Instead of amending the legislation governing the Bank or pressuring the governor to resign over a policy dispute, in which Coyne and Towers agreed the government had final say, the Conservative government declared the governor's position vacant. When the Senate (an appointed body) refused to vote on the Bill,[31] the governor resigned (Rymes, 1994; Laidler and Robson, 1993).

Coyne's successor, Louis Rasminsky, previously the deputy-governor, clarified the Bank's position in the wake of the Coyne affair. Henceforth, the Bank would be responsible for monetary policy and, in the event of a conflict with the government over monetary policy, it would require that the minister issue a directive which would compel the Bank to follow the government's wishes. The statement, while only issued in 1961, became enshrined in the 1967 version of the Bank of Canada Act. The 'directive', as it has often been called, not only gave the Bank more independence, by forcing the minister of finance to publicly air disagreements with the Bank over monetary policy, but it increased its accountability by clearly spelling out its ultimate responsibility over monetary policy.

While Rasminsky's successor, Gerald Bouey, presided over problems similar to those facing his US counterpart, Arthur Burns, his performance was equally mixed. An accountant by training, his tenure is notable for the 'Saskatoon manifesto' in which a 'strategy of gradualism' was adopted whereby the Bank, using monetary targeting, would gradually reduce money growth and, therefore, inflation. The failure of this policy (though inflation did fall substantially toward the second half of his tenure), for both technical and policy reasons, provided Bouey's successor with the opportunity to move the Bank of Canada in an entirely new direction.

The crisis in inflation which affected the US also affected Canada but, by the time John Crow became governor in early 1987, the fight over inflation had seemingly been won. As deputy-governor, he experienced both the stagflation that monetary policy wrought and he set out to guarantee the gains from lower inflation. The thrust of the Bank's policy was first outlined in a public lecture in 1988 in which, without hesitation, he outlined the goals of monetary policy:

> Monetary policy should be conducted so as to achieve a pace of monetary expansion that promotes stability in the value of money. This means pursuing a policy aimed at achieving and maintaining stable prices (Crow, 1988: 4).

Laidler and Robson argue, however, that it was not until explicit inflation targets were agreed to between the Bank and the Finance department, and outlined in the Budget of 1991 (but not put into the Bank of Canada Act), that some form of price stability (in reality low and stable inflation) was agreed upon (Laidler and Robson, 1993: ch. 7).[32] The political feelings toward price stability were also no doubt facilitated by growing international concerns over Canada's rising debt and the growing fraction of the debt held by foreigners. It was, therefore, a fiscal crisis, rather than a purely monetary one, which led to greater harmony between the Bank and the federal government's policies.

When the newly elected Liberal government chose not to reappoint Crow in 1993 it was not so much because of a disagreement over the desirability of low and stable inflation but perhaps because of the governor's insistence that zero inflation be included in the target range of acceptable inflation rates instead of the original 1–3 per cent target range. The fact that the deputy-governor, Gordon Thiessen, was appointed in 1994 signalled some continuity in the 'price stability' policy, as did the agreement to extend the 1–3 per cent inflation targets to 1998. Ultimately, however, the fiscal constraints which emerged under the previous government tightened further and so, in effect, left the incoming government with little choice but to pursue existing monetary policies. This is evidenced by public statements of the governor, as well as by emphatic statements about the importance of meeting the inflation targets (Bank of Canada, 1995).

Discussion

Political scientists and economists are divided about the role of personalities and politics in the history of central banking. A reader who focused only on the previous section of this paper would surely be tempted to conclude that personalities matter a great deal in the history of US and Canadian central banking. By contrast, someone interested only in the econometric analysis of time series would be rather less sanguine about the importance of either personalities or politics. Instead, it would appear that a few defining events have more to do with the path taken by macroeconomic time series than with either the CEOs of the two central banks considered in this paper or with electoral and partisan politics.

Is there then a conflict of sorts between the data and history? I would argue that this is not the case. Even those academic authors (for example, Kettl, 1986) who place a great deal of weight on the role played by the CEO (in this case of the Fed), as do more popular histories of the Fed (for example, Greider, 1987 and Deane and Pringle, 1995), point out that, more often than not, the interests of the politicians merge with those of the central banks by virtue of necessity and the realization that their interests are common ones. When disagreements do arise, they tend to produce defining moments in the history of the central bank.

It is also interesting to note that the tremendous interest shown toward personalities at the helm of central banks is more of an American phenomenon perhaps because in the relatively short history of the Bank of Canada, the great issues of who is responsible for monetary policy and what are its goals were more or less eventually settled early on. The only occasion when a dispute between the government and the central bank arose was when the rules of responsibility were not sufficiently clear. In this respect, the Fed, in the sense of Goodhart (1988), faced a longer 'evolutionary' process than the Bank of Canada. Moreover, and again unlike the Fed, the Bank of Canada was not born out of a crisis but out of political need (for example, see Bordo and Redish, 1990). What then is the source of the potential conflict between the historical and econometric evidence?

If I were to hazard a guess, part of the problem is that many economists are wedded to the Barro–Gordon (Barro and Gordon, 1983) model in which the inflation bias of governments that arises because of the inconsistency of optimal plans can only be resolved through central bank independence. However, growing empirical evidence (for example, see Johnson and Siklos, 1996) suggests that this is not the correct way to think about what central banks do, be they independent in the statutory sense or not. Central banks, especially in the post-Second World War era, behave more like each other than their statutes would lead us to believe.

This brings us to the next vital question about central banking in North America and elsewhere. If, despite the vast institutional differences between the two central banks considered in this paper, overall macroeconomic performance is similar in the two countries, are institutional arrangements irrelevant? This is certainly the view articulated by Posen who argues that opposition to inflation by the financial sector in particular, and financial wealth holders more generally, placed the necessary and sufficient discipline on central banks (Posen, 1995). Bordo, Jonung and Siklos (1996) point out that the common development of institutional change in the financial sector is one of the principal determinants of similarities in business cycles since the late nineteenth century in at least five industrialized countries (Canada, US, UK, Sweden and Norway). But this does *not* lead to the conclusion that institutional structure is irrelevant because, like the Barro–Gordon approach, the 'irrelevance' view ignores the role of fiscal policy in the economists' jargon or politics in the political scientists' approach.

Therefore, if institutional structure matters, then there must be a flaw in the set-up of both the Fed and the Bank of Canada which produced such comparable economic development overtime.[33] It is for this reason that the search for 'Monetary Salvation' (Fischer, 1994) has been going on with proposals ranging from Rogoff's conservative central banker (Rogoff, 1987), Walsh's contracting approach (Walsh, 1995 also see Walsh, 1995a), or Fischer's legislative approach (Fischer, 1994). Rogoff suggested that, if governments could not be trusted to produce the socially desirable level of inflation, then one way to deal with the problem would be to appoint a central banker likely to deliver a rate of inflation lower than the politicians would otherwise have chosen themselves. One difficulty with this proposal is that if society cannot trust governments to deliver the socially optimal inflation rate why should they be entrusted to appoint a relatively more conservative central banker? The conservative central banker may work in theory but, as the history of both central banks has shown, central bank CEOs can only resist political pressures in the very short run and, in most cases, wish to be reappointed.

The contracting approach is appealing but it faces two difficulties. First, the technical problem of defining performance measures. Generally, these will have escape clauses which will not enhance credibility in the event of crisis. Again, history has shown that the defining moments of a central bank's history occur precisely at such times when the contract is least likely to be useful. A second difficulty is that such contracts generally do not exist in the private sector. If performance contracts of the kind Walsh is advocating are 'optimal' in some sense, then why do such contracts not exist more often for CEOs of large firms?

The legislative approach, which involves legislating a specific objective for the central bank to attain, offers the best solution because, on the surface, it seems clear and measurable and, so long as the goal is low or zero inflation, the appropriate path to follow. Again, however, existing proposals build in escape clauses for events such as supply shocks and have difficulty in defining the measure of inflation that is to be the goal of monetary policy. In this sense, the legislative approach has the same flaws as the contracting approach and offers no improvement over the current statutory arrangements between central banks and government. Instead, if the legislative approach is to be followed there should be no escape clauses (or at least very few of them) and the goal of inflation should be stated in terms of the measure that the public has come to understand and use, namely the CPI, despite the latter's shortcomings.

Conclusions

Attempting to draw broad conclusions from an exploration of central banking in the US and Canada is a daunting and somewhat presumptuous task. It is made more difficult still because of the apparent conflict between the econometric evidence and the historical evidence.This much, however, is clear. The mere introduction of central banking did not, by itself, usher periods of excessive inflation or sustained economic growth or reduce the volatility of these macroeconomic aggregates. Nor is it the case that the personalities of the CEOs of the Fed or the Bank of Canada can consistently explain overall economic performance any more than electoral or partisan changes over time.[34]

Rather, success in economic terms is better evaluated at particular defining moments in history, usually associated with some economic crisis. Institutional considerations do matter, but again only (and not always) when there is sharp disagreement between the monetary authorities and their political masters, or when a landmark change occurs, and not necessarily one reflected in the statutes of the central bank.

What is abundantly clear from the historical record is that CEOs of the central banks in the US and Canada usually had a keen sense of when to push for reform and when to pull back from confrontation and, when confrontation was inevitable, the central bank usually triumphed even if this led to the resignation or replacement of the CEO.

It is also the case that fundamentally different central banking institutions can produce remarkably similar economic records. This being so, I suspect that part of the reason is that legislatures in both countries have not precisely defined the manner in which success or failure is to be measured. To overcome this problem does not require a contract, or a central banker more 'conservative' than the politicians under whom he or she will serve, nor declarations of formal autonomy or independence, but instead a clear description of how the objectives of monetary policy are to be measured and ways that are likely to be well understood by the public. This also means that devices such as escape clauses should be avoided. After all, it seems somewhat of an 'overkill' to permit a central bank to achieve an inflation rate within a specified range[35] as well as, in effect, choosing the most convenient price level indicator with which inflation is to be measured. Finally, the contracting approach places the entire responsibility on the CEO for the failure to reach a specific inflation goal. Yet, monetary policy is usually decided upon by a Board of several members and making the CEO take the blame introduces moral hazard problems where none currently exist.

Notes

1. Research for this paper was conducted while I was a Visiting Professor at UCSD whose hospitality is gratefully acknowledged. Financial support from the Social Sciences and Humanities Research Council of Canada (grant 410–93–1409) is also appreciated. An earlier version was presented at the Conference of the European Association for Banking History, 'The Emergence of Modern Central Banking: 1918 to the Present', Évora,

Portugal, May 1996. Richard Sylla and Eugene White provided useful comments on an earlier draft.

2. Obviously, space constraints prevent a fuller description of the relevant events. Readers should consult the many textbooks on the subject. For the US, see, for example, Mayer, Duesenberry and Aliber (1993); for Canada, consult Siklos (1994).
3. Clearly, political influences also lurked in the background as the populist movement pressured the government to provide stability in the financial sphere to its constituents.
4. Via the Banking Acts of 1933 and 1935.
5. Until 1991, the legislation specifically applied to so-called chartered banks. This distinction was dropped with the Bank Act of 1991 although not all financial institutions are covered by this piece of legislation. See Siklos (1994, ch. 17).
6. Nominally, it is the Board of Directors which is responsible. It includes the governor, the Senior Deputy governor, and regional representatives (currently two from Ontario and Quebec and one representative from six other Provinces, as well as an ex-officio representative from the Department of Finance. The senior Bank officials are part of the so-called Governing Council (see below). Howitt (1993) provides more institutional background about Bank of Canada operations.
7. Havrilesky (1995a) defines accountability according to whether the central bank is responsible, formally or informally, for inflation performance; whether it adheres to some intermediate target (such as for monetary growth); and according to whether the central bank regularly publicly discusses its policy plans. It would seem to me that in many respects all central banks satisfy Havrilesky's accountability criteria in one way or another. Bernanke and Mishkin (1992) point out that while most central banks in the industrial world published or professed to aim for some intermediate target during the 1970s and 1980s, few of them actually corrected for deviations of the target or simply let the target drift over time. Havrilesky gives the Fed a total score of 1 for the 1966–75 period, 2 for the 1976–85 period, and a maximum of 3 for the 1986–93 period. By contrast, the Bank of Canada receives scores of 0, 1 and 1 for the same period. The coding is surely incorrect for Canada in the 1986–93 period since the Bank clearly meets all of the accountability objectives spelled out by Havrilesky.
8. Now the responsibility of the Governing Council of the Bank of Canada.
9. The Bank of Canada does, however, make available extracts from the minutes of the meeting of the Board of Directors although actual monetary policy is ruled by a group of senior bank officials as pointed out earlier.
10. Items 1 to 4 capture the appointment procedures of the Chief Executive Officer of the central bank (CEO). Items 5 to 7 deal with monetary policy formulation, while item 8 captures the objectives the central bank is legislated to follow. Items 9 to 16 define the limitations to lending by the central bank to the government and the financial sector in general.
11. It is somewhat puzzling, therefore, that Cukierman's coding of **conf** in Table 1 remains unchanged since the directive was enshrined in the Bank of Canada *Revised Statutes of Canada, 1967*.
12. It proved impractical to update the list beyond 1980 given the sheer size

and number of government documents relating to Federal Reserve activities and the Congressional oversight role of this institution.

13. Annual data, for example, will mask the within-year impact of central bank actions or the role that political considerations might play in central bank behaviour. By contrast, monthly data are unavailable for many macroeconomic aggregates, let alone for samples stretching back to the introduction of the two central banks being considered here. Therefore, much of the evidence discussed in this section is based on quarterly data for both countries, which are available for the US since the creation of the Fed, but only since the mid-1950s for Canada. As is well known, there has been considerable debate about the basis on which pre-Second World War (that is, pre-1939) data have been constructed (for example, see Romer, 1986, 1988, 1989, 1994). Unfortunately, empirical tests using different data sets would only be possible at the annual frequency, which is inappropriate for the present study.
14. An appendix is available from the author which provides the technical details.
15. Prior to 23 August 1935 Chairman and Vice-Chairman were designated Governor and Vice-governor, respectively.
16. In the sense that forecasts of economic outcomes are not derived from some explicit model of the economy which an economist is attempting to replicate. Although elections are held irregularly in Canada, the argument continues to hold because politicians still attempt to improve economic performance before an election or, rather, the prospects of an election are higher the better the current economic performance.
17. The exact shape of the political business cycle is ill-defined in the literature (Beck, 1991). I experimented with different specifications for the dummies but the results reported here are based on definitions consonant with most studies in this literature.
18. Given the wide variety of variables measuring political influences on the macroeconomic variables of interest, the chosen variable, if statistically significant, was selected as the one which, in the regressions, resulted in the smallest sum of squared residuals.
19. The moving average terms in the regressions in Part A of the table are consistent with active attempts by the Fed to stabilize all indicators, except, not surprisingly, government spending. There is some evidence of this in the regressions with electoral variables but the effect is far less widespread and the MA terms are quantitatively much smaller than those shown in part A. This suggests that the Fed is the principal actor in stabilizing economic shocks, to inflation, output and unemployment in particular.
20. The personalities of the Secretary of the Treasury could be said, in some instances, to be as important as the personality of the CEO of the Fed. Examples include McAdoo and Glass (1913–20), who were instrumental in the creation of the Fed and the writing of the Act.
21. The other ex-officio member was the Comptroller of the Currency, one of whom, David Crissinger, became Chairman of the Board subsequently.
22. I am thinking here of the 'direct action program' of 1928. See Chandler (1958) and Wheelock (1991) for the details.
23. And may have explained the onset, severity and perhaps even the length of the Great Depression. See Eichengreen (1992).

24. This led Woolley (1984: 109) to state that presidents get the 'monetary policy they want from the Federal Reserve' in order to ward off Congressional interference, although historical and econometric evidence about this issue is generally inconclusive. Kettl (1986: 94) documents the number of meetings between Martin and the President in the 1953–68 period. Relatively few meetings were alone. More frequent were meetings which included members of the Council of Economic Advisors, the Treasury, the Fed and the director of the Budget. During the Kennedy administration these were christened the Quadriad Meetings.
25. He served on the Board until 1936.
26. This accusation has certainly been levelled at Martin, the longest-serving Board chairman so far, Burns, as well as at Greenspan, as this is written.
27. As in the conflicts between Martin and Johnson in 1965 (Sylla, 1988 and Woolley, 1984: 116–17) over interest rate increases. Martin had a habit of not disclosing in advance to the Administration discount rate changes, while Burns did so regularly. Martin outlasted Burns in office by a considerable margin.
28. The October 1987 crash is one 'event' which is difficult to model with the available data because of its brevity thereby illustrating the potential drawback of analysis based solely on a time series analysis.
29. His views on the subject are also clear from his remarks in Capie, Goodhart, Fischer and Schnadt (1994).
30. Friedman and Schwartz (1963: 250–51n) essentially repeat the same comment.
31. More precisely, the Senate argued that the governor did not misbehave and recommended against passage of the Bill to vacate his office.
32. Johnson (1990) argues that discrepancies between fiscal and monetary policies were large enough to make the goal first outlined by Crow in 1988 impractical.
33. One other possibility for the common business cycle development of the two countries is that Canadian economic policy and outcomes are largely determined by the US. There is certainly some evidence of interdependence (for example, Burdekin and Burkett, 1992) but it is not, in my opinion, sufficiently strong to explain entirely common business cycle movements which are shared with other countries less dependent on US trade.
34. In a manner of speaking, this conclusion parallels that of Eichengreen (1995) in his exploration of alternating exchange rate regimes over time.
35. Though central banks such as those of New Zealand and Canada attempt to aim for the mid-point of such ranges.
36. $(1-\tau)\varepsilon_t$ then is the portion generated by central bank actions but not immediately observable by either the economist or the central bank observer.
37. Whether this is correct or not has important implications for modelling central bank behaviour but the issues are beyond the scope of this paper. See, however, Johnson and Siklos (1996).
38. If $\theta = -1$ then the process in question becomes trend stationary.

References

Alesina, A. (1988), 'Macroeconomics and politics' in Fischer, S. (ed.), *Macroeconomics Annual 1988*, Cambridge, MA, MIT Press.

Alesina, A. and Roubini, N. (1990), 'Political cycles: evidence from OECD countries', *Review of Economic Studies*, vol. 59, October 1990.

Alesina, A. and Sachs, J. (1988), 'Political parties and the business cycle in the United States, 1948–84', *Journal of Money, Credit and Banking*, 20.

Aufricht, H. (1961), *Central Banking Legislation*, Washington, DC, International Monetary Fund.

Bank of Canada (1995), *Monetary Policy Report*, May.

Barro, R. and Gordon, D. (1983), 'Rules, discretion and reputations in a model of monetary policy', *Journal of Monetary Economics*, 12.

Beck, N. (1991), 'The Fed and the political business cycle', *Contemporary Policy Issues*, 9.

Bernanke, B. and Mishkin, F. (1992), 'Central bank behavior and the strategy of monetary policy: observations from six industrialized countries', in Blanchard, O. and Fischer, S. (eds), *Macroeconomics Annual 1992*, Cambridge, MA, The MIT Press.

Bollerslev, T. (1986), 'Generalized autoregressive conditional heteroskedasticity', *Journal of Econometrics*, 31.

Bollerslev, T., Chou, R. and Kroner, K. (1992), 'ARCH modelling in finance', *Journal of Econometrics*, 52.

Bordo, M.D. and Jonung, L. (1981), 'The long run behavior of the income velocity of money: a cross country comparison of five advanced countries, 1870–1975', *Economic Inquiry*, 19.

Bordo, M.D. and Jonung, L. (1987), *The Long-Run Behavior of the Velocity of Circulation: The International Evidence*, Cambridge, Cambridge University Press.

Bordo, M.D., Jonung, L. and Siklos, P. (1997), 'Institutional change and the velocity of money: a century of evidence', *Economic Inquiry*, 35, October.

Bordo, M.D. and Redish, A. (1987), 'Why did the Bank of Canada emerge in 1935?', *Journal of Economic History*, June.

Bordo, M.D. and Redish, A. (1990), 'Credible commitment and exchange rate stability: Canada's inter-war experience', *Canadian Journal of Economics*, May.

Bordo, M.D., Rockoff, H. and Redish, A. (1994), 'The US banking system from a northern exposure: stability versus efficiency', *Journal of Economic History*, 54, June.

Burdekin, R.C.K. and Burkett, P. (1992), 'The impact of US economic

variables on Bank of Canada policy: direct and indirect responses', *Journal of International Money and Finance*, 11.
Burdekin, R.C.K. and Siklos, P.L. (1999), 'Exchange rate regimes and shifts in inflation persistence: does nothing else matter?', *Journal of Money, Credit and Banking*, 31, May.
Cairns, J.P. and Binhammer, H.H. (1965), *Canadian Banking and Monetary Policy*, Toronto, McGraw-Hill.
Capie, F., Goodhart, C., Fischer, S. and Schnadt, N. (1994), *The Future of Central Banking*, Cambridge, Cambridge University Press.
Chandler, L.V. (1958), *Benjamin Strong: Central Banker*, Washington, DC, The Brookings Institution.
Chandler, L.V. (1971), *American Monetary Policy 1928–1941*, New York, Harper and Row.
Crow, J.W. (1988), 'The work of Canadian monetary policy', *Bank of Canada Review*, February.
Cukierman, A. (1986), 'Central bank behavior and credibility: some recent theoretical developments', *Review of the Federal Reserve Bank of St Louis*, 68.
Cukierman, A. (1992), *Central Bank Strategy, Credibility and Independence: Theory and Evidence*, Cambridge, MA, The MIT Press.
Cukierman, A. and Meltzer, A. (1986), 'A theory of ambiguity, credibility and inflation under discretion and asymmetric information', *Econometrica*, 53.
Deane, M. and. Pringle, R. (1995), *The Central Banks*, New York, Viking.
Eichengreen, B. (1992), 'Designing a central bank for Europe: a cautionary tale from the early years of the Federal Reserve', in Canzonin, M.B., Grilli, V. and Mason, P.R. (eds), *Establishing a Central Bank: Issues in Europe and Lessons from the US*, Cambridge, Cambridge University Press.
Eichengreen, B. (1995), 'The endogeneity of exchange rate regimes', in Reis, J. (ed.), *International Monetary Arrangements in Historical Perspective*, London, MacMillan.
Fischer, S. (1994), 'Modern central banking', in Capie, F., Goodhart, C., Fischer, S. and Schnadt, N. (eds), *The Future of Central Banking: The Tercentenary Symposium of the Bank of England*, Cambridge, Cambridge University Press.
Friedman, M. (1962), 'Should there be an independent monetary authority?', in Yeager, L.G. (ed.), *In Search of a Monetary Constitution*, Cambridge, MA, Harvard University Press.
Friedman, M. (1977), 'Inflation and unemployment: Nobel Lecture', *Journal of Political Economy*, 85, June.
Friedman, M. and Schwartz, A. (1963), *A Monetary History of the United States, 1870–1960*, Princeton, Princeton University Press.

Goodhart, C. (1988), *The Evolution of Central Banks*, Cambridge, MA, The MIT Press.

Gordon, H.S. (1961), 'The Bank of Canada in a system of responsible government', *Canadian Journal of Economics and Political Science*, 27, February.

Gordon, R.J. (ed.) (1986), *The American Business Cycle: Continuity and Change*, Chicago, The University of Chicago Press.

Greider, W. (1987), *Secrets of the Temple: How the Federal Reserve Runs the Country*, New York, Simon and Schuster.

Havrilesky, T. (1990), 'The influence of the federal advisory council on monetary policy', *Journal of Money, Credit and Banking*, 22.

Havrilesky, T. (1995), 'Restructuring the Fed', *Journal of Economics and Business*, 47.

Havrilesky, T. (1995a), 'Central bank autonomy, central bank accountability and inflation performance', unpublished manuscript, Duke University.

Hawtrey, R.G. (1970), *The Art of Central Banking*, 2nd edition, New York, Kelley.

Hibbs, D. (1977), 'Political parties and macroeconomic policy', *The American Political Science Review*, 71.

Howitt, P. (1993), 'Canada', in Fratianni, M. and Salvatore, D. (eds), *Monetary Policy in Developed Economies*, 3, Handbook of Comparative Economic Policies, Westport, CT, Greenwood Press.

Hyman, S. (1976), *Marriner Eccles, Private Entrepreneur and Public Servant*, Stanford, CA, Graduate School of Business.

Jamieson, A.B. (1953), *Chartered Banking in Canada*, Toronto, Ryerson Press.

Johnson, D.R. (1990), 'The zero inflation target: do Wilson and John Crow agree?', *Canadian Public Policy*, 14.

Johnson, D.R. and Siklos, P.L. (1996), 'Political and economic determinants of central bank behaviour: are central banks different?' *Economic Inquiry*, October.

Kettl, D.F. (1986), *Leadership at the Fed*, New Haven and London, Yale University Press.

Laidler, D.E.W. and Robson, W. (1993), *The Great Canadian Disinflation*, Toronto, C.D. Howe Institute.

Leacy, F.H., Urquhart, M.C. and Buckley, K.A.H. (eds) (1983), *Historical Statistics of Canada*, 2nd edn, Ottawa, Ont., Statistics Canada.

MacRae, D. (1977), 'A political model of the business cycle', *Journal of Political Economy*, 85.

Mayer, T., Duesenberry, J. and Aliber, R. (1993), *Money, Banking and the Economy*, 5th edn, New York, W.W. Norton.

Memoranda Concerning the Federal Reserve Board taken from the

Diaries of Charles S. Hamlin (1984), Washington, DC, Library of Congress.

Nordhaus, W. (1975), 'The political business cycle', *Review of Economic Studies*, 42.

Perron, P. (1994), 'Non-stationarities and non-linearities in Canadian inflation', in *Economic Behaviour and Policy Choice Under Price Stability*, Ottawa, Bank of Canada.

Posen, A. (1995), 'Declarations are not enough: financial sector sources of central bank independence', in Bernanke, B.S. and Roteinberry, J.J. (eds), *Macroeconomics Annual 1995*, Cambridge, MA, The MIT Press.

Pusey, M.J. (1974), *Eugene Meyer*, New York, Knopf.

Report of the Royal Commission on Banking and Finance (1964), Ottawa, Queen's Printers.

Rogoff, K.F. (1987), 'Reputational constraints in monetary policy', in Brunner, K. and Meltzer, A.H. (eds), *Carnegie–Rochester Conference Series on Public Policy*, 24, Amsterdam, North Holland.

Rogoff, K.F. and Siebert, A. (1988), 'Equilibrium political business cycles', *Review of Economic Studies*, 55.

Romer, C. (1986), 'Is the stabilisation of post-war economy a figment of the data?' *American Economic Review*, 76.

Romer, C. (1988), 'World War I and the post-war depression: a reinterpretation based on alternative estimates of GNP', *Journal of Monetary Economics*, 20.

Romer, C. (1989), 'The prewar business cycle reconsidered: new estimates of gross national product, 1869–1908', *Journal of Political Economy*, 97, February.

Romer, C. (1994), 'Remeasuring business cycles', *Journal of Economic History*, 54, September.

Rymes, T.K. (1994), 'On the Coyne–Raminsky directive and responsibility for monetary policy in Canada', in Siklos, P.L. (ed.), *Varieties of Monetary Reforms: Lessons and Experiences on the Road to Monetary Union*, Boston, Kluwer Academic Publishers.

Siklos, P.L. (1992), 'Politics and US business cycles: a century of evidence', unpublished manuscript, Wilfrid Laurier University.

Siklos, P.L. (1993), 'Income velocity and institutional change: some new time series evidence', *Journal of Money, Credit and Banking*, 25, August.

Siklos, P.L. (1994), *Money, Banking and Financial Institutions: Canada in the Global Environment*, Toronto, McGraw-Hill Ryerson Ltd.

Siklos, P.L. (1994a), 'Central bank independence in Eastern Europe: a preliminary investigation', in Szekely, J. and Bonin, J.P. (eds), *Development and Reform of the Financial System in Central and Eastern Europe*, London, Edward Elgar.

Siklos, P.L. (1995), 'Establishing central bank independence: recent experiences in developing countries', *Journal of International Trade and Economic Development*, 4, November.

Sylla, R. (1988), 'The autonomy of monetary authorities: the case of the US Federal Reserve System', in Toniolo, G. (ed.), *Central Banks' Independence in Historical Perspective*, Berlin and New York, Walter de Gruyter.

Timberlake, R. (1993), *Monetary Policy in the United States*, Chicago and London, The University of Chicago Press.

Urquhart, M.C. and Buckley, K.A.H. (1965), *Historical Statistics of Canada: Revised Edition*, Ottawa, Statistics Canada.

Volcker, P. (1994), 'The human factor and the Fed', in Colander, D.C. and Daane, D. (eds), *The Art of Monetary Policy*, Armonk, NY, M.E. Sharpe.

Volcker, P. and Gyohten, T. (1992), *Changing Fortunes: The World's Money and the Threat to American Leadership*, New York, Times Books.

Walsh, C. (1995), 'Recent central bank reforms and the role of price stability as the sole objective of monetary policy', in Bernanke, B.S. and Rotenberg, J.R. (eds), *Macroeconomics Annual 1995*, Cambridge, MA, The MIT Press.

Walsh, C. (1995a), 'Optimal contracts for central bankers', *American Economic Review*, 85(1).

Walsh, G.O. (1981), *Federal Reserve Act of 1913: with Amendments and Laws Relating to Banking*, Washington, DC, US Government Printing Office.

Wells, W.C. (1994), *An Economist in An Uncertain World: Arthur F. Burns and the Federal Reserve, 1970–78*, New York, Columbia University Press.

Wheelock, D.C. (1991), *The Strategy and Consistency of Federal Reserve Monetary Policy, 1924–1933*, Cambridge, Cambridge University Press.

White, E.N. (1983), *The Regulation and Reform of the American Banking System, 1920–1929*, Princeton, Princeton University Press.

Wicker, E. (1993), 'United States', in Fratianni, M.V. and Salvatore, D. (eds), *Monetary Policy in Developed Economies*, Vol. 3, Handbook of Comparative Economic Policy, Westport, CT, Greenwood Press.

Wicker, E. (1966), *Federal Reserve Monetary Policy, 1917–33*, New York, Random House.

Woolley, J.T. (1984), *Monetary Politics: The Federal Reserve and the Politics of Monetary Policy*, Cambridge, Cambridge University Press.

Data appendix

US data

All data are quarterly or annual. For the quarterly data the data until 1982:4 are from the appendix in R.J. Gordon (1986), *The American Business Cycle: Continuity and Change*, Chicago and NBER, University of Chicago Press. Data were updated from sources given in Gordon, namely the US Department of Commerce's *Survey of Current Business* and the *Federal Reserve Bulletin.*

Canadian data

All quarterly data are from CANSIM, Ottawa: Statistics Canada.

Technical appendix

It is assumed that the series under consideration have a simple autoregressive representation of the form:

$$A(L)x_t = \mu + \beta I_t + \nu_t \tag{2.1}$$

where μ is the mean of a series, ν_t an error term satisfying the usual properties (i.e. zero mean stationarity), and $A(L)$ is an autoregressive (AR) distributed lag operator of order k (i.e. $A(L) = 1 - p_1L - \ldots - p_kL^k$). I represents a set of interventions, defined here as consisting of dummy variables to capture the possibility that the mean of the time series, μ, can change across regimes variously defined below. It is well known (e.g. see Perron, 1994) that ν_t in (2.1) is likely to contain a moving average component. Again, following Perron (1994), assume that the central bank responds only to a portion of the shocks ν_t as part of its active role in monetary policy. Define the aggregate shock the economy experiences as ε_t. The magnitude $\tau\varepsilon_t$, where $0 < \tau < 1$, represents the fraction (τ) of the total shock ε_t unanticipated by the central bank.[36] Now, suppose that because of lags in obtaining information or uncertainty about the nature or source of the shock (i.e., whether it is of the permanent or transitory variety), the central bank is not assumed to completely affect $\tau\varepsilon_t$ but instead to react in the following manner:

$$\nu_t = \varepsilon_t - \delta\tau\varepsilon_{t-1} \tag{2.2}$$

Part of the justification for specification (2.2) is that the central bank can only observe ε_t in period ε_{t-1}.[37] Equation (2.2) also describes a first-order moving average process. Since it is not the intention of this paper to separately identify the δ and τ parameter, rewrite (2.2) as:

$$\mu_t = \varepsilon_t + \theta\varepsilon_{t-1} \tag{2.3}$$

Thus, if $\theta = -1$, then the central bank intervenes to completely offset the contemporaneous shock θ_t.[38] At the other extreme, $\theta = 0$ signifies that no moving average is present and, therefore, there is no active intervention by the central bank. While we expect the central bank to respond to (short-run) shocks in carrying out its normal monetary policy duties, estimates of β in (2.1) should provide us with some indication about how other factors, namely the CEO of the central bank, political influences in the form of electoral or partisan effects, or major economic shocks (e.g. wars, depression, oil price changes) separately affect the time series under investigation. In generating empirical results, equation (2.1) was estimated in all cases as an AR of order three with a moving average (MA) term of order one.

Additional tests By focusing on the performance of mean indicators of economic performance we potentially omit another source of influence by personalities and politics, namely their impact on the *volatility* of macroeconomic aggregates. As Friedman (1977) pointed out in his Nobel Lecture, and has subsequently been confirmed by a vast amount of empirical evidence, levels of economic activity can directly or indirectly be influenced by the volatility of inflation and output growth.

To ascertain the significance of this feature of central bank performance, I sought to determine whether some measure of volatility might influence inflation and output growth in particular. In order to do so I augmented (2.1) with a measure of conditional variance. This results in the following specification:

$$A(L)x_t = \mu + \beta_0 I_t + \beta_1\sigma_t^2 + \nu_t \tag{2.4}$$

where:

$$\sigma_t^2 = \beta_2 + \beta_3\sigma_{t-1}^2 + \beta_4\nu_{t-1}^2 \tag{2.5}$$

Equations (2.4) and (2.5) are jointly estimated and the result is known as a GARCH (for Generalized Autoregressive Conditional Heteroskedasticity) in the mean model (see Bollerslev, 1986 and Bollerslev, Chou and Kroner, 1992 for a survey). Specifically, and following the existing literature, the variance of a time series (σ^2) is assumed to be a function of a constant (β_2), last period (forecasted) volatility (β_3,) and the squared residual from last period (β_4). For this reason, (2.5) is labelled a GARCH (1,1) model. Figure 8.A1 presents the relevant evidence. The GARCH term from equation (2.5), to be more precise, is the one step ahead standard deviation for each observation in the sample. The observation at time *t* is the forecast using information at *t*–1. For inflation, the GARCH effects were separately estimated for the pre- and post-Second World War periods while (2.5) was estimated for the full sample in the case of output growth. The last two plots are based on Canadian data.

Turning to the US post-Second World War evidence, first we see that inflation volatility is high around the turn of the Fed–Treasury Accord and around the oil price shocks but there is no obvious pattern or consistent variation in volatility around election times or during specific terms of Fed chairmen. There is a noticeably sharp peak in 1967–68 which may be related to mounting fiscal pressures created by the war in Vietnam and the breakdown of gold sales by the gold pool members (Volcker and Gyohten, 1992: 342–3). As for the pre-Second World War era, there are noticeable increases in volatility around the 1916 and 1920 elections although the collapse of the boom in 1920 may have had much to do with it. There are also relatively small increases in volatility around the time of active open market operations conducted by the Fed in 1924 and 1927 (called the 'Strong Rule' by Wicker, 1993: 202), as well as a much sharper rise in volatility as the country emerged out of the Depression. As for output, the plot confirms what was hinted at in Figure 8.3 namely that output volatility is considerably higher before the Second World War than in the post-war era. Volatility is more or less stationary after the mid-1950s until the late 1970s; thereafter it displays a definite downward trend which may be associated with the Volcker–Greenspan eras. It should be noted, however, that the GARCH coefficient in (2.4) is not statistically significant in any of the US specifications where the vector *I* consists of dummies for the CEOs of the Fed (results not shown).

The Canadian evidence does reveal that inflation volatility is highest around the time of the Coyne affair as well as around the time of the announcement of formal inflation targets in the 1991 Budget Speech. Nevertheless, it takes almost a year before volatility falls and is seen to rise again at the end of Crow's tenure and the debate about his reappointment, in 1994. The results for output growth roughly parallel those of inflation except that there is a much milder response to uncertainty surrounding Crow's reappointment. As with the US case, none of the GARCH terms were found to be statistically significant in (2.4).

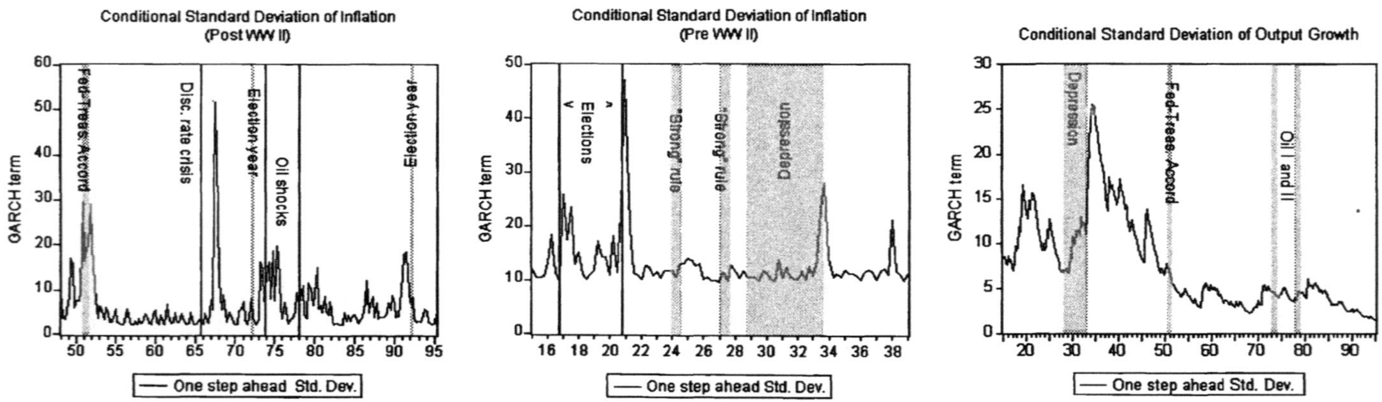

8.A1 Conditional standard deviations of inflation and output growth for the US and Canada

Note: Based on joint estimates of (2.4) and (2.5) where I = CEOs. For US inflation the post-war sample has one lag for inflation and includes an MA(1) term; for the pre-war sample an AR(2) is estimated and no MA terms are included. For US real GNP growth an AR(3) with no MA term is estimated. The Canadian inflation equation contains an AR(3) and an MA(1) while the output growth equation contains no MA term.

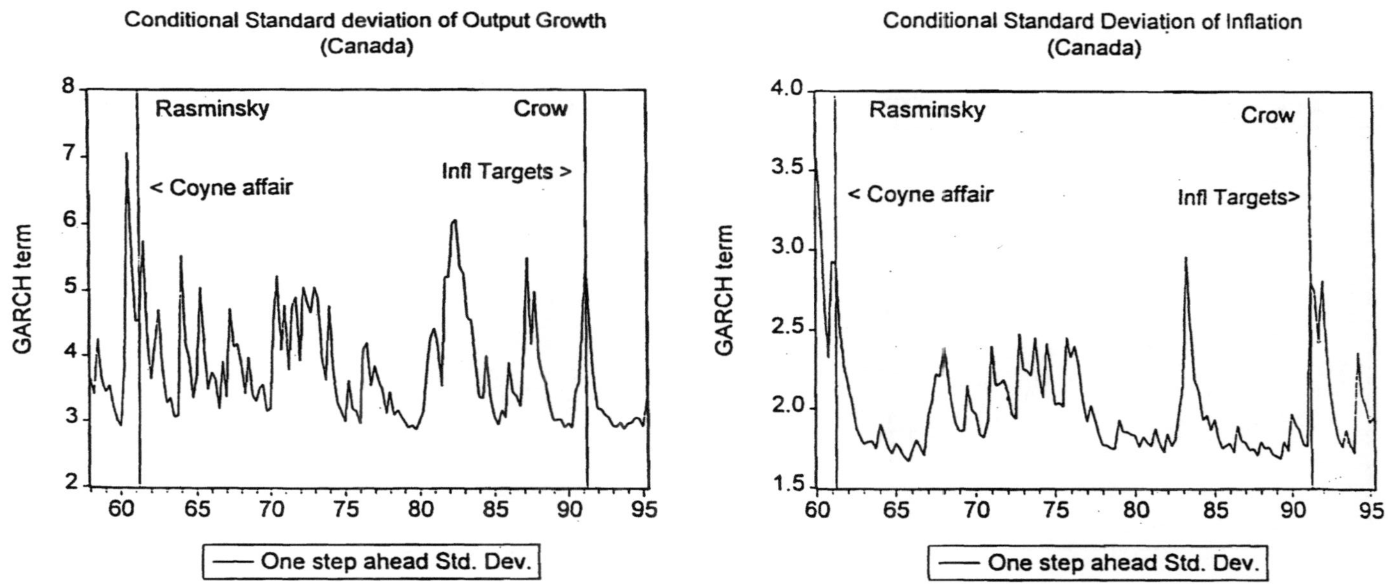

8.A1 continued

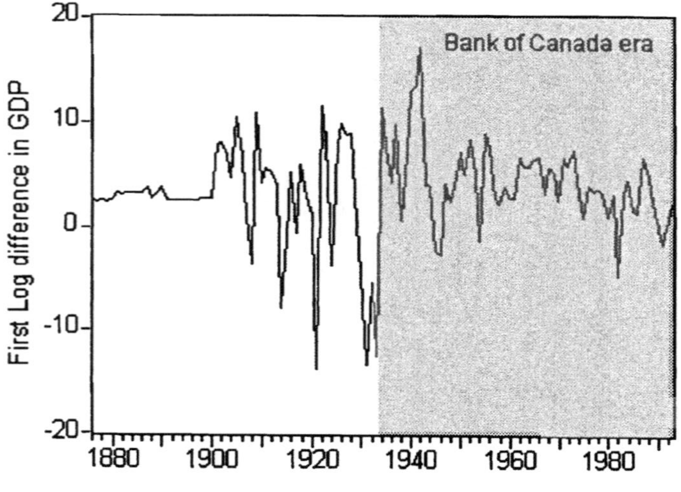
First Log difference in GDP
20
10
0
-10
-20
1880
1900
1920
1940
1960
1980
Bank of Canada era

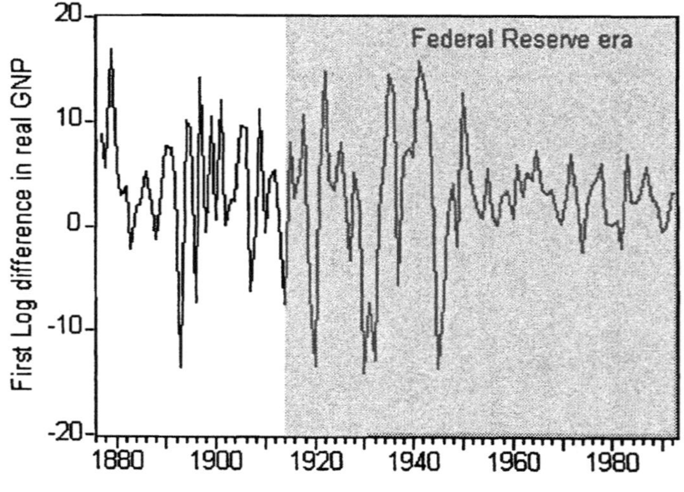
First Log difference in real GNP
20
10
0
-10
-20
1880
1900
1920
1940
1960
1980
Federal Reserve era

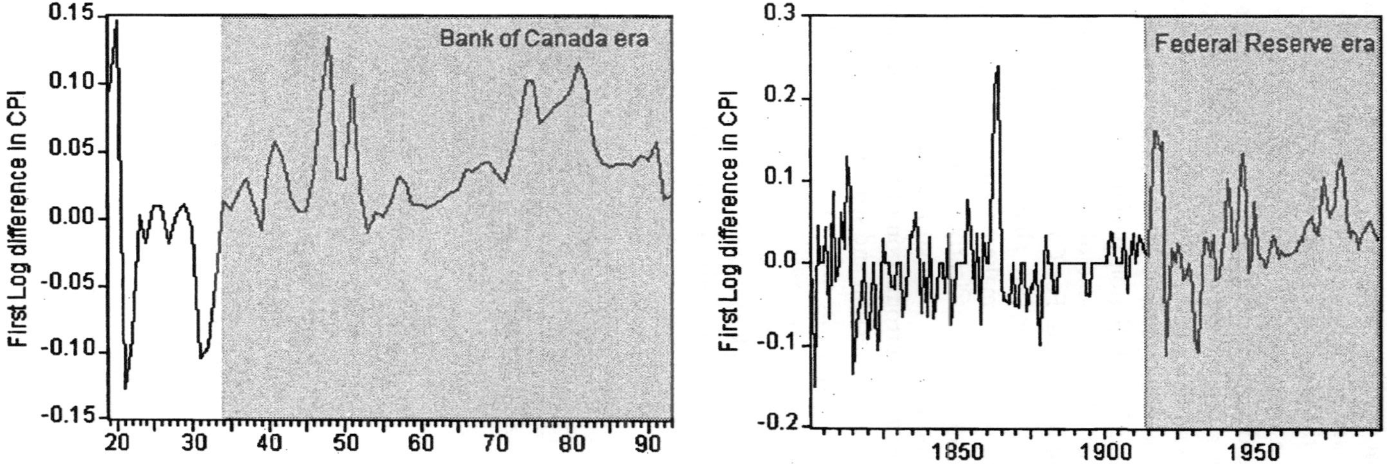

8.A2 Inflation and output growth performance before and after central banking

Source: See Figure 8.A1.

The era before central banking Another way of gauging the role and influence of central banking is to examine overall economic performance before and after the creation of the Fed and the Bank of Canada. Figure 8.A2 presents a descriptive comparison of inflation and output growth for the US and Canada using annual data. The shaded areas identify periods when a central bank existed. Clearly, average inflation rates are both higher and less volatile several years after the creation of these two central banks while output growth is less volatile but only after the Second World War. Inflation performance seems to be more strongly related to the abandonment of the gold exchange standard than with the creation of the Fed. For Canada, inflation rates began to rise in the early 1950s until they are sharply reversed in the 1980s. Overall then, it seems difficult to make an abrupt distinction between pre and post-central banking eras. Clearly, there are a variety of experiences in the post-central banking era that require an explanation or an exploration beyond the mere introduction of these institutions. Indeed, as shown in Table 8.A2, the direction and size of electoral and recession effects on output and inflation (the only variables available for a sufficiently long pre-Fed sample) are not vastly different then for the entirety of the Fed era. Similarly, inflation and output persistence in Canada, before the formation of the Bank of Canada, is not vastly different from the era which follows it (also see Burdekin and Siklos, 1999).

Table 8.A1 Pre-central banks summary statistics

Variable	Indicator	Coeff.	Std dev.
A. US (quarterly data 1876.1–1913.4)			
PRES	y	0.198	0.113
MA(1)		0.983	0.013
PRES	p	4.791	2.786
MA(1)		–0.687	0.219
RCESSION	y	–3.609	1.283
MA(1)		0.364	0.226
RCESSION	p	–3.639	1.002
MA(1)		0.771	0.103
B. Canada (annual data 1915–33)			
y_{t-1}	y	0.241	1.068
p_{t-1}	p	0.384	0.204
WW1		0.085	0.040

CHAPTER NINE

The Emergence of Central Banks in Latin America: Are Evolutionary Models Applicable?[1]

Carlos Marichal and Daniel Díaz Fuentes

This chapter is a preliminary effort to stimulate a debate on the comparative study of the origins of central banking in Latin America, especially in Argentina, Brazil and Mexico, with emphasis on an institutional framework analysis.[2] The chapter also attempts to link some of these problems with the ongoing discussion among European economic historians on the origins and evolution of central banking in Europe from the nineteenth century, most notably as developed on a comparative basis by Charles Goodhart and by historians of the early history of central banks in other European countries (Goodhart, 1988).[3] We propose that the antecedents and early history of central banking in Latin America are distinct and that it is misleading to think strictly in terms of evolutionary models both with respect to the origins of these banks, as well as to their initial operations beginning in the 1920s and 1930s.

The emphasis in this chapter is on the analysis of certain long-run features of banking structures and monetary regimes in the three largest Latin American economies – Argentina, Brazil and Mexico – as well as on the political and economic factors which played a major, direct role in the establishment of central banking practice and institutions. Our study indicates that the contrasts are clearly as important as the parallels.

In the first part of the chapter, emphasis is placed on the analysis of the emergence of large 'national' banks from the 1880s onwards which were closely tied to their respective governments and which did in fact carry out some central banking functions well before the establishment of formal central banks. But none of these large government banks became a central bank. These kinds of institutional financial innovations – which are studied in the second part of the chapter – came much later. Central banks were established in Mexico in 1925, in Argentina in 1935, and in Brazil as late as 1965, as a result of specific economic and political circumstances, although in some cases there is evidence of a progressive but prolonged process of banking reforms. Latin American financial history is more abrupt and often more surprising than a stage-by-stage perspective could lead us to believe.

Despite rejection of an evolutionary model, the data presented here certainly suggests that, from the late nineteenth century onwards, there was considerable experimentation with forms of central banking throughout the region, as is revealed by the study of the institutional functions of certain 'national' banks (publicly and privately owned), the practice of monetary agencies (especially in the 1900–14 period) and the different policies adopted under succeeding monetary regimes. This historical experience was certainly an important precedent to the formulation and development of modern central banking in the three nations under study, although the process was not linear.

We should also emphasize that this chapter does not deal in detail with the history of central banking in the post-1940 period but rather with the historical antecedents in order to provide a general description of how central banking emerged in Argentina, Brazil and Mexico.

Historical antecendents to central banking

Origins of government banks in Latin America in the late nineteenth and early twentieth centuries

The first part of this chapter focuses on the role of the series of 'national' banks which emerged during the second half of the nineteenth century in Argentina, Brazil and Mexico and which performed some of the functions typical of central banks. These 'national' banks were closely connected to the government and in some cases came to enjoy a monopoly of note issue. At the same time, these 'national' banks also provided commercial services and dealt with the public. The rate of rediscounting was one of their most important tools, but this function was again restricted by the government.[4] However, it should also be noted that between 1900 and 1914 the 'national' banks were also complemented by the creation of a series of monetary agencies – in Argentina and Brazil known as the *Caja de Conversión or Caixa de Conversão* – and in Mexico as a monetary and exchange commission.

The focus on the role of these 'national' banks in the late nineteenth century and up to 1914 also raises certain important but understudied issues in Latin American banking history such as: (1) free banking versus monopoly of issue of bank notes; (2) the management by 'national' banks of the current accounts of the government and service of internal and external debts; and (3) finally, the debate over the gold standard and the initial instruments put in practice in the early twentieth century to attempt to regulate monetary circulation and hard currency reserves.

We begin with a succinct account of the early development of Latin America with emphasis on the emergence of the first 'national' or 'government' banks.[5]

Although Latin America had a succession of relatively short-lived banking experiments in the early nineteenth century, it was not until past the mid-century that banking began to take root in the leading ports and capitals of the vast subcontinent.[6] By the early 1870s, financial markets were operating in Rio de Janeiro, Santiago, Valparaíso, Buenos Aires and Lima with a certain dynamism, as manifest in the diversification and initial institutionalization of financial activities. In each of these as yet relatively small urban centres, a number of commercial banks began operations, approximately a dozen in Rio de Janeiro and Buenos Aires respectively, and half a dozen or more in Santiago and Lima. At the same time, primitive but operative stock exchanges were set up in those cities, as well as a series of insurance and complementary financial-service firms.[7]

Already from this era, a few commercial banking institutions, which were closely linked to national governments, began to stand out. The *Banco do Brasil* – refounded in 1850 – was to dominate Brazilian domestic banking until the end of the nineteenth century.[8] The *Banco de la Provincia de Buenos Aires*, created in 1854, soon controlled much of local credit for commerce in the Argentine capital and for agriculture and ranching in the rich hinterland of Buenos Aires. This bank dominated (but did not monopolize) the issue of bank notes and handled most of government finance for both the provincial and national governments.[9]

Not surprisingly, it was also from this period that debates began on the institutional and legal models believed most adequate for the development of local banking systems. In most Latin American countries, there were already two different schools of thought, which corresponded broadly to those in favour of 'free-banking' and only limited regulation, and those who were advocates of more strict regulation and monopoly (or predominance) of issue by a great state bank, in the style of the Banque de France.

'Free-bankers' such as Souza Franco, the finance minister of Brazil in 1857, argued that the first system allowed for more rapid growth and diversification of the banking sector. Similar arguments were advanced by Juan Bautista Alberdi in Argentina and, from the 1860s, by the disciples of the influential French economist, Courcelle Seneuil, in Chile.[10]

While the ideologues of free banking tended to gain space in the Latin American press, in practice the incipient banking structures in

Argentina, Brazil and Chile tended to be dominated by one or two large banks closely linked to the respective government, dominating the issue of bank notes, handling government accounts and taking charge of service of the internal and external public debts.[11]

In the 1880s there was a renewed boom in banking in the larger Latin American nations, which began first in the capital cities and then by the end of the decade began to spread to the more commercially dynamic provincial centres in Argentina, Brazil, Chile and Mexico.[12] From the point of view of the traditional historiography of Latin America, the 1880s are seen both as the age of consolidation of national government under oligarchic structures, as well as a golden age for the export economies. It is often argued that it was the new political stability which allowed for the expansion of the economies, but it is more rarely observed that the modernization of finance and banking contributed forcefully to a more stable and stronger national political administration. In effect, the expansion of national banks proved to be a key element in facilitating 'national' government, so lacking in previous decades. In this sense, a possible avenue for future research would be to explore the hypothesis that institutional innovation in the banking sector could induce improvements in the efficiency of management of the state fiscal and financial administration in Latin America at different historical moments.[13]

While the structure of banking varied from country to country the parallels between the 'national' banks were important, especially in exercising functions as bankers to the government. The dominance of one or two large banks (with close links to the respective public administrations) from the end of the nineteenth century can be observed in the cases of Brazil, Argentina and Mexico among others (Marichal, 1997). Naturally, we must ask why this was a common tendency among the principal economies of Latin America. We venture to suggest that it may be attributed to the advantages acquired by those banks which had a monopoly of note issue and/or dominant control of government financial accounts. Moreover, such advantages were particularly important in monetary and credit markets that were still relatively small and limited with respect to the number and volume of financial instruments traded. Alliances with the state were therefore fundamental. A privileged relation with the government (precisely at the time where a national administration was becoming consolidated) would appear to have provided important comparative advantages to certain institutions in the banking sector.[14]

On the other hand, and reciprocally, there were great advantages for finance ministers in promoting the creation of 'national' banks since they brought about a sharp drop in many transaction costs of financial transactions carried out by governments and further allowed important savings as a result of the drop in interest rates which followed on the establishment of such banks. In the first half of the nineteenth century, information costs (on fiscal and debt matters) had been quite substantial and, being accompanied by high interest rates, had diminished the efficiency of the respective state administrations.[15] The broadening of money markets and the creation of new banks effectively brought down the price of money (interest rates) generally speaking and, specifically, reduced the costs of the credits required by the government for short-term overdrafts or medium-term loans.[16] With the creation of 'national' banks, governments opened large accounts with them which allowed for substantial overdrafts at small cost, facilitating the payment of expenses by all public agencies in any part of the country. This increased flexibility was accompanied by the improved handling of the internal debt, with lower interest rates and less dependency on money lenders.

The 'national' banks also provided increased access to foreign funds, through external loans, at more reasonable costs, and simultaneously broadened their own commercial networks.[17] In the 1880s, in Argentina, for example, banking was heavily concentrated in the city of Buenos Aires, and, furthermore, dominated by two 'government' banks, namely the *Banco de la Provincia de Buenos Aires* and the *Banco Nacional*: in 1885 these two banks controlled 67 per cent of the capital, 41 per cent of the metallic reserves, 64 per cent of the loans and 89 per cent of the note issue of all banks in the capital.[18]

In Brazil, the predominance of the *Banco do Brasil* was clear until the end of the 1880s, as it held sway in the realm of capital, deposits and note issue.[19] It should be noted that the relation between reserves and total note issue was apparently similar to that of the Argentine banks, but actually the Brazilian banks (initially) proved to be more conservative in this regard since most of the notes were issued by the national treasury rather than by the banks. None the less, the stability of the Brazilian banking system was undermined in the late 1880s when two other banks (with special issuing privileges) were established. According to Stephen Topik: 'By September, 1890, the three banks, the *Banco do Brasil,* the *Banco dos Estados Unidos do Brasil* and the *Banco Nacional* controlled by means of their privileges, and through other banks which they owned, 95 per cent of all bank notes in circulation' (Topik, 1987: 31).

Quite different was the situation in Mexico, the Latin American nation where banking took longest to develop and where, from the outset, the banking structure proved most concentrated. It was only in the mid-1880s that a banking infrastructure was established in Mexico City where one great institution, the *Banco Nacional de México,* initially dominated. In 1885, it held close to 80 per cent of total capital, deposits and loans of the capital's banking firms. The *Banco Nacional de México* was a privately-owned and managed bank, but at the same time it was put in charge of a great number of government financial affairs. It handled a large current account for the finance ministry, it provided the service of the internal and external debts of the republic and it made regular medium-term advances, when the government was in urgent need of funds.[20]

None the less, the creation of such large banking companies with such close links to governments also posed a series of formidable dangers. For instance, the financial boom of the 1880s and the consequent phase of prosperity led political and economic elites to fancy that they could do no wrong. However, their excursions into speculative ventures were pregnant with catrastrophe.

The financial crisis of the 1890s and its impact on banking developments

The close alliances between governments and certain large banks proved to be the cause of bankruptcy and the origin of political and financial crises of severe impact. The early 1890s witnessed bank failures and stock exchange crashes (accompanied by political revolutions) in Argentina and Brazil. In various cases these crises were linked to extreme mismanagement of state banks and, as a result, the relationships between state and banks were restructured. Paradoxically, however, in Argentina, Brazil and Mexico these ties were not weakened but rather strengthened. Thus, the symbiotic evolution of national governments and the largest 'national' banks continued into the twentieth century.

The banking crises of the early 1890s were accompanied by major social convulsion and both political and economic crises. In the Argentine case, the banking crisis of 1890/91 (which coincided with a foreign debt crisis) lasted a year and a half and was extremely violent (Martí, 1990). The two largest state banks, the *Banco Nacional* and the *Banco de la Provincia de Buenos Aires*, collapsed, as did ten regional banks owned by provincial governments (Marichal, 1989). In other words, all the banks closely linked to the Argentine government went under, an indication of the perils implicit in such relationships. On the other hand, relatively few private banks went bankrupt, although the number of mercantile firms that did so was quite large.[21]

At the end of 1891, with the creation of the *Banco de la Nación de Argentina*, the financial situation began to improve. In practice, the success of the new national bank in establishing itself at the heart of the

Table 9.1 Banking structure in Argentina, 1854–91

Bank/Type of bank	Dates
Banco de la Provincia de Buenos Aires	1854–91
Private banks (Buenos Aires, Rosario Córdoba)	1863–
Banco Nacional	1873–91
Banks of ten provincial governments	1873–91
Mortgage State Banks	1873–91

Table 9.2 Banking structure in Argentina, 1891–1929

Bank/Type of bank	Dates
Private banks	1863–
Banco de la Nación	1891
Provincial bank reorganized	1900
Mortgage banks reorganized	1900
Caja de Conversión	1891–1914

Argentine financial system was quite surprising for, in a short time, it not only became the largest bank in the capital but also proceeded to establish branches in virtually all important provincial cities and large towns. This was due in large measure to the export boom of the years 1890–1914, but it also reflected the success of the extremely cautious policies of the new bank's managers who maintained extremely high metallic reserves, to make sure that a financial crisis like that of 1890–91 would not be repeated.

In Brazil, during the extraordinary stock exchange boom of 1889–91 known as the '*Encilhamento*', the position of the *Banco do Brasil* was weakened by increasing competition with the two large banks which had obtained note-issue privileges from the government. The rivalry intensified as of December 1890, when the two rival banks, the *Banco dos Estados Unidos do Brasil* and the *Banco Nacional*, proceeded to fuse into one giant financial enterprise called the *Banco da República*. None the less, the fusion also reflected the increasingly unstable economic situation and the need to pool resources in order to avoid a panic. In 1891, bankruptcies began to multiply in Rio de Janeiro in the midst of an orgy of speculation. A generalized financial collapse came in 1892 as dozens of old and new companies toppled. In order to shore up public and private credit, a new restructuring plan was put into force, leading to the fusion of the old *Banco do Brasil* with the new

Table 9.3 Banking structure and monetary agencies in Brazil, 1905–23

Bank/Type of Bank	Dates
Bank of Brazil	1905
Caixa de Conversão	1906–14
Provincial State Banks	
Private Banks: Rio, São Paulo, Minas, Bahia	
Rediscount office of Bank of Brazil	1914–23

Table 9.4 Banking structure and monetary agencies in Mexico, 1896–1914

Bank/Type of Bank	Dates
National Bank of México	1884
Private bank in the provinces	
Other private banks in Mexico City	
Commission of Money and Exchange	1905–14
Central bank (clearing agency)	1900–10

Banco da República.[22] Eventually, the reforms gave place to the configuration of the *Banco do Brasil* in 1905, an institution which was destined to dominate Brazilian banking during much of the twentieth century.

Finally, in the Mexican case it may be observed that while the financial crisis of the early 1890s was less severe, it also reflected the close links established between a great bank (*Banco Nacional de México*) and the government. A few years later, in 1897, Limantour ratified the first comprehensive Mexican banking law which promised to allow for a more federalist financial structure, but in practice the *Banco Nacional* continued to be the most important bank and the one most heavily engaged in the administration of government finance.

Some Latin American financial experts would later argue, with the apparent advantage of hindsight, that it had been the lack of adherence to the gold standard in the 1880s that had led to the crisis of the 1890s. This is, however, a debatable issue, for in fact the financial debacles of the early 1890s were a more complex affair and were also closely linked to a series of major, concurrent errors in bank practice and strategy in diverse Latin American countries.

Bank management problems in Latin America, at this early stage, arose in good measure from a misunderstanding of monetary and public debt problems, although it could also be argued that the lack of central banks, as such, was a factor. Contemporary bank directors also had an inadequate understanding of monetary inflation with inconvertible currency (as was the Argentine case after 1885) or with monetary systems with inadequate metallic reserves, as in Brazil.[23] In Mexico, on the other hand, this pitfall was avoided because of the small volume of bank notes issued and the relatively large silver monetary reserves of the major banks, but problems did arise as a result of the falling value of silver in relation to gold, a fact which also tended to increase the weight of the service on foreign debts and investments.

The shift to the gold standard after the turn of the century

Following the crises of the 1890s, a new financial consensus became dominant throughout Latin America. The view that it was necessary to adopt formally the gold standard in order to avoid the financial instability of the very recent past (as well as to attract new flows of foreign capital) rapidly gained strength. By the turn of the century, the response of key sectors of the financial elites in several major countries was therefore to press for the adoption of the gold standard, accompanied by advocacy of maintaining high metallic reserves in relation to bank note issues.

The generalized adoption of the gold standard in various Latin American countries and the creation of new mechanisms to ensure its functioning in a stable fashion was quite a remarkable phenomenon. It may have contributed to spurring an unprecedented volume of foreign investments in the region and to initiating a relatively long period of three decades, in which bank panics became infrequent, particularly in Argentina and Brazil.

None the less, before 1914 there were few specific proposals for the creation of central banks.[24] Rather, a two-pronged strategy tended to be adopted in both Argentina and Brazil which included strengthening the main 'government' bank and adopting a high reserve policy accompanied by the creation of *cajas de conversión* (monetary exchange agencies) which were basically in charge of regulating gold-currency reserves in accord with the fluctuating demand for gold. The analysis of the role of the various monetary agencies (*cajas de conversión*) during the 1900–14 period would seem to be of some comparative interest since they were quite similar to present day currency boards.

In Argentina, the gold standard was formally adopted in 1899, following a long period of restructuring of the public banking sector, as well as of public-sector external debts as a result of the financial collapse of 1890 (better known as the Baring Panic).[25] The recovery of the Argentine economy was surprisingly rapid and during the 1890s large export surpluses allowed both public and private sectors to cover their very considerable external obligations without problems. As a result, Argentina regained the confidence of international financial markets, and by the end of the decade adoption of the gold standard became feasible.

The stabilization of the Argentine economy was closely linked to two banking reforms. The first was the creation of the *Banco de la Nación Argentina* in 1891 which quickly became both government banker and the largest commercial bank in the country, setting up branches in all the provinces. The second, simultaneous reform was the creation of a *caja de conversión* to deal with the banking crisis. The agency was initially set up in 1891 to retire the bank notes of the large number of state banks that had collapsed. The vast circulation of such notes both in Buenos Aires and in each of the provinces (issued by provincial government banks on a vast scale between 1887 and 1890) posed a major problem as these bills had effectively lost their nominal value and were highly depreciated. In order to attempt to salvage the credit system, the government resolved to create a heterodox banking/monetary agency (the *caja de conversión*) to which the national finance ministry allocated the national gold bonds which had served as basis to the vast, currency issues of the provincial state banks in the late 1880s. The *caja* imposed strict discipline on these banks, retiring most of the bank notes issued and eventually liquidating the majority of the old government banks, including the *Banco Nacional* and the *Banco de la Provincia de Buenos Aires*.

This same *caja de conversión* was transformed in 1899 into a formal monetary agency. Henceforth, generally speaking, both public and private sector banks sold their gold holdings (accumulated as a result of trade surpluses) to the monetary agency, which in exchange gave them paper money (backed by the gold reserves of the *caja*). The value of the Argentine gold peso was maintained until 1914, when as a result of a local banking panic and the fall in trade caused by the outbreak of the First World War, the government decided to leave the gold standard, returning to it only in 1927, and then opting out again for inconvertibility after 1931.

While the *caja de conversión* fulfilled one of the functions of a central bank, others were exercised, until the mid-1930s, by the *Banco de la Nación*. These would later be noted on the occasion of the creation of the central bank in 1935:

> In addition to its tasks as commercial bank and lender to the government, the *Banco de la Nación* added that of holder of the government's fiscal and financial accounts, that of Clearing Bank

> and even that of fulfilling certain tasks typical of a central bank. It is known, in effect, that an important group of banks (in the 1920s) considered their holding of treasury bills in accounts in the *Banco de la Nación* as reserves, against which they could issue credits.[26]

In other words, in the first three and a half decades of the twentieth century, some of those functions which today are characteristic of central banks were exercised in Argentina by a combination of the *caja de conversión* and the *Banco de la Nación*; and in periods of inconvertibility, by the *Banco de la Nación* alone, utilizing a monetary exchange office.

In the case of Brazil, a similar monetary and banking scheme was adopted following the monetary reform of 1905 which brought about the adoption of the gold standard, the reorganization of the *Banco do Brasil*, and the creation of the *Caixa de Conversão* in 1906.[27] This office (based on the Argentine model) carried out foreign exchange transactions which maintained the predetermined value of the *mil-réis*: it was based within the *Banco do Brasil* and continued to operate until the end of the first period of the formal gold standard which lasted until 1914, when the operations of the Conversion Office were suspended.[28]

During this period, as Gail Triner argues, the money supply and therefore credit operated in close relation to the trends and discipline of the foreign exchange markets. But in the succeeding years of 1914–24, the Brazilian government abandoned the gold standard and eased credit and the money issue. As she points out, during the First World War and the years immediately following:

> The economy experienced both growth and price inflation. The Treasury funded facilities to increase bank credit in 1914, 1915 and 1918. The first such attempt took the form of direct loans to banks; then in 1915 and 1918 the *Banco do Brasil* rediscounted the notes of other banks based on special Treasury programs. The years from 1921 to 1923 saw large scale monetary expansion through the rediscount Office in the *Banco do Brasil* (Triner, 1996: 10).

After 1923, on the other hand, the money issue was limited by the *Banco do Brasil* which closed its Rediscount Office and at the same time contracted money and credit. Then, between 1927 and 1929, a new attempt was made to re-adopt the gold standard but, as Peláez and Suzigan argue, the currency was not fully convertible, leading the Treasury to abandon its efforts to sustain the gold standard at the same time as the international economic crash of 1929 came to a head (Peláez and Suzigan, 1976: 187–9).

Monetary and banking trends in Mexico were quite different, as the country moved from the silver standard to the gold standard as a result of monetary reform in 1905, although again there are some parallels with the Argentine and Brazilian cases. During the 1890s, there had been a running battle between proponents of the silver standard, basically exporters and industrialists, and the advocates of gold, among which were importers, managers of big foreign firms and some bankers. None the less, the steady fall in the price of silver tended to favour the groups preferring the gold standard and generated increasing pressure to modify the monetary regime, as the government external debt service was becoming increasingly costly and foreign investors were growing wary of investing more money in an economy tied to a depreciating currency. By the turn of the century, and after the large loan of 1898 which converted all the foreign debt (in gold) into lower-interest bonds, finance minister José Yves Limantour began to press hard for the adoption of the gold standard. A monetary advisory commission, which included both Mexican and North American entrepreneurs and economic experts, was set up to review the options and finally drew up the blueprint for the monetary reform of 1905.

As a result of that reform, a monetary agency called the *Comisión de Moneda y Cambios* was set up to receive gold from the banks in exchange for gold certificates, which were to serve as partial metallic reserves of bank note issue; the banks were also expected by law to hold a high level of metallic reserves to support their respective note issues. Additional research is needed to establish the exact mechanisms used by the government to finance the *Comisión de Moneda*, but it is clear that a key factor was the large fiscal surpluses in gold that Limantour had accumulated between 1900 and 1905 and which were deposited in the accounts of several large banks in New York, London and Berlin.

Economic historians have not yet carried out sufficient research to establish the precise impact of the monetary reform on the Mexican economy, which in 1907 suffered the scissors effect of a domestic banking crisis and the repercussions of the great economic crisis of that year in the United States which spilled across the Rio Grande. Between 1910 and 1913, the increasingly unstable political situation did not provoke a new financial crisis, but in 1914, after the assassination of Madero and the rise to power of General Victoriano Huerta, capital flight gained strength, the *Comisión de Moneda* lost much of its gold and pressure accumulated which would lead to the abandonment of the gold standard. A weakening of regulations governing the metallic reserves of the banks took place as well. As revolutionary conflicts deepened and each of the various armies issued inconvertible (and rapidly depreciating) currency, the monetary situation became chaotic and the banking system began to sink rapidly. In late 1915, the administration of Venustiano Carranza set up a new banking and monetary commission which took over all the metallic reserves of Mexican banks and spurred a return to a monetary system based essentially on the circulation of silver. Soon after, the government closed the majority of Mexican banks, although a few of the larger ones, like Banamex, managed to weather the political and economic storms of the revolutionary era.

'Money doctors' and the projects for central banks in Argentina, Brazil and Mexico

The first part of this chapter has shown that, during the second half of the nineteenth century, 'national' banks performed some of the functions typical of central banks. Nevertheless, it was not until the 1920s that the first central banks were established in Latin America, beginning with the Andean nations. The principal motivation for their creation was to facilitate the return of these economies to the gold standard. The role of foreign policy advisers in the creation of central banks in Andean countries has been examined by Drake (1989), who has analysed in detail the role of the 'money doctors', in particular the various American missions headed by Professor Walter Kemmerer to Colombia (1923–33), Chile (1925–32), Ecuador (1925–33), Bolivia (1927–32) and Peru (1930–33) (Seidel, 1972; Eichengreen, 1989; Drake, 1989).

However, the cases of Argentina, Brazil and Mexico proved quite different, for while there were missions by 'money doctors' – by the Director of the Bank of England, Sir Otto Niemeyer, to Brazil (1931) and to Argentina (1933) – which in some ways resembled Drake's definition of 'money doctoring', there were important differences from the Andean cases of the 1920s.[29] This section analyses the principal factors that influenced the creation of central banks in Argentina, Brazil and Mexico, ending the account at that historical moment in each case. Our argument is that these three large Latin American economies did not restore the gold standard or create formal central banks principally on the advice of 'money doctors' from abroad. In the case of Mexico, the advice of Kemmerer in 1917 was not taken seriously (Kemmerer, 1940). Brazil and Argentina received Niemeyer's recommendations after the collapse of the gold standard, but in the first case the formal central bank was not created until 1965, and in Argentina the internal debate was more influential than the foreign counsel. Finally, we argue that the key difference when comparing the establishment of central banks in Latin America is the level of institutional development in each country, and particularly the differences in the economic situation of the three countries under consideration.

Before entering into a discussion of the actual proposals for the creation of central banks, it is important to take into account contemporary conceptions of monetary regimes in Latin America. The system of the gold standard (1819–1914) is an important reference point because all the succeeding agreements on fixed exchange rate systems (Bretton Woods, European Monetary System) have been inspired by its advantages (Eichengreen, 1987; 1994). In theory, the gold standard rule (fixing the price of the currency in terms of gold) would limit monetary expansion in the international economy and create stability in price levels. In practice, the objective of full employment was subordinated to external objectives (Krugman and Obstfeld, 1994: ch. 18).

During the First World War, many governments, in particular those of belligerent countries, were forced into inconvertible currency. As had happened in previous times of war, governments financed part of their military expenses by borrowing from their banks, which led to monetary expansion. Thus, after the war, the price levels were higher in these countries, and some of them continued a policy of monetary expansion to finance reconstruction, which was followed by inflation and hyperinflation (Aldcroft, 1985). After the war, there was an aspiration to return to the 'rules of the game' of the gold standard. One of the consequences of the First World War was an accumulation of a significant proportion of the world's gold in the hands of the new largest creditor. The United States rapidly restored the gold standard in 1919 but the United Kingdom delayed restoring it until 1925 at the prewar parity. Though British price levels had been falling since the end of the First World War, they were still higher than before the war (Williams, 1930; Moggridge, 1972).

Perceiving that world gold reserves were insufficient after the war, the League of Nations called for the adoption of a 'gold exchange standard' in which countries, including those in Latin America could hold currencies of large countries such as Britain (pound-gold) (Martín Aceña, 1982; Krugman and Obstfeld, 1994: 533–4). Policy makers in Argentina, Brazil and Mexico belatedly adopted the gold standard (Brazil in December 1926, Mexico in February 1927 and Argentina in August 1927) but their membership was inspired more by circumstance than by conviction. For Brazil and Argentina, this was a way to facilitate access to foreign finance, while for Mexico it was the only way to stabilize the discredited post-revolutionary monetary system (Triffin, 1944).

During the 1920s, in addition to the 'money doctors' from the United States who visited Andean countries with recommendations for the establishment of a central bank, there were a number of international organizations which also advocated this project. For instance, monetary agreements were part of the International Economic Organisation of the League of Nations which promoted the gold standard and the creation of central banks, between 1922 and 1931.

With the onset of the Great Depression, holders of pounds throughout the world lost confidence in their convertibility into gold (Cassel, 1936). The change of monetary policy of the Federal Reserve Board in 1928 was the beginning of the end of the gold standard for the periphery.[30] Capital flight and a loss of reserves obliged Argentina to abandon it in December 1929, Brazil in November 1930 and Mexico in July 1931. Britain was forced to leave the gold standard in September 1931. The United States abandoned the gold standard in 1933 but returned to it in 1934 (with a depreciation from 20.7 dollars to 35 dollars per ounce). Other governments also used administrative controls or multiple exchange-rates in order to allocate the scarce foreign exchange reserves to different uses. Trade barriers and deflation in the developed countries led to Latin American governments defaulting on their foreign debt (Marichal, 1988). After the United Kingdom abandoned the gold standard, the Brazilian and Argentinian authorities implemented multiple exchange-rate controls in September and October 1931, in order to allocate reserves and avoid fluctuations in the money supply. These measures were considered temporary in both cases, but in Argentina they lasted longer (Salera, 1941).

In Latin American countries, budgetary restrictions, associated with fiscal dependence on their foreign trade, resulted in the modification of national bank institutions (Díaz Fuentes, 1993). In Mexico, the *Banco de México* was transformed into a central bank in 1935–36, and in Argentina, new central bank legislation was passed in 1935 in order to finance the fiscal deficit. In general, the banking reforms did not imply a shift in the private or semi-public control of the banks, but instead meant that they had more leeway to lend to the public and perform rediscounting to the other banks.

The case of Argentina

The creation in 1935 of the *Banco Central de la República Argentina* (BCRA), Argentina's central bank, was not the result of a sudden, unexpected decision, nor one which responded primarily to the recommendations of a foreign advisor, as may have been true for other cases such as the Andean countries. The economic environment into which the BCRA was born contrasted sharply with the circumstances of the 1920s, and a comparison of the periods helps to highlight the differences in functions and characteristics of central banks created in the

1920s and those established one decade later. Reforms adopted after the Great Depression and the abandonment of the gold standard determined the dominant financial and monetary rules in the country.

The Argentine authorities suspended the gold standard in August 1914,[31] but this did not imply monetary reform because, despite the restriction on gold flows, there was no monetary expansion without gold reserves. When the United States entered the war there was a financial shortage, and Argentina became a creditor, primarily due to its exports to belligerent countries. From the end of the war to 1927, Argentine monetary policy reflected the fluctuation of balance of payments on both the current and capital accounts. From 1923 to 1930, Argentina increased its foreign debt to the United States from 93 to 340 million dollars (Peters, 1934: 127). Its reserves increased from 775 million dollars in 1927, to 1047 million dollars in 1928; in contrast, in 1929 they declined by 297 million dollars. When the gold standard was suspended in December 1929, the authorities considered this a temporary situation (Prebisch, 1985).

Although Argentina did not have a central bank before 1935, some central bank functions were performed in a decentralized way by other institutions (Cortés Conde, 1985; 1988). *The Banco de la Nación Argentina* carried out rediscount operations for other commercial banks and was closely linked to the government. Initially, the *Caja de Conversión* issued notes in exchange for gold, and later, in some circumstances, in exchange for government bonds and commercial notes. From 1931, the Treasury's fund of foreign exchange was administered by the *Banco de la Nación* (Office for the Control of Exchange).

When considering the factors in favour of the creation of a central bank in Argentina, it is important to look beyond the influence of foreign advisors. There were already many ideas and proposals locally for the creation of a central bank when Niemeyer was requested by the Argentine financial authorities to visit Buenos Aires on an official advisory mission in 1933 (Olarra Jimenez, 1968). Moreover, Argentinian policy makers looked to the antecedents and experiences of the newly created or reformed central banks in other countries. Indeed, two decades before Niemeyer's visit to Argentina, as a consequence of the First World War, various politicians and ministers had already suggested the necessity of merging the *Banco de la Nación* and the *Caja de Conversión* (Hueyo, 1938; Salera, 1941; Vilaseca, 1988). Piñero and Molinas, for instance, proposed a project whereby the *Banco de la Nación* would be converted into a central bank. President Irigoyen warned in 1917 that: 'The National and Foreign Institutions established in this country lack the foresight of a banking regime' and in the same year, Ramos Mejía claimed that it was necessary to organize a banking regime within a large central institute since the *Banco de la Nación* was a commercial institution, with the only difference that it was the property of the state and the *Caja de Conversión* performed mechanically, without discernment or efficiency. He said that a 'bank of banks' needed to be created, by transforming the *Caja de Conversión* and converting the *Banco de la Nación* into one section of a central bank. Additionally, Damian Torino proposed that the *Banco de la Nación* and the *Caja de Conversión* be merged in order to control credit and to put an end to the destabilizing effects of drains on the gold reserves in the country and Enrique Uriburu, finance minister, presented a similar project with the objective of resolving the Treasury's problems. Finally, financial crisis and the collapse of the gold standard reinforced the arguments promoting greater governmental intervention in the economy and the creation of a central bank (Lascano, 1970; O'Connell, 1984).

The Niemeyer report of 1933 recommended the creation of a private central bank which should be organized as a limited company.[32] Given that some of the functions of the proposed bank were already being performed by the *Banco de la Nación*, the *Caja de Conversíon* and the Treasury, Niemeyer's proposals for the central bank's functions really only amounted to an attempt to centralize banking functions in order to improve the implementation of monetary and fiscal policies. Indeed, it could be argued that the Niemeyer report was requested to reinforce internal projects; to counteract possibly the suspicion that inflation would be generated as a consequence of the creation of such an institution; and gain more financial support or reduce the uncertainty of investors and foreign banks in the circumstances prevalent in the 1930s. It is worth noting that Argentina was one of the few countries in the world that continued servicing its foreign public debt, probably due to pressures from Britain and also because it was hoped that this would give it easy access to capital (Peters, 1934; Phelps, 1938).

In the final analysis, the creation of the BCRA must be understood in the context of the financial reforms undertaken by Federico Pinedo, finance minister from 1934, which were much more influential than Niemeyer's proposals (Prebisch, 1985; 1986). Pinedo attempted to clean up the banking situation and exercise better control of the financial system by constituting the *Instituto Movilizador de Instituciones Bancarias* (IMIB). There were significant differences between Pinedo's proposals and Niemeyer's recommendations for the creation of a central bank.[33] Fundamental to Pinedo's reform was the necessity of maintaining reserves in the face of capital flight given that Argentina was an agrarian exporting country – a concern that continues to be valid today despite the fact that the country has changed (Prebisch, 1959; Pinedo, 1961). The procyclical process implied that during stages of abundance of gold (as a result of increased exports and foreign investment) the money supply expanded and credit was relaxed (Williams, 1920, 1929; Ford, 1958). This created monetary expansion which surpassed the original increase in exports and foreign investment, and encouraged a growth in imports and a disequilibrium in the trade balance. Although this situation could be sustained temporarily with foreign investment flows, in the end, the flows inverted and destabilized the balance of payments. Capital flight and the withdrawal of foreign reserves led to abandoning the gold standard and to the application of exchange controls (Salera, 1941; Díaz Fuentes, 1994). This situation had repeated itself under distinct regimes and conditions and thus it was thought that a central bank, which held reserves and controlled credit, could defend monetary stability in particular, and the economy in general.[34]

The objectives of the new central bank would be: to maintain reserves in order to regulate the consequences of the export cycle and foreign capital flows; to regulate money supply in accordance with the real evolution of the economy; to promote liquidity and credit by inspection and verification; to be a financial agent to the government and be its advisor in credit operations and in the issue and administration of debt. Its principal functions would be to issue notes, buy and sell gold and foreign exchange, provide sight deposits without interest, rediscount notes to the banks, make advances to banks within limits and act as an agent for similar foreign institutions, and act as the government's financial agent, performing operations in the open market, through buying or selling government bonds to banks.

The BCRA would not be permitted to participate in commercial firms, to buy shares or buy properties not for its own use. The minimum reserve which would support the money supply and deposit liabilities would be 25 per cent (90 per cent in gold). If the reserve fell below one-third for more than 60 days, or for 90 days within a financial year, dividends would not be distributed in this year. The banks would deposit two thirds of their legal reserves in the central bank (law 12156) which would constitute the funds for rediscounting, compensation and advancing operations (BCRA, 1935; Vilaseca, 1988). Furthermore, as a government agent, it could not subscribe to its operations nor guarantee them. Advances to the government would be limited to 10 per cent of official deposits accumulated in the last three years, which would only be used to finance the short-term deficit.

The Brazilian case

The economy of the early Brazilian Republic was characterized by inflation, financial chaos, and by the consequent 'orthodox' stabilization plan put into place by the Ministry of Finance (1898–1906). There were two main schools of thought in the economic debate of this period. On the one hand, there was the 'orthodox' group which supported the coin issue and promoted the appreciation of the exchange rate (by returning to the parity of 1846 and adjustment by deflation). On the other hand, there were the 'developmentalists', who encouraged note issuing and sought to impose a more 'realistic' adjustment of the exchange rate without deflation (Peláez and Suzigan, 1976).

Monetary policy depended crucially upon the exchange rate, which in Brazil was tied to government-sponsored programmes for the coffee sector. Thus, the rules of the gold standard were first adopted in December 1906, with the creation of the *Caixa de Conversão*. This was one of the results of the Agreement of Taubaté, made in February 1906, between the governors of the coffee-producing states of São Paulo, Minas Gerais and Rio de Janeiro, which drew up a scheme whereby the price of coffee and the exchange rate would be stabilized (Villela and Suzigan, 1973). However, adherence to the gold standard was partial, since the *Caixa de Conversão*'s issue of notes at an exchange rate of 15 pence for 1000 *réis* co-existed with an inconvertible fiduciary money issued by the Treasury. The mechanism of conversion depended on the inflow of foreign reserves, which were restricted by the onset of the First World War, so that in 1914 the *Caixa de Conversão* was closed down, and, as a consequence, the Treasury was allowed to issue more inconvertible money (Silber, 1956).

After the war, between 1923 and 1926 monetary policy was influenced by the 'real bills doctrine'. This called for linking the expansion of the payments system and credit to legimitate productive activities. Flexible monetary mechanisms would be created, preferably through the establishment of a central bank, so that monetary expansion would be responsive to the needs of production, and not to the needs of the Treasury or to finance the public deficit (Neuhaus, 1974). The proponents of this doctrine pointed to the United States' Federal Reserve System (1914) and the *Reichsbank* as antecedents which had endeavoured to adjust the flow of money according to the necessities of business.

Proposals for the creation of a central bank in Brazil were encouraged by Batista, the president of the *Banco do Brasil* between 1914 and 1918 and the finance minister between 1919 and 1922.[35] In his opinion, it was necessary to improve monetary control by eliminating the erratic interference of the Treasury and by transferring these functions to a Central Bank through a reorganization of the *Banco do Brasil* (De Paiva Abreu, 1976). Moreover, ideas conducive to the creation of a central bank were promoted by the campaign of the League of Nations at the Brussels conference in 1920 and in Geneva, in 1922, as well as by the advice of its experts to various European governments (League of Nations, 1921; Triffin, 1944).

The first step for the establishment of a central bank was the founding of the *Carteira de Redescontos* (CARED) by the *Banco do Brasil* in November 1920. The CARED was allowed to rediscount commercial notes, and although it had an original limit on its issue of 100 000 *contos*, it had a notable compensatory effect during the recession of 1920–21 and in the financing of the third programme of coffee valorization between 1921 and 1924 (Peláez, 1971; Neuhaus, 1974).

Advocates of the creation of a central bank found their first spokesman in Arthur Bernardes, who took up the project as part of his presidential campaign. Once elected in 1922, he promoted the transformation of the *Banco do Brasil* into a central bank inspired by the *Reichsbank*, which would follow the 'real bills doctrine' retaining one-third of its reserves in gold and two-thirds in commercial notes. However, the experience was short-lived (1923–26).

Brazil's next president, Washington Luís (1926–30), suspended the functions of the central bank designed by the previous administration, through the creation of an organ that promoted the full and free convertibility of money in circulation into gold at a fixed exchange rate. This would be achieved by a Stabilization Fund (*Caixa de Estabilização*) similar to that of 1906–14 (inspired by the French stabilization programme and the ideas of Gustav Cassel). According to Neuhaus (1974), Washington Luís considered this measure a provisional one, to create the reserves to establish an orthodox central bank in 1928. However, the onset of the Great Depression postponed his plan. Brazil was forced to abandon the gold standard in November 1930, and the authorities closed the stabilization fund and withdrew its notes, while a proportion of the bills of the *Banco do Brasil* were maintained for the Treasury (Banco do Brasil, 1930; Peláez, 1968; Cardoso, 1979).

Abandonment of the gold standard as a consequence of the Great Depression was a radical rupture with the economic policies of the first Republic, and brought with it a period marked by the intervention of the state in the economy (Villela and Suzigan, 1973). Monetary policy in 1929 and 1930 was restrictive, reserves fell from 690 000 to 279 000 *mil réis*, and the reserve requirements were increased. In 1930, the CARED of the Banco do Brasil was reopened, which affected the monetary base through rediscounting operations of commercial notes and the financing of acquisitions for the storage of coffee by the *Direcção Nacional do Café* (Peláez, 1969; 1971).

Before 1930, Brazilian economic policy had been characterized by the stabilization of the exchange rate and the coffee 'valorization' policy.[36]

A great proportion of the financial requirements for the latter were obtained from the international markets. This dependence of the valorization policy upon foreign finance made it a requirement that British missions assess the country's payment capacity and recommend the policies it should follow to assure the regular service of debt. But the coffee valorization policy entered a crisis of overproduction and surplus of stock in 1927–28 and, after the beginning of the Great Depression, financial conditions made it still more difficult to sustain the policy (Cardoso, 1979). Despite these circumstances, in April 1930, the São Paulo government obtained the only foreign loan issued in London in 1930. This loan totalled 20 million pounds nominal but the actual receipts were only 8.5 million pounds. The loan was not enough to maintain the coffee policy, but the Washington Luís administration maintained the *mil réis* on the gold standard and, as a consequence, there was an inflow of capital and a total loss of gold reserves in 1931 (Souza Reis, 1934; De Paiva Abreu, 1975; Cardoso and Dornbusch, 1989).

In 1931, Rothschild, the London banker, proposed that the concession of a new loan required a technical assessment of the economic situation of the country and an analysis of the measures that must be adopted to assure the debt repayment capacity. This recommendation led to Niemeyer's financial mission to Brazil in 1931 which was important for its influence on economic policy-making in Brazil during the 1930s. The mission was not an isolated case for Brazil, since there were immediate precedents in the Montagu (1923–24) and D'Abernon (1929) missions, but it was the most important one in terms of financial and central banking policy advice for the country during the 1930s.[37] In the Niemeyer case, conditionality consisted basically in the stabilization of the exchange rate and the creation of an orthodox central bank (Niemeyer, 1931).

In 1931, however, there was a significant change in Brazilian monetary policy, as the *Banco do Brasil* was authorized to increase its circulation by 300 000 *mil reis*, but only 170 000 were issued; in part, this was used to support the coffee sector. In 1932, there was a regional rebellion the cost of which was assumed by the government, representing a Treasury bond expansion of 400 000 *mil réis*. The *Caixa de Mobilização Bancária* (CAMOB), created in 1932, allowed commercial banks to regain liquidity by receiving their overdue credits as a result of the Great Depression. In 1933, the *Banco do Brasil* was granted a monopoly of exchange rate control.

Subsequently, as part of the policies of the *Estado Novo* of Getulio Vargas (1937–45), the *Carteira de Crédito Agrícola e Industrial* (CREAI) was created in 1938 as a branch of the *Banco do Brasil*, with the objectives of promoting investment in industrial, agricultural and infrastructural sectors and also in 'national defense' (Skidmore, 1982). Policies during this period were clearly procyclical (expansionary) and were influenced by the 'real bills doctrine', which held that monetary expansion would lead to a financing of 'productive activities' and would not have inflationary effects (Neuhaus, 1974).

Financing the deficit during the Second World War had direct consequences on inflation, due to the lack of coordination over the issue of money and credit. This situation, after the Bretton Woods agreements, led to the creation of the *Superintendencia da Moeda e do Crédito* (SUMOC) in 1945. Until this moment, the *Banco do Brasil* had assumed powers in monetary and financial matters and had acted as a development bank by supporting governmental programmes to promote industry and agriculture (Neuhaus, 1978). The principal functions of SUMOC had been to regulate the money issue and the requirements of the Treasury; to act as a depository for the legal reserves of commercial banks; to regulate the bank's rate of rediscount; to operate in the open market using government bonds; to supervise the debt of commercial banks with CARED and CMOB; and finally to inspect and control banking activity in general.

The 'incestuous' relationship of the SUMOC with the *Banco do Brasil*, whereby the latter had to put into practice the decisions taken by the former, annulled any possible beneficial effects of an independent monetary policy. Instead of holding the reserves deposited by commercial banks on the orders of SUMOC, the *Banco do Brasil*, used these resources to expand its own operations. In this way, the credit capacity of the *Banco do Brasil* was amplified and that of commercial banks restricted, without controlling effectively money supply. During the 1950s and 1960s, SUMOC's efforts were also frustrated by government decisions to pursue developmentalist policies excessively by financing them with the money issue.

In 1942, however, the money issue to finance the Treasury's deficit was limited by legislation. Until the creation of the central bank, which revoked this legislation, the Treasury paid an overdraft advance to the *Banco do Brasil* which generated extraordinary issues of CARED, authorized by the government through special legislation. But the debate between impersonal rules and the discretionary power of the monetary authorities cannot be applied to the Brazilian case before the creation of the central bank. There was neither one nor the other, as monetary policy was subject to the federal budget deficit. Between 1958 and 1964, various programmes of stabilization were implemented, but their failure resulted in a rise of inflation to 164 per cent in the last of these years.

To control inflation was one of the objectives of the dictatorship which seized power in 1964. The regime adopted a gradualist option and tried to reduce the expansion of the payments system, particularly by lessening the growth of the monetary base as a principal instrument of control over the money stock. To this end, the government deficit was reduced by restrictions on federal spending and the issue of indexed bonds, and in 1965 a reform of banking was enacted which eliminated the SUMOC and created the central bank and the *Conselho Monétario Nacional* (Neuhaus, 1978: Rabbello and Ronci, 1991). The function of the central bank would be to programme the annual expansion of the payments system by establishing a monetary target which would make the money stock compatible with anticipated rates of inflation and the growth of GDP. At the same time, its functions were amplified, and the range of instruments of monetary policy at its disposal increased, including open market operations with short-term bonds.

The case of Mexico

Central banking in Mexico has its antecedents in the nineteenth century, but the most important influences can be found in the post-revolutionary period. While in the international arena it was the First World War which precipitated the collapse of the gold standard, in Mexico, it was first and foremost the outbreak of the Revolution in 1910 which forced its abandonment. The system of 'free banking', legislated in 1905, had exacerbated the financial chaos before the Revolution. If, in the post-war years, there was an international aspiration to return to the gold standard, in the case of Mexico there was additional incentive to liquidate and clean up the old banking and financial system, as well as a desire to create new financial institutions which responded to revolutionary demands (Brothers and Solis, 1966).

There is strong historical evidence to show that the creation of a central bank in Mexico was not the result of a sudden decision, nor a 'top-down' decision emanating from the government. Indeed, there was a desire to create a government-controlled single issuing bank when the Mexican Constitution was written in 1917 (Fernández Hurtado, 1976). The creation of the *Banco de México* (1925), which enjoyed only some of the functions of a central bank, was delayed by eight years, and its consolidation as a central bank took another ten years. This bank was born in the aftermath of the Revolution under rather unusual conditions. Old monetary, financial and banking rules persisted, but in addition, as an inheritance of the Revolution, money issued by various political authorities generated financial chaos (Cárdenas and Manns, 1989).

Monetary instability was exacerbated during the revolutionary conflicts (1910–17). When General Carranza's troops seized Mexico City in 1914, they started to issue notes which they called *constitucionalistas*. Their intention was to finance military spending, and the *constitucionalista* was given legal tender although in a decree of the period 21 types of notes were also recognized as legal tender. As a result of excess circulation and public confusion, the *constitucionalista* note was depreciated (Manero, 1957).

In September 1915, Carranza withdrew his authorization for banks to issue money unless they conformed to the General Law of Institutions of Credit, which had been passed ten years earlier. Moreover, he established a commission to inspect and regulate the activities of the 24 banks which existed. This commission found that only nine operated in line with this law. Between 1916 and 1921, 15 banks were seized and their banking credit suspended (López Rosado, 1965). At the same time, the inspection committee proposed the creation of a 'national bank' which would have a monopoly of issue.

Another failed attempt by the authorities to stabilize the monetary system occurred in May 1916 when they adopted a new note, the so-called *infalsificable*, which also rapidly depreciated (Manero, 1957: 108). From 1917 to 1930, the monetary system (silver and gold) was exclusively metallic (Martínez, 1954).

As the new Revolutionary government started to undergo consolidation at the beginning of the 1920s, the banking system was reorganized. However, at the same time, competition remained among different banks, and financial instability continued into the middle of the decade. The constitutional debates of 1917 gave rise to a proposal to create a government-controlled central bank with a monopoly of issue. Among the Constitutionalists, there was a broad consensus about this proposal, but there were disagreements about the degree and type of government control that would be exercised over the bank and whether it would be exclusively state-owned or private interests could participate (Manero, 1957: 129). When the Constitution was approved, the executive immediately took the initiative and created a bank of issue and discount (Rodríguez Garza, 1995). This project corresponded to that of constitutionalist R. Nieto, and had aspects in common with the *Banco de México* to be created later. However, given the chaos of the banking system, the uncertainty on the part of the public and the scarcity of resources available to create the bank, the latter foundered.

In January 1921, General Obregón decreed that the banks seized in 1916 could return to operation (Torres Gaitán, 1980: 157). This initiative was considered a step towards creating the bank of issue as outlined in the Constitution, but it would not be until February 1924, with the first banking Convention, that more detailed legislation began to be discussed to establish the framework for the future of the banking system (Manero, 1957; Rodríguez Garza, 1995).

As of the second half of the 1920s, a more favourable institutional framework was outlined in order to apply monetary policies.[38] On 2 January 1925, the *Comisión Nacional Bancaria* was created. In April of the same year, the government made gold and silver money legal tender and in September the *Banco de México* was established. In August 1926, the new law for institutions of credit and banking establishments was passed.

The *Banco de México* started activities with the monopoly of issue. It was organized as a limited company owned 51 per cent by the federal government, while private banks and individuals could only subscribe for up to two per cent of capital. The bank's issue could not exceed the double of its reserves of precious metals and foreign exchange (INEGI, 1990: 635 and BANAMEX, 1934). However, from the time of its creation, the money in circulation in the economy (M1/GDP) was reduced[39] and the bank did not issue notes because they continued to be discredited by the public.

In February 1927, the Mexican authorities decided to adopt the gold standard. As money in circulation continued to be both silver and gold, there was the possibility of a flexible exchange rate. Legally, the monetary system was based on the gold standard, but silver continued to be the most heavily used currency, and the predominant exchange rate was of the silver *peso* with the dollar. The government tried to maintain the legal quotation by increasing the supply of gold coins while restricting that of silver coins, as much for the changes in prices of metals as for the disequilibrium in the balance of payments (Torres Gaytán, 1980).

Between 1926 and 1931, Mexico's current account balance deteriorated due to the orthodox monetary policy which led to an appreciation of the *peso*, and also due to exogenous factors, including the fall of petrol and mineral export prices, transfers made by agreements on the external debt, and the economic crisis in the United States (FitzGerald, 1980; 1984). Monetary restriction and the appreciation of the *peso* after 1926 coincided with a decline in exports and GDP which had started already before the Great Depression (Torres Gaytán, 1980). The restrictive monetary policy was maintained once the Great Depression started, and the financial crisis led to drains on reserves and a drastic contraction in money supply – the means of payment were reduced by at least a half during 1930 and 1931.

By May 1931 the situation was no longer sustainable. Banks were pressured by their customers in the fear that the government would declare the *peso* inconvertible into gold. Reform of the monetary system was delayed until July 1931, by which time the monetary system was virtually exhausted. Then, the government had no other alternative but to abandon the gold standard and devalue the currency. In the face of scarce reserves, the exchange rate was floated until June 1932, when it reached a parity of around 3.6 *pesos* per dollar, similar to that maintained until March 1938.

Money supply increased again when silver was coined and notes were issued in 1932. In order that the *Banco de México*, directed by the former president Calles, could increase the circulation of notes and silver coins, various laws were reformed, such as the *Constitutiva del Banco de México*, and that of the Institution of Credit and Credit Exchange, which allowed for the creation of a network of private banks. These new laws allowed the *Banco de México* to be the central issuing bank (BANAMEX, 1978: 100–103; Fernández Hurtado, 1976). At the outset, its notes were used to pay overdue salaries of public employees, but later they were used as the normal method of payment. Between 1932 and 1933, the coinage of silver rose to 89 million *pesos* and note issue to 53 million. In 1931, notes constituted only 0.5 per cent of the primary means of payment, but this increased to 10.5 per cent in 1932 and reached 34.8 per cent by 1935. In addition, the devaluation of the *peso* (by 67 per cent between 1929 and 1933) changed relative prices and encouraged import substitution (Cárdenas, 1987: 260–80).

These profound changes of exchange rate policy did not imply an open rejection of monetary orthodoxy, since the authorities announced that the benefits of seignorage would be conserved to increase the reserves backing the note issue, assuming that the circulation could not be constituted exclusively with notes, as in other countries (BANAMEX, 1978).

The favourable effects of this monetary policy were apparent with the recovery in 1933. External factors also contributed later to its success. When the United States abandoned the gold standard in April 1933, the *Banco de México* established a fixed exchange rate policy of 3.6 *pesos* to the dollar which allowed the continuity of parity until March 1938. The monetary policy adopted by Roosevelt raised the international prices of gold and silver and stimulated Mexican production of these metals (BANAMEX, 1978). In April 1935, the price of silver in the United States rose to such a level that the metallic value of the Mexican *peso* was greater than its nominal value. In reaction, the Mexican authorities decoupled the monetary system from the fluctuations of the price of silver, and substituted the silver *peso* for notes and coins of other metals of lesser quality. This new monetary reform meant that gold and silver coins were abolished as a means of payment, while it was established that henceforth the single legal currency would be *Banco de México* notes.

Once the price of silver declined, the new finance minister E. Suárez, approved a new 'Organic Law' of the *Banco de México* in August 1936, as well as a new monetary law whereby silver coins returned into circulation and were convertible into notes (Turrent Díaz, 1982). The *Banco de México* was reorganised under new legislation (Manero, 1957), which in general would be kept in place for the next half century.[40] In relation to the composition of the reserves it was decided that these would consist of 80 per cent gold and foreign currency, with a maximum of foreign exchange of 10 per cent, and 20 per cent in silver. The total of reserves would not be less than 100 million *pesos*, nor go below 25 per cent of notes issued.

The monetary reform of 1932 did not limit the transformation of the financial system to the transformation of the *Banco de México* into a central bank. It also stimulated the creation of powerful sectoral institutions of credit, including the *Banco Nacional Hipotecario y de Obras Públicas* (1933), the *Nacional Financiera S.A.* (1934) and the *Banco Nacional de Comercio Exterior* (1937).

At the beginning of 1939, a new reform of the 'Organic Law' of the *Banco de México* was passed, whose objective was to limit government credit and make it independent. According to the new legislation, the government would obtain finance through certificates of the Treasury. In addition, current account deposits of private individuals were no longer to be kept in the *Banco de México*, but transferred to commercial banks. At the same time, the central bank was given the faculty to issue certificates of payment, in order to attract savings and restrict the circulation of money according to the evolution of the balance of payments. For these last changes, the law of credit institutions was reformed.

In sum, the evolution of the monetary system in Mexico since the post-revolutionary period exhibits the following characteristics. At the beginning of the 1920s, monetization was reduced and the banking system was destabilized. Halfway through the decade, institutions were created which gave greater stability to the financial system, including the creation of the *Banco de México*. In the second half of the 1920s, the government continued an orthodox monetary policy, which was strengthened with the adoption of the gold standard, from February 1927 to 1931. After the onset of the Great Depression, the same policies were continued until June 1931, when reserves became almost exhausted. From 1932, monetary reforms were introduced gradually which gained the confidence of the public, since the demand for notes and silver coins increased. Once orthodox monetary policy was abandoned, a policy of a fixed exchange rate to the dollar was adopted which lasted until the petroleum industry was expropriated in March 1938.[41] Monetary reform in 1932 was crowned by success, when the United States abandoned the gold standard in April 1933, and decided to increase its reserves by buying silver in 1934. As Mexico was a producer of silver, it was favoured with the increase in the price of silver, to the extent that in 1935, the metallic value of its silver coins was higher than their nominal value. The government modified the monetary law and the Organic Law of the *Banco de México* in August 1936, which conferred on it the functions of a central bank, and these remained in place until 1986. At the end of the 1930s, the functions of the central bank were made independent from government finances. But these financial and banking reforms were not limited to the functions of a central bank, since other, important entities for sectoral credit were also created, which would subsequently play a significant role in financing the development of the economy.

Conclusions

While we have only focused on the three largest nations in Latin America, this chapter clearly suggests that the emergence of central banking in Latin America did not follow one path but rather several different trajectories. Generally speaking, some central banking functions were fulfilled from the late nineteenth century by a series of 'national' banks, being complemented by the regulation of gold reserves in the 1900–14 period by *cajas de conversión* – which were in many regards similar to modern currency boards. Following the First World War, projects for the creation of central banks were debated broadly throughout Latin America but it was first in the Andean countries that they were set up, whereas the creation of central banks in Argentina, Brazil and Mexico was slower and more complex. It can be argued, in fact, that it was largely as a result of the depression of the 1930s that central banking came to the fore in these nations as a prerequisite both for monetary policy as well as for the different banking systems, but even so political factors continued to be of great importance in the policy-making decisions related to central banking in these three nations. None the less, as has been noted, increasing practice and experimentation with central banking functions eventually did prove conducive to the emergence of central banking in Latin America.

Notes

1. The authors have divided the responsibility for the paper into two parts: Marichal, for the first part, and Díaz, for the second.
2. The most important recent work developing this comparative framework is Drake (1989).
3. Also see Tedde (1988) on the origins of Spanish central banking; Plessis (1985) on the historical evolution of the Banque de France; and on the Bank of England the classic work by Clapham (1944). See additional up-to-date bibliographical references in Pohl (1994).
4. Even in those countries without a formal central bank, the natural evolution of pyramiding of (smaller) bank reserves, and the concentration and centralization of reserves in some major central commercial banks or bank occurred. In those countries where a single commercial bank dominated, it tended to assume quasi-central-bank functions. In those countries where the pyramiding-centralization was concentrated in a group of powerful banks, the clearing house which they had established and ran assumed certain quasi-central-banking functions. See Timberlake (1984), Goodhart (1995: 76).
5. Initially, the 'national' banks reviewed were privately owned banks but later, as in the case of the *Banco de la Nación de Argentina* (from 1891) or the *Banco do Brasil* (after 1905), they tended to become government-owned. The *Banco Nacional de Mexico* (established in 1884) was, however, always privately owned. All of these large banks handled government accounts and carried on a very extensive commercial business in the respective countries.
6. Among the earliest banking experiments those that stand out are the first *Banco do Brasil* (1808–29), the *Banco de Buenos Aires* (1822–26) and its successor the *Banco Nacional* (1826–35), although a number of additional financial institutions were also established in other countries of the region such as the *Banco de Avío* (1830–40) in Mexico. All were government-owned banks except for the *Banco de Buenos Aires*. On the *Banco do Brasil*, see Pelaez (1975) and Levy and Ribeiro de Andrade (1970); on the *Banco de Buenos Aires* and *Banco Nacional*, see Amaral (1977 and 1982) and Garrigós (1873); on the *Banco de Avío*, see Potash (1965).
7. The stock exchanges of Rio de Janeiro and of Valparaíso/Santiago de Chile were the most active and sophisticated, on both of which more than thirty companies traded stock by the late 1860s. See Levy (1977) and Oppenheimer (1976).
8. A discussion of the banking developments in Brazil in the 1860s can be found in Andrade (1987). In the late 1880s and early 1890s, the *Banco do Brasil* went through a series of fusions with two other banks, which together dominated the Rio de Janeiro financial market. Later, in 1905, the *Banco do Brasil* was reorganized and restructured into the banking firm which still today is the largest in Brazil. See Barroso and Gustavo (1983) and Topik (1987).
9. This included management of government bank accounts, issuing internal debt on the local financial market and taking charge of the service of both internal and external debts. See Garrigós (1873), Lamas (1886) and the detailed annual accounts of the provincial bank in the annexes to the annual *Memorias* of both the finance ministry of the province of Buenos

Aires and that of the national government of Argentina. The latter can be located in the library of the Ministerio de Economia in Buenos Aires and there are microfilm copies in the Library of Congress in Washington.

10. For the Brazilian debate see Ferreira Soares (1865a). For the Argentine debates see Cortés Conde (1985) who reviews the parliamentary discussions of banking in 1863; on the influence of Courcelle Seneuil in Chile from 1860 see Subercaseaux (1922). For an overview, see Marichal (1994).
11. A similar conflict took place in Mexico in the mid-1880s: the lawyers of the *Banco Nacional de Mexico* were advocates of a monopoly of issue by that bank. See Macedo and Sánchez Gavito (1885). Their rivals, the *Banco de Londres y Mexico*, were more inclined to free banking. See Casasús (1900).
12. By the end of the 1880s there were at least fifteen important commercial banks in Rio de Janeiro and sixteen in Buenos Aires and a lesser number in other Latin American cities. In Argentina there were also some ten official provincial banks and another dozen private banking institutions in various provincial cities. In Brazil provincial banking in the late 1880s was concentrated in the North-east and in São Paulo, although a few small banking firms could be found in other regions. Among the few studies on regional banking in this period see Saes (1986).
13. If we look more specifically at fiscal administration, it is clear that the creation of national banks with numerous agencies was a significant institutional innovation with important and positive effects upon state finance. For example, the collection and movement of tax revenues (and government funds in general) proved much swifter and surer in the 1880s as a result of the establishment of bank agencies in many secondary cities and ports. The collection of funds continued to be handled by fiscal agents but they now had more secure places to safeguard such funds. Moreover, finance ministers now counted on more complete and quicker information on how much money was available throughout the nation and could dispose of it more effectively. In combination with telegraphs and railroads, banks substantially improved the efficiency of the state fiscal and financial administration. See Marichal (1994).
14. In this regard, moreover, it seems appropriate to recall the comment of the late banking historian, Jean Bouvier, who insisted on paying special attention to the role of the state in the economy, for as he noted 'What has the state been in the 19th and 20th centuries but the largest enterprise in the economy? By reason of the mass of its employees, the enormous nature of its business and the great movement of funds ... the state has always been the most influential of economic agents' (Bouvier, 1978).
15. A particularly notorious example of the negative effects of the lack of adequate information of supply and costs of money can be found in the review of Mexican state finances before 1860. See Tenenbaum (1987).
16. In the case of Mexico City, for example, interest rates in the 1870s fluctuated between 10 and 14 per cent, but from the early 1880s, with the establishment of several large banks, rates dropped to between 6 and 10 per cent. Obviously, this benefited both the private and the public sectors. For an analysis of trends in the 1880s, see Marichal (1995).
17. The *Banco Nacional* in Argentina, for example, negotiated various foreign loans in the 1880s for the national government as did the *Banco Nacional de México*. For details, see Marichal (1989: ch. 5).

18. The best statistics on Argentine banking in the 1880s are to be found in the official reports of Agote (1887).
19. There is no detailed monograph specifically on the *Banco do Brasil* in the last third of the nineteenth century despite its importance. Melo Franco (1979) is a traditional institutional work but only deals with the first half of the nineteenth century.
20. See the essays by Batiz, Ludlow and Marichal in Ludlow and Marichal (1986). Also see Ludlow and Silva (1993).
21. The most important private bank to collapse was the *Banco Carabassa*, subsequently absorbed by the Bank of London and River Plate. The other merchant and financial firms that went under suffered as a result of both the decline in trade, the fall in real estate prices and the fall of the state banks with which they had conducted business. For details see Marichal (1989: ch. 6).
22. For antecedents and details see Barroso and Gustavo (1983) and Topik (1987).
23. It should also be noted that the accumulation of foreign debt by state banks, which was only payable in gold (a common feature of Argentine finance in the late 1880s) led to perilous situations as the balance of payments situation worsened. When the metallic reserves of banks evaporated and as foreign currency and gold disappeared from local money markets, there was no way of continuing the service on foreign debts. As a result, a number of banks found their international sources of credit and capital frozen, and were soon subject to severe international pressures to start payments despite the critical situation in the balance of payments.
24. However, see experiments in Colombia and Peru. The best single monograph on central bank history in one nation is that on Colombia: *Banco de la República de Colombia* (1990), 2 vols. On Peru see Quiroz (1989) and his essay in Marichal and Tedde (1994).
25. The Argentine debt re-negotiations of the 1890s were the largest and most complex up to that date of any Latin American nation. For a review of the debt re-negotiations of provincial and national external debts in the 1890s, which led to the issue of more than £35 million of new bonds in exchange for the old bonds see Marichal (1989: ch. 5). For details on the banking crisis in Buenos Aires in 1890 see Martí (1990).
26. This is a quote from the presidential address to the Argentine Congress in 1935 proposing the creation of the Central Bank. See *Banco Central de la República Argentina* (1972: vol. 2, 631–2).
27. For details see Peláez and Suzigan (1976: 153–5); Neuhaus (1974: 17–27) and Fritsch (1988: 16–18).
28. The Conversion Office was formally closed in 1920 after six years of suspension.
29. That Argentina and Brazil should have requested and received recommendations from Niemeyer under the auspices of Rothschild, after the Great Depression, reflects the British, rather than the American, influence in these countries.
30. A discussion on the subject can be found in Friedman and Schwartz (1963), Hamilton (1987), Temin (1989) and Romer (1992).
31. This was after the longest period on the Gold Standard, starting with the *Ley de Convertibilidad* (1899) that came into effect in 1903; see Williams

(1920), Peters (1934), Phelps (1938), and Ford (1958). Probably the best definition of the Argentinian monetary system is that of finance minister A. Hueyo (March 1932–July 1933): 'sporadic gold-standard' (1938).

32. Its principal functions would be to issue notes, regulate credit and bank reserves, maintain monetary stability, act as a financial agent of the government and approve the issue of public debt. See Niemeyer (1933).
33. Pinendo's proposals included: (1) up to 20 per cent of total gold reserves could be held in the form of foreign exchange (Niemeyer did not establish a foreign exchange limit); (2) measures were not considered to adjust the relation of reserves to money issued by means of adjusting rediscount rates (Niemeyer recommended raising rates when the ratio of reserves to money supply fell below 33 per cent); (3) rediscount operations should be guaranteed by one institution only in addition to the soliciting bank (Niemeyer suggested that two institutions act as guarantors).
34. The central bank would be directed by a 14-member board. The president and vice-president had a seven-year mandate (which was longer than the period of the presidency of the Republic), both of whom would be elected on the proposal of the bank's shareholders by the government and in accordance with the Senate. The other 12 directors had a three-year mandate. The government, the *Banco de la Nación* and the provincial banks would have one representative, foreign banks two and national private banks three.
35. Batista considered that an independent central bank should regulate money and credit according to the requirements of business. The treasury had failed to fulfil these functions, since it had many overlapping functions. On the one hand, its main responsibility was monetary and it used this function to finance the government deficit. At the same time the government was vulnerable to pressure groups. Batista believed that money issued by the Treasury was 'artificial', since it was legal tender, but the reserves of a central bank would be backed up by real wealth, in gold or foreign exchange obtained from legitimate transactions, and consequently the central bank's circulation would be less inflationary than that coming from the Treasury. Moreover, while it should be noted that a central bank would have the means to reach the desired return to the gold standard, the majority of 'civilized countries' were using money issued by a central bank and not by the Treasury.
36. Both policies were supported by the coffee lobby that dominated the national and key local state governments, whose purpose was to avoid the appreciation of the currency (*mil réis*) and maintain a stable coffee income. The 'valorization' policies were applied in 1906–1907 and from 1921 to 1939.
37. Niemeyer was 'voluntarily' invited by the Brazilian Goevernment after Rothschild's proposal to condition further credit. He was not a disinterested expert, his prescriptions were traditional of an adjustment policy to assure debt payment, and the only new element was the institution of an independent central bank, an idea that was not new in the country. See De Paiva Abreu (1976 and 1984).
38. The creation of new financial institutions was not limited to those performing central banking functions – the *Banco Nacional de Crédito Agrícola* and four regional cooperative banks (ejidales) were also established. See BANAMEX (1978) and *Banco Nacional de Comercio Exterior* (1988).

39. Accurate monetary statistics for the period 1910–24 are not available, but our estimation of the relation M1/GDP shows that this was low: 8.8 per cent in 1925, of which 76 per cent was in coin, 0.3 per cent in notes and 23.7 per cent in sight deposits (Díaz Fuentes, 1994, using the methodology developed by Tortella Casares, 1974).
40. The functions of the reformed contral bank were: (1) the regulation of the issue of currency and the control of the quantity of money and credit for monetary policy purposes; (2) managing the country's international reserves; (3) to act as banker to the commercial banks including lender of last resort; and (4) to continue to act as the banker to the government. See Tello (1984).
41. See Knight (1990) on the expropriation of the petroleum company.

References

Agote, P. (1887), *Informe del presidente del crédito público nacional sobre la deuda pública, bancos, acuñación de moneda y presupuestos*, 4, Buenos Aires, G. Kraft.

Albert, B. (1988), *South America and the First World War: The Impact of War on Brazil, Argentina, Peru and Chile*, Cambridge, Cambridge University Press.

Aldcroft, D.H. (1985), *From Versailles to Wall Street, 1919–1929*, Berkeley, University of California Press.

Aldcroft, D.H. (1991), 'Las consecuencias económicas de la guerra y de la paz (1919–1929)', in Cabrera, M., Juliá, S. and Martin Aceña, P. (eds), *Europa en Crisis 1919–1939*, Madrid, Pablo Iglesias, pp. 1–28.

Amaral, S. (1977), 'Comercio y crédito: el Banco de Buenos Aires, 1822–1826', *América*, 2, (4), Buenos Aires.

Amaral, S. (1982), 'El Banco Nacional y las finanzas de Buenos Aires. El curso forzoso y la convertibilidad del papel moneda en 1826', in *Actas del VI Congreso Internacional de Historia de América*, Buenos Aires: Academia Nacional de la Historia, 5.

Andrade, A.M. (1987), *1864: Conflito entre metalistas e pluralistas*, Master's thesis, Universidad de Rio de Janeiro, 1987.

Banco do Brasil (1930), *Relatório*, Rio de Janeiro.

Banco Central de la República Argentina (1935–1940), *Memoria Anual*, Buenos Aires.

Banco Central de la República Argentina (1972), *La créacion del Banco Central y la experienca monetaria argentina entre los años 1935–1943*, Buenos Aires.

Banco de México (1938), *Informe Anual 1937*, México.

Banco Nacional de Comercio Exterior (1988), *Historia del BANCOMEX, 1920–87*, México, BANCOMEX.

Banco Nacional de México (BANAMEX) (1934), *Quinuagesimo Aniversario de su Fundación*, México, Cultura.

Banco Nacional de México (BANAMEX) (1978), *Examen de la situación económica de México, 1925–1976*, México.

Banco de la República de Colombia (1990), *El Banco de la República: antecedentes, evolución y estructura*, Bogotá.

Barroso, F. and Gustavo, H. (1983), *Reforma monetária e instabilidade durante a transição republicana*, Rio de Janeiro.

Bouvier, J. (1978), 'Histoire financiére et problémes d'analyse des dépenses publiques', *Anales ESA*, (2).

Brothers, D.S. and Solis, L. (1966), *Mexican Financial Development*, Austin, University of Texas Press.

Caja de Conversión (1891–92, 1897), *Memoria de la Caja de Conversión*, Buenos Aires.

Cárdenas, E. (1984), 'The Great Depression and industrialisation: the case of Mexico', in Thorp, R. (ed.), *Latin America in the 1930s: The Role of the Periphery in World Crisis*, Oxford, Macmillan–St Antony's College.

Cárdenas, E. (1987), *La industrialización mexicana durante la Gran Depresión*, México, El Colegio de México.

Cárdenas, E. (1992), 'La política económica en la época de Cárdenas', *Econometric Society*, México.

Cárdenas, E. and Manns, C. (1989), 'Inflación y estabilización monetaria en México durante la Revolución', *El Trimestre Económico*, 55 (217).

Cardoso, E.A. (1979), 'Celso Furtado revisitado: a década de 30', *Revista Brasileira de Economia*, 33(3).

Cardoso, E. A and Dornbusch, R., (1989), 'Brazilian debt crises: past and present', in Eichengreen, B. and Lindert, P. (eds), *The International Debt Crisis in Historical Perspective*, Cambridge, MA, MIT Press.

Casasús, J. (1900), *Las instituciones bancarias en México*, México.

Cassel, G. (1936), *The Downfall of the Gold Standard*, London, Oxford University Press.

Clapham, J.H. (1944), *The Bank of England: A History*, Cambridge, Cambridge University Press.

Cortés Conde, R. (1985), 'The export economy of Argentina, 1880–1920', in Cortés Conde, R. and Hunt, S. (eds), *Latin American Economies: Growth and the Export Sector 1880–1930*, New York, Holmes & Meier.

Cortés Conde, R. and Hunt, S. (1988), *Dinero, deuda y crisis, evolución fiscal y monetaria en la Argentina*, Buenos Aires, Sudamericana.

De Paiva Abreu, M. (1975), 'A dívida pública externa do Brasil, 1931–1943', *Pesquisa y Planejamento*, 5(1).

De Paiva Abreu, M. (1976), 'The Niemeyer mission: an episode of British financial imperialism in Brazil', Working Paper, Centre of Latin-American Studies.

De Paiva Abreu, M. (1984), 'La Argentina y Brasil en los años treinta. Efectos de la política económica internacional británica y estadounidense', in Thorp, R. (ed.), *Latin America in the 1930s: The Role of the Periphery in World Crisis*, Oxford: Macmillan–St Antony's College.

Díaz-Alejandro, C. (1970), *Ensayos sobre la economía argentina*, Buenos Aires, Amorrortu.

Díaz Fuentes, D. (1993), *Las políticas fiscales de Argentina, Brasil y México durante la Gran Depresión*, Madrid, Instituto de Estudios Fiscales.

Díaz Fuentes, D. (1994), *Crisis y Cambios Estructurales en América Latina: México, Brasil y Argentina durante el período de entreguerras*, México, Fondo de Cultura Económica.

Drake, P. (1989), *The Money Doctor in the Andes*, Durham & London, Duke University Press.

Eichengreen, B. (1987), 'Macroeconomics and history', in Field, A. (ed.), *The Future of Economic History*, Kluwer-Nijhoff, Boston.

Eichengreen, B. (1989), 'House calls of the money doctor: the Kemmerer missions to Latin America, 1917–1931' in Calvo, G. et al. (eds), *Debt, Stabilization and Development, Essays in Memory of C. Diaz-Alejandro*, Oxford University Press.

Eichengreen, B. (1994), *International Monetary Arrangements for the 21st Century*, The Brooking Institute, Washington.

Fernández Hurtado, E. (ed.) (1976), *Cincuenta años de banca central*, México, Fondo de Cultura Económica.

Ferreira Soares, S. (1865a), *Elementos da Estatística comprendendo Theoría da Sciencia e a Sua Aplicação a Estatística Commercial do Brasil*, Rio de Janeiro.

Ferreira Soares, S. (1865b), *Esboço ou Primeiros Traços da Crise Commercial da Cidade do Rio de Janeiro em 10 de Setembro de 1864*, Rio de Janeiro.

FitzGerald, E.V.K. (1980), 'A note on capital accumulation in Mexico: the budget deficit and investment in finance', *Development and Change*, 11(3).

FitzGerald, E.V.K. (1984), 'Restructuring through the Great Depression: the state and capital accumulation in Mexico, 1925–1940', in Thorp, R. (ed.), *Latin America in the 1930s: The Role of the Periphery in World Crisis*, Oxford, Macmillan–St Antony's College.

Ford, A. (1958), 'Flexible exchange rates and Argentina 1885–1900', *Oxford Economic Papers*, (10).

Friedman, M. and Schwartz, A.J. (1963), *A Monetary History of the United States, 1867–1960*, Princeton, NJ, Princeton University Press.

Fritsch, W. (1988), *External Constraints on Economic Policy in Brazil, 1889–1930*, Pittsburgh, PA, University of Pittsburgh Press.

Garrigós, O. (1873), *El Banco de la Provincia de Buenos Aires*, Buenos Aires.

Goodhart, C. (1988), *The Evolution of Central Banks*, Cambridge, MA, The MIT Press.

Goodhart, C. (1995), *The Central Bank and the Financial System*, London, Macmillan.

Hamilton, J.D. (1987), 'Monetary factors in the Great Depression', *Journal of Monetary Economics*, (19).

Hueyo, A. (1938), *Argentina en la Depresión Mundial*, Discursos y conferencias, Buenos Aires, Ateneo.

INEGI [Instituto Nacional de Estadística, Geografía e Informática] (1990), *Estadísticas Históricas de México*, México, INEGI.

Jones, C. (1973), *British Financial Institutions in Argentina, 1860–1914*, Doctoral Thesis, University of Cambridge.

Kemmerer, E.W. (1940), *Inflation and Revolution. Mexico's Experience of 1912–17*, Princeton.

Knight, A. (1990), 'México 1930–1946', in Bethell, L. (ed.), *Latin America Since 1930. México, Central America and the Caribbean*, 7.

Krugman, P. and Obstfeld, M. (1994), *International Economics*, Harper Collins.

Lamas, A. (1886), *Estudio histórico y cientifico del Banco de la Provincia de Buenos Aires*, Buenos Aires, El Nacional.

Lascano, M.R. (1970), *El crecimiento económico, condición de la estabilidad monetaria en la Argentina*, Buenos Aires, EUDEBA.

League of Nations (1921), *The Recent International Conference at Brussels, 25th February 1921*, Geneva.

Levy, M.B. (1977), *Historia da Bolsa de Valores do Rio de Janeiro*, Rio de Janeiro, IBMEC.

Levy, M.B. (1985), 'Fundamentos do Sistema Bancário no Brasil: 1834–1860', *Estudos Económicos*, 15, Special Edition.

Levy, M.B. and Ribeiro de Andrade, A.M. (1980), 'A Gestão Monetária na Formaçao do Estado Nacional', *Revista Brasileira do Mercado des Capitais*, Rio de Janeiro, 6(17).

Llona, A. (1990), *Chilean Monetary Policy, 1860–1925*, PhD thesis, Boston University, reproduced by UMI Dissertation Services.

López Rosado, D. (1965), *Historia Económica de México*, Pormaca, México.

Ludlow, L. (1986), 'La primera etapa de formación bancaria (1864–

1897)', in Ludlow, L. and Marichal, C. (eds) (1986), *Banca y Poder en México, 1800–1925*, México, Grijalba.

Ludlow, L. and Silva, J. (eds) (1993), *Los negocios y las ganancias: de la colonia al México moderno*, México, Instituto Mora.

Macedo, P. and Sánchez Gavito, I. (1885), *La cuestión de los bancos*, México.

Maddison, A. (1991), 'Economic and social conditions in Latin America, 1913–1950', in Urrutia, M. (ed). *Long-Term Trends in Latin American Economic Development*, New York, Inter-American Bank of Reconstruction and Development.

Manero, A. (1957), *La revolución bancaria en México*, México.

Marichal, C. (1988), *Historia de la Deuda Externa en América Latina*, Madrid: Alianza.

Marichal, C. (1989), *A Century of Debt Crises in Latin America: From Independence to the Great Depression, 1820–1930*, Princeton, NJ, Princeton University Press.

Marichal, C. (1994), 'Modelos y sistemas bancarios en América Latina en el siglo XIX, 1850–1880' in Marichal, C. and Tedde, P. (eds), *La formación de la banca central en España y América Latina*, Madrid: Banco de España

Marichal, C. (1995), 'Foreign loans, banks and capital markets in Mexico, 1880–1910' in Liehr, R. (ed.), *The Public Debt in Latin America in Historical Perspective*, Berlin, Vervuert.

Marichal, C. (1997), 'National banks and nation-building in Latin America, 1850–1900', in Teichova, A. (ed.), *The Rise of Banking: Essays in International Comparative Economic History*, Cambridge University Press.

Marichal, C. and Tedde, P. (eds) (1994), *La formación de la banca central en España y América Latina*, Madrid: Banco de España, serie rojo, two volumes.

Marti, G. (1990), 'Argentina. La crisis de 1890. Endeudamiento externo y crack financiero', *El Trimestre Económico*, 57(228).

Marti, G. (1992), 'La Argentina y la convertibilidad monetaria: una experiencia histórica con el régimen del patrón oro, 1883–1885', *El Trimestre Económico*, 59(235).

Martín Aceña, P. (1982), *La política monetaria en España, 1919–1935*, Madrid, Instituto de Estudios Fiscales.

Martínez, R. (1954), *Teoría monetaria y del crédito*, México, Cátedra.

Melo Franco, Afonso A. de, et al. (1979), *Historia do Banco do Brasil*, Rio de Janeiro, four volumes.

Moggridge, D.E. (1972), *British Monetary Policy 1924–1931: The Norman Conquest of $4.86*, Cambridge, Cambridge University Press.

Moggridge, D.E. (ed.) (1980), *The Collected Writings of John Maynard Keynes*, London, Macmillan–Cambridge University Press.

Neuhaus, P. (1974), *A Monetary History of Brazil, 1900–1947*, PhD thesis, University of Chicago.

Neuhaus, P. (1978), 'A inflação brasileira em perspectiva histórica', *Revista Brasileira de Economia*, 32 (2).

Niemeyer, Sir O.E. (1931), *Report to the Brazilian Government*, London.

Niemeyer, Sir O.E. (1933) 'Report to the Argentinian Government', *Revista Económica* [1934], 7(5–6).

O'Connell, A. (1984), 'Argentina into the Depression: problems of an open economy', in Thorp, R. (ed.), *Latin America in the 1930s: The Role of the Periphery in World Crisis*, Oxford, Macmillan–St Antony's College.

O'Connell, A. (1985), 'Free trade in one (primary producing) country: the case of Argentina in the 1920s', in Di Tella, G. and Platt, D. (eds), *The Political Economy of Argentina, 1880–1946*, Oxford, Macmillan Press.

Olarra Jimenez, R. (1968), *Evolución monetaria argentina*, Buenos Aires, EUDEBA.

Oppenheimer, R. (1976), *Chilean Transportation Development: the Railroad and Socio-economic Changes in the Central Valley*, PhD thesis, University of California.

Paiva Abreu, M. de, (1976), 'The Niemeyer mission: an episode of British financial imperialism in Brazil', Working Paper, Cambridge, Centre of Latin American Studies, University of Cambridge.

Paiva Abreu, M. de (1984), 'Argentina and Brazil during the 1930s: the impact of British and American international economic policies', in Thorp, R. (ed.), *Latin America in the 1930s: The Role of the Periphery in World Crisis*, Oxford, Macmillan–St Antony's College.

Peláez, C.M. (1968), 'A Balança Comercial, a Grande Depressão, e a Industrialização no Brasil', *Revista Brasileira de Economia*, 22.

Peláez, C.M. (1969), 'Acêrca da Política Governamental, da Grande Depressão e da Industrialização no Brasil, *Revista Brasileira de Economia*, 23(3).

Peláez, C.M. (1971), 'Análise econômica do programa brasileiro de sustentação do café, 1906–1945: Teoria, Política e Medição', *Revista Brasileira de Economia*, 25(4).

Peláez, C.M. (1975), 'The establishment of banking institutions in a backward economy: Brazil, 1800–1851', *Business History Review*, 49(4).

Peláez, C.M. and Suzigan, W. (1976), *História Monetária do Brasil: análise da política comportamento e instituições monetárias*, Rio de Janeiro, IPEA-INPES.

Peters, H.E. (1934), *The Foreign Debt of the Argentine Republic*, Baltimore, MD, Johns Hopkins Press.

Phelps, V. (1938), *The International Economic Position of Argentina*, Philadelphia, PA, University of Pennsylvania Press.

Pinedo, F. (1961), *Siglo y medio de economía argentina*, Mexico, Centro de Estudios Monetarios Latinoamericanos.

Plessis, A. (1985), *La politique de la Banque de France sous le Second Empire*, Geneva.

Pohl, M. (ed.) (1994), *Handbook on the History of European Banks*, London, Aldershot.

Potash, R. (1965), *Historia del Banco de Avío y Fomento de la Industria, 1830–1841*, México, Fondo de Cultura Económica.

Prebisch, R. (1959), 'Commercial policy in the under-developed countries', *American Economic Review*, Papers and Proceedings, 49(2).

Prebisch, R. (1985), 'Argentine economic policies since the 1930s: Recollections', in Platt, D. and Di Tella, G. (eds), *The Political Economy of Argentina, 1880–1946*, Oxford, Macmillan Press.

Prebisch, R. (1986), 'Five stages in my thinking on development', in Meier, G. and Seers, D. (eds), *Pioneers in Development*, Washington, DC, Oxford University Press/World Bank.

Quiroz, A.W. (1989), *Banqueros en conflicto: Estructura financiera y economía peruana, 1884–1930*, Lima, Centro de Investigación de la Universidad del Pacifico.

Rabello, P. and Ronci, M. (1991), 'Sixty years of populism in Brazil', in Dornbusch, R. and Edward, S. (eds) *The Macroeconomics of Populism in Latin America*, Chicago, The Chicago University Press.

Rodríguez Garza, F. (1995), 'La nacionalización de la política monetaria durante el período de entreguerras', in *Orígenes del pensamiento económico en México*, México, El Colegio de México.

Romer, C.D. (1992), 'What ended the Great Depression', *Journal of Economic History*, 52.

Rosenzweig, F. (1989), 'La evolución económica de México, 1879–1940', *El Trimestre Económico*, 56(221).

Saes, F. (1986), *Crédito e bancos no desenvolvimento da economia paulista, 1850–1930*, São Paulo, Instituto de Pesquisas Economicas.

Salera, V. (1941), *Exchange Control and the Argentine Market*, New York, Columbia University Press.

Seidel, R.N. (1972), 'American reformers abroad: the Kemmerer missions in South America, 1923–1931', *Journal of Economic History*, (32).

Silber, S. (1956), *Historia Monetária do Brasil*, São Paulo, Brasiliense.

Skidmore, T. (1982), *Politics in Brazil 1930–1964, An Experiment in Democracy*, Oxford, Oxford University Press.

Societé des Nations (1931), *Deuxième Rapport Provisoire de la Delegation de l'Or du Comité Financier*, Geneva.

Societé des Nations (1933), *La Conférence Monétaire et Economique (London)*, Geneva.

Societé des Nations (1934), *Revue de la Situation Economique Mondiale en 1933–34*, Geneva.

Souza Reis, F.T. (1934), *A depressão comercial e o funding-loan de 1931*, Rio de Janeiro, Lobato e Cia.

Subercaseaux, G. (1922), *Monetary and Banking Policy of Chile*, Oxford, Clarendon Press.

Tedde, P. (1988), *El Banco de San Carlos, 1782–1829*, Madrid, Banco de España/Alianza Editorial.

Tello, C. (1984), *La nacionalización de la banca en México*, México, Siglo XXI.

Temin, P. (1989), *Lessons from the Great Depression, The Lionel Robbins Lectures for 1989*, Cambridge, MA, The MIT Press.

Tenenbaum, B. (1987), *The Politics of Penury in Mexico, 1821–1856* Albuquerque, University of New Mexico.

Thorp, R. (ed.) (1984), *Latin America in the 1930s: The Role of the Periphery in World Crisis*, Oxford, Macmillan–St Antony's College.

Timberlake, R.H. (1984), 'The central banking role of clearinghouse associations', *Journal of Money, Credit and Banking*, 16(1).

Topik, S. (1987), *The Political Economy of the Brazilian State, 1889–1930*, Austin, University of Texas.

Topik, S. (1988), 'La revolución republicana en Brasil: ¿la burguesía en el poder?' *Siglo XIX*, 3(5), January–June.

Torres Gaytán, R. (1980), *Un siglo de devaluaciones del peso mexicano*, México, Siglo XXI.

Tortella Casares, G. (1974), 'Las magnitudes monetarias y sus determinantes' in Tortella, G. (ed.) *La banca española en la restauración*, Madrid, Banco de España.

Triffin, R. (1944), 'Central Banking and Monetary Management in Latin America', in Harris, S. (ed.), *Economic Problems of Latin America*, New York, McGraw Hill.

Triner, G.D. (1994), *Banking and Brazilian Economic Development: 1906–1930*, PhD thesis Columbia University.

Triner, G.D. (1996), *Banking on the Periphery, 1906–1930*, paper presented to Cliometrics Panel 1996, ASSA Conference.

Turrent Díaz, E. (1982), *Historia del Banco de México*, México, Banco de México.

Urrutia, M. (ed.) (1991), *Long-Term Trends in Latin American Economic Development*, New York, InterAmerican Bank of Reconstruction and Development.

Versiani, F.R. (1984), 'Before the Depression: Brazilian industry in the 1920s' in Thorp, R. (ed.), *Latin America in the 1930s: The Role of the Periphery in World Crisis*, Oxford, Macmillan–St Antony's College.

Vilaseca, H. (ed.) (1988), *Banco Central de la República Argentina sus primeros cincuenta años*, BCRA, Buenos Aires.

Villela, A.V. and Suzigan, W. (1973), *Política do governo e crescimento da economia brasileira, 1889–1945*, Rio de Janeiro, IPEA-INPES.

Williams, J.H. (1920), *Argentine International Trade Under Inconvertible Paper Money, 1880–1900*, Cambridge, Harvard University Press.

Williams, J.H. (1929), 'Latin American foreign exchange and international balance during the war', *Quarterly Journal of Economics*, 33.

Williams, J.H. (1930), 'Reparations and the flow of capital', *American Economic Review*, Papers and Proceedings, vol. 20.

PART III
International Institutions and Central Banking

CHAPTER TEN

The International Monetary Fund and Central Banking[1]

Harold James

The IMF may appear to fit only rather poorly in the context of a conference on the emergence of modern central banking, since it is clearly not a central bank constituted on an international scale. It is, however, a financial institution, lending to and borrowing from governments. Certainly, the initial wartime vision of John Maynard Keynes went much further and envisaged the creation of a new international money by the proposed Clearing Union; and Harry Dexter White's original mission for a World Bank included note issue (to replace gold) as well as the functions of an ordinary commercial bank (Oliver, 1971). In the 1960s, as the international monetary system became dangerously over-dependent on the dollar, new proposals were made for satisfying the world's need for reserves. Some aspects of the Special Drawing Right (SDR) proposals in the 1960s revived the initiative for an international currency, but the SDR was deliberately so restricted in its use as to make it a non-money available only to governments (and solely in particular circumstances and with particular obligations). The SDR was in fact devised as a solution to the problem of a general shortage of reserve assets, a problem which has quite clearly not existed since the beginning of the 1970s.

As realized under the terms of the Bretton Woods agreements, the IMF does not create money or regulate its creation in a way characteristic of central banks. Neither is it directly involved in the regulation of international banking systems – often a task that has been assumed by central banks on the national level. These design elements can be explained historically in terms of the assumption prevailing at Bretton Woods that the monetary mechanisms of the past had failed and also that there would be no major private financial flows across national frontiers. Trade imbalances, however, might lead to problems on the external account; and the IMF was intended to act as a mechanism for helping central banks to deal with their external accounts under these circumstances.

The IMF's origins lay in the perception of a failure of central banks in the inter-war period: in the memory of the imposition of intolerably harsh deflation as part of adjustment in a fixed rate system. The resources of the Fund were to be used to make adjustment less painful and less socially and politically contentious. In addition, the provision of a mechanism for discussing exchange rate changes in the event of a 'fundamental disequilibrium' was intended to remove one of the causes of inter-war monetary difficulties.

For the first period of the IMF's activity, during the so-called period of the Bretton Woods regime, the best way of thinking of the IMF and its functions is not so much as an institution, but as the institutional embodiment of a system of rules. In this era, private capital movements at first played only a minor role. The founding fathers of Bretton Woods, in fact, had believed that private international flows had been pernicious in the inter-war economy and both hoped and expected that they would be severely limited in the post-war world. When a large-scale international capital market developed in the later 1960s, it produced large flows responding to incompatibilities between different national policies, and, in the end, brought down the traditional Bretton Woods order.

After the collapse of the Bretton Woods or par value system (of fixed but adjustable exchange rates), the presence of a rapidly growing private sector capital market changed the character of the IMF, and it had to begin to consider the tasks that had traditionally been those of central banks dealing with money and capital markets in a national context. In particular, it had to deal with sudden reversals of confidence on capital markets, and to act as a lender of last resort on the international level. Secondly, it began also – in part as a result of the need for lender of last resort activities – to consider questions of international capital markets and their supervision. The logic of what John Williamson has called the 'non-system' pushed the IMF to become more like an international central bank in these two respects (Williamson, 1983: 103).

The IMF and capital markets

The construction of the post-war international monetary system, built around the IMF, came as a result of a general agreement that a repetition of the economic and political nationalism of the 1930s could and should be avoided. The inter-war experience had provided a vivid and terrifying demonstration of how the collapse of the economic order could bring about political and social fragmentation. In the new order, a commitment to keep stable but adjustable exchange rates would eliminate the temptation to engage in competitive devaluation. Controls on capital movements would eliminate the big speculative flows that had destroyed the exchange rate regime of the inter-war period. The essential insight of the new vision was that harmonious inter-state relations involved a willingness to agree on the surrender of some aspects of national sovereignty.

The agreements produced at Bretton Woods combined a vision of a liberal world economy with a rule. The rule's primary purpose was to constrain national economic policies in cases where otherwise the interaction of different national strategies might cause disaster for the world as a whole (in currency policy, competitive devaluations; in trade policy, the application of protectionism). Apart from this, it would preserve the policy-making options ('sovereignty') of nation-states. At the time of Bretton Woods, a vivid memory of the 1930s saw the requirements of the international order as frequently in conflict with the imperative of building a more just and a more stable domestic order. The conference aimed at providing a solution to this dilemma. The main attraction of the rule was that it was impersonal and largely automatic. States were obliged, under the terms of their legislation accepting Bretton Woods, to maintain fixed exchange rates. The pursuit of inappropriate policy would lead to danger signals in the form of balance of payments imbalances. A state could then either take corrective action (adjustment), if necessary with the assistance of the resource pool created in the International Monetary Fund; or, if it was judged that the imbalance reflected a fundamental disequilibrium, the exchange rate could be altered with the approval of the Fund. The commitment to keep the exchange rate fixed would by itself provide sufficient limitation of the room for national policy manoeuvre. A further function of the Fund was to create, through the quota mechanism, an additional pool of reserves which functioned analogously to a credit union (Kenen, 1986). The goal was to ensure that, in a period in which a general shortage of reserves existed outside the United States, this limitation would not stand in the way of the movement toward liberalized trade and exchange convertibility.

This system had a strong element of automaticity, but one which would and could never be total. The principle of surveillance by the Fund developed out of the necessity of judging whether a member country's needs and policy objectives corresponded to a situation in which the use of the Fund's resources would be appropriate; as well as out of the commitment of members to consult, if they maintained the transitional regime (under Article XIV of the Articles of Agreement) in which exchange controls might still be tolerated. In other words, the Fund, as a financial institution, was required to use its lending to promote a specific outcome. Its resources were to be used 'to facilitate the expansion and balanced growth of international trade, and contribute thereby to the promotion and maintenance of high levels of employment and real income and to the development of the productive resources of all members'. The Articles of Agreement also recognized the importance of the new body in the exchange of information and views. Its purposes had already been defined as 'to promote international monetary cooperation through a permanent institution which provides the machinery for consultation and collaboration on international monetary problems'.

The basic commitment to liberalization inherent in the acceptance of convertibility laid the foundations for a system which created unprecedented rates of economic growth, and increased prosperity throughout much of the world. However, there were two major surprises. First, the new institution never controlled world liquidity (and indirectly the world money supply) in the way originally envisaged. As the global economy grew, IMF quotas accounted for ever smaller shares of international reserves. Even the new IMF 'money' of the 1960s, the SDR, which actually reproduced quite faithfully the intentions of the founders of Bretton Woods, came to represent only a very small part of the world's reserves. Instead national authorities, and increasingly also the substantially uncontrolled operations of the Euro-markets, created their own money.

The second development largely unforeseen at Bretton Woods – one which in fact contributed greatly to the dynamism of the world economy, but also altered the character of the monetary order – was the emergence of large capital movements, freeing money from national control. The original agreements had involved an obligation to liberalize current accounts, but – among other considerations – the primary rule (fixed exchange rates) involved the necessity, or at least the possibility, of controlling capital flows. When the world returned to nearly general convertibility at the end of the 1950s, and accepted the corresponding Article (Article VIII) of the Fund's Articles of Agreement, this meant convertibility on current account only. However, even at this early stage, substantial capital movements developed. The access to resources they brought constituted one of the main incentives to many countries to adopt convertibility. Capital movements brought not just the possibility of increasing national investment levels, but were also often associated with flows of skills and technology. This was true of Spain in the late 1950s, and then of Latin American countries (where the initial experiment in convertibility was often unsuccessful) and East Asia (where some spectacular successes occurred).

As capital flows developed, the problems of monetary management became more complex. One instance of the new difficulties was the effect of capital inflows on the domestic money supply. Another example was that capital flows allowed a financing of current account deficits. Initially current account deficits were believed to be the major problem requiring international action; but capital flows might make them less of a problem. Inflows – foreign borrowing – could offer an easy and at least temporary alternative to immediate adjustment. Obviously, such flows depend on the verdict of the lenders – the market – and cannot necessarily be maintained indefinitely, particularly if the resources are chiefly used to pay for increased consumption. The availability of capital often simply offered the possibility of making a choice about a time-frame for adjustment; but governments (often with limited political time-horizons reaching to the next elections) wanted to take advantage of such a choice and defer the adjustment as a problem to bequeath to their successors. As a result, there were temptations not to recognize underlying economic problems. The new difficulties were the underlying rationale for the extension of IMF consultations to include also the member countries who had gone over to full convertibility under Article VIII of the Articles of Agreement. Such consultations might give advance notice of the likely emergence of economic problems. Throughout the 1960s, the international community repeatedly tried to develop a systematic approach to 'early warning signs' and this is indeed a discussion that is still with us.

At the same time, the availability of funds on capital markets altered the demand for liquidity. In cases where confidence was maintained, there would be sufficient liquidity as a consequence of private lending. Such funds, however, would not be available exactly when they were needed – in a crisis. In cases where confidence disappeared, the Fund became more necessary than ever as a substitute for the private market, as a way of financing imbalances and restoring expectations of stability: in short, as a reserve centre or a lender of last resort. There are two ways of providing such assistance. The first, immediate support in the case of a market panic, in order to forestall an imminent market failure, is undertaken by central banks or by the central bankers' central bank, the BIS. The second, in which policy changes as well as a persuasion of financial markets are required in order to restore confidence, after a market failure has already taken place, has been the domain of the IMF. This intervention too is associated with the supply of resources. (The IMF could potentially play a larger role in the former operation also – perhaps not so much directly, by trading on its own account, but by using its resources to help to unwind the substantial swap positions built up by central banks in cases of intervention when they combat speculative attacks. In effect, this would mean strengthening the reserve position of central banks.)

Until the 1970s, the IMF regularly intervened in the aftermath of currency crises arising out of current account imbalances, and provided an additional source of reserves. The United Kingdom IMF crises of 1967 (with a sterling devaluation) and 1976 could be taken as examples. In the 1980s, when the IMF no longer dealt with industrial countries, since these were confident in their ability to meet their needs on the capital markets, a new type of situation arose with regard to some developing countries. In these cases, in restoring confidence, the IMF had to involve itself directly with the markets, and could not rely simply on policy advice to governments alone (although the latter still constituted the principal element in the IMF's statutory task of surveillance of the international monetary system). Crises began to occur because of shifts in the capital account, rather than from the current account imbalances for which the IMF Articles of Agreement provided a remedy. At the time of Bretton Woods, it had been assumed that capital account problems would be simply dealt with through the imposition of capital controls.

The IMF as lender of last resort

The most dramatic learning experiences of the IMF as a lender of last resort occurred with respect to two rather different crises, but which coincidentally arose in the same country: the Mexican crises of 1982 and 1994–95. Before each of these crises, the commercial banking world had convinced itself that the IMF was an increasing irrelevance on the stage of international finance – perhaps good only for organizing an Annual Meeting to serve as a backdrop for bankers' pitches to their governmental clients.

In the late summer of 1982, the announcement of difficulties in servicing Mexico's external debt led immediately to fears of a collapse of the entire international banking system, since exposure to Mexico and other troubled debtor countries amounted to substantially more than the capital of many major banks. At this point, the IMF was quite ill-prepared to act as a lender of last resort in the sense identified by Kindleberger (Kindleberger, 1978). Usually the lender of last resort needs to act very quickly and decisively in the face of a sudden crisis. The IMF makes decisions in its Executive Board, subject to voting by Executive Directors who consult their national authorities (and, in the case of the elected Executive Directors, usually a substantial number of national governments). These decisions, as in the Mexican case, depend on an often lengthy negotiation of the reform programme with the borrowing country. On the other hand, central banks, with their traditions of secrecy and clear operational guidelines, are able to act very speedily; and, in the Mexican crisis, both the US Federal Reserve and the central bankers' central bank, the BIS, did act extremely promptly in August 1982. But they wanted assurance that they would not be left on their own, and that their short-term assistance would be used to galvanize the rest of the financial community. This was the task that the IMF set itself. The Managing Director of the IMF, Jacques de Larosière, put his own prestige on the table – committing the Executive Board, in effect, to follow his advice. In an emergency, the Board had to act in a different and more expeditious way than that to which it was not only accustomed but also committed through the Articles of Agreement.

The major mission involved in this exercise lay in building new institutional bridges very rapidly within the international financial community, and to Mexico and then to other debtor countries, as well as within the politically bitterly divided Mexican government. Assistance from the IMF and central banks, on the one hand, and the stabilization of bank credit, on the other, were made mutually dependent on each other.

The Chairman of the Federal Reserve Board, Paul Volcker, and the influential co-chairman of the Banks' Advisory Committee (a body formed to handle the Mexican debt crisis), William Rhodes (of Citibank), argued that there should be no new money from the banking system unless Mexico could come to an agreement with the IMF. The Mexican example came to be a model, in this as in many other regards. For each country, a separate bank committee of 12 to 14 banks was established to negotiate a new schedule of payments. Each bank on the committee had the task of keeping the other creditor banks in its country or region informed and under pressure to agree.

The IMF, instead of appearing (as many bankers had previously believed) as a fringe institution in a world which could be quite adequately managed by the private financial sector, now took on the task of coordinating the global system. Its negotiations with Mexico represented a bracket that would hold the world of money and the world of sovereign states together.

The letter of intent for a three-year extended facility prepared by Mexico as a result of those negotiations was signed on 10 November. It involved 450 per cent of Mexico's IMF quota, or around $3.7 billion. For its implementation, the Fund had to borrow substantial additional resources. As was usual, the programme depended on domestic policy performance criteria, but also on an agreement over external debt. Under the terms of the agreement, the budget deficit would be cut from 16.5 per cent of GNP in 1981 to 8.5 per cent in 1983, 5.5 in 1984 and 3.5 by 1985. The current account deficit would be expected to fall from

$13 billion in 1981 to $6.5 billion in 1982 and $4.25 billion in 1983. The agreement would, in addition, be dependent on a rescheduling accord with the commercial creditors.

The calculations of the IMF involved a substantial element of new money. On its own, the IMF could clearly not provide all of it. De Larosière initially shocked bankers meeting in the New York Federal Reserve building, on 16 November 1982, with a statement that the Fund arithmetic could not work without a sizeable contribution from the banks. Instead of bailing out the banks, the IMF would be 'bailing them in'. De Larosière then explained the details of the Mexican and Argentine figures. For Mexico, a total of $8.3 billion would be required over the course of 1983, of which $1.3 billion would come from the IMF and $2 billion from the United States and other governments. Then de Larosière added that the rest – $5 billion – was to be the contribution of the bankers, in order to 'make the amortization schedule compatible with the orderly execution of the Fund program'. The banks would have to agree to this additional funding, which amounted to a 7–8 per cent increase in their exposure, by 15 December 1982, one week before the Executive Board vote on the Mexican Extended Fund Facility. (De Larosière pointed out that, in 1981, bank exposure to Mexico had been increased by 46 per cent.) In addition, the banks might have to deal with interest arrears. The procedure of providing new funds was known by a variety of names, most politely 'concerted lending', more clearly as 'involuntary lending', and mostly (by the bankers) as 'forced lending'.

During the meeting, at which no representative of the US administration was present, the president of the Federal Reserve Bank of New York, Anthony Solomon, explained the consequences for banking regulation. He added that 'there is always a question of political will of the borrowing nations but the IMF has considerable experience in these matters.' When loans accompanied and depended on an agreed Fund programme and when they 'facilitated the adjustment process', bank supervisors would raise no objections. On the same evening, Paul Volcker made the same point in a speech in Boston in which he urged both banks and the 'relevant authorities and financial institutions' to deal more effectively with a threat 'essentially without precedent in the post-war world. In such cases, where new loans facilitate the adjustment process and enable a country to strengthen its economy and service its international debt in an orderly manner, new credits shouldn't be subject to supervisory criticism' (*Wall Street Journal*, 1982: 2).

In effect, here was a triangular conflation of the functions of an international arbiter, a domestic regulator, and the market. First, the IMF had become, for practical purposes, a part of the domestic regulatory mechanism of US banking. Linkage of loans with IMF programmes could offer a way of avoiding the consequences of non-accruing or non-performing loans. Or, to put it another way, the definitions of what constituted sound banking were being rewritten in accordance with the requirements of the world financial system as a whole. Secondly, the banks themselves became part of the IMF's international surveillance exercise. Their funds greatly enhanced the facilities that the IMF could hold out as the reward to a country for the successful completion of a programme – in effect for rejoining the international financial system. An agreement with the IMF was supposed to have a 'catalytic' effect on the private sector. And finally, the IMF would do the work that the banks had hitherto neglected to perform themselves: negotiate sound criteria for the use of funds, which would make economic stabilization and adjustment possible and would allow for banks to be repaid. In order to get this service, however, the banks would have to pay the price of putting up additional resources. By acting in this way, the IMF ensured that lending continued, and that the cutting off of external credit did not produce a world depression of the type experienced in the past. In 1825, 1857, 1890, or most spectacularly and most damagingly in 1929, global depression followed the breakdown of credit markets. 1982 did not join this unhappy list of dates.

On 30 November 1982, the New York based Banks' Advisory Committee agreed to the proposed terms of the bank contribution. The 90-day emergency moratorium would be extended until the end of 1984 for 1983 and 1984 maturities, with repayment over eight years and a four-year grace period. In addition, banks would commit an additional 7 per cent of their existing exposure (for six years, at a rate 2⅛ per cent above US prime rate).

The individual banks involved were subjected to great pressure to agree to the committee's terms. Any single bank could have brought down the rather delicate structure by declaring a default, and thus triggering automatically a default for all the other bank credits through the cross-default clause that formed a standard part of loan agreements. In part, the pressure on banks not to extricate themselves was applied in the United States by the Federal Reserve and, in other countries, by other central banks. The authorities might threaten increased regulatory attention to banks which did not comply (Madrid, 1990: 98–9). In Europe, the Governor of the Bank of England, Gordon Richardson, arranged meetings for de Larosière with the leading figures of European commercial banking. Initially, many argued that 'it will be a tough job to get new money', and that 'the real job is to get official money'. One European banker complained that 'normally a bank says "stop" when it is stuck'. It required, in consequence, considerable persuasion to move the bankers. The advantage of the IMF appeared in its position as an international juridical institution created under the general international treaties which also governed the United Nations. In a situation in which many of the participants were acutely aware of the costs and risks involved, the IMF could give advice, persuade, encourage and cajole, without running any risk that it could be sued by those who followed its advice. The major money centre banks also took their own part in persuading other institutions, in particular the smaller regional banks which desperately wanted to extricate themselves from Latin American lending.

De Larosière announced that for the IMF Board to approve the programme, a 'critical mass' of 90 per cent of the $5 billion would be required from the banks. The bank package was indeed put in place by 15 December 1982, and in the following week the governments also made their $2 billion available through state export banks (such as the US Export–Import Bank, the Japanese Export–Import Bank, the Compagnie française pour l'assurance du commerce exterieur, Hermes in Germany, and the UK Export Credit Guarantees Department). As a result, the Fund extended arrangement was approved by the Executive Board on 23 December. By 23 March 1983, the commercial banks' $5 billion had been fully achieved, with 526 banks across the world participating.

The international banking side of the Mexican rescue was an undoubted success, and the immediate fears in 1982 of international collapse were avoided. The domestic, Mexican side of the package was less well conceived. The first programme, of 1982, imposed an unexpectedly severe collapse of output; and in 1985–86 a new approach to Mexican reform was required. Even that was problematical. It can be argued that Mexican reform would have been better served by a Brady-style write-off approach to external debt at an earlier stage, perhaps as early as the mid-1980s after banks had been able to build some reserves against losses. As it was, the Brady plan only came late in the day – in 1989, which was too late. But for 1982, at the outbreak of the debt crisis, such an approach would have been unthinkable because of the catastrophic effect on the international banking system following what would have been a complete destruction of banks' capital.

The crisis of 1994–95 followed a period of euphoric confidence in Mexico's prospects and a surge of foreign direct investment but also of portfolio flows. This new Mexican 'miracle' raised very intricate problems of how the financial sector and the exchange rate should be managed. In particular, when the return of flight capital and the resumption of capital inflows brought upward pressure on the exchange rate, and the exchange rate was used as an anti-inflationary instrument, a risk arose that the result might be a reappearance of the old problems of an external rate sufficiently high to serve as a deterrent to domestic activity and a disincentive to exporters. The political stakes attached to the maintenance of the exchange rate produced a taboo on discussion of the parity in the Mexican administration – a taboo that has often characterized pegged rate systems.

When the Mexican exchange rate over-valuation was corrected at the end of 1994 with an ill-prepared devaluation, at the same time as a large quantity of public sector short-term instruments needed to be renewed, a new financial panic showed the extent of the instability of the financial system. The large current account deficit (over 8 per cent of GDP) that had been financed in 1994 by private capital inflows now appeared unsustainable. The magnitude of the deficit was a deterrent to further inflows. Mexico also produced a knock-on blow to other economies, in a manner analogous to the spread of the 1982 debt increase to other middle-income developing countries. In early 1995 there was a 'tequila effect' not only in Latin American economies with large current deficits, but also in East Asian emerging markets. The risk was met by a $17.8 billion IMF stand-by programme (amounting to an unprecedented 688 per cent of Mexico's quota in the IMF), in combination with $20 billion from the US Stabilization Fund and $10 billion from the G-10, after intense high level diplomacy involving chiefly the US Treasury and the IMF's Managing Director, Michel Camdessus.

Fundamentally, however, Mexico's fiscal position was much stronger than it had been in the crises of the 1980s. In addition, and most importantly, a wide-ranging structural reform had already been implemented. The private character of much of the debt and of the capital inflows meant that the losses inevitably associated with adjustment were distributed more widely. A critical difference which made the new inflows less destabilizing than those of the big commercial bank debt boom of the 1970s is the dispersion of risk produced as a consequence of privatization and of economic reform. This dispersion led to a debate on whether the rescue operation was really necessary, with the Europeans taking a particularly critical stance. Those hostile to the IMF–United States rescue operation claimed that the contagion effects were exaggerated, that the rescue represented a bailout of the creditors using 'OPM' (Other Peoples' Money) to achieve American policy goals, and that the longer-term consequence would be to create a moral hazard problem with regard to emerging market debt.

The IMF drew a quite different lesson about the consequences of financial globalization and the vulnerability of the system to confidence shocks. The speed with which the IMF programme had to be put together in January 1995 illustrates the way in which globalization requires faster responses: the IMF programme was already fully in place by 1 February 1995. The 1982 crisis became public in August 1982, but the discussions with the banks about the IMF programme only occurred in November and December. In 1995 much more rapid action was required because the number of actors was so much greater: the crisis could not be solved by corralling the investors (in innumerable mutual and pension funds) in the way taken by de Larosière and Volcker just over a decade earlier. This consideration imposed a greater immediate burden on the IMF and the US government to act to tackle the crisis and limit the extent of contagion. In the longer term, it made the crisis easier to tackle than 1982 had been, and Mexico very soon was able to return to international capital markets as a borrower.

The IMF and capital markets

Both Mexican crises clearly raised difficult issues in regard to the management and supervision of private sector flows – banking operations in the case of the 1980s, portfolio flows in the 1990s.

The explosion of short-term lending after the collapse of the par value system and after the massive current account imbalances produced by the oil shocks had already alarmed the IMF in the 1970s. The most intensive discussion of the dangers of recycling the oil-produced imbalances occurred at the beginning of the process, when recycling was actually functioning surprisingly well. Perhaps the ease with which the problem was apparently solved in the mid-1970s made the world in general too complacent in the aftermath of the second oil price shock of 1979, whose negative impact on many developing country borrowers was intensified by the abrupt anti-inflationary change in the monetary policy of the United States (sometimes referred to as the 'Volcker shock').

Initially, in 1974, the Fund's *Annual Report* had worried about whether private banks would be able to finance the recycling process (IMF, 1974: 26 and IMF, 1975: 19). By 1976, the *Report* noted the 'sudden escalation' of borrowing after 1973, and warned that: 'Many borrowing countries, however, have become potentially vulnerable to any significant change in their access to external credit, or to any seriously adverse shift in their export earnings. This vulnerability is heightened by the eroding effects of inflation on the real value of external reserves, which are now quite low in relation to current and prospective imports' (IMF, 1976: 20, 22). The then Managing Director of the IMF, Johannes Witteveen, delivered warnings both in public and in private. In spring 1976, he told a conference that: 'Competitive enlargement of this role of private banks might well foster a climate of all-too-easy borrowing by deficit countries, thus facilitating inflationary financing and delaying the adoption of needed adjustment policies. [...] In general, therefore, a very careful and balanced policy by the international banks is needed' (Witteveen, 1976). Later in the year, he told the Interim Committee at the Fund meeting in Manila that 'commercial bank lending should not be so easily available that it made the need for adjustment less clear, and hence caused the authorities to accumulate larger debts than were desirable.' In 1977, US officials noted Witteveen's concern about international bank lending: 'He is worried that incentives favoring bank lending abroad may be too attractive, that such lending is essentially uncontrolled, that it leads to international liquidity creation (as countries borrow foreign currency to add to their reserves), and that its continuation may permanently prevent another SDR allocation.'[2] The same theme appeared in statements at the Annual Meeting. Since there was a danger of a resurgence of inflation, the world required 'more stress on the adjustment of external positions and less emphasis on the mere financing of deficits' (IMF, 1976a: 16–17).

Some of this concern was shared by central banks and banking regulatory authorities. In 1977, the chairman of the Federal Reserve Board, Arthur Burns, proposed compiling a list of questions on the current indebtedness of borrowing countries, and on the content of bank lending. When the BIS discussed the Burns suggestion with individual banks, the response was largely hostile. Almost all the bigger banks opposed such intervention, and declared themselves fully 'satisfied with their present information on, and methods of assessing, country risk situations. The recommendation of a checklist of questions would appear to reflect on their past lending policies and would therefore be resented by them.' Other banks believed simply that they should not provide information to regulators, but that the 'official' institutions such as IBRD, IMF or BIS should have the 'job' of putting together information. As a result, the Burns and BIS discussions for the moment led nowhere.[3]

Such advice from national and international regulators was very unpopular with the intended subjects of regulation. Bankers did not see why they should not lend, and came to believe that the Fund's advice was obsolete, outmoded and appropriate only to an era when capital markets had not reached their current levels of sophistication and integration. The market, rather than multilateral institutions, held out the best way of solving the world's problems. In addition, the same feature which eventually made the IMF quite effective as a crisis manager in 1982 – its juridical independence of national authorities – made it wholly unsuited to the role of regulator of banks in a national context.

Finance ministers in deficit countries felt equally strongly that warnings about financing and invocations to adjust were quite inappropriate.

One of the attractions of the Euro-markets was that it allowed them to ignore the warnings of the IMF. Vast resources opened up which involved virtually no foreign control. As one astute comment noted, 'probably no international capital market in history has had a lower degree of political interference, to the dismay of "strategic minds" like that of Dr Kissinger' (Bacha and Diaz-Alejandro, 1982: 140). In the IMF Interim Committee, in 1976, Mario Enrique Simonsen, the Finance Minister of Brazil, said that 'he was rather disturbed by Mr Witteveen's reference to commercial banking: banks should naturally be cautious in lending, but not only to foreign countries.' In the following year, he was even more explicit in his insistence that the Fund should not give advice or attempt to influence the private sector: 'While they [the developing countries] would certainly welcome the technical assistance of the Fund and other institutions, in helping them to improve their own statistical and informational systems, the developing countries continued to feel that the Fund could play no useful role as a purveyor, to the private sector, of judgments, analyses and forecasts' (IMF, 1976b and 1977).

In the course of the 1970s, the proportion of developing countries' current account deficits financed by the IMF was lower than it had been in the 1960s (5.1 per cent rather than 7.5 per cent). On the other hand, debt incurred through commercial banks clearly affected the outcome of Fund programmes, and the Fund needed to take private liabilities into account. In 1979, the Fund agreed that if the size or growth rate of external indebtedness might affect the design of a Fund-sponsored adjustment programme, performance criteria for the programme should include foreign loans with a maturity over one year (and in exceptional circumstances, non trade-related loans under one year might be included).

In being more specific about particular debt situations, the IMF ran into a basic problem in international financial and monetary management (or 'surveillance' as the process is termed in the IMF's 1978 revised Articles of Agreement). Public warnings – as opposed to confidential advice – bring the risk of setting off exactly the crisis which it might be hoped to avoid. It is not difficult to imagine the consequences of an explicit IMF warning on the level of Mexican indebtedness in the summer of 1982, or on the exchange rate management of Mexico in the summer of 1994. However, very frequently, even the provision of useful confidential advice on issues as market-sensitive as external indebtedness or exchange rates is difficult because of the risk of leakage.

The outbreak of the 1980s debt crisis immediately shattered the complacency of the later 1970s, and encouraged a renewed interest in financial regulation across frontiers. One important US initiative extended the regulatory debates that had taken place in the course of the

1970s. It was now thought that banking supervision should be carried out internationally in a more systematized and open way than the tentative, informal and secret coordination and exchange of regulatory experience carried out in the framework of the Basle Committee on Banking Regulation and Supervisory Practices (which had begun functioning in 1974). Part of the pressure came from domestic opinion in the United States and from the widespread fear that a solution to the international debt problem would involve a bail-out of the banks. The consequent reluctance of the US Congress in 1983 to increase IMF quotas (as part of the Eighth General Review), in the wake of the Latin American debt crisis, could only be overcome through a legislative measure which extended control of banking. The International Lending Supervision Act (November 1983) gave US regulatory authorities the legal right and the obligation to 'cause banking institutions to achieve and to maintain adequate capital by establishing minimum levels of capital.' It also included a request for American regulators to pursue a convergence of international bank capital standards. Subsequent negotiations, first with the United Kingdom, then with Japan and the other G-10 members, produced a set of standards embodied as the Basle Accord of 1988.[4]

The Accord required an 8 per cent ratio of recognized capital to credit-weighted risk exposure by the end of 1992. Five different categories of relative riskiness were established, with loans to OECD/GATT official borrowers having a zero risk weight, and loans to non-OECD/GATT governments having a 100 per cent weight. Like any arbitrary categorization, this system encountered obvious objections: would it not, for instance, act as a deterrent to developing country borrowing, but also to borrowing by industrial corporations, and would it not make lending to industrial country governments too attractive? There exists both a scope and a demand for the evolution of a more sophisticated and sensitive system of standards.

In addition, by the early 1990s a new financial innovation came to play a part analogous to that of commercial bank lending in the late 1970s and early 1980s. At that time, the growth of international financial intermediation had been neglected by national regulators, in part out of fear of affecting the competitive position of their own banks in the international market place through over-tight control. Over a decade later, such bank lending constituted much less of a systemic risk. But the threat now came from the largely unregulated growth of newer financial innovations: derivatives markets. These involve a separation and sale of various components of risk. In this way they lower individual risk, and have been an important cause of the major growth of international capital movements. At the same time, many experts argue that they contain an increased systemic risk (it is possible to imagine a chain effect of defaults and bankruptcies).[5] Unlike bank lending, this off-balance sheet activity has not in general been the concern of the BIS. The IMF, as part of its surveillance mission, produced the first major account of the systemic dangers posed by derivative markets.[6] More effective action, however, depends on the willingness of national authorities to act together in concert in this area of supervision and regulation.

Conclusion

Many of the most interesting reform initiatives suggest making the IMF resemble a central bank more closely. They range from the relatively modest, such as strengthening the financial resources of the Fund to make it more effective as a lender of last resort, through to the more utopian idea of a single world currency with the IMF as the central bank (Cooper, 1984).

The development of capital markets, especially since the early 1970s, has certainly brought the IMF much closer to the traditional concerns of central banks with crisis management and supervision of financial systems – but without much formal preparation of such a role. Indeed, the major initiatives at the time of the two Mexican crises were unanticipated and highly personal. In both cases, the Managing Directors took considerable risks and also encountered considerable criticism.

Regulatory initiatives are also less a question of a legal definition of the IMF's responsibilities and more a matter of IMF economists using information and publications, such as the *World Economic Outlook* and the surveys of *International Capital Markets,* as a way of sensitizing opinion and thereby shaping behaviour. Capital markets have a large appetite for information, and the IMF will increasingly have to satisfy that appetite in order to survive institutionally. The regular supply of information allows markets to make more informed judgments of government policies, and helps to depoliticize the process of reaching judgments. In this way, it could be argued, it involves the markets in the IMF's traditional surveillance function. The discussion of the role of the IMF in facilitating the rapid supply and dissemination of accurate information on macroeconomic variables, including internal and external indebtedness, government spending and money supply had already begun before the *peso* crisis of 1994–95; but that experience put the issue at the top of the agenda for the IMF, as well as for the 1995 G-7 summit in Halifax.

The suggestions were embodied in 1996 in a new 'special data dissemination standard' (SDDS), to which members of the IMF having or seeking access to international capital markets may subscribe on a voluntary basis. The data assembled in this way are made available through an electronic bulletin board on the Internet. Increasing numbers of countries will need to sign on to the SDDS as a way of reassuring markets and securing access to international capital. But the technical issues involved in providing a great deal of data swiftly enough are highly complex. Moving in this direction will also cost a great deal. One recent estimate of the cost of modernizing statistical and data-collecting agencies throughout the world to conform with the new standards is $150 billion, a cost which will have to be carried largely by the participating countries (*Neue Zürcher Zeitung*, 1996: 23).

Such provision and dissemination of information on financial conditions will also bring the IMF into increased contact with other international institutions performing similar roles. During the first 50 years of the IMF's existence, the critical institutional relationship was frequently that across 19th Street in Washington – with the World Bank. For the next 50 years, the link with markets will be crucial and, in terms of regulation, the vital issue will be the contacts between Washington and Basle.

Notes

1. The IMF archival material used in this paper is documented fully, and the arguments extended further in James (1996).
2. Gerald D. Ford Presidential Library, Arthur Burns papers B72, IMF Witteveen facility, Ted Truman, 2 November 1977, Background Material for Witteveen luncheon.
3. Burns papers, B3, B15 1976–8, 27 October 1977 Lamfalussy cable to Burns.
4. See Cohen, B.J. (1986), *In Whose Interest? International Banking and American Foreign Policy;* New Haven: Yale University Press; Norton, J.J. (1989) 'Capital adequacy standards: a legitimate regulatory concern for prudential supervision of banking activities?', *Ohio State Law Journal*, 49, p. 1325; Granirer, D. (1994), 'A modern great power concert: New York, Tokyo, and the political economy of international financial regulatory cooperation', Princeton PhD; and Goldstein, M. et al. (1982), *International Capital Markets: Developments, Prospects and Policy Issues,* Washington DC, International Monetary Fund, pp. 10–15.
5. For instance, Corrigan, G.E. (1992), 'Challenges facing the international community of bank supervisors', *Federal Reserve Bank of New York Quarterly Review*, 17(3), pp. 1–9.
6. Goldstein, M. et al. (1993), *International Capital Markets Part II: Systemic Issues in International Finance*, Washington DC: International Monetary Fund. The survey notes that 'Some of the recent products may not be well understood either by senior management of banks or by supervisers of securities firms' (p. 28).

References

Bacha, E.L. and Diaz-Alejandro, C.F. (1982), 'Tropical reflections on the history and theory of international financial markets' in Helleiner, G.K. (ed.), *For Good or Evil: Economic Theory and North–South Negotiations*, Toronto: University of Toronto Press.

Cooper, R.N. (1984), 'A monetary system for the future', *Foreign Affairs*, Autumn.

IMF (1974), *Annual Report.*

IMF (1975), *Annual Report.*

IMF (1976), *Annual Report.*

IMF (1976a), *Annual Meetings, Summary Proceedings.*

IMF (1976b), *Interim Committee meeting*, 2 October 1976.

IMF (1977), *Interim Committee meeting*, 24 September 1977.

James, H. (1996), *International Monetary Cooperation Since Bretton Woods*, New York, Oxford University Press and IMF.

Kenen, P.B. (1986), *Financing, Adjustment and the International Monetary Fund*, Washington DC: Brookings Institution.

Kindleberger, Charles P. (1978), *Manias, Panics and Crashes*, New York, Basic Books.

Madrid, R.L. (1990), *Overexposed: US Banks Confront the Third World Debt Crisis*, Washington DC: Investor Responsibility Research Center.

Neue Zürcher Zeitung, 'Entwicklung durch Informatik', 17 May 1996.

Oliver, R.W. (1971), *Early Plans for a World Bank*, Princeton Studies in International Finance No. 29, Princeton, Princeton University Press.

Wall Street Journal (1982), 'Volcker Offers Plan to Reduce Debt Strain on Developing Nations, Cut Default Risk', 17 November 1982, p. 2.

Williamson, J. (1983), 'Keynes and the international economic order', in Worswick, D. and Trevithick, J. (eds), *Keynes and the Modern World: Proceedings of the Keynes Centenary Conference, King's College, Cambridge*, Cambridge, Cambridge University Press.

Witteveen, J. (1976), 'The IMF and the international banking community', Address to the Financial Times Conference, New York, 29 April.

CHAPTER ELEVEN

Sixty-five Years of Central Bank Cooperation at the Bank for International Settlements

Gunter D. Baer

Introduction

The Bank for International Settlements (BIS) is the oldest international financial institution and has, since its foundation in 1930, been the principal centre for cooperation among central banks. The Bank has been able to play this role by combining its operational banking and agency functions with that of a meeting-place for central bank officials.

From the outset, the BIS has understood its stated object of promoting cooperation and providing services to central banks as an invitation to bring central banks together, to facilitate their exchange of views and collaboration and, whenever possible, to provide practical assistance. As experience has shown, the Bank's scope for doing so has been strongly influenced by monetary and financial developments in the countries of its member central banks and, in particular, the role that these central banks were able to play in these developments. Cooperation at the BIS is thus to a significant extent a reflection of the history of monetary and financial relations and of how central banks, and with them the BIS, have responded and adapted to new challenges.

However, a review of history from the angle of the BIS is inevitably selective and cannot therefore present a balanced account of international economic and financial cooperation. Such cooperation has been undertaken in a large number of groups and forums, the agendas of which were set by an interest in specific topics or in response to particular events. Many interesting and important developments, such as the debate about the SDR or the eventful days of the Plaza and Louvre Agreements, are left out of the account in this review. Although they were also discussed extensively in Basle and covered in detail in BIS *Annual Reports*, the real debates, negotiations and actions surrounding such events took place elsewhere. When looking at examples of cooperation at the BIS, an attempt has therefore been made to focus primarily on those situations where the Bank and its member central banks were called upon to help mend cracks in international monetary relations or where financial market trends demanded the attention of central banks and their cooperation at the BIS.

Some institutional characteristics of the BIS

The ability to render different types of services to central banks owes much to the legal structure given to the BIS. It is, on the one hand, an institution based on international treaties, founded by central banks and endowed with the necessary privileges and immunities. On the other hand, it is a limited company, with an issued share capital and which operates in the financial markets[1] and whose commercial activities are subject to the jurisdiction of the ordinary courts.[2] However, although the BIS has a share capital, shares and shareholders, a Board of Directors and a General Meeting, it differs very significantly from an ordinary limited company and, although the BIS is located in Basle, Switzerland, it is subject neither to the Swiss Federal Law concerning Banks and Savings Banks nor to the provisions of Swiss company law.

The complex legal character of the Bank[3] was not untypical of that of many central banks in 1930, but was also chosen deliberately in the light of the exceptional circumstances and of the specific reasons for the establishment of the BIS. The Young Plan of 1929, designed to resolve the problem of German reparation payments, had foreseen the creation of an international institution to act as trustee in the execution of the plan. This role was entrusted to the BIS after the Young Plan was adopted at the Hague Conference in January 1930.

However, the Hague Agreements merely created an opportunity to establish an international central bank institution. The need for and the desirability of having an institution through which central banks could exchange views and consult each other had already been voiced on several occasions since the turn of the century. It is therefore not by chance that the Bank's objects as listed in the Statutes are first and foremost 'to promote the cooperation of central banks and to provide additional facilities for international financial operations'. Indeed, when giving their reasons for recommending the creation of a new bank, the experts drawing up the Young Plan wrote: 'Especially it is to be hoped that it [the Bank] will become an increasingly close and valuable link in the cooperation of central banking institutions generally – a cooperation essential to the continuing stability of the world's credit structure' (BIS, 1935: 41).

The BIS today has 32 member central banks from industrial countries (the legal status of Yugoslavia's membership being suspended), which hold 84 per cent of the Bank's issued capital. The remainder is in private hands, reflecting the decision of three founding members – the central banks of the United States, France and Belgium – to place their subscription partly or fully in the market. However, while private shareholders receive the same annual dividend as central banks, they are not entitled to vote, this right being reserved exclusively for the central bank of the country in which the relevant national issues of shares were initially subscribed. For all practical purposes, the BIS is thus an institution owned and managed by central banks.

The formative years

After the Bank took up its operations on 17 May 1930, it was to be little more than a year before its initial functions as a trustee with respect to international financial settlements were reduced to being 'primarily of a formal character involving only an incidental handling of relatively small sums' (BIS, 1934: 37). The Hoover moratorium of July 1931 and the Lausanne Agreement one year later had *de facto* put an end to the inter-governmental debt payments to be made under German (and other) reparation obligations. Moreover, in July 1934, Germany also suspended unilaterally all payments for the international loans placed in the market under the Dawes and Young Plans, terminating the BIS's role as fiscal agent to the trustees of those loans.

These developments have, of course, to be seen against the background of the much wider and more profound deterioration in the economic and financial situation. The crash on Wall Street in autumn 1929, the banking crises in Austria and Germany in 1931, and the subsequent outflow of short-term capital from central Europe and the concomitant exchange market turmoil, all pointed to the existence of deep-seated imbalances. As each country sought its own salvation and resorted to various forms of protectionist measures such as tariffs, quotas, bilateral trade and compensation agreements and exchange controls, world trade contracted at a frightening speed and accelerated the economic downturn, culminating in the Great Depression.

The starting conditions for the Bank could hardly have been worse. The rapid disintegration of multilateral relationships needed to be countered by cooperation and joint action. However, attempts to stem the tide proved futile. Rescue operations, involving the Bank as lender or as organizer and coordinator, were stopped quickly and the prevailing climate of economic isolationism left little room for effective central bank cooperation at the BIS.

One consequence of the unfortunate events of the early years was that they made it necessary for the Bank almost immediately to define its policies with regard to the provision of financial assistance and, more importantly, which basic principles should govern international financial relations and central bank cooperation.

The need to formulate its views on the conditions under which financial support should be granted arose in the spring of 1931 when the collapse of the *Oesterreichische Credit-Anstalt* necessitated emergency aid to the National Bank of Austria, and when one month later large-scale withdrawals of funds from central Europe prompted the BIS to organize assistance to the *Reichsbank* and other central banks. Recognizing the need for more fundamental adjustment, the BIS stressed in its *Annual Report* that 'at no time were these credits regarded as remedies, but merely as facilities giving the chance for corrective or defensive measures to be taken' (BIS, 1932: 8). When in September the sterling crisis erupted and the Bank was again faced with a decision as to whether to provide support, it concluded that 'credit-giving, alone, was insufficient to bridge the economic difficulties or to maintain currencies against the swift current of capital withdrawal and flight engendered by the more general realisation of the existing disequilibrium in the international balance of payments, a deepening business depression, and a crisis of confidence of almost panic proportions' (BIS, 1932: 9). On the basis of this reasoning the Bank refused new advances, and, with the spreading deterioration in underlying conditions elsewhere, 'suspended the policy of being a substantial new credit-giver to sundry central banks' (BIS, 1932: 9). A distinction was thus drawn between financial support in situations of liquidity shortages and that in the case of fundamental imbalances. Although later experience would confirm that this distinction was not easy to make in all circumstances, the policy adopted in 1931 together with the techniques developed at that time remained basically the same when the Bank was called upon to provide financial assistance in later years.

The second development which obliged the Bank to determine a position of principle was the rapid departure from the gold standard after the sterling crisis and the spread of trade and exchange controls. Already in 1932 the Bank made its attitude clear: 'Exchange control, with or without clearing arrangements, forces trade into a kind of strait-jacket, leaving little or no room for the play of such economic forces, price changes and other factors as normally tend to re-establish equilibrium' (BIS, 1932: 14). This theme was developed further in subsequent *Annual Reports*, which argued forcefully for a liberal and multilateral trading system and orderly monetary conditions, understood at the time to mean the restoration of the gold standard: 'The gold standard is not an end in itself. It is a machinery and a medium for permitting, facilitating and enhancing the exchange of goods, capital and services, internally and externally' (BIS, 1934: 54). Although, over the years, it proved unrealistic to hope for a reinstatement of the gold standard, the firm belief in the greatest possible freedom of trade and international payments and in market forces as an allocative mechanism has unequivocally guided the Bank in its analysis, advice and recommendations.

A third development which induced the Bank to articulate its understanding of central bank cooperation was the declining scope for cooperation in a situation of continuing disintegration. In its 1935 *Annual Report*, the Bank devoted a full special chapter to the topic of central bank cooperation, and the conclusions reached in that study have, as time has shown, influenced profoundly its approach towards cooperation and have in many respects set its agenda during the 60 years which have passed since then. Starting from the observation that cooperation does not mean simply financial support but that 'the real kernel of central bank collaboration ... is or should be evident in continuous and daily practice' (BIS, 1935: 41), the chapter states that the need for cooperation arises from the identity of tasks and the interdependence of policies and actions. It defines the main areas of cooperation as monetary theory, problems and practice, and the management of the exchange rate. It sets out the objectives – the maintenance of purchasing power and stable exchange rates. And it proposes as methods of cooperation meetings, exchanges of views and mutual consultations. Although drafted with a view to preserving a monetary system anchored in the gold standard, the considerations and recommendations made in that chapter are as valid and valuable today as they were at the time they were written.

To give practical effect to the conclusions drawn in that chapter, the Bank took steps to make meetings at the BIS a more effective vehicle for building mutual acquaintanceship and understanding among central bank officials, and created the Monetary and Economic Department to strengthen the Bank's analytical capabilities and set up a system for collecting and exchanging statistical data. The effect of these changes was visible primarily in the quality of the Bank's *Annual Report*, which became a highly regarded and for many years unrivalled publication on world financial and economic developments. The impact on promoting cooperation had to await more propitious circumstances after the Second World War.

The restoration of multilateralism and the road to currency convertibility

With the outbreak of the Second World War, the activities of the BIS were reduced to a minimum and, in conformity with a decision adopted in the autumn of 1939, no meetings of the Board of Directors took place during the war and the Annual Meetings were all held by proxy (BIS, 1946: 6). For a number of reasons, perhaps most significantly because no need was seen for a central bank institution to exist alongside the International Monetary Fund, the final declaration of the Bretton Woods Conference in July 1944 contained a resolution that the BIS be liquidated.[4] This recommendation was never put into effect and, in fact, on the occasion of the First Annual Meeting of the Boards of Governors of the IMF and the IBRD, in October 1946, first contacts were made leading to an exchange of information and cooperation in research, especially by putting the expertise of the Bank's Monetary and Economic Department at the disposal of the IBRD (BIS, 1947: 8).

Although the IMF accepted, in December 1946, the parities proposed by 32 of its members and announced on that occasion that exchange transactions would begin on 1 March 1947, it was clear that the prevailing circumstances did not permit the implementation of the Bretton Woods design and that the road to convertibility would be long and difficult. However, it was precisely these difficulties, or rather the efforts to overcome them, which presented the BIS with an opportunity to demonstrate its usefulness to the international community. This opportunity came to some extent fortuitously when in November 1947 five European countries signed an agreement on multilateral compensations. 'The first draft of this agreement had provided for the Fund [IMF] to act as clearing agent, but in the absence of a Fund representative at the meeting an offer from the BIS to undertake this function was accepted' (Horsefield, 1969: 215).

The possibility of falling back on the very agency function which had been so important at the time of its creation, marked the entry of the BIS into the struggle with one of the most burning problems of the immediate post-war period. Already during the war, but especially thereafter, bilateral trade agreements had proliferated. While such agreements were helpful in getting goods moving between countries, the limits they placed on further growth in trade soon became apparent. They not only distorted trade patterns and exacerbated the underlying disequilibria, but if a debtor position was incurred under such arrangements, this tended to prompt import cuts to save scarce gold and dollar reserves. The multilateral compensation scheme of 1947 for which the BIS was invited to act as agent was the first in a series of attempts by European countries to design a mechanism for offsetting bilateral deficits with bilateral surpluses. However, neither this scheme nor the subsequent Intra-European Payments Agreements were particularly successful in a situation of large structural imbalances in debtor–creditor relations and Europe's pronounced deficit *vis-à-vis* the United States. The breakthrough came only in 1950 with the European Payments Union, which achieved full multilateralization of payments through a complete netting of all bilateral payments positions at the end of each accounting period. Initially only modest proportions of the surpluses and deficits resulting from the monthly clearing were settled in gold, dollars or other convertible currencies, while the major part was automatically converted into credit through the EPU up to predefined ceilings. However, over time, as members' external reserve positions strengthened, the balances to be settled in reserve assets were progressively increased, gradually nudging the EPU members towards immediate settlement and thereby leading them to convertibility. The success of the EPU rested not only on its technical features and the pragmatic implementation of the scheme. It owed as much, as several crisis situations demonstrated (Kaplan and Schleiminger, 1989), to the willingness of the members to cooperate and accept policies and domestic adjustment measures recommended by the EPU's Managing Board.

Having once got its foot in the door, the BIS became a welcome partner in all the schemes aimed at multilateralizing trade and payments. It accepted the role of agent on condition 'that its duties should be purely of a technical nature and without political implications of any kind' (BIS, 1949: 221). In practical terms the involvement of the BIS meant that it received from each participant reports of its positions *vis-à-vis* the other members of the scheme and determined for each participant the respective surpluses and deficits. Moreover, the BIS was authorized to debit and credit the accounts of the central banks for the purposes of the payment mechanism. In its capacity as agent, the BIS also carried out the liquidation when the EPU was wound up at the end of 1958.

The BIS thus provided the technical backbone of the EPU and allowed it to operate without a permanent staff. This made the BIS an important integral part of the arrangement and helped it to prove its usefulness. But more importantly, the BIS also benefited in an indirect way from the success of the EPU, in that the return to convertibility strengthened the role of central banks and thereby created new opportunities for the BIS to contribute more actively to cooperation in other fields.

The turbulent years of the Bretton Woods system

With the liquidation of the EPU, and its successor, the European Monetary Arrangement, only playing a marginal role for the settlement of some residual balances channelled through that system, the agency function exercised by the BIS once again diminished in importance. But there was now a growing need for international cooperation as the return to convertibility and the progressive move towards a more liberal trade and payments system was not accompanied by the expected smooth functioning of the Bretton Woods system. Very soon strains became apparent which, on the one hand, gave rise to discussions on the possible need to adapt or reform the system and, on the other, required steps to subdue the rising tensions. Although this is perhaps an oversimplification, the 1960s saw an evolving division of labour in managing the Bretton Woods system in which conceptual issues relating, for instance, to the adjustment process between surplus and deficit countries or the supply of international liquidity were dealt with mainly by the IMF, but the practical fire-fighting to contain crisis situations fell to the central banks, frequently operating in the framework of the BIS.

The Bretton Woods system as it had evolved by 1960 rested on two basic pillars: firstly, the commitment of the US authorities to maintain the gold parity of the dollar (fixed since 1934 at $35 per ounce) and to buy gold from, or sell gold to, the monetary authorities of other countries at this parity in unlimited amounts; and secondly, the undertaking by other countries to maintain their currencies' parity *vis-à-vis* the dollar within a margin of plus or minus one per cent. The lasting stability of this arrangement depended ultimately on reasonably balanced external positions and, to the extent that temporary surpluses and deficits needed to be financed, on an adequate supply of international liquidity, that is gold, as the ultimate settlement means. Neither of these two conditions, however, was sufficiently fulfilled when free convertibility allowed market forces to come into play: the supply of newly minted gold which could have found its way into official US gold holdings was too small and the willingness to hold dollars (after all an attractive alternative given the return from investment) instead of gold was dependent upon confidence in the ability to convert such dollars into gold at the guaranteed price.

This was no problem as long as there was a shortage of dollars and the United States retained its strong external payments position. However, when the pattern of underlying payments positions began to shift at the end of the 1950s in the wake of diverging economic policies and changes in relative competitiveness, the US balance of payments weakened and so did the ability of the United States to meet its dollar conversion obligation. Signs of strain were evidenced when, in October

1960, the price of gold on the (free) London gold market moved above the dollar's gold parity. This flare-up was temporarily checked by intervention by the Bank of England, facilitated by an understanding with the US monetary authorities. But pressures re-emerged less than a year later, opening up an almost constant battle to defend the official price of gold as well as individual currencies' parities *vis-à-vis* the dollar. The situation had changed from a dollar shortage to a dollar glut. A contingency plan to counter pressures on the gold price had in fact already been discussed at monthly BIS meetings and an informal agreement, initially kept confidential but later known as the Gold Pool, had been reached. Under this agreement the Bank of England intervened to keep the price on the London market in line with the official gold price, with gold losses being shared among eight central banks in accordance with an agreed formula. The dollar proceeds resulting from interventions could be presented to the United States for conversion.

The meetings of the members of the Gold Pool were normally held at the BIS, which also collected and distributed to the Pool members the data on the gold demand and supply required to assess the market situation in London. The Gold Pool worked reasonably well for the first three years, not least because significant new supplies of gold were added by Russian gold sales. However, the underlying private demand for industrial, but also speculative, purposes continued to rise. In 1965 the US payments situation deteriorated as a result of spending for the Vietnam war, in 1966 Russian gold sales ceased and in 1967 sterling was devalued. Against this background, the private demand for gold exploded. The crisis came to a head in March 1968 and it was decided to close the London market. The central bank governors of the countries active in the gold market met in Washington to review the situation and issued a communiqué noting that 'the US Government will continue to buy and sell gold at the existing price of $35 an ounce in transactions with monetary authorities'. The two-tier market – for official gold at the dollar parity, and at a price freely determined by private demand and supply – was born.

The Gold Pool arrangements were, however, only one of the instruments employed to defend the dollar parity. In 1962, a network of mutual support facilities in the form of bilateral short-term credit lines was set up between the US monetary authorities, on the one hand, and other major central banks and the BIS, on the other. The purpose was to provide quickly mobilizable funds to accommodate short-term reversible capital flows and thereby prevent at least temporarily dollar balances from being presented for conversion into gold.

The possibility of large-scale recourse to IMF credit by the United States gave rise in the same year to the introduction of the General

Arrangements to Borrow (GAB). When the IMF was established it seemed inconceivable that the United States would ever have to seek assistance from the Fund, but in 1961, owing to the persistent weakness of the US payments position, this had become a realistic possibility. However, a drawing on the IMF by its largest shareholder to ward off a speculative attack would have been virtually impossible in view of the IMF's limited stock of convertible currencies. In order to supplement the Fund's resources the ten most important industrial countries agreed under the GAB to place certain amounts in national currency at the disposal of the IMF in the event of any one of the GAB participants wishing to borrow from the Fund. Since 1963 the members of the GAB have, as the 'Group of Ten', become the principal forum for the discussion of international monetary questions.

This institutional framework, initially built primarily with a view to defending the dollar parity, soon needed to be used for the management of payments problems in the industrial world. In fact, partly reflecting the bouts of dollar weakness but frequently also intra-European imbalances, all major currencies were subjected to exchange rate pressures in the 1960s. In particular sterling, burdened by the legacy of its former reserve currency role, needed to be supported by various central bank arrangements organized at the BIS. In 1961 considerable temporary foreign exchange resources were made available by a number of European central banks, and in 1968 and 1969, under the two so-called Group Arrangements, substantial amounts were provided through the BIS by major central banks to protect sterling against the withdrawal of short-term sterling liabilities to foreign central banks. Special support operations were also mounted at the BIS for the Italian *lira* in 1964, and the French *franc* in 1968 when a wave of social and industrial unrest caused growing exchange market nervousness. How interrelated many of these events were became clear, for instance, after the 1964 *lira* crisis. It had been overcome in large measure through a bilateral credit from the Federal Reserve. But owing to the relatively weak position of the US currency at that time, the dollars provided to the Bank of Italy ended up mainly in the reserves of other central banks which did not necessarily want them.

The realization that, as a consequence of the Fed's action, other central banks had involuntarily extended credit to the United States underlined the need for more information on financing flows. In the framework of the G-10 it was thus decided to establish a system of multilateral surveillance under which the G-10 countries would report data on the financing of their external surpluses and deficits to the BIS on a monthly basis. The multilateral surveillance exercise was conducted regularly from late 1964 onwards at meetings of the G-10 in

Basle and of the OECD Working Party No. 3. The Bank introduced the discussion with an analytical assessment.

The financing operations of the 1960s were, like those in the early years of the BIS, not designed to remedy the underlying situation. They were regarded mainly as a first line of defence to buy time for more fundamental action or they formed indirectly part of a set of policy measures which, however, were frequently not in the hands of the central bankers gathering in Basle. While occasionally successful, in many instances the crisis management through the provision of support facilities, often supplemented by exchange and capital controls but inadequately underpinned by 'too little too late' domestic policy adjustment, failed to restore lasting stability and ended in painful parity changes. However, these efforts established a framework of institutionalized international cooperation, a significant part of which took place in the informal and discreet meetings at the BIS. The activities of the Gold Pool formed a focal point at the monthly meetings, and from these meetings evolved later the Gold and Foreign Exchange Committee. The setting-up of the swap network brought officials from the Federal Reserve into the sphere of the BIS, where ever since 1962 they have been regularly attending the monthly meetings. But most significantly, the G-10 central bank governors coming together in Basle developed into a closely-knit group for international monetary cooperation.

The emergence of the international banking market

August 1971 marked, as we know now, the definitive breakdown of the Bretton Woods system. An attempt to establish and defend the new exchange rate structure negotiated in the Smithsonian Agreement, at the end of 1971, proved short-lived, and by spring 1973 a generalized system of 'managed floating' had emerged. The hopes of the 'Committee of Twenty' for a fundamentally reformed system based on stable but adjustable par values were dashed by the dramatic rise in oil prices in 1973–74. But given the strong dissent and the deadlock about the question of adjustment versus asset settlement (James, 1996: 246ff.), it is highly unlikely that even in the absence of this 'force majeure' any agreement could have been reached.

On the other hand, the hopes of the advocates of flexible exchange rates were also disappointed. The promised equilibrating effects of exchange rate movements offering freedom in domestic economic management did not materialize. Admittedly, the huge oil-price-induced payments imbalances gave floating exchange rates little chance to prove their worth, but when the dislocations caused by the oil shock had been digested, a market-induced quasi-automatic return to stability still did not occur. The need to cooperate remained and, in fact, grew as inflation problems, recession and external disequilibria prompted the authorities to intervene massively in the exchange markets and, contrary to earlier expectations, resulted in an even greater demand for official reserves.

Cooperation under the auspices of the BIS followed in part the same pattern as in previous years: discussions of adjustment problems and the role of monetary policy in a system of managed floating figured prominently on the governors' agenda and, in 1977, a third Group Arrangement was concluded at the BIS to help the United Kingdom to relieve pressure on official reserves arising once again from withdrawals of sterling balances.

However, from the perspective of the BIS the most significant development was the surge in euro-currency market activity. The modest scale of euro-currency business in the late 1950s had grown by the mid-1970s into a mature wholesale market for banking funds. This was caused in part by expanding world trade and the migration of banks wishing to follow their multi-national customers; but more importantly, it reflected the banks' response to the incentives generated by capital controls (such as the interest equalization tax and the voluntary credit restraint programme of the United States) and monetary policy regulations (such as Regulation Q, limiting interest payments on US domestic bank deposits and minimum reserve requirements). After the move to managed floating rates, euro-market activity was boosted further by the recycling of petro-dollars and, in the latter part of the 1970s, by the weakness of the dollar leading to huge outflows of funds from US banks into the euro-market. In parallel, the market became more sophisticated by creating new instruments to strengthen the banks' opportunities for borrowing (through negotiable CDs and floating rate bonds) and for investing (such as roll-over credits and syndicated credits). Backed by an efficient inter-bank market, the euro-market had developed into a worldwide market and a source of credit to both developing and industrial countries.

The BIS, which in 1963 had started collecting statistical data on the foreign currency assets and liabilities of commercial banks in the G-10 countries (except the United States) and in subsequent years had extended the coverage with respect to both the geographical area of reporting banks as well as the contents of the statistics, became a pioneer in monitoring the evolution of the market and analysing its implications. The rapid expansion of the market – as was remarked at the time, anything that grows by 25 to 40 per cent per annum warrants close attention – initially raised questions of a macroeconomic nature.

From 1971 onwards, these issues were examined regularly at meetings of the G-10 governors on the basis of analytical work by the BIS and of a newly established Euro-currency Standing Committee of senior central bank officials chaired by the General Manager of the BIS. The focus was first of all on whether the euro-markets had destabilizing consequences for the international economy, for instance through liquidity-creating effects which could exacerbate inflation and/or significantly reduce balance-of-payments constraints, or through generating exchange rate instability by acting as a channel for speculative capital flows (Mayer, 1979). No definitive conclusions were reached and the question of control of the euro-markets remained controversial. None the less, as a precautionary measure, the G-10 central banks agreed in 1971 to refrain from placing their official reserves in the euro-market.

The concerns about excessive liquidity creation and overfinancing abated, however, when the 1973–74 oil-price explosion created financing requirements for the resultant external deficits. Instead of being viewed as an undesirable source of financial instability, the market was now appreciated for its ability to re-channel smoothly enormous amounts of funds from oil-exporting surplus countries to deficit-ridden oil importers. Indeed, the market performed this service so well that it quickly raised new concerns, this time about the soundness of banks' balance sheets. The deteriorating payments position of the debtor countries threatened to impair the quality of banks' assets, and the short-term nature of the deposits from oil-exporting countries exposed banks to the danger of sudden withdrawals. Moreover, although not directly related to euro-business, the failure of the Herstatt bank in June 1974 (causing losses on foreign exchange transactions due to settlement failure) illustrated the potential fragility of international banking and 'rattled' confidence in the euro-market. In September, the G-10 governors issued a statement confirming their responsibility for the international banking market and their willingness and ability to help in case of need. In response, market sentiment improved slowly, but the potential prudential problems remained a matter of concern.

The G-10 governors therefore established, in December 1974, a new Committee on Banking Regulations and Supervisory Practices (now known as the Basle Committee on Banking Supervision) at the BIS, inviting senior officials from central banks and other authorities with formal supervisory responsibility to look into the implications for banking supervision arising from the increasing internationalization of banks' activities. Over the years this Committee has come to exercise considerable influence, even though it never possessed any formal supranational supervisory authority or legal powers.

The first recommendations of the Committee were derived from the recognitions that the internationalization of banking needed to be matched by a corresponding internationalization of banking supervision and that no bank, regardless of where its operations took place, should escape supervision. The view of how the responsibilities for the supervisors of internationally active banks should be appropriately divided was expressed in the 1975 so-called 'Concordat', which defined the role of the parent and host authorities in the supervision of foreign banking establishments. A second issue was how to monitor banks on a worldwide basis. This motivated the Committee's extensive work on developing guidelines for the supervision of internationally active banks.

From the debt crises to the globalization of financial markets

At the end of the 1970s, after many years of high and rising inflation, the industrial countries moved rather abruptly to a policy of monetary restraint, driving interest rates temporarily to record levels. This had a profound impact on the global economy and proved to be a watershed for financial market development. The surge in interest rates sharply dampened economic activity, gave rise to a pronounced and prolonged upward movement of the dollar and contributed to severe external imbalances among the major industrial countries. The combination of high interest rates and an unusually deep recession had bitter consequences for broad groups of debtors, in particular the developing countries which had borrowed substantial amounts from banks in the preceding years of low or negative real interest rates and rapid growth of export earnings. The sudden deterioration in debt service ratios, aggravated by political disturbances and massive capital flight left many debtor countries unable to meet their debt service obligations. By the second half of 1982 the world was faced with a serious international debt crisis with potentially dangerous implications for the health of the international banking sector, heavily exposed to the debtor countries.

In addition to the IMF, governments and central banks, the international effort to contain the crisis and keep the international financial system afloat also involved the BIS, which participated in 1982–83 in a number of rescue operations by providing bridging credits to the central banks of Mexico, Brazil, Argentina and Yugoslavia as part of the pre-financing of those countries' drawings on IMF facilities. However, already in 1984, the BIS – echoing views expressed in somewhat similar circumstances in 1931 – noted in its *Annual Report* that this kind of first-aid treatment was no longer called for (BIS, 1984: 152). The solution had to be sought in the establishment of confidence in the longer-term viability of the borrowers' economies and through the provision of funds at the appropriate maturities. The BIS pointed out that it was not a suitable vehicle for the realization of such aims because its resources could not be immobilized in medium and long-term lending although they could, within limits, be used to help the IMF indirectly in promoting adjustment.

Large-scale official financing (with a key role played by conditional IMF credits), debt rescheduling and officially induced extension of additional credits from banks, as well as the debt strategies initiated by the US Treasury Secretaries Baker and Brady, and, finally, new techniques involving debt conversions and debt service reduction, all succeeded in keeping the debt crisis under control. By the early 1990s, the problems were largely overcome. However, the shock of having part of their assets frozen as a consequence of the debt crisis, together with the experience of sharply rising interest rates, volatile exchange rates and changing patterns of financing external payments disequilibria, left a marked impact on the internal banking sector and financial markets in general. In fact, the developments in the early 1980s, now reinforced by the dismantling of controls and regulations as well as rapid progress in information and data-processing technology, set in train a process of financial revolution. Within a few years the traditional demarcation lines between different kinds of financial asset in the international and the domestic market, between different financial institutions, and between intermediation in the banking and the securities markets became blurred, foreshadowing the move towards a genuinely global financial market.

The repercussions of the debt crises were felt most directly in a strong trend towards 'securitization', that is the intermediation of a growing share of credit flows through the securities markets. This involved to a significant extent the banks themselves. They became important participants in these markets, partly to improve the marketability and liquidity of their book, which had been impaired by the immobility of a substantial part of their assets, including short-term claims, partly also because they sought longer-term funding of such claims through recourse to the bond market. In addition, the securities business was boosted because prime borrowers could raise funds more cheaply in these markets than from banks.

The second prominent development in the early 1980s was the growing importance of off-balance-sheet transactions. To some extent this reflected banks' efforts to increase fee income as their margins came under pressure. More significantly, the volatility of interest and exchange rates in conjunction with technological advances triggered a wave of financial innovations. Various new or greatly improved derivative instruments, such as futures, forward rate agreements, interest rate and currency swaps and options were developed to unbundle and shift risks, and banks, becoming active users or market-makers for such hedging devices, sharply increased their off-balance sheet exposure.

Finally, the process of deregulation and liberalization which got underway in the 1980s, entailing the removal of fiscal barriers, interest rate restriction and exchange controls, linked domestic and international markets. The seeds of globalization were sown as financial institutions began to operate in an increasingly more free, integrated and competitive environment.

The tendencies which became apparent in the first half of the 1980s gathered speed thereafter and have continued until today. Further steps towards liberalization, a growing propensity for worldwide investment, the desire to manage better the risks associated with changes in asset prices in the wake of stock market shocks and bond market disturbances, further advances in electronic data processing and the introduction of screen-based trading systems spurred financial market activity, sparked more financial innovation and, in particular, triggered vigorous growth of the market for derivative financial products.

The emerging network of international financial markets and the range of new financial products lowered intermediation costs and helped market participants to hedge against unwanted interest and exchange rate risks and thereby to concentrate on the management of their core business activities. This should have contributed to a more efficient process of resource allocation. Moreover, by pooling financial resources, the markets gained in depth and liquidity and strengthened their ability to absorb shocks. These developments had, however, two implications for central banks. Firstly, they narrowed the degree of national autonomy in policy-making and affected the strategy and operating procedures of monetary policy. Secondly, as the linkages between markets grew closer, the potential for disturbances being transmitted widely increased and heightened the threat posed by systemic risk. The two issues were discussed extensively in meetings at the BIS and led to a number of initiatives.

The possible impact of the changing financial environment for the conduct of monetary policy was examined on various occasions by the G-10 central banks, especially against the background of the growing role of private international payment and settlement arrangements and the growth of derivatives markets. On the whole, the studies undertaken did not find supportive evidence that the effectiveness of monetary policy had been impaired, even though the changes in financial markets had made necessary some adaptations in the manner in which policies had to be implemented. These findings were made public in a 1994 report prepared by a sub-group of the Euro-currency Standing Committee which concluded that the expanding derivatives markets were unlikely to have altered the transmission channels of monetary policy or the efficacy of traditional monetary policy instruments.

In contrast, the analysis of risks emanating from changing financial markets showed that a response needed to be formulated at the international level and that central banks and supervisory authorities had to take on collectively the responsibility for ensuring the stability of the globalizing financial system. Several committees and working groups of the BIS addressed issues relating to the soundness of financial institutions, as well as to the robustness of the clearing and settlement process.

In order to build a system of adequate safeguards at the level of individual banking institutions, three interrelated courses of action were followed. Firstly, the Basle Committee on Banking Supervision published in 1994 a number of risk management guidelines, which stressed the responsibility of senior management for the appropriate handling of risks associated with the new hedging instruments. The recommendations ranged from practical proposals for internal risk control to an appeal to senior management to develop a proper understanding of the complexity of the instruments and the risks involved. Secondly, a 1994 report by a working group of the Euro-currency Standing Committee recommended that financial institutions regularly disclose quantitative information on off-balance sheet exposures. The purpose was to enhance the usefulness of published accounts and thus to enable market participants to assess better the nature and size of risk taken by counterparties. Thirdly, the regulatory framework was strengthened, both by adapting the procedures for supervision and by proposing requirements for an adequate capital cushion and minimum standards to be met by internationally active banks. The 1975 Concordat on the sharing of supervisory responsibilities was amended twice, and in 1988 the Basle Committee reached an agreement on a risk-weighted capital-assets ratio to bolster banks' capacity to withstand potential losses on a 'level playing-field'. This recommendation was implemented through national legislation in a large number of countries. While the 1988 accord dealt primarily with credit risk, a new proposal, addressing the risk of losses from movements in exchange rates, interest rates and other market prices was published in January 1996.

The second major line of defence against systemic risk was to ensure that a shock originating at the level of one large market participant or market disruptions could not be propagated through the payment and settlement mechanisms. As the volume of cross-border financial transactions multiplied, financial institutions resorted increasingly to bilateral or multilateral netting arrangements to reduce interbank payment flows and credit exposures. The basic weakness of such schemes was that, without adequate safeguards, the inability of one participant to meet settlement obligations when due could cause other participants to fail. This could set in motion a chain reaction, with defaults on settlement obligations resulting in widespread insolvencies. Central banks had always been the guardians of the integrity of payment systems at the national level. But there was no such oversight for the emerging private international clearing and payment mechanisms. Following two reports on netting arrangements prepared by expert groups at the BIS in 1988 and 1990, the central banks adopted recommendations on a set of minimum standards for international clearing systems and on principles for cooperative oversight. The Committee on Payment and Settlement Systems established by the G-10 central banks in 1990 carried out various studies on issues relating to large-value interbank transfer systems, risks in securities settlement systems and cross-currency settlement risks.

In spite of the various safeguards introduced in recent years and the improvements made in risk management, large and well-publicized losses were occasionally incurred by users of derivative products. This gave new impetus to a debate about potential dangers arising from the globalization of financial markets. However, so far, the studies have found no evidence that the losses could be attributed to market failures; they were caused rather by inadequate internal controls or inappropriate use of derivative instruments, and the conclusion in official circles remained that existing regulations, complemented by further efforts to improve internal controls, external transparency and market functioning should be sufficient to contain systemic risks (BIS, 1995: 183).

The search for an international response to the globalization of markets greatly increased the need for central bank cooperation, the most visible sign of which was a marked expansion of meeting activities at the BIS. In the absence of formal powers such cooperation had to rely essentially on commonly developed proposals and recommendations which were then implemented at national levels. None the less, the central banks came to exert a degree of influence they had probably never enjoyed before during the 65 years of consultation and collaboration at the BIS.

The BIS and European monetary cooperation

A historical review of central bank cooperation would not be complete without at least a passing reference to the Bank's close association with the process of intra-European monetary integration. In fact, for a period of more than 30 years, ending only with the move of the European Monetary Institute to Frankfurt in November 1994, the BIS provided the home for European central bankers and the technical infrastructure of European exchange rate arrangements. The operational support entailed essentially the performance of agency functions, starting in June 1973 for the European Monetary Cooperation Fund (EMCF). The EMCF never assumed, as initially envisaged, any direct responsibility for the functioning of the agreement on the narrowing of the margins of exchange rate fluctuations (the 'snake'), which had been set up a year earlier as one of the few practical steps following the adoption of the Werner Report's recommendations on monetary union. The EMCF remained an empty shell and the task of multilateralization of positions resulting from interventions in the 'snake' and of administering the associated financing mechanisms was carried out by the BIS. This was also the case when, in the context of the introduction of the European Monetary System (EMS) in March 1979 the functions of the EMCF were extended to the creation of official ECUs against contributions of gold and dollars.

The policy discussions surrounding the management of the exchange rate mechanisms were conducted by the Committee of Governors of the EEC central banks, which had been established in 1964. From the beginning, the Committee, supported by a secretariat from the BIS, met in Basle in the framework of the regular monthly BIS meetings.

The Committee started on a modest scale, with its initial role being confined to holding consultations concerning the general principles and broad lines of policy of the EEC central banks. Over the years, however, it became a very effective group for close cooperation and, whenever possible, coordination of monetary policies. After several years of remarkable stability in the EMS, the Committee could not prevent the dramatic exchange market crises of autumn 1992 and July 1993 which led to the *de facto* abandonment of an effective exchange rate constraint. However, over the years, the discussions in the Committee had produced a strong convergence of views on the objectives of monetary policy and the desirable institutional features of a central bank. These views in fact influenced decisively the framework for economic and monetary union as embodied in the Maastricht Treaty. The model of an independent central bank committed to price stability – an idea which was not easily acceptable to many governments at the time – had already been advocated in the 1989 Delors Report at the instigation of the central bank governors who served in a personal capacity on the Delors Committee. The recommendations were developed further by the Committee of Governors in their draft proposal for the Statute of the future European System of Central Banks, which was adopted virtually without any changes. The fact that these activities could take place outside the European Community was a clear sign of the trust and confidence the BIS enjoyed as host of the European central bankers.

Concluding observations

The value of international cooperation is rarely questioned. None the less, it is not always easy to pinpoint when cooperation has been successful – at least beyond the counterfactual argument that in the absence of cooperation things would have been worse.

Central bank cooperation at the BIS has often been associated with the Bank's technical facilities, which enabled it to mount spectacular support operations in moments of crisis management or to render, less spectacularly and behind the scenes, services as agent for various forms of financial arrangements. However, the Bank's most important role in promoting cooperation has been that of bringing central bankers together and fostering, through the meetings held in Basle, a climate of trust and understanding among the participants.

The success of this approach has depended largely on international developments. For many years the services and assistance sought from the BIS have reflected the need to react quickly and flexibly, frequently by means of stop-gap measures, to the tensions that flared up under the Bretton Woods system. The need for this kind of firefighting persisted when new economic upheavals erupted after the constraints of fixed exchange rates had been lifted. However, the concomitant changes in the international financial system have demanded increasingly forms of central bank cooperation which, without reliance on formal powers but working through recommendations and guidelines, could meet the challenges of globalizing markets. In this respect, the approach of the BIS in operating through discreet and informal meetings is certainly an example of successful international cooperation.

Notes

1. As this review focuses on cooperation involving primarily BIS member central banks, no reference is made to the role of the BIS as a bank. It should be noted, however, that at present more than 100 central banks and international financial institutions from all over the world place deposits with the BIS and that these business relations have been a significant element in establishing contacts beyond the circle of member central banks. While the BIS offers a wide range of banking services, it does not accept

private sector deposits, nor is it permitted to make advances to governments or to open current accounts in their name.
2. See Art. 55 of the Statutes of the BIS: 'In all cases ... the bank may proceed or be proceeded against in any court of competent jurisdiction.'
3. For a more detailed description see Giovanoli (1990).
4. Resolution V of the Final Act of the Bretton Woods Conference, reads: 'The United Nations Monetary and Financial Conference recommends the liquidation of the Bank for International Settlements at the earliest possible moment', in *Proceedings and Documents of the United Nations Monetary and Financial Conference*, Bretton Woods, New Hampshire, vol. 1, July 1944 (Washington, 1948). The Final Act, however, was not an international agreement imposing obligations on parties but merely a final record of the discussions and resolution V, as opposed to other resolutions of the Final Act, was neither acted upon nor ever incorporated into a ratified treaty.

References

BIS (1932), *Second Annual Report*, Basle.
BIS (1934), *Fourth Annual Report*, Basle.
BIS (1935), *Fifth Annual Report*, Basle.
BIS (1946), *Sixteenth Annual Report*, Basle.
BIS (1947), *Seventeenth Annual Report*, Basle.
BIS (1949), *Nineteenth Annual Report*, Basle.
BIS (1984), *Fifty-fourth Annual Report*, Basle.
BIS (1995), *Sixty-fifth Annual Report*, Basle.
Giovanoli, Mario (1990), 'The role of the Bank for International Settlements', in *Festschrift in Honor of Sir Joseph Gold*, Heidelberg.
Horsefield, Keith J. (1969), *The International Monetary Fund 1945–65*, Vol. I, Washington, DC.
James, Harold (1996), *International Monetary Cooperation since Bretton Woods*, Oxford.
Kaplan, Jacob J. and Schleiminger, Günther (1989), *The European Payments Union*, Oxford.
Mayer, W. Helmut (1979), 'Der Eurowährungsmarkt, seine makroökonomische Problematik und Auswirkungen' in *Aussenwirtschaft*, Heft 1.

PART IV
The Emergence of Modern Central Banking from 1918 to the Present

CHAPTER TWELVE

Concluding Comments

Barry Eichengreen

In conjunction with the meeting for which the papers in this volume were prepared, the European Association for Banking History mounted a remarkable book display. It presented what is possibly the most extensive collection ever assembled of institutional histories of central and commercial banks. That display reminded participants that their topic, the emergence of modern central banking, is hardly uncharted terrain. Virtually every important bank has its official history, and many are the subject of unauthorized biographies.

What then remains to be added by the volume at hand? For one thing, the preceding chapters point up the limitations of the official-history model. Histories of national central banks all too frequently fail to capture what is distinctive about their subject. One way of removing the blinkers imposed by the case-study approach is to adopt a comparative perspective. Comparative history disciplines scholarly speculation: counter-examples rule out otherwise plausible hypotheses, while regularities highlight explanations with the widest applicability. The chapter by Carl-L. Holtfrerich and Toru Iwami, for example, underscores the limitations of interpretations of the structure and conduct of post-Second World War German and Japanese central banking that emphasize the influence of the occupation authorities. Japan had closely followed the German example before the Second World War. In so far as both countries were then occupied by the same military power, the United States, which even delegated the task of reshaping their monetary arrangements to the same individuals, such as Joseph Dodge and William Draper, it is striking that their central banking institutions evolved subsequently in very different ways.

While paired case studies are useful, more comprehensive comparisons must be undertaken to advance significantly the state of knowledge. Admittedly, this is easier said than done; aspiring to synthesize a myriad of national experiences threatens to render the scholarly enterprise intractable. One solution is to concentrate on functional comparisons: to focus on the evolution of the lender of last resort function, for example, or on the history of supervisory and regulatory responsibilities.

Whatever the strategy, a comparative perspective is essential if we are to understand what drives changes in the structure of monetary-policy-making institutions, given the abundance of available explanations for the phenomenon at hand. The chapters by Michael Collins and Mae Baker, and Lars Jonung and Tarmo Haavisto emphasize the influence of ideas in the conduct of monetary policy. That by Pierre Siklos emphasizes the importance of personalities in cases where the central bank statute and political circumstances leave freedom for individual action. Siklos, Cosma Gelsomino in his chapter on the Bank of Italy, and Carlos Marichal and Daniel Díaz Fuentes in their chapter on Latin America all point to the influence of historical experience. But while each of these interpretations is plausible, a wide comparative net must be cast to assess their generality.

A variation on this theme is the role of crisis in institutional development. Collins's chapter on the Bank of England lays considerable stress on the roles of the 1866, 1890 and 1907 financial crises in the development of the Bank of England's lender of last resort function. Siklos similarly highlights the impetus lent by the 1893 and 1907 financial crises to the founding of the Federal Reserve System. An analogous story can be told about the impact of the Great Depression on the debate that led to the establishment of the Bank of Canada. Gunter Baer emphasizes how crises occurring soon after the creation of the Bank for International Settlements powerfully shaped that institution's attitude toward such issues as exchange control, bank insolvencies and international lending. Economic historians, naturally enamoured of examples of path dependence (where passing events have highly persistent effects), do not have to stretch far to interpret the evolution of modern central banking in this light.

The comparative perspective lent by the papers collected here cautions against underestimating the power of emulation and example when seeking to comprehend the evolution of national monetary arrangements. Cosma Gelsomino makes much of the power of German example in the design of Italian monetary institutions. Turning to the inter-war period, the United States, in the peculiar incarnation of Edwin Kemmerer, Princeton professor and eminent 'money doctor', did much to convince Latin American countries, in episodes that are admirably discussed by Marichal and Díaz Fuentes, to adopt central banking statutes and institutions that resembled those of their neighbour to the north. The Bank of England and UK Treasury, operating through the offices of the League of Nations and the personages of Montagu Norman and Otto Niemeyer, played not dissimilar roles in Eastern Europe, as described by Aurel Schubert. The successful track records of the Federal Reserve System and the German *Bundesbank* have surely done much to encourage the recent trend toward central bank independence. And the resemblance of the statute of the European System of Central Banks to the *Bundesbank* law suggests that emulation and example are hard at work today.

The role of central bank independence, though by no means neglected, deserves still further study. Several of the chapters here provide detailed accounts of relations between central banks and governments, but without the kind of rigorous analysis, based on numerical indices of central banks' legal and economic independence, featured in the literature of recent decades. Recently, Beth Simmons has constructed analogous indices for the inter-war years and shown that these are significantly related to monetary policy outcomes. Some readers will object that central bank independence cannot be measured identically in different historical periods, and all would presumably agree with Pierre Siklos that characterizing the economic and political autonomy of central banks requires more than an analysis of the major provisions of central bank statutes. Siklos points to the importance of subsidiary legislation, but he could have equally emphasized the extent to which a given degree of statutory independence can have different effects in different historical settings. Some contributors to the literature on contemporary central banking have argued that central bank independence has different effects in federal political systems. Others have suggested that its effects depend on the structure of national financial systems, for example on the prevalence of universal or unit banking. Still others submit that central bank independence has particularly beneficial effects when paired with corporatist labour market institutions.

Siklos makes a start in addressing these issues when he places the debate over the independence of the Federal Reserve System and the Bank of Canada in the context of the political and financial environment in which they operated. Schubert's discussion of the fragility of financial systems in Central and Eastern Europe and their implications for central bank independence can be thought of in a similar way. So too can Jonung and Haavisto's point that free capital markets are a prerequisite for effective central bank independence. But these are interactions on which systematic historical research has barely begun. Other historians will insist that monetary policy outcomes depend not just on the structure of central banking institutions and on the economic environment in which they are situated but also on the attitudes and personalities of the individuals with access to the levers of policy. Milton Friedman and Anna Schwartz made this point when they ascribed the failure of US monetary policy in the Great Depression to the untimely death of Benjamin Strong. One can detect echoes of their view in the chapter by Siklos and in the passages on the Bank of Spain in the chapter by Pablo Martín Aceña and Olivier Feiertag. But focusing exclusively on the individual at the helm (the CEO, as Siklos calls him) runs the risk of slighting the influence of bureaucratic politics within the central bank itself. Just as 'principal-agent slippage' can give the governor of the central bank the freedom to tailor policy to his personal preferences, the need to delegate responsibility for formulating and implementing policy decisions similarly empowers staff. Part of the story of US policy in the Great Depression, after all, was the conflict between the Federal Reserve Bank of New York and the Board of Governors in Washington, DC, over who would provide leadership within the institution; and conflict among district reserve banks, the Chicago and New York banks in particular, over how interventionist that policy should be. Similarly today, there are well-known differences in the voting patterns of district reserve bank presidents and members of the Federal Reserve Board, with the former evincing more reluctance than the latter to tailor discount rates to macroeconomic conditions. The same contrast is evident in the voting behaviour of *Landeszentralbank* presidents and members of the *Bundesbank* Board. This reminds us that central banks are not unitary organizations and that historians should not treat them as such.

The issues grow more complex when we extend our purview to relations between central banks. While central bank cooperation is a hardy perennial of the historical literature, the papers in this volume significantly extend existing scholarship on the subject. They highlight the extent to which regime-preserving cooperation involved the participation of not just central banks but private banks as well. This point is prominent in Jaime Reis's chapter on the Bank of Portugal. It is clear in Marc Flandreau's account of the role of the Rothschilds in the operation of the late nineteenth-century gold standard.[1] These studies open up an important line of inquiry, suggesting questions like the following: How prevalent was international cooperation between central and private banks? Which central banks had access to private support? Under what conditions were private banks inclined to extend it, and why did they view it as in their interest?

The chapters on the International Monetary Fund by Harold James and on the Bank for International Settlements by Gunter Baer raise rather different questions. Compared to national central banks, it is less clear how the historical roles of these institutions should be conceptualized. James suggests that the IMF, at least during the Bretton Woods period, should be thought of as the institutional embodiment of a system of rules. This is too literal an interpretation for my taste. I would suggest that the new institutional economics provides a more illuminating way of thinking about the functions of the IMF and the BIS. The characterization would go as follows. By providing a venue for the ongoing, systematic exchange of information and ideas, this view suggests, the two institutions foster consensus formation. The procedures they follow serve an agenda-setting function that lends precedence to some conceptualizations above others. Expert analyses informing their proceedings further define the parameters of discourse and decision making. The written record and recollections of permanent staff permit these processes to endure beyond the terms in office of any particular set of elected officials.

Interest in the history of the BIS and IMF derives, in part, from the controversy over the future of these organizations. Since the end of German reparations (in the case of the BIS) and the collapse of the Bretton Woods system of pegged but adjustable exchange rates (in the case of the IMF), they have been organizations in search of a mission. One possible mission, whose existence has not gone unnoticed by those who inhabit the front offices of these institutions, involves the acquisition of international central banking functions, and international lender of last resort responsibilities in particular. The Mexican rescue of 1995 has been cited as evidence of the need for an international lender of last resort. The sceptical rejoinder has two strands. First, that the existence of an international lender of last resort would create more problems than it solves; it would give rise to moral hazard, encouraging countries to follow risky financial strategies that would only provoke more financial crises. Second, that crises in fact tend to be limited to the countries in which they originate; there is little risk of cross-border contagion of a sort that threatens the international financial system.

This last hypothesis is clearly one that cries out for testing against historical evidence. For example, the financial difficulties experienced by countries around the world between 1890 and 1893 have been interpreted both in terms of cross-border contagion and, alternatively, as the common but functionally distinct responses of separate national financial systems to a global economic downturn. The 1931 financial crisis in Central Europe has been analysed in terms of contagion from Austria to Germany but also as separate, functionally unconnected crises in neighbouring countries. This is a question on which the jury remains out and one on which additional research is warranted.

Finally, the papers in this volume suggest that the title of the conference at which they were presented, 'The Emergence of Modern Central Banking, 1918 to the Present', was too restrictive. Understanding the evolution of central banking necessarily means starting earlier. In the advanced industrial countries with which these papers are concerned, modern central banking did not suddenly take root in 1918. By then, the institutions and attitudes shaping the structure, conduct and performance of twentieth-century central banks had already undergone an extended process of evolution. Even in the United States, where the Federal Reserve System was only established on the eve of the First World War, the controversy surrounding the first and second Banks of the United States profoundly influenced the structure and policies of their twentieth-century successor. It is fortunate that, in writing their papers, contributors so readily disregarded the chronological limitation imposed by the conference title.

Notes

1. This paper, which was presented at the Évora conference, has been published in *Economic History Review* (November, 1997) as 'Central bank cooperation in historical perspective: a sceptical view'.

Index